MOTIVATIONAL PSYCHOLOGY OF HUMAN DEVELOPMENT

Developing Motivation and Motivating Development

ADVANCES IN PSYCHOLOGY

131

Editor:

G. E. STELMACH

ELSEVIER
Amsterdam – Lausanne – New York – Oxford – Shannon – Singapore – Tokyo

MOTIVATIONAL PSYCHOLOGY OF HUMAN DEVELOPMENT

Developing Motivation and Motivating Development

Edited by

Jutta HECKHAUSEN

Max Planck Institute for Human Development
Centre for Lifespan Psychology
Berlin, Germany

2000
ELSEVIER
Amsterdam – Lausanne – New York – Oxford – Shannon – Singapore – Tokyo

ELSEVIER SCIENCE B.V.
Sara Burgerhartstraat 25
P.O. Box 211, 1000 AE Amsterdam, The Netherlands

First edition 2000

Library of Congress Cataloging in Publication Data
A catalog record from the Library of Congress has been applied for.

ISBN: 0 444 50601 2
ISSN:0166-4115 (Series)

♾ The paper used in this publication meets the requirements of ANSI/NISO Z39.48-1992 (Permanence of Paper).
Printed in The Netherlands.

Contents

Acknowledgments

This edited volume is based on the "Motivational Psychology of Ontogenesis" conference held at the Max Planck Institute for Human Development in Berlin, Germany, May 8–10, 1998. The authors of chapters in this book are scholars from three interrelated areas of psychology, namely developmental psychology, motivational psychology, and applied psychology in the areas of educational, occupational, and family research.

I am grateful to a number of people and institutions for their contributions to the conference and to this volume. First, I thank Paul B. Baltes, Director of the Center for Lifespan Psychology, Jürgen Baumert, Director of the Center for Educational Research, and the Max Planck Institute for Human Development in Berlin for hosting and providing financial support for the conference. I also thank Ulrich Knappek for his excellent work on the administrative tasks involved in organizing the conference. I am much indebted to Anita Todd for her most professional copyediting of the chapters. Finally, Dagmar Stenzel and Madeline Hoyt deserve my gratitude for producing the camera-ready book manuscript.

Contributors

Hans Bierhoff, *Ruhr University Bochum*
Bruce D. Burns, *Michigan State University, East Lansing*
Doris Fay, *University of Giessen*
Michael Frese, *University of Giessen*
Alexandra M. Freund, *Max Planck Institute for Human Development, Berlin*
Jutta Heckhausen, *Max Planck Institute for Human Development, Berlin, and University of California at Irvine*
Hugo M. Kehr, *University of Munich*
Olaf Köller, *Max Planck Institute for Human Development, Berlin*
Andreas Krapp, *University of the Federal Armed Forces, Munich*
Julius Kuhl, *University of Osnabrück*
Günter W. Maier, *University of Munich*
Heinz Mandl, *University of Munich*
Rolf Oerter, *University of Munich*
Reinhard Pekrun, *University of Regensburg*
Falko Rheinberg, *University of Potsdam*
Elke Rohmann, *Ruhr University Bochum*
Lutz von Rosenstiel, *University of Munich*
Klaus A. Schneewind, *University of Munich*
Axel Schölmerich, *Ruhr University Bochum*
Inge Seiffge-Krenke, *University of Mainz*
Rainer K. Silbereisen, *University of Jena*
Robin Stark, *University of Munich*
Clemens Trudewind, *Ruhr University Bochum*
Regina Vollmeyer, *University of Potsdam*
Bettina S. Wiese, *University of Darmstadt*
Margit Wiesner, *University of Jena*

Motivational Psychology of Human Development – J. Heckhausen (Editor)

Introduction

Jutta Heckhausen

Motivational Psychology of Ontogenesis: An Emerging and Integrative Area of Research

The idea for this book on *Motivational psychology of human development: Developing motivation and motivating development* grew out of the conference "Motivational Psychology of Ontogenesis" held at the Max Planck Institute for Human Development in Berlin, Germany, in May 1998. This conference focused on the interface of development and motivation and, therefore, brought together scholars from three major areas in psychology: (1) developmental psychology across the life span, (2) motivational psychology, with its classical models as well as more recent process-oriented approaches to motivation and volition, and (3) research on the key social contexts for lifespan development, that is, institutions of family life (psychology of family and social relations), education (educational psychology), and work (industrial and organizational psychology). This combination of fields in psychology represents the potential influence of development on motivation, and the potential role motivation plays in development and its major contexts of family, work, and school. Thus, contributors were chosen to apply motivational models to diverse settings of human everyday life and in various age groups across the life span, ranging from early childhood to old age.

In the context of the increased attention to process-oriented approaches to human behavior, motivational processes have become a key and hot topic in developmental and personality psychology, as well as in cognitive psychology. The authors contributing to the volume have been selected so as to represent a consensual and coherent conceptual model of motivation, the action-theoretical approach. This approach has its foundations in expectancy-value models of motivation and also draws on an interactive (person × situation) perspective on the effects of interindividual motive differences on goal-directed behavior. This motivation and action-theoretical approach is particularly well developed in Europe (especially in the German speaking countries), where the relevant theoretical traditions have thrived on the continual attention and support of the scientific community, and therefore, has brought about innovative theoretical conceptions and empirical paradigms (e.g., state and action orientation, volition). In the United States, motivational phenomena have recently received a stunning upsurge of attention, after an extended phase of decreased investment in both education and research in this area. Thus, contributions from the European research tradition in motivational psychology should be most informative and stimulating for researchers and students in this field throughout the world.

Motivational Psychology of Ontogenesis: Interface of Motivation and Development

The interface of motivation and development comprises of two perspectives: the influence of motivation on development, and the development of motivation in human ontogeny. Both these perspectives are addressed in this book.

The role of motivation in development has long been a topic of heated debate and still raises much controversy. Traditionally, the extreme positions of biological and situational determinism were confronted with conceptions that assert the unique capacities of humans to exert a free will, and thus determine their behavior and development. However, nowadays most researchers do not take a unidimensional or extreme position in this regard. Instead, the individual's motivation is, on the one hand a product of, and on the other hand, a producer of development.

What the individual can do and which goals one can pursue is not simply a matter of an individual's free choice, but to a large extent constrained by the biology of maturation and aging, and by the opportunities society provides at different ages and at different positions in the system of social strata. Becoming a world-class athlete is not a suitable goal for one's late thirties, and a top management position will not be attainable in one's early twenties. Biology and society together furnish an age-graded sequence of opportunities to attain important developmental goals in terms of life transitions and psychological growth. This age-graded structure of opportunities is not just a constraint to the individual's free expression of will. Instead, the age-graded opportunity structure provides a time-organized scaffold the individual can use as a timetable to guide his or her goal engagement and disengagement. Thus, the degrees of freedom provided by biological and societal canalizations of development can be actively used by the individual. To the extent that the individual uses them, they become realized as adaptive constraints of development (Heckhausen, 1999). It is the individual, and her active pursuit of developmental goals and agendas, that brings to bear the biological and societal potential for ontogenesis. This way, individual, biology, and society are the components of a dialectical system that generates patterns of development and life courses. As part of this dialectic, the individual has the potential to deviate from normative life-course patterns, but only at the large expense of investing many resources to swim against the stream in one regard (e.g., outstanding artistic career) while sacrificing developmental potential in other domains.

Adaptive Function of Motivation: Evolutionary Considerations

Homo sapiens has evolved as a species with unprecedented variability and flexibility in the regulation of behavior and ontogeny. Humans have evolved with the ability to flexibly adapt to a great range of environmental conditions, and in particular with the ability to generate new patterns of behavior. Much of this behavioral and ontogenetic plasticity is based on the phylogeny of mammals, a biological strata characterized by open behavioral programs (Mayr, 1974). This plasticity opens behavioral patterns both in terms of concurrently available behavioral options and—even more important for ontogenetic change—in terms of acquiring new behavioral patterns.

However, the variability and flexibility of human behavior also has costs. The costs of variability are incurred by the need to regulate and actively organize behavior on-line such that it is effective in mastering the challenges of survival and reproduction. Thus, behavior that is not determined by preprogrammed stimulus-response patterns is bound to become disorganized, oscillating in its responses to fluctuations in external stimuli, and thus, grossly ineffective in catching prey, defeating a rival, soliciting a mate, and caring for offspring. What is needed is a system of directing behavior such that it remains flexible yet is systematically selected with regard to a specific goal state toward which it is conducive. This is achieved by motivation. In its earliest form, without conscious representations of goal states, it may have been a need state that gave rise to emotional processes that predispose the organism to need-relevant behavior (e.g., searching for prey; Schneider & Dittrich, 1990). The more advanced form involves the mental representation of a goal state the organism tries to attain. Goal-directed striving allows for behavioral flexibility in adjusting the behavioral means to the specific situational conditions while at the same time organizing the direction of behavior with regard to the goal state. This also implies that motive systems such as the one for achievement and mastery function not only in the "Here and Now," but across longer time intervals and even independently of current need states. Thus, motivation can address long-term outcomes of behavior and, therefore, also one's own development.

From Developing Motivation ...

Research on the development of motivation has traditionally been focused on childhood, and in particular on achievement motivation in school contexts (e.g., Dweck, 1998; Heckhausen, 1982; Nicholls, Cheung, Lauer, & Patashnick, 1989; Pintrich, Brown, & Weinstein, 1994; see also Rheinberg, Vollmeyer, & Burns, Chap. 4, this volume). Other approaches have broadened the scope of this research field to include early childhood precursors of motivational systems (e.g., curiosity, anxiety as precursors of hope and fear in achievement motivation) and have extended the scientific agenda beyond childhood into adolescence, adulthood, and old age (Carstensen, 1993; Kuhl & Fuhrmann, 1998; Ryan & Deci, 2000).

For age groups beyond childhood, when biological maturation has played out its role, institutions of family, education, and work become increasingly influential in shaping motivational profiles. It seems appropriate to assume that motive systems, such as the ones concerning achievement, aggression, or affiliation, themselves undergo a life-course trajectory of development (see e.g., Heckhausen, 1986). Across the life span the priorities between motives shift. Moreover, which aspect of a motive system is most salient changes across the life course (e.g., Carstensen, 1993). For instance, the intimacy and social acceptance aspects of the affiliative motive system may be more important in early adulthood, while the aspects of social companionship and generativity may gain salience in old age (Lang, 1999, 2000). These shifts in componential emphasis within a motive system probably reflect life-course changes in opportunity structures and biological (e.g., endocrinological changes) adaptations, analogous to the way that the increasingly cognitively accomplished and experienced child gets access to more and more challenging concepts of event interpretation and learning about her own ability.

... to Motivating Development

Since 1981 when Richard Lerner and Nancy Busch-Rossnagel published their much-cited volume *Individuals as producers of their development* (Lerner & Busch-Rossnagel, 1981) the topic has received ever-growing interest. Concepts such as personal goals and strivings (Brunstein, 1993; Emmons, 1986), developmental goals (Heckhausen, 1997; Nurmi, 1992), developmental regulation, and intentional self-development (Brandtstädter & Lerner, 1999) capture the reasoning that individuals make attempts to shape their own development and also cope with developmental changes occurring without their active influence. The ability to regulate one's own development in itself is a product of developmental advances in terms of anticipating long-range future changes, and selecting and using suitable action means and regulatory strategies. Moreover, the individual has to take into account and skillfully use the age-graded opportunities for realizing important life goals at the right time when biological and societal factors foster goal attainment.

Specific Areas of Research Addressed in This Book

Together, the two aspects, motivation of development and the development of motivation, make up a new and promising area of research: the motivational psychology of ontogenesis. The focus of this book is on the influence motivational processes have on the individual's development in different age-groups and institutional settings (e.g., school, workplace), while the development of motivation provides the conceptual and empirical background to this complex topic.

The chapters are organized around topical areas defined by a certain theoretical construct (e.g., the attachment/exploration system) or a specific developmental ecology (e.g., school). Within these topical areas the individual contributions come from either a primarily developmental or a primarily motivational perspective. Thus, in a common field of behavioral phenomena the two complementary approaches are juxtaposed and integrated. There are four topical sections, which are briefly described in the following paragraphs.

Attachment, Curiosity, and Anxiety as Motivational Influences in Child Development

The three contributions in this section address the role of emergent motive systems and action-regulation in developmental change during early childhood. Clemens Trudewind discusses the central role of curiosity and anxiety as evolved and adaptive systems of human motivation. Based on these conceptual considerations, Trudewind investigates the influence of the early motivational systems of curiosity and anxiety on subsequent cognitive development by means of longitudinal research in non-delayed and Down's-syndrome children. It is shown how the two systems do not simply oppose each other but unfold a regulatory dialectic that is particularly promotive of cognitive development in early childhood and at early mental ages (demonstrated with mentally retarded children).

Axel Schölmerich tackles a closely related, long-standing, yet unresolved topic of attachment research in his review of constructs and evidence in the field of attachment and behavioral inhibition. The key question here is how attachment patterns and related phenomena of behavioral inhibition influence the early steps in motivational development.

Rolf Oerter develops a perspective of Tätigkeitspsychologie (activity psychology) based on long-standing conceptual traditions in Western and Eastern European (particularly Russian) action and activity theory. The proposed generalized human frame motivation is conceptualized as a culturally informed behavioral regulator of children's activity.

Motivation, Emotion, and Interests in School Learning

This section is dedicated to the important and long-standing topic of motivational influences on school learning. This area may be the most developed, due to the great advances in conceptual and empirical research on achievement motivation, both in Europe and in the United States. It is all the more interesting to see the recent advances and debates in this area of investigation.

Falko Rheinberg, Regina Vollmeyer, and Bruce Burns develop an expanded cognitive model of motivation to learn that prominently features self-regulated learning strategies as mediating processes between general inter-individual differences in motive strength and orientation on the one hand, and school achievements on the other hand. This model of learning motivation incorporates phenomena and constructs, some of which are also addressed by other research approaches to learning motivation, thus allowing for a conceptual juxtaposition of propositions favored by different theoretical perspectives.

One theoretical perspective that recently has been elaborated and received much attention is the concept of learning motivation by interest. Interest is conceived as an enduring person-object relationship. Andreas Krapp develops this perspective according to which the motivation to learn is fuelled by interest in learning topics. According to the interest approach, learning motivation is content specific, and in this sense intrinsic. School achievement and the effectance of certain teaching styles and school environments are viewed as mediated by differential levels of intrinsic learning motivation based on differing interest in the topic.

Olaf Köller takes up the issue of goal orientations in achievement behavior as task-centered versus ego-centered. This issue has received much attention in international achievement motivation research and is closely related to Carol Dweck's work on learning versus performance goals (Dweck, 1998; Dweck & Leggett, 1988). Köller shows that developmental trends from a predominant task orientation to a predominant ego orientation may be reversed for higher age groups of adolescents depending on real-life contingencies (school vs. work life). These age-differential trends in goal orientations may also imply that at different ages, task versus ego orientations yield more adaptive developmental outcomes.

Reinhard Pekrun calls attention to positive and negative emotions in school settings, which hold a key function in the motivation and effective organization of achievement activities. He proposes a new social cognitive model of achievement emotions, which gives a central role to cognitive mediation, since standards of quality defining achievement are socio-culturally transmitted. Pekrun's model of achievement emotions builds on the conceptual tradition of expectancy-value models in achievement motivation research (see review in Heckhausen, 1991), yet extends it to include not only expectancy about achievement behavior, but also situation outcome and control expectancies.

Robin Stark and Heinz Mandl discuss the potentials and limits of current approaches to situated learning for the process analysis of motivational influences on learning. The authors use the learning setting and challenge of teaching empirical research methods to students in the social sciences. A number of parameters are specified, in particular the learning goals, promotive motivational task features, and multiple paths to efficient motivation-learning systems.

Motives, Goals, and Developmental Tasks as Organizers of Developmental Regulation

In this section, a set of six chapters covers motivational concepts (i.e., motives, goals, developmental tasks) as basic units of motivated behavior and, thus, as organizers of individuals' attempts to influence their own development and life course. Each of these contributions addresses the dynamic of societally provided norms and developmental timetables and the individual's active efforts to take charge of her development. The segment of the life span covered is fairly extensive with the contributions addressing adolescence and early adulthood through late midlife, presumably a continuously active field for developmental regulation.

Julius Kuhl presents a comprehensive theory of personality and its development that focuses on adaptive and in particular on maladaptive affective fixations in childhood. Kuhl proposes that these early fixations give rise to chronically ingrained dispositions to interpret certain situations as challenges or anxiety provoking with regard to the major motives of achievement, power, and affiliation. In this way, motivational styles determine operant motivated behavior throughout life. Kuhl also offers extensively developed assessment instruments to measure the various components of motivational processes that play a role in self-development.

In my own chapter, I develop a model of developmental regulation across the life span that is based on the life-span theory of control (Heckhausen & Schulz, 1995). Developmental regulation of the individual is organized in action cycles of engagement and disengagement with developmental goals, such as career promotion or family building. In adaptive regulation, these action cycles are synchronized with age periods, during which biological and societal opportunities for attaining the respective developmental goal are favorable. A particularly challenging regulatory task is the shift from urgent engagement before passing a developmental deadline to disengagement when the deadline has been passed.

Bettina Wiese and Alexandra Freund address the developmental regulation of young adults with regard to managing conflicts between the family and the work domain. According to the model of selection, optimization, and compensation (SOC model; Baltes & Baltes, 1990), usage of these processes promotes successful development. The findings reported by Wiese and Freund support the proposition of the SOC model that it is adaptive to set priorities. While most of their subjects report parallel or simultaneous goal structures, those who give sequential priority to career goals also report better subjective well-being.

Two further chapters address adolescents' developmental regulation with regard to major developmental tasks of adolescence. Developmental tasks are by definition universal and normative. Thus, the issue of interindividual differences in motivation for mastering them appears counter-paradigmatic. However, substantial differences in the effectiveness and age-timing of normative developmental transitions have been found that call for explanation in terms of individual- or subgroup-specific developmental ecologies and in terms of interindividual differences in the motivation for mastering developmental tasks. Inge Seiffge-Krenke asks the question whether discrepancies between normative age-timing and one's own developmental status motivate active efforts to catch up in developmental attainments. The age-timing of developmental task mastery in adolescents with and without chronic health problems (juvenile diabetes) demonstrates the important motivational effects of discrepancies between normative and self-related timing.

Rainer Silbereisen and Margit Wiesner contrast East- and West-German adolescents' developmental ecologies in terms of opportunities and pressure for accelerated versus delayed developmental task mastery. They find differential impacts of biographical burdening (e.g., separation of parents) and peer group integration in East- and West-German developmental contexts, as well as some convergence between the two parts of Germany in this regard.

Work, Love, and Children: Individual Motivation and Societal Conditions for Mastering Developmental Tasks in Adulthood

The final section addresses the key developmental tasks of adulthood in the domains of work, love, and parenting. Successful and less adaptive patterns of development in these domains are identified as well as potential facilitating and debilitating conditions both in terms of developmental ecology and the individual's personality. Lutz von Rosenstiel, Hugo Kehr, and Günter Maier discuss the major motivational theories with regard to their capacity to capture processes in organizational socialization, as well as interindividual and interorganizational differences in these processes. Specifically, the authors present findings on university graduates' career entry and leadership training, which show the individual entering a career as an active agent and coproducer of her organizational socialization. Critical aspects in the motivational and volitional pursuit of personal work goals are identified that mediate organizational integration.

Doris Fay and Michael Frese argue for an important interindividual difference variable in achievement motivation, namely, personal initiative. For processes of work socialization the authors propose sequential developmental influences between perceived personal control at the work place, self-efficacy, control aspirations, and personal initiative, which can be verified in both causal directions.

Hans-Werner Bierhoff and Elke Rohmann identify patterns of cross-age stability and change for different styles of romantic love that reflect age-graded developmental tasks as well as stability in pronounced personality styles (e.g., possessive). Clear linear trends were identified only for two styles of love. Romantic love style decreases across adulthood, while pragmatic styles of love become increasingly common.

Finally, Klaus Schneewind studies young couples' management strategies with regard to bearing and raising children. The chapter covers a whole array of key questions in this regard, such as the issue of availability of child care, investment in the work domain, and the question of what makes a child a stressor for his family. Findings from a quasi-experimental longitudinal study of young couples reveal that initial personality differences account for substantial differences in intentions for childbearing versus childlessness. Moreover, relationship quality proves to be a decisive factor in the couples' capacity to cope with the challenges of parenthood.

Perspectives for a Motivational Psychology of Ontogenesis

The chapters of this book provide fascinating insights into the ways in which people at various ages and in diverse developmental settings manage to stay in control of their motivational and emotional resources and, thereby, preserve their ability to take active control of their own development. Not only during periods of growth but also during phases of challenge and threat, individuals across the life span are agents, who by pursuing their own goals and agendas bring to life the ontogenetic potential of the human species.

However, we have to keep in mind that this impressive control potential may also have its limits. For instance, at the end of life frailty and disease often take their toll: Action potential and thus control and quality of life are severely impaired (e.g., Schulz, Heckhausen, & O'Brien, 1994). Under such conditions, the power of human agency fails, and neither hope can overcome these constraints nor optimism put them in perspective. It is particularly the limits of human agency and willpower that reveal the nature of human motivation. Motivation is a psychic instrument for action in the real world. It is this function of motivation that phylogeny has optimized. When the effectance of action is gone, motivation has lost its function and thus its power. The enjoyment of success, subjective well-being, and flow—all these phenomena are not adaptive in and of themselves. They are adaptive to the extent that they enhance, maintain, and protect internal resources for control, effective action in our material and social environments, and thus successful development across the life span.

References

Baltes, P. B., & Baltes, M. M. (Eds.). (1990). *Successful aging: Perspectives from the behavioral sciences.* Cambridge, UK: Cambridge University Press.

Brandtstädter, J., & Lerner, R. M. (Eds.). (1999). *Action and self-development: Theory and research through the life span.* Thousand Oaks, CA: Sage.

Brunstein, J. C. (1993). Personal goals and subjective well-being: A longitudinal study. *Journal of Personality and Social Psychology, 65,* 1061–1070.

Carstensen, L. L. (1993). Motivation for social contact across the life-span: A theory of socioemotional selectivity. In J. Jacobs (Ed.), *Nebraska Symposium on Motivation.* (Vol. 40, pp. 205–254). Lincoln: University of Nebraska Press.

Dweck, C. S. (1998). The development of early self-conceptions: Their relevance for motivational processes. In J. Heckhausen & C. S. Dweck (Eds.), *Motivation and self-regulation across the life span* (pp. 257–280). New York: Cambridge University Press.

Dweck, C. S., & Leggett, E. L. (1988). A social-cognitive approach to motivation and personality. *Psychological Review, 95,* 256–273.

Emmons, R. A. (1986). Personal strivings: An approach to personality and subjective well-being. *Journal of Personality and Social Psychology, 51,* 1058–1068.

Heckhausen, H. (1982). The development of achievement motivation. In W. W. Hartup (Ed.), *Review of child development research* (Vol. 6, pp. 600–668). Chicago: University of Chicago Press.

Heckhausen, H. (1986). Achievement and motivation through the life span. In A. B. Sorenson, F. E. Weinert, & L. R. Sherrod (Eds.), *Human development and the life course: Multidisciplinary perspectives* (pp. 445–466). Hillsdale, NJ: Erlbaum.

Heckhausen, H. (1991). *Motivation and action.* New York: Springer.

Heckhausen, J. (1997). Developmental regulation across adulthood: Primary and secondary control of age-related challenges. *Developmental Psychology, 33,* 176–187.

Heckhausen, J. (1999). *Developmental regulation in adulthood: Age-normative and sociostructural constraints as adaptive challenges.* New York: Cambridge University Press.

Heckhausen, J., & Schulz, R. (1995). A life-span theory of control. *Psychological Review, 102,* 284–304.

Kuhl, J., & Fuhrmann, A. (1998). Decomposing self-regulation and self-control: The volitional components inventory. In J. Heckhausen & C. S. Dweck (Eds.), *Motivation and self-regulation across the life span* (pp. 15–49). New York: Cambridge University Press.

Lang, F. R. (1999). Soziale Orientierungen im Erwachsenenalter und Alter [Social orientations in adulthood and old age]. In W. Hacker (Ed.), *Zukunft gestalten. Bericht über den 41. Kongreß der Deutschen Gesellschaft für Psychologie* (pp. 384–392). Lengerich, Germany: Pabst Science Publishers.

Lang, F. R. (2000). Endings and continuity of social relationships: Maximizing intrinsic benefits within personal networks when feeling near to death? *Journal of Social and Personal Relationships,17,* 157–184.

Lerner, R. M., & Busch-Rossnagel, N. A. (Eds.). (1981). *Individuals as producers of their development: A life-span perspective.* New York: Academic Press.

Mayr, E. (1974). Behavior programs and evolutionary strategies. *American Scientist, 62,* 650–659.

Nicholls, J. G., Cheung, P. C., Lauer, J., & Patashnick, M. (1989). Individual differences in academic motivation: Perceived ability, goals, beliefs, and values. *Learning & Individual Differences, 1,* 63–84.

Nurmi, J.-E. (1992). Age differences in adult life goals, concerns, and their temporal extension: A life course approach to future-oriented motivation. *International Journal of Behavioral Development, 15,* 487–508.

Pintrich, P. R., Brown, D. R., & Weinstein, C. E. (Eds.). (1994). *Student motivation, cognition, and learning: Essays in honor of Wilbert J. McKeachie.* Hillsdale, NJ: Erlbaum.

Ryan, R. M., & Deci, E. L. (2000). Self-determination theory and the facilitation of intrinsic motivation, social development, and well-being. *American Psychologist, 55,* 68–78.

Schneider, K., & Dittrich, W. (1990). Evolution und Funktion von Emotionen [Evolution and function of emotions]. In K. R. Scherer (Ed.), *Enzyklopädie der Psychologie: Psychologie der Emotion* (pp. 41–114). Göttingen, Germany: Hogrefe.

Schulz, R., Heckhausen, J., & O'Brien, A. T. (1994). Control and the disablement process in the elderly. *Journal of Social Behavior and Personality, 9,* 139–152.

PART ONE

Attachment, Curiosity, and Anxiety as Motivational Influences in Child Development

Motivational Psychology of Human Development – J. Heckhausen (Editor)

1 Curiosity and Anxiety as Motivational Determinants of Cognitive Development

Clemens Trudewind

The period between the third and the seventh year of life is an important transitional phase for cognitive and motivational development. The basis for acquiring and structuring domain-specific knowledge is formed. Researchers have intensively examined the development of strategies, social cognitions, metacognitions, capabilities of self-regulation, planning, problem solving and first operational systems. In contrast, the development of motive systems in this stage has been dealt with in a much poorer manner. Even the question of the motivational basis of developmental change in the different cognitive domains is widely overlooked. The myth of the total social determination of child development makes the competent adult responsible for instructing and motivating in the "zone of proximal development." So the recourse to the "active organism" becomes mere lip service because the specific driving and inhibitory forces for the child's self-determined activity have seldom been discussed and even more seldom been systematically studied.

Since the 1950s curiosity and exploratory behavior have been regarded as components in an independent behavioral system built in the course of evolution. In many developmental theories curiosity is seen as a central explanatory construct for cognitive developmental changes (Berg & Sternberg, 1985; Bowlby, 1969; Case, 1984, 1985; E. Gibson, 1988; J. Gibson, 1979; Piaget, 1952, 1972), so it is more astonishing that up to now there has been so little empirical evidence for the relationship between the strength of the curiosity disposition and the development of cognitive competencies. One reason for that surely is the difficulty in measuring individual differences in the structure and strength of the curiosity motive; another is Piaget's dictum that affective-motivational and cognitive processes are inseparably connected (Piaget, 1972).

However, Berg and Sternberg (1985) discussed the relationship of curiosity and cognitive development in an extensive review article. They presented empirical data about the relationship between reactions to novel stimuli and situations in infancy and early childhood and measures of intelligence in later developmental periods. They then called into question the widely accepted assumption that the development of intelligence is discontinuous in the first years of life and that interindividual differences in this phase are unstable. They interpreted the data as proof that the child's reaction to novelty is not only a continuous condition of intellectual performance but also a constant condition for individual differences in cognitive development. The interest in novelty and the ability to deal with it competently continue to be integral components of individual differences in intelligence over the whole life span. Berg and Sternberg (1985) distinguished two components in the process of dealing with novelty:

(1) A motivational component representing the affective, energizing aspect of novelty. This component is expressed by interest in, curiosity for, and preference for new stimuli, new tasks, and new aspects of the environment.
(2) A cognitive or information-extraction component that is responsible for the isolation, evaluation, and acquisition of relevant information and its assimilation to earlier experiences.

According to this view, the significance of a strong disposition towards curiosity for cognitive development is due to the stronger preference curious children have for new stimuli or situations. Curious children also develop more strategies of information extraction, focus their attention unerringly on informative aspects of situations, and attempt to explore these situations by active manipulation. Furthermore, they show higher persistence when searching for assimilative information than less curious children. Therefore, the relationship between the strength of the curious motivation and intellectual competence should become obvious in situations in which the child has to discover the relevance of numerous unfamiliar elements for problem solving. One important motivational tendency that perhaps moderates the relationships between curiosity disposition and learning by experiences, has not been discussed by Berg and Sternberg (1985). This is the anxiety disposition. It has been argued from an ethological point of view that a behavioral system that focuses on exploring and approaching new stimuli and situations has adaptive advantages only if this system is inhibited by an antagonistic system that buffers or delays an uncontrolled approach to unknown, potentially risky objects (Hinde, 1966). W. James (1890) had already conceptualized neophobia, the fear of novelty, as such a system.

In the following passage the results of some studies will be discussed, in which the relationship between curiosity motive and anxiety motive on the one hand, and manifest exploratory behavior and the ability to remember and solve problems on the other, were examined. These studies are part of the motivational and developmental psychological research program of our research group at the Ruhr University at Bochum.

Measurement of Curiosity and Anxiety Disposition in Preschool Children

The problem of the functional relationships between curiosity and anxiety dispositions on the one hand, and cognitive development on the other, can only be solved if it is possible to measure individual differences in the strength and structures of the two motives. However, motives as dispositional variables are not observable but can only be derived from the manifest motivated behavior. To be able to derive the differences in the strength of motives from differences in observable anxious and exploratory behavior in a controlled assessment situation one must assume that the incentive conditions for the motives in question are similar for all individuals. To derive strength of motives from observed behavior in everyday situations one has to take care that a representative sample of the curiosity- or anxiety-instigating situations is chosen (cf. Trudewind & Schneider, 1994). As such conditions are realizable only to limited extent, we have developed three methods of measuring the curiosity motive and two methods of measuring the anxiety disposition: a parents' questionnaire for each motive (Trudewind, Matip, & Berg, 1992; Trudewind & Schneider, 1994), a puppet show-technique with systematic observations of the child's exploratory behavior (Lange, Massie, & Neuhaus, 1990; Trudewind & Schneider, 1994), a checklist for systematic observation of anxious behavior in free-play situations in nursery school (Lugt-Tappeser & Schneider, 1986), and a test battery to encode the exploratory behavior in standardized instigation of the curiosity motive by new objects (Schneider, Trudewind, Mackowiak, & Hungerige, 1993).

The parents' questionnaire is based on the registration of exploratory behavior in ecologically key situations for exploration at home. Parents had to judge on a 4-point Lickert scale the typicalness of the described curiosity behavior for the assessed child in these age-specific everyday situations. Three scales can be derived by factor analysis from the 35 items. The scales are moderately correlated and can, therefore, be combined to a total score for overall curiosity. But each scale also measures specific components of the curiosity motive.

The *first scale* was interpreted as the *epistemic curiosity* scale. The behaviors specified here indicate a desire to gain insight, knowledge, and understanding (e.g., "My child always asks how things work"). The *second scale* represents behaviors of information gathering via looking, manipulation, and trial-and-error behaviors (e.g., "Very often my child refuses to pass a building site and insists on watching everything"). It was called the *perceptive and manipulative curiosity* scale. The *third scale* measures tendencies to look for interesting, exceptional, or surprising events and for hidden objects and secrets (e.g., "When I return from shopping, my child immediately wants to see what is in the shopping bag"). This scale represents *searching for stimulating events.* The first two scales represent facets of specific curiosity, the last one also measures aspects of diversive curiosity (Berlyne, 1960) or sensation-seeking tendency (Zuckerman, Kolin, Price, & Zoob, 1964).

To measure anxiety disposition we also constructed a parents' questionnaire based on the same principles as the curiosity questionnaire. It also represents three scales that can be combined to a total score for the strength of the anxiety motive.

The *first scale* of the anxiety questionnaire measures *social anxiety and shyness.* The behaviors specified here indicate fear, withdrawal, and behavior inhibition in social situations (e.g., "My child often is not able to utter a sound for greeting an adult"). The *second scale* represents passive or avoidance behavior in situations with a risk of physical harm (e.g., "My child very seldom climbs to the top of a climbing frame"). The scale was named *fear of physical impairment.* The *third scale* indicates *cognitive anxiety, worry, and apprehension.* The items indicate fears of cognitively represented objects, situations, or events (e.g., "My child fears ghosts and fairy-tale figures").

Strength of Curiosity and Anxiety Motive and Manifest Exploratory Behavior

In a series of studies we examined the relationship between the curiosity and anxiety dispositions measured in this way and the manifest exploratory behavior instigated in a standardized manner. As standard stimuli we used the drawer-box and the Banta-box from the curiosity test battery (Schneider et al., 1993). The drawer-box has 25 drawers containing small toys or everyday objects. The Banta-box is a 45 × 32 × 32 cm-sized coloured box with 11 different pieces that can be manipulated and inspected. The different forms of exploratory behavior (showing, inspecting, touching, manipulating, and asking), the

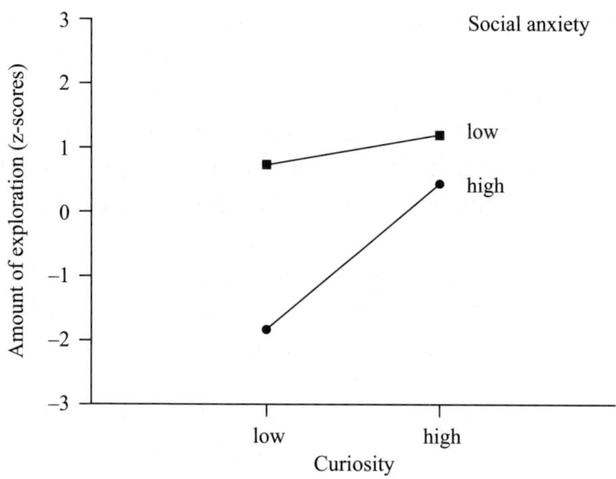

Figure 1. Amount of exploration as a function of the strength of curiosity and social anxiety disposition.

duration of exploration, and the latency for the first manipulation are coded online.

In almost all the studies with preschool children we found interactions between the curiosity and the anxiety disposition on the manifest exploratory behavior. However, the interaction was not always found for the whole sample but only for subgroups, mainly for the boys or the younger children—usually those aged three to five.

The interactions between curiosity and anxiety were not always uniform either, but their forms varied depending on the age and sex of the subjects and the way the curiosity motive was instigated. We also found different patterns of relationships depending on which of the scales of curiosity and anxiety disposition were examined. Nevertheless, a basic pattern of the interaction between the curiosity and anxiety motive on exploratory behavior becomes evident, as shown in Figure 1.

Figure 1 shows the results of a study with three- to six-year-old children carried out by Schacht (1998). She coded the manifest exploratory behavior of the children confronted with the drawer-box. The figure shows the means of the total exploration score depending on the strength of the social anxiety and the curiosity disposition. The highly anxious children explore significantly less than the children with low anxiety tendencies. The interaction between curiosity and social anxiety is marginally significant. Children with low dispositional curiosity who also have a high dispositional anxiety explore less than all the other groups. Anxiety seems to inhibit exploratory behavior, but in a minor degree if the curiosity motive is strong. The interaction term for the boys is higher than the one for the girls, a result, replicated in different studies. So the extent of inhibiting the exploratory behavior by high dispositional anxiety depends on the strength of the curiosity motive if the curiosity incentives of the situation are constant.

Dornow (1997) studied how the variation of curiosity incentives influences the relationships between the motive dispositions and the manifest exploratory behavior. As a curiosity incentive she chose the Banta-box whose incentive strength she tried to vary by an additional experimental intervention. In short videos she introduced the Banta-box either as a boring old box or as an exiting, interesting and mysterious new object before confronting the children with it. Then she observed the three- to six-year-old children exploring the Banta-box. Children with low anxiety disposition reacted sensitively to this additional curiosity incentive (Figure 2).

When the incentive value of the box was increased by the video, the interaction between curiosity and anxiety disposition, which was observed in many other studies, vanished. Under this condition only the two main effects for the curiosity and anxiety disposition were significant: Highly curious chil-

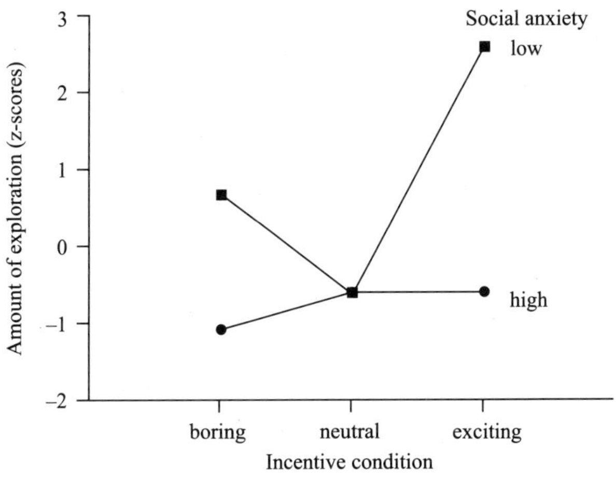

Figure 2. Amount of exploration as a function of the strength of social anxiety disposition and curiosity incentive condition.

dren explore more than children with low curiosity disposition, and children with low social anxiety explore more than children with high social anxiety.

All our results make evident that a specific pattern of functional relationship between anxiety and curiosity disposition on exploratory behavior cannot be generalized too far. Though in most studies high anxiety seems to inhibit the exploratory behavior this effect is not observable in all subsamples. Younger children (three to five years) and boys are affected more often. But children with a high anxiety disposition often show uninhibited exploratory behavior if the strength of their curiosity motive and/or the curiosity incentives are high. We are not yet able to build a model which integrates the different patterns of results.

Curiosity, Anxiety, and Cognitive Competencies

Nevertheless, we searched for the patterns of relationships between motive dispositions and cognitive performances. Gibas and Scheps (1995) observed four- to seven-year-old preschool children watching a curiosity-stimulating puppet show. The amount of their observable information-gathering behavior (e.g., their involvement in the show, their focusing of attention, their facial expressions of astonishment and surprise etc.) in each of the 22 curiosity-

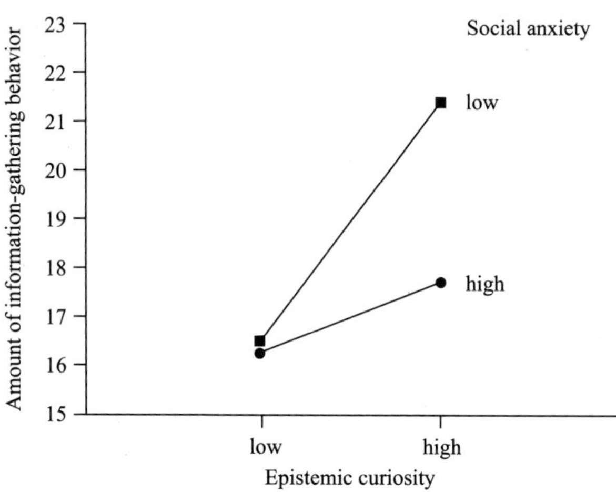

Figure 3. Amount of information-gathering behavior in a puppet show as a function of the strength of epistemic curiosity and social anxiety disposition.

instigating episodes of the puppet show was rated and summed up. This measure was analyzed by a 4-factorial ANOVA using age, sex, and the strength of curiosity and anxiety disposition as independent variables in a $2 \times 2 \times 2 \times 2$ design. Beside other effects there was a significant interaction between epistemic curiosity and social anxiety, which is shown in Figure 3.

As the figure shows, the means in the information-gathering behavior were higher for all groups of children with high strength of curiosity motive. But the angle of gradient is much smaller for children with high anxiety disposition. In this situation the observable information-gathering behavior of children with high epistemic curiosity is depressed if their social anxiety disposition is strong.

After the puppet show 28 questions were used to examine how much of the contents the children remembered. It was a priori differentiated between questions that examined the remembrance of facts and questions that measured the depth of processing and the understanding of the story. The hypothesis that highly curious children pick up more pieces of information and process them on a deeper level than less curious children was not confirmed. The prediction that a strong anxiety motive inhibits this deeper processing also did not receive empirical support.

On the contrary, as Figure 4 shows, in the younger group of children (48 to 64 months of age) highly anxious subjects understood and remembered the

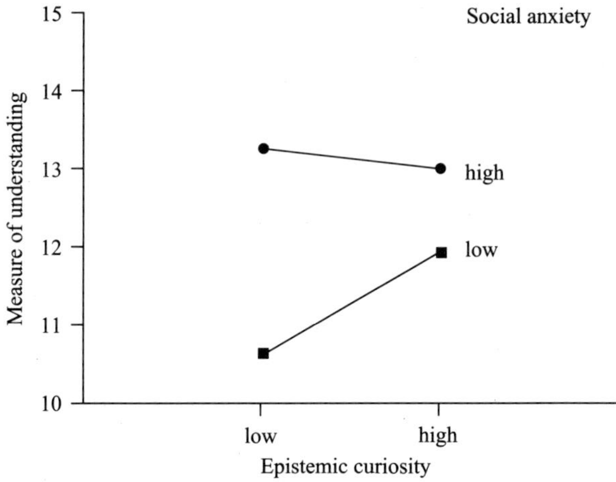

Figure 4. Understanding of the story as a function of the strength of epistemic curiosity and social anxiety disposition for the younger group (48–64 months).

story significantly better than the less anxious children. In the group of older children (65 to 80 months of age), however, there was no significant relationship between the motive dispositions and understanding and remembering. For the recall of pure facts we did not find any significant relationship with the motive dispositions (see Trudewind, Gibas, & Scheps, 1996).

In a following study by Babioch (1998) the children had to remember (free recall) or recognize visually or tactilely the objects of the drawer-box that they had explored before without announcement of the memory test. It could be shown that the memory performance highly depends on the number of explored objects, which also results from an interaction between the strength of the curiosity and the anxiety motive. But the number of remembered or recognized objects relative to the number of explored objects did not depend on the strength of anxiety. With younger children, however, there is a positive relationship between the strength of curiosity disposition and the performance in the free recall test. The author interprets this relationship as an indicator for the promoting influence of the curiosity motive on the development of encoding, storing, and retrieving. Given that the relationship between the strength of curiosity disposition and the performance of free recall was found to be weak for the older children and as there is no relationship of this variable with the performance in the visual and tactile recognition test in both age groups the results can be interpreted in the following way: A strong curiosity motive energizes the long-lasting exploration of the objects while a strong anxiety disposition more likely inhibits the exploration if the strength of the curiosity motive is not simultaneously very high (see Figure 1). A high strength of curiosity only boosts those memory abilities that depend on cognitive processes or structures that are currently in a critical developmental stage. This applies to the processes of encoding, storing, and retrieving for the four- to five-year-old children. The development of these cognitive abilities might be boosted and accelerated by the transaction with new objects motivated by the curiosity motive. Memory performances like visual recognition that are based on cognitive processes, developed in earlier stages, are processed automatically in our sample's period of age. Therefore, we do not expect and do not really find any influence of the curiosity motive on the recognition measures, neither for the older nor for the younger children of our sample.

Berg and Sternberg (1985) had expected the boosting effect of a high curiosity disposition in the domain of problem-solving. Schubert and Ballin (1995) reported evidence for this hypothesis in a study in which preschool children had to fetch down an object that hung from a cross-beam out of the

children's reach. A number of auxiliary materials were available that children could use to solve the problem. As a measure of performance in this problem-solving task the weighted number of subproblems that were completely or partially solved without help was assessed. The analysis of this measure by ANOVA showed a highly significant main effect for the curiosity motive.

Children with high curiosity solved more subproblems than children with low curiosity disposition (see Figure 5). Further, there was a highly significant main effect for the anxiety disposition that shows that highly anxious children solved fewer subproblems. In addition, we found a significant interaction between curiosity and anxiety on problem-solving ability (see Trudewind, Schubert, & Ballin, 1996). In this type of problem solving, high dispositional anxiety seems to impair problem-solving performance only if children are simultaneously low in dispositional curiosity. However, in children with high curiosity and high anxiety disposition mainly their curiosity disposition seems to be stimulated by this situation. The stimulated curiosity systems sensitizes the children for the relevant pieces of information, enabling a goal-oriented activity. This study did not show a significant role of advanced motoric-manipulative skills in the children with high dispositional curiosity. But, there are indicators that improved processes of information gathering and structuring more likely result in a better problem-solving performance of the children with high dispositional curiosity. In a further experimental condition the curi-

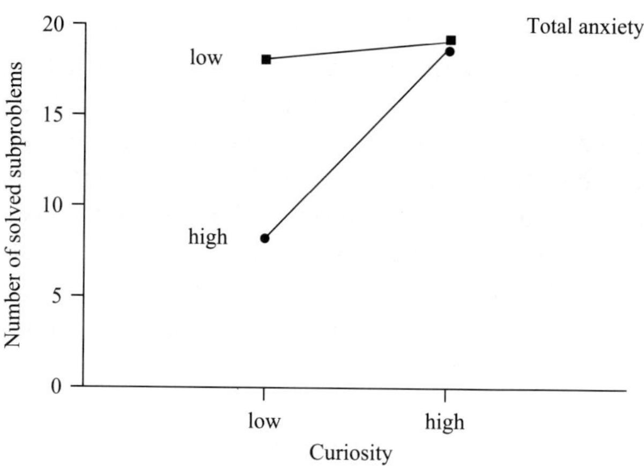

Figure 5. Number of solved subproblems as a function of the strength of curiosity and social anxiety disposition.

osity motive was additionally stimulated by a frog's croaking released periodically from the object. In this condition even the children with low dispositional curiosity increased their level of activity. But this increase only resulted in an increment of redundant but not goal-oriented problem-solving activities as an analysis of the process variables shows. Their level of problem-solving performance was not affected by the additional curiosity incentive. So we can conclude that less curious and highly anxious children have deficits in information-gathering strategies and operations.

The study proves that the strength of dispositional curiosity is positively related to problem-solving ability. High dispositional anxiety impairs problem-solving performance only if children are simultaneously low in dispositional curiosity, that is, children whose intensity of exploration with new objects is reduced, as it was shown in other studies (see Figure 1). In contrast to Berg and Sternberg's (1985) assumption that high dispositional curiosity might effect cognitive abilities cumulatively in such a way that the differences in problem-solving abilities between children with low and high dispositional curiosity increases with age, the opposite effect was shown in this study. The differences in this problem-solving ability between these two groups decrease with increasing age. That could mean that children with below average dispositional curiosity might have enough chances to acquire the necessary abilities over time. So the main function of a high dispositional curiosity might be the acceleration of developing cognitive structures in their early phase of establishment. It is possible that children with low dispositional curiosity must be supported more by competent adults who have to instruct and motivate the children.

If these assumptions are right the influence of the curiosity motive on cognitive development should be more evident

(1) in such developmental variables with a long-lasting genesis demanding a high level of self-regulated activities and
(2) for children whose speed of development generally is delayed. These children need more experiences to figure out new knowledge and operations. In this group the amount of exploratory behavior motivated by dispositional curiosity should be more closely related to cognitive abilities than in the group of children with normal rates of development.

Curiosity, Anxiety, Exploratory Behavior, and Problem-Solving Ability in Down's Syndrome Children

The last assumption was examined in a study comparing the relationships between curiosity, anxiety, exploratory behavior and problem-solving abilities in a group of Down's syndrome children and in one of non-delayed children.

In our study we examined 34 Down's syndrome children (19 boys and 15 girls) aged between 6;8 and 14;10 years with a median of 10;6 years. A parallelized sample of 34 non-delayed children (17 boys and 17 girls) was taken from nursery schools, aged between 2;3 and 6;8 years with a median of 3;10 years. The samples were parallelized according to their developmental age measured with the Snijders-Oomen Nonverbal Intelligence Test (SON-R 2 1/2-7; Tellegen, Winkel, & Wijnberg-Williams, 1996). The anxiety and curiosity disposition of each child was measured by the parents' questionnaire ELFRANA. While exploring the drawer- and the Banta-box the children's manifest exploratory behavior was assessed by systematic behavior observation. A measure for the intensity of exploration was built by summing up the standardized number of manipulations, inspections, opened drawers, the manipulated pieces of the Banta-box as well as the duration of exploration and the latency for the first manipulation. For both groups the internal consistency of the scale was Cronbach's alpha = .84. The problem-solving ability was measured by confronting the children with eight mechanical problems. Each one had to be solved in two to four minutes. The problems demanded manipulations of the objects to overcome blocked goal attainments or barriers. For example, the children had to use a small stick to pull a longer one closer which helped them to reach a Teddy bear behind a barrier out of their reach. Or they had to undo a wing screw which was blocked by a bolt to get a visible object in a closed box. Each completely solved problem was credited with two points, partially solved problems with one point. As a measure of problem-solving ability, the averaged points for the treated problems were calculated.

Similarities and Differences Between Down's Syndrome and Non-Delayed Children in Curiosity and Anxiety Disposition and Manifest Exploratory Behavior

First we compared the measures of the curiosity and anxiety dispositions and their subscales of the two samples. There were no significant differences in the means of the total score for the two dispositions. However, differences in the means of some subscales were significant.

Parents of Down-syndrome children assessed their children's epistemic curiosity and their social anxiety to be lower than the parents of the non-delayed children did, but cognitive anxiety was assessed to be higher in Down's syndrome children. Down's syndrome children ask less but simultaneously they show a smaller amount of social inhibition than the non-delayed children of the same status in cognitive development. However, they show more anxiety in imagined threats.

Thus, we can say that there is no difference in the total score for the curiosity and anxiety motive between Down's syndrome and non-delayed children but there are important differences in the structure of the curiosity and anxiety motive. Such differences could also be observed in the structure of manifest exploratory behavior.

Compared with the non-delayed children the Down's syndrome children's time of exploring the drawer-box was significantly shorter but their time of exploring the Banta-box was longer. The latency for the first manipulation in both subtests was also shorter. This indicates a lower level of conflicting tendencies in dealing with new objects. The higher number of manipulated pieces of the Banta-box and the total number of manipulations show the more intensive exploration of this object by the Down's syndrome children.

An important question of this study refers to the functional relationship between the dispositional curiosity and anxiety, manifest exploratory behavior, and the acquisition of problem-solving competencies of Down's syndrome and non-delayed children. To examine the relationship between the curiosity and anxiety motive and manifest exploratory behavior in both groups a $2 \times 2 \times 2$ ANOVA with the total score for exploration as a dependent variable was conducted. The epistemic curiosity and the social anxiety (median splitted each for the subgroups separately) and the sample (Down's syndrome vs. non-delayed children) are the independent variables. To control the influence of the developmental age this variable was used as a covariate. This analysis shows a highly significant positive effect of the developmental age ($F(1;59) = 9.13$; $p = .004$), a main effect for the sample ($F(1;59) = 15.50$; $p = .000$) and a marginally significant interaction between sample, epistemic curiosity and social anxiety ($F(1;59) = 3.06$; $p = .086$). The interaction is shown in Figure 6.

We can see that Down's syndrome children explore more intensively than the control group. But more important is that social anxiety does not inhibit manifest exploratory behavior in the Down's syndrome sample as it does in

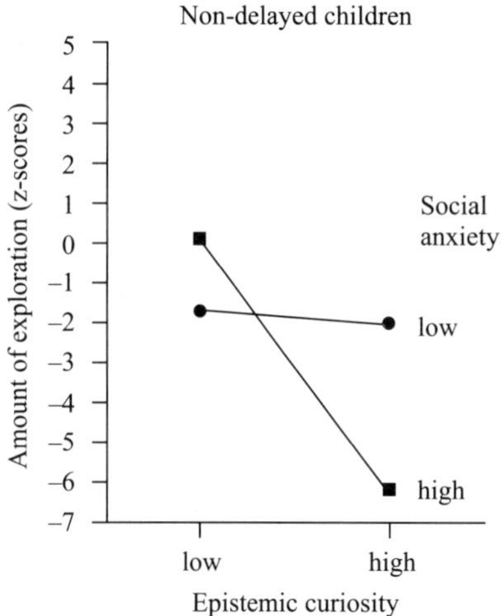

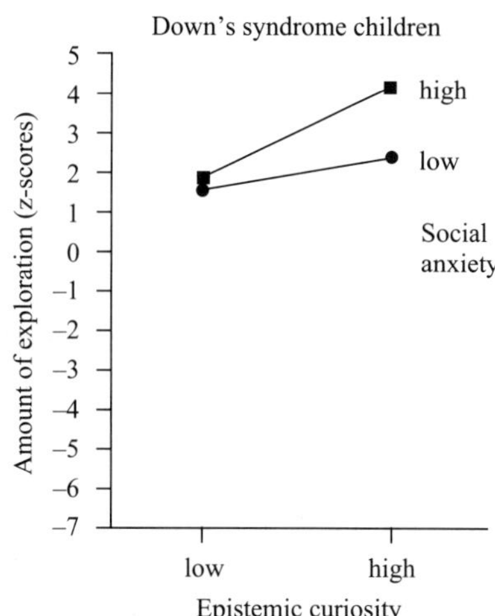

Figure 6. Amount of exploration as a function of the strength of epistemic curiosity and social anxiety disposition for non-delayed and Down's syndrome children.

the non-delayed group. On the contrary it seems to intensify the exploratory behavior presupposing the child's epistemic curiosity is high.

The following explanation for this pattern of relationships is possible: The curiosity motive of dispositionally highly curious and highly anxious children is strongly stimulated by the new object. Simultaneously, the anxiety system is activated by the social situation and the strange object. Both tendencies increase the subjective uncertainty. As the level of dispositional social anxiety is lower in Down's syndrome children than in non-delayed children, the first group can reduce the subjective uncertainty by intensifying their exploratory behavior. For the younger non-delayed children the level of subjective uncertainty may be so high that a conflict between curiosity-motivated approaching and anxiety-motivated avoidance tendencies is possible, resulting in a reduction of exploratory behavior. The longer latency for the first manipulation of the non-delayed children supports this speculation.

Correlations Between Motive Dispositions, Manifest Exploratory Behavior and Problem-Solving Abilities

For the Down's syndrome and the non-delayed children we next examined if there are differences in the patterns of relationship between anxiety, curiosity and manifest exploratory behavior, on the one hand, and problem-solving abilities on the other hand. Therefore, we computed for each sample the Pearson correlations between the total scores and the subscales for the curiosity and anxiety disposition (parents' questionnaire) and the scores for the manifest exploratory behavior (drawer-box, Banta-box, and total score). For the non-delayed children all curiosity scales correlate negatively—though statistically not significant—with the exploratory scores. For the Down's syndrome children, however, all curiosity scales correlate positively—for the Banta-box even statistically significant—with the exploratory scores. For the scales of the anxiety motive we only found a statistically significant correlation between the fear of physical impairment and exploratory behavior of the non-delayed children which, however, was positive.

Neither for developmental age nor for problem-solving ability did we find significant correlations with the anxiety scales in either group. For the curiosity scales we only found positive correlations between the epistemic curiosity scale and developmental age ($r = .47$; $p = .005$) and problem-solving ability ($r = .38$; $p = .025$) in the group of Down's syndrome children. In the group of non-delayed children this correlation was near zero. This is a first indication that Down's syndrome children profit more in their cognitive development from a high curiosity disposition than non-delayed children. Down's syndrome children need—roughly speaking—twice as much time for the development of cognitive structures than non-delayed children. Therefore, self-generated experiences are more important for these children. We assumed that the strength of a dispositional variable that energizes and directs the intensity and persistency of environmental transactions and fosters the acquisition of strategies to extract and process information should be more highly correlated to cognitive abilities in a group of Down's syndrome children than in a group of non-delayed children. The reported correlations support our hypothesis.

For the non-delayed children it could not be shown that the curiosity motive is important for predicting problem-solving ability. There was a close relationship between the amount and intensity of manifest exploratory behavior in the experimental situation and problem-solving performance, both in the Down's syndrome children ($r = .36$; $p < .05$) and in the non-delayed children ($r = .56$; $p < .01$). Similar relations were found for the amount of exploration and the children's developmental age ($r = .31$; $p < .05$ for Down's syndrome children and $r = .43$; $p < .05$ for non-delayed children).

As there are very close relationships between cognitive developmental age and problem-solving ability in both samples ($r = .70$ for the non-delayed and $r = .85$ for the Down's syndrome children) and as there are significant correlations between exploratory behavior and problem-solving ability, we tried to isolate the influence of the motive dispositions and the exploratory behavior on problem-solving ability by stepwise regression analyses for the two groups separately. For the regression analyses all subscales of the curiosity and anxiety motive and the different variables of the manifest exploratory behavior were taken. The total score of the problem-solving tasks was the criterion variable. In Table 1 the significant variables for the prediction of the problem-solving performance are listed.

In the group of non-delayed children two variables of the manifest exploratory behavior are significant predictors for problem-solving ability. The number of manipulations can be regarded as an indicator for the intensity of exploratory behavior. The number of opened drawers characterizes how systematically and exhaustively a new object is explored. The variation in these measures is a product of the interaction between the curiosity and anxiety dispositions and the subjective incentives of the new object (see Figure 6). Children who explore this object systematically, exhaustively, and with high intensity more easily find the correct solution in our problem tasks. The relative

Table 1
Significant Predictors in Stepwise Regression Analyses for the Problem-Solving Ability in Non-Delayed and Down's Syndrome Children (for each sample: $n = 34$)

Predictor variables	*B*	*Beta*	*T*	*p*
Non-delayed children*				
Number of manipulations on the objects of the drawer-box	.0012	.4172	2.840	.008
Number of opened drawers	.0267	.3540	2.409	.022
Down's syndrome children**				
Epistemic curiosity	.0548	.4836	3.166	.004
Number of opened drawers	.0275	.3900	2.771	.010
Time of exploration of the Banta-box	.1759	.2968	1.924	.064
Searching for stimulating events/sensation seeking	–.0481	–.4809	–3.006	.005

* $R = .593$, adjusted $R^2 = .310$; ** $R = .678$, adjusted $R^2 = .385$.

stable curiosity and anxiety dispositions observed by the parents in everyday situations do not explain an additional part of the variance of the problem-solving ability. In contrast to the non-delayed children "epistemic curiosity disposition" and the dispositional "tendency of searching for stimulating events" are the best predictors for problem-solving ability in the group of Down's syndrome children. Corresponding to the former group the "number of opened drawers"—the measure for systematic, planned, and exhaustive exploration—also explains a significant part of the criterion variable in the group of Down's syndrome children. A further statistically important predictor variable is the time of exploring the Banta-box, a measure for persistency in exploring new objects.

In addition, the stepwise regression analysis for the Down's syndrome children brought out a further remarkable result. The beta coefficient for the subscale "searching for stimulating events/sensation seeking" of the curiosity disposition shows a negative sign. As the Pearson correlation between this variable and the criterion variable problem-solving ability is near zero ($r = -.09$; $p > .30$), we can conclude that this variable functions as a suppressor variable. This will be understandable when we look closely at the different goal orientations of the two subscales: The items of the "searching for stimulating events"-scale characterize a curiosity behavior directed towards the approach or production of surprising events or effects, which leads to short-term increase in the level of activation. The items of the "epistemic curiosity"-scale, however, characterize a behavior directed towards gathering and processing of information which leads to a better knowledge and understanding of new objects or events. This behavior often demands effort and persistence. If for some Down's syndrome children with cognitive and motoric impairments the physical and psychical costs for this behavior are too high, the incentive value for epistemic curiosity behavior may decrease, and they develop a preference for curiosity behavior that primarily provides regulation of activation. As a consequence, the acquisition of knowledge and cognitive competencies might be delayed or inhibited for these children.

The results of a 2 × 2 ANOVA with the Down's syndrome children's data, using the score for problem-solving ability as the dependent variable and the strength of "epistemic curiosity" and the tendency of "searching for stimulating events" as independent variables (median split, six cases meeting the median were excluded) support this interpretation. Besides a significant main effect for "epistemic curiosity" there was a significant interaction between "epistemic curiosity" and "searching for stimulating events" ($F(1;24) = 6.102$; $p = .021$). Figure 7 shows the means of problem-solving performance

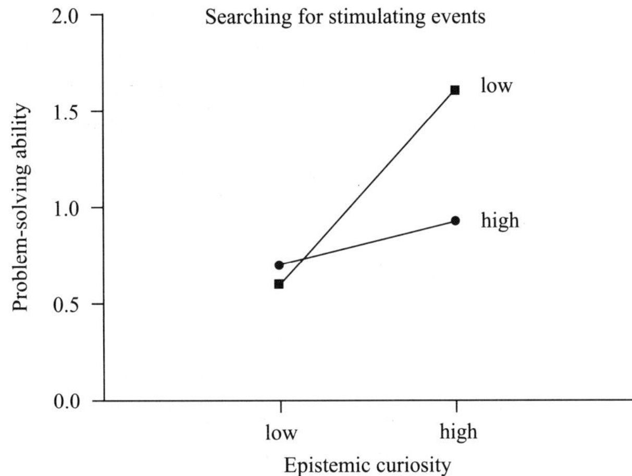

Figure 7. Problem-solving ability as a function of the strength of epistemic curiosity and searching for stimulating events in Down's syndrome children.

depending on the strength of "epistemic curiosity" and "searching for stimulating events."

Down's syndrome children with high dispositional epistemic curiosity show better problem-solving performances than children with low scores in this variable. But the difference is considerable for the subgroup with low tendencies for searching stimulating events only. If children with high scores in epistemic curiosity simultaneously have a high need for stimulation and rapidly changing impressions their transactions with new objects or events might be frequent but superficial. For this group the same amount of observable exploratory behavior leads to a lower rate in the acquisition of declarative and procedural knowledge resulting in lower problem-solving competencies.

Summary and Conclusions

Our functional-analytic approach for studying the relationships between curiosity, anxiety, exploratory behavior and cognitive development has shown a lot of interesting, not trivial results. Nevertheless, some conclusions are possible that may suggest an orientation for further research. They refer to (a) the measurement of individual differences in dispositional curiosity and anxiety, (b) the relationship between the strength of dispositional curiosity and anxiety and manifest exploratory behavior, and (c) the functional relationships between motives, situational incentives, and cognitive competencies especially for the development of problem-solving abilites.

Measurement of Individual Differences in Dispositional Curiosity and Anxiety

In our functional-analytic approach we conceptualize curiosity and anxiety as very basic motive systems that have important functions for the acquisition of experiences, knowledge, and operations. They help us deal with the demands of new and changing environments. The function of high dispositional curiosity for cognitive development, especially for problem-solving abilities of preschoolers (mostly dealt with in our studies), appears to lie in stimulating and energizing active transactions with the environment. This stimulation results from an instigation of curiosity motivation through situational cues (e.g., new objects). Our first assumption of the general function of high dispositional anxiety was that exploratory behavior would be blocked to reduce subjective uncertainty instigated through the same situational cues (e.g., new objects).

To demonstrate empirical evidence for these assumptions it is necessary to measure interindividual differences in the strength of motive dispositions. Our different approaches for the measurement of the motives (systematic behavior observations in free play situations and under standardized stimulation conditions, parental assessment of motive specific behavior in everyday situations) result in valid scales for the strength of curiosity and anxiety disposition (Lugt-Tappeser, Trudewind, & Schneider, 1992; Schneider et al., 1993; Trudewind & Schneider, 1994). We found fewer covariations between the curiosity and anxiety measures. This supports our assumption that curiosity and anxiety are motive systems that are independent to a large extent. On the other hand, we found different scales for the two motives that represent distinct facets of the disposition. These scales are intercorrelated to a certain extent, but they show different functional relationships to exploratory behavior and cognitive competencies. Especially the differentiation between epistemic curiosity and the tendency toward searching for stimulating events/sensation seeking was found to be important in our study with Down's syndrome children. In a factor analysis of exploratory behavior Henderson and Moore (1979) found two factors which they called breadth versus depth of exploration. They interpreted these factors as "differences in mode and style of exploration" (Moore, 1985, p. 4). In contrast, we assume that epistemic curiosity and searching for stimulating events are different dispositional tendencies with distinctive goals and processes of affect regulation. They correspond to Berlyne's (1960) distinction between specific and diversive curiosity. We further assume that they are based on the same behavioral system developed in the course of evolution but differentiate ontogenetically depending on individual experiences and socialization factors. They have different consequences for exploratory behavior and its cognitive effects as has been shown in the studies reported above.

Relationships Between the Strength of Dispositional Curiosity and Anxiety and Manifest Exploratory Behavior

In our studies we did not find a uniform pattern of relationships between measures of curiosity and anxiety and measures of manifest exploratory behavior. The best predictors for different forms of exploration were the measures of epistemic curiosity and social anxiety. Our measure for social anxiety disposition seems to include fear of new objects (neophobia) and fear of strangers. In contrast to the hypothesis that high dispositional anxiety generally blocks exploratory behavior we found that this was only true for children with low dispositional curiosity. If the motivational state of the curiosity system is high there seems to be a primacy of the approach tendency, and the differences in exploratory behavior between high- and low-anxiety children disappear. Although this form of interaction could neither be shown in all our studies nor for all subgroups (age, sex), it was the most frequent pattern of relationship we found. To date there have been no differentiated models that enable us to integrate the different results. More empirical evidence is necessary. But in this model the anxiety disposition cannot be conceptualized as a general behavior inhibition system.

Curiosity, Anxiety, and the Development of Cognitive Competencies

Henderson (1994) analyzed the relationship between general measures of higher cognitive abilities (intelligence test scores) and behavioral, self-report- or rating-measures of curiosity and exploration. Summarizing, the results of different studies he concluded "that overall, the existing evidence for a relationship between individual differences in intelligence and individual differences in curiosity and exploratory behavior is not very impressive" (Henderson, 1994, p. 217). Numerous investigations found an impairment of scholastic performance through high anxiety (for an overview, see Bittmann, 1980; Krohne, 1982; Markgraf-Stiksrud, 1989). But there are almost no empirical findings on the interplay of curiosity and anxiety as the basic motives in the formation of experiences and the acquisition of cognitive competencies. In the studies reported in this chapter we found some evidences for influences of different levels of the curiosity and the anxiety motive on cognitive abilities (memorizing, understanding, and problem-solving) and their interaction (see also Beckmann & Trudewind, 1997). In contrast to the assumption of Berg and Sternberg (1985) that high curiosity disposition boosts the development of cognitive abilities cumulatively we can interpret our findings in another way. For preschool children high curiosity disposition seems to accelerate the acquisition of cognitive structures and operations in an early stage of their development.

Children with low dispositional curiosity develop these competencies at a slower rate (perhaps with more help from competent adults) so that at a later developmental stage no differences between the two groups were found. The fact that for Down's syndrome children with delayed cognitive development the scale of epistemic curiosity disposition predicts the problem-solving ability much better than for non-delayed children supports this interpretation. It emphasizes—especially for Down's syndrome children—the importance of a behavioral system that motivates, energizes, and directs the self-determined transactions with the environment.

The function of a high anxiety disposition for the acquisition of cognitive structures and operations seems to be similar to the function for manifest exploratory behavior. The competencies of highly anxious children are impaired if their curiosity disposition is simultaneously low. Therefore, this interaction effect might be mediated through the amount, persistence, and well-planned nature of explorations in everyday situations as we could conclude from Babioch's (1998) study reported above. On the other hand, the younger children in the puppet-show study show better information processing and memorizing performances if their dispositional anxiety is high, independent of their epistemic curiosity disposition (see Figure 4).

To understand the role of curiosity and anxiety in the cognitive development in the preschool years further conceptual and empirical clarification is needed. The development of procedures to measure the specific components of the motive systems, systematic variations of the incentives to stimulate the motives, and studying a broader range of tasks and cognitive functions are necessary steps in a research program to demonstrate and to explain motivational influences on cognitive development.

References

Babioch, A. (1998). *Neugier, Angst und Gedächtnis im Vorschulalter—Zusammenhang zwischen Motiven, Exploration und Behalten* [Curiosity, anxiety, and memory in preschoolers—Relationship between motives, exploration, and memory performance]. Unpublished master's thesis, Ruhr University, Department of Psychology, Bochum, Germany.

Beckmann, J., & Trudewind, C. (1997). A functional-analytic perspective on affect and motivation. *Polish Psychological Bulletin, 28,* 125–143.

Berg, C. A., & Sternberg, R. J. (1985). Response to novelty: Continuity versus discontinuity in the developmental course of intelligence. *Advances in Child Development and Behavior, 19,* 1–47.

Berlyne, D. E. (1960). *Conflict, arousal, and curiosity.* New York: McGraw-Hill.

Bittmann, F. (1980). Zusammenhänge zwischen Angst und schulischer Leistung [Relationships between anxiety and school performance]. *Zeitschrift für Empirische Pädagogik, 4,* 161–190.

Bowlby, J. (1969). *Attachment and loss.* London: Hogarth Press.

Case, R. (1984). The process of stage transition: A neo-Piagetian view. In R. J. Sternberg (Ed.), *Mechanisms of cognitive development* (pp. 19–44). San Francisco, CA: Freeman.

Case, R. (1985). *Intellectual development. Birth to adulthood.* New York: Academic Press.

Dornow, K. (1997). *Neugier, Angst und Anreiz: Motivationale Determinanten des kindlichen Explorationsverhaltens* [Curiosity, anxiety and incentive: Motivational determinants of children's exploratory behavior]. Unpublished master's thesis, Ruhr University, Department of Psychology, Bochum, Germany.

Gibas, D., & Scheps, C. (1995). *Messung der kindlichen Neugiermotivation* [Measuring curiosity motivation in children]. Unpublished master's thesis, Ruhr University, Department of Psychology, Bochum, Germany.

Gibson, E. J. (1988). Exploratory behavior in the development of perceiving, acting, and the acquiring of knowledge. *Annual Review of Psychology, 39,* 1–41.

Gibson, J. J. (1979). *The ecological approach to visual perception.* Boston, MA: Houghton Mifflin.

Henderson, B. (1994). Individual differences in experience-producing tendencies. In H. Keller, K. Schneider, & B. Henderson (Eds.), *Curiosity and exploration* (pp. 213–225). Berlin, Germany: Springer.

Henderson, B., & Moore, S. G. (1979). Measuring exploratory behavior in young children: A factor analytic study. *Developmental Psychology, 15,* 113–119.

Hinde, R. A. (1966). *Animal behaviour: A synthesis of ethology and comparative psychology.* London: McGraw-Hill.

James, W. (1890). *The principles of psychology* (Vol. 2). New York: Holt, Rinehart & Winston.

Krohne, H. W. (1982). Die Rolle der Angst in Lern- und Leistungsprozessen [The role of anxiety in learning and achievement]. In B. Treiber & F. E. Weinert (Eds.), *Lehr- und Lernforschung* (pp. 221–241). München, Germany: Urban & Schwarzenberg.

Lange, D., Massie, M., & Neuhaus, C. (1990). *Entwicklung eines Puppenspielverfahrens zur Erfassung des Neugiermotivs bei Vorschulkindern* [Development of a puppet show instrument to measure the curiosity motive in preschool children]. Unpublished master's thesis, Ruhr University, Department of Psychology, Bochum, Germany.

Lugt-Tappeser, H., & Schneider, K. (1986). *Die Entwicklung einer Zeichenliste für die Erfassung von Ängstlichkeit bei Vorschulkindern* [Development of an observation method to measure anxiety in preschool children] (Tech. Rep. No. 5). Bochum, Germany: Ruhr University, Department of Psychology.

Lugt-Tappeser, H., Trudewind, C., & Schneider, K. (1992). *Die Marburger Angstzeichenliste. Ein Beobachtungsverfahren zur Erfassung der Ängstlichkeit im Vorschulalter* [Marburg Anxiety Scale. A method of observation to measure anxiety in preschoolers] (Report No. 106). Marburg, Germany: University of Marburg, Department of Psychology.

Markgraf-Stiksrud, J. (1989). Leistung und Angst—Leistungen über Angst? Literaturbericht [Achievement and anxiety—Achievement through anxiety? A report of literature]. *Zeitschrift für Pädagogische Psychologie, 3,* 57–65.

Moore, S. G. (1985, August). *Exploration in young children: Stability, variability and social influence.* Paper presented at the Symposium on Facets of Exploratory Activity in Childhood, APA Conference, Los Angeles, CA.

Piaget, J. (1952). *The origins of intelligence in children.* New York: International Universities Press.

Piaget, J. (1972). The relation of affectivity to intelligence in the mental development of the child. In S. I. Harrison & J. F. McDermott (Eds.), *Childhood psychopathology* (pp. 167–175). New York: International Universities Press.

Schacht, A. (1998). *Neugier, Angst und Gedächtnis im Vorschulalter: Einfluß der Motive auf das Explorationsverhalten* [Curiosity, anxiety, and memory in preschoolers: Influence of motives on exploratory behavior]. Unpublished master's thesis, Ruhr University, Department of Psychology, Bochum, Germany.

Schneider, K., Trudewind, C., Mackowiak, K., & Hungerige, H. (1993). *Die Entwicklung einer Testbatterie zur Erfassung des Neugiermotivs bei Vorschulkindern* [Development of a test battery to measure the curiosity motive in preschoolers] (Tech. Rep. No. 83). Bochum, Germany: Ruhr University, Department of Psychology.

Schubert, U., & Ballin, U. (1995). *Entwicklung von Neugier und Problemlösen im Vorschulalter* [Development of curiosity and problem solving in preschoolers]. Unpublished master's thesis, Ruhr University, Department of Psychology, Bochum, Germany.

Tellegen, P. J., Winkel, M., & Wijnberg-Williams, B. J. (Eds.). (1996). *Snijders-Oomen Nonverbaler Intelligenztest SON-R 2 1/2-7* [Non-verbal test of intelligence SON-R 2 1/2-7]. Amsterdam/Lisse: Swets & Zeitlinger.

Trudewind, C., Gibas, D., & Scheps, C. (1996). *Wie regulieren Neugier- und Angstdisposition das Neugierverhalten und die Informationsaufnahme im Vorschulalter?* [How do curiosity and anxiety disposition regulate exploratory behavior and information gathering in preschoolers?] (Tech. Rep. No. 89). Bochum, Germany: Ruhr University, Department of Psychology.

Trudewind, C., Matip, E. M., & Berg, P. (1992). *Elternfragebogen zur Erfassung der Neugier und Ängstlichkeit (ELFRANA 3592)* [Parents' questionnaire to measure curiosity and anxiety (ELFRANA 3592)]. Bochum, Germany: Ruhr University, Department of Psychology.

Trudewind, C., & Schneider, K. (1994). Individual differences in the development of exploratory behavior: Methodological considerations. In H. Keller, K. Schneider, & B. Henderson (Eds.), *Curiosity and exploration* (pp. 151–176). Berlin, Germany: Springer.

Trudewind, C., Schubert, U., & Ballin, U. (1996). Die Rolle von Neugier und Angst als Basismotivationen der frühkindlichen Erfahrungsbildung [The role of curiosity and anxiety as basic motives for learning in young children]. In C. Spiel, U. Kastner-Koller, & P. Deimann (Eds.), *Motivation und Lernen aus der Perspektive lebenslanger Entwicklung* (pp. 15–30). Münster, Germany: Waxmann.

Zuckerman, M., Kolin, E. A., Price, L., & Zoob, I. (1964). Development of a Sensation-Seeking Scale. *Journal of Consulting Psychology, 28,* 477–482.

Motivational Psychology of Human Development – J. Heckhausen (Editor)
2000 Elsevier Science B.V.

2 Attachment and Behavioral Inhibition: Two Perspectives on Early Motivational Development

Axel Schölmerich

Abstract

Both attachment theory and the theory of behavioral inhibition offer explanations for individual differences in the degree to which children actively engage with the social and physical world. This engagement is an important mechanism of the child's future development on a motivational as well as cognitive level. The theory of behavioral inhibition postulates a generalized fear of novelty for those individuals with an "inhibited" physiology. Attachment theory, on the other hand, explains a low orientation to the physical surroundings with the activation of the more powerful attachment behavior system, which allows exploration only during relative security (e.g., while no attachment behaviors are activated).

Similarities and differences of both perspectives are illustrated in exploring concepts relevant for task-oriented behavior, exploration, and mastery motivation. The attachment perspective offers some empirical evidence relevant for the development of object-oriented activity, and the inhibition perspective contributes information on stability expectations, especially for fear and negative emotions. The inhibition perspective offers no studies on motivated object-oriented behavior (e.g., exploration and problem solving) outside the situations used to assess inhibition itself. It is argued that future research should pay more attention to complex interactions of self-regulatory and socializing influences to explain motivational development.

Early Motivational Development

Researchers within the motivational tradition have frequently emphasized that motives are basic phenomena whose existence does not need to be explained. One example here is H. Heckhausen (1980) who criticized two theoretical positions based on socialization theory: One can be summarized as the assumption that an achievement motive will only develop under certain conditions in the individual socialization, and the other describes the achievement motive as a mere by-product of the development of social motives. He quotes Crandall, Katkowsky, and Preston to illustrate this position: "The basic goal of achievement behavior is the attainment of approval and the avoidance of disapproval." (cited in Heckhausen, 1980, p. 640) The motivational perspective, as developed by H. Heckhausen, posits that the development of achievement-related motives is influenced by socialization variables (e.g., age-appropriateness of achievement challenges) but follows its own developmental logic. Precursors of mature achievement behavior are early mastery experiences (White, 1959), such as *"Funktionslust"* (Bühler, 1919), which differ from mature achievement motivation in that they organize behavior not from a desired end-state, but from within the behavior itself. With the latter in mind, Harter (1978) emphasized the role of regular reinforcement for the development of mastery motivation. Such reinforcement should be given for attempts as well as successes. White's (1959) original idea of effectance motivation was conceptualized as an innate tendency to explore and interact with the environment in an effective way, which does not exclude socializing refinements per se but keeps the focus on the self-regulatory aspects of such a motivational system. The unsolved task that remains for developmental psychology is to study the interaction of self-regulatory functions with social-interactive experiences in early childhood to gain a better understanding of early motivational development.

From this perspective, our research should try to identify factors that either enhance or limit the motivational development of the individual. The literature on longer-term development of effectance, achievement, and curiosity cannot be reviewed here; most of the existing studies are retrospective and the time span covered is relatively brief. However, to illustrate the basic models of connecting motivational development with other aspects of development I will focus on two concepts especially relevant in early development, namely attachment and behavioral inhibition.

Three Models

It may be helpful to illustrate the increasing complexity of possible relationships between antecedents and consequences with three models (see

Figure 1). All three are simplifications: The contents of the components serve as mere examples, and the models are not supposed to represent every single study that was ever performed.

Model 1 describes a somewhat naive theoretical position, yet a relatively large proportion of existing empirical studies are based on this type of theoretical expectation. Here, security of attachment serves as an example of an antecedent for a variety of developmental outcomes (cognitive competence, motivation, exploration, social competence). Some of these studies will be summarized below. Note that for the purpose of this illustration, security of attachment could be replaced with behavioral inhibition, temperament, or any

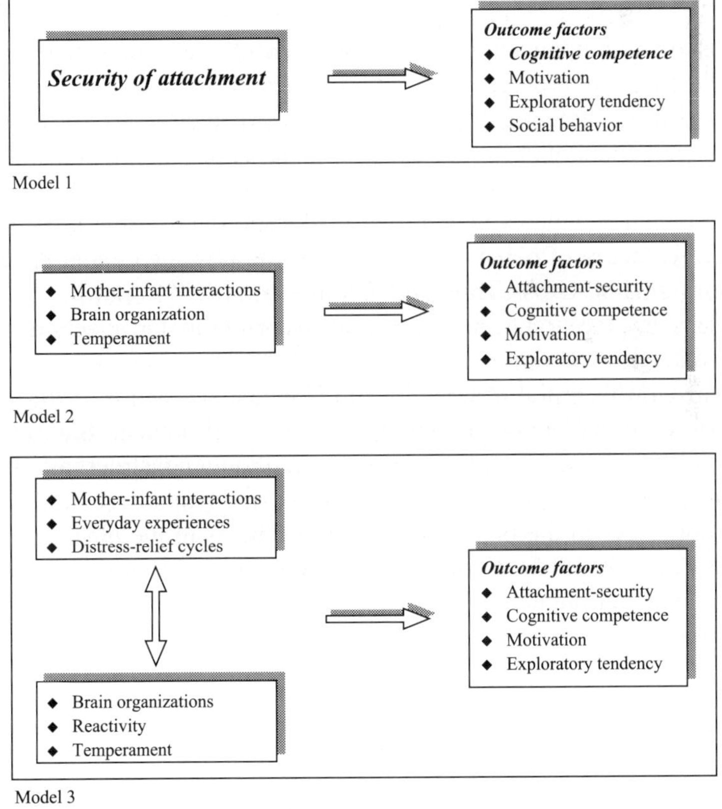

Figure 1. Three theoretical models.

other concept from the figure. The important aspect is that one concept is used to predict one or several others. Model 2 differs from the first one in that it includes several concepts on the antecedent side. Here, the type of mother-infant interaction is seen as one of several factors that influence developmental outcomes. Security of attachment is then one of the consequences (among motivational and cognitive factors) of antecedents both within the child and the dyad. The third model assumes no direct influences from antecedents but suggests that the interaction between specific preconditions in the child and the interactive environment predicts the developmental outcomes, here—security of attachment, motivational dispositions, and the tendency to explore. Again, the concepts used as examples are interchangeable.

The Attachment Perspective

The most obvious connection to motivational concepts within attachment theory is the question of object exploration. The conceptualization is the centerpiece of the attachment-exploration balance (Ainsworth, 1970). Infants and toddlers were thought to be free to explore the world, if their attachment system is not activated. However, to this day attachment researchers tend to focus on the attachment behaviors and treat exploration with some neglect—typically as a category of behaviors that cannot be subsumed under attachment, or, as Grossmann, Grossmann, and Zimmermann (1999) put it: "Seen from our wider view, the strange situation assesses primarily the attachment side of the attachment-exploration balance." (p. 762) This may seem surprising, since Ainsworth's initial observations in Uganda (Ainsworth, 1967) focused on the different patterns of exploration of the environment. She referred to White's (1959) sense of competence (a *motivational* construct) as a by-product of the infant's experience with a sensitive and responsive mother, which should spill over to the baby's approach to objects in the physical environment (Ainsworth, 1985). I will briefly summarize the available literature on exploration as formulated in the attachment research paradigm in the following section.

Central Points of Attachment Theory

Based on their experiences with their primary caregivers, children construct an inner working model of what they can expect from the social environment.

This forms the basis of not only social relationships but a wider array of psychological functions (Grossmann et al., 1999). Especially prominent experiences here are those with a negative emotional undertone, in which the parents provide relief from distress, commonly known as the distress-relief cycle (Lamb, 1981). Upon repeated experience of prompt care, infants develop the expectation that care providers are reliable and that expression of their own felt state influences the environment, thus providing an early model of effectancy (Harter, 1981). One aspect of the dyadic interaction is contingency, indicating the degree of timely coordination between events, which appears first in social interaction. Keller, Lohaus, Völker, Cappenberg, and Chasiotis (1999) have suggested differentiating contingency experiences from warmth in parent-child interactions in a model that explains cultural variation in the internal working models. No specific hypotheses on the independent influence of both components on exploratory behavior have been formulated within that model. However, it may be fruitful to follow this line of thinking to separate effectance-oriented behavior (with a stronger link to contingency) from security of exploration under conditions of fear (with a stronger link to warmth) in the future.

Issues in Studying Exploration From the Attachment Perspective

Quantitative and Qualitative Differences. The central problem with approaching novel events in the environment—the very core of human acquisition of information—is that it may lead to interesting events, and/or instigate mild or even intense fear. Within attachment theory, the emphasis is on a continuous open approach to the world as evidenced in the Adult Attachment Interview (Main, Kaplan, & Cassidy, 1985). Felt security of the child is the main determinant of the attachment-exploration balance. According to this theory, the presence of the mother will—regardless of type of attachment—allow the child to explore more than without mother, and—here is where the bulk of the research has been performed—a securely attached child will explore more (or qualitatively better) than an insecurely attached one, simply because the latter one will be constantly preoccupied by an activated attachment system. Thus, the question of engaging with the environment becomes a matter of a secure base, both in a binary way (with mother, without mother) and a qualitative way (with a base offering more or less security).

Confoundation of Competence With Caretaker Support. The continuity of adaptation is the focus of a classic study (Matas, Arend, & Sroufe, 1978; Sroufe, 1978), in which toddlers were classified as securely or insecurely attached to their mothers using the Strange Situation (Ainsworth, 1970; Ainsworth, Blehar, Waters, & Wall, 1978) at 18 months of age. Subsequently, the children were seen again as toddlers at 24 months of age, and their free-play behavior, compliance with maternal suggestions during a clean-up task, and problem-solving behavior were investigated. Results indicated a high degree of continuity, with securely attached infants showing more spontaneous symbolic play, less oppositional behavior during the clean-up task, and better problem-solving abilities (including getting help from mother when needed). Also, maternal supportive behavior was higher in the securely attached group. This, of course, raises questions regarding the interpretation of the findings, since the performance lead of the securely attached toddlers may also be driven by the actual support in the problem-solving situation or more competent coaxing of the toddlers into compliance during the clean-up session. While the authors claim that "such an interpretation does not seem likely" (Matas et al., 1978, p. 556), it should be noted that the mothers' behavior plays a crucial role in those results. For example, the supportive presence of the mother and the quality of maternal assistance are about twice as high in the securely attached group (B) than in the insecurely attached (A – avoidant type and C – ambivalent type), while the performance gains for the secure group are of much smaller magnitude (e.g., percent of compliance B: .57 vs. A: .39 and C: .40; enthusiasm B: 9.22 vs. A: 6.08 and C: 7.70). Interestingly, the authors also identify a "temperamental" factor, which consists mainly of negative emotionality (crying, negative affect, frustration, and "saying no"). No significant differences between secure and insecure infants were found in intelligence (Bayley Mental Developmental Index).

Integration of Different Attachment Relationships Into the Inner Working Model. Within attachment theory, the central regulative function for exploratory behavior is rooted in the social environment. Grossmann et al. (1999) have suggested using the term "security of exploration" as an integral part of the security of attachment, a position in clear opposition to theorists who had suggested that any exploratory behavior is driven by fear (Halliday, 1966; Russel, 1973). When we use attachment theory to predict object-oriented behavior an unsolved problem remains: The inner working model represents several different attachment relationships with different attachment figures, and no single coherent integration rule is available. Thus, we do not know what to expect when an infant, who maintains an insecure relationship with her mother and a secure one with her father, engages in object exploration in the absence of both mother and father (e.g., in a day-care setting). This leads to difficulties in comparing security-based concepts to typical motivational or approach-avoidance concepts, which do not include significant others in describing individual differences in the exploration of the environment. Three such integration rules for different attachment relationships to different caretakers (assume now a secure relationship with mother and an insecure one with father) can be suggested:

(1) *Hierarchical:* The relationship to the most important figure (mother) is most powerful and others (father) are subsumed, thus providing security expectations in absence of both figures.
(2) *Domain-specific:* Contextual information is used to determine which relationship becomes activated in a situation (mother in care-giving situations, and father in play episodes).
(3) *Additive:* Different types of security relationships can complement each other (expected security = security with mother + security with father). No research on this important issue is currently available.

Direct Influences of Maternal Interactional Style on Competence. Another line of relevant evidence of the development of competence comes from the work of Hoppe-Graff and his colleagues (Hoppe-Graff & Engel, 1996). They showed that the emergence of symbolic play (which is a major developmental milestone in the refinement of sophisticated object-engagement) was preceded in time by the use of symbolization within mother-infant interactions. While we may not want to agree with their far-reaching conclusion that symbolic play activity is mainly socially co-constructed, it seems relevant to include relationships of the socialization type in our considerations. In our context, it may be that different types of children rely on different types of support from the social environment to regulate approach-avoidance conflicts in engaging with novel objects.

Differences Based on the Modality of Exploration. Another neglected issue in the research on the development of exploration and effectance motivation are the different modalities of contacts with the environment. Keller and her colleagues (Keller, Schölmerich, Miranda, & Gauda, 1987) have suggested differentiating a proximal modality (object manipulation or tactile exploration) from a distal one (visual inspection and epistemic behavior). This distinction takes different degrees of physical proximity to the potentially fear-inducing novel stimuli into account. While proximal modes require physical approach and contact, the distal modality operates from a distance and may thus be more appropriate for fearful situations—or inhibited children. In their longitudinal study, no significant predictors of the amount of exploratory behavior (between 8 months and 4 years) could be identified on the basis of very extensive analysis of mother-infant interactions (measured repeatedly during the first year of life); however, the use of different modalities was linked to mother-infant interaction in that more sensitively attuned interactions would lead to greater proportions of manipulative exploration.

Strange Situation Attachment and Toy Play. Mastery-related behavior can be observed in a variety of settings. One study used a toy play situation and investigated the influence of attachment status as assessed by the Strange Situation as well as maternal control style in interactions between 12 and 20 months (Frodi, Bridges, & Grolnick, 1985). The authors found that the toddlers' competence at play and their persistence was related to maternal control style. Mothers who supported autonomy had children who were more persistent and competent, and higher levels of maternal sensitivity were also associated with higher levels of persistence and competence. Unfortunately, the authors do not provide sufficient detail to assess the independent contribution of both correlated (average $r = .53$) scales. Both securely attached (B) and avoidant (A) children were more persistent than ambivalent children. However, it should be noted that the correlations were only modest, ranging from $r = .28$ ($p < .10$) for maternal controlling-autonomy supportive style and competence at 12 months to $r = .45$ ($p < .01$) for maternal controlling-autonomy supportive style and persistence at 20 months. Likewise, the differences in competence and persistence between the securely and insecurely attached infants were generally small in magnitude. Moreover, while the competence difference at 12 months shows A-classified infants at a disadvantage and B- and C-classified infants equally competent, at 20 months, A- and B-classified infants are equally competent, but C-classified infants show a disadvantage. Consistently, however, persistence is higher for both A- and B-classified and lower for C-classified infants. In addition, no longitudinal relationship was found between attachment status at 12 months and any of the mastery-related measures at 20 months. This study contradicts findings that are frequently taken to indicate the overarching influence of attachment status on a host of secondary developmental variables (Grossmann et al., 1999). Recall the study by Sroufe and colleagues (Matas et al., 1978; Sroufe, 1978) described above. Among the problematic aspects is that the Sroufe group used an assessment of competence that included maternal interactive support and emotional rapport with the infant, which is likely to have much conceptual and measurement overlap with variables relevant for the development of attachment. Therefore, significant relationships may be in part artefactual.

In another study that also focused on toy play in relation to attachment status in a non-risk sample (Maslin, Bretherton, & Morgan, 1986; Maslin-Cole & Spieker, 1990), results were somewhat similar to the ones reported by Frodi et al. (1985). Both A- and B-classified toddlers showed higher levels of engrossment with symbolic toys than did C- or D-classified toddlers, (the D-classification was recently introduced and describes the degree of disorganization of the child's behavior; see Main & Solomon, 1986, 1990) but this was only true at 25 months of age, not at 18 months. Again, persistence was not related to attachment at any age. This pattern of findings with respect to engrossment was roughly replicated in a high-social risk sample (Spieker & Morisset, 1986), but here the authors found a surprising result with respect to persistence: A-classified infants were significantly more persistent and competent than were B-classified infants in structured mastery tasks. It is interesting to note that in the non-risk sample, no significant relationships between maternal sensitivity (reduction of frustration) and motivational measures were apparent. The observed differences pointed in the opposite direction: High persistence and goal-directed behavior were related to lower sensitivity ratings (and higher intrusiveness).

Exploratory Behaviors and Attachment in the Home. The most prominent instrument that measures toddler attachment is the Attachment Q-Set (AQS; Waters & Deane, 1985; Waters, 1987). It has been used in a number of studies looking at antecedents (e.g., Schölmerich, Lamb, Leyendecker, & Fracasso, 1997; Seifer & Schiller, 1995) as well as consequences of attachment. Its major advantage is that it allows the assessment of a variety of aspects of child behaviors in the context of the child's home. To illustrate the richness of the item set and to alert the reader to issues of measurement overlap when using this instrument in conjunction with motivational/effectance or behavioral inhibition (see below) oriented instruments, I list those items relevant for exploration and social inhibition. I find it important to note that studies with such instruments can overcome limitations inherent in using laboratory-based assessments only. The numbers in parentheses indicate the value of the item in terms of how relevant this item is in assessing security (range from 0 to 9) based on the established expert sort describing the maximally secure child. A value of 4.5 would be a neutral item, positive values larger than the midpoint indicate security, and values lower than the midpoint indicate insecurity.

(a) Items related to behavior with physical objects:

30. Child easily becomes angry with toys **(2.25)**.
40. Child examines new objects or toys in great detail. Tries to use them in different ways or to take them apart **(6.75)**.
57. Child is fearless **(4.50)**. *Low: Child is cautious or fearful.*
82. Child spends most of his play time with just a few favorite toys or activities **(4.00)**.
85. Child is strongly attracted to new activities and new toys **(7.75)**. *Low: New things do not attract him away from familiar toys or activities.*

(b) Items related to behavior with social objects:

49. Runs to mother with a shy smile when new people visit the home **(6.50)**. *Low: Even if he eventually warms up to visitors, child initially runs to mother with a fret or a cry. ** Middle if child doesn't run to mother at all when visitors arrive.*
50. Child's initial reaction when people visit the home is to ignore or avoid them, even if he eventually warms up to them **(3.25)**.
51. Child enjoys climbing all over visitors when he plays with them **(5.00)**. *Low: Doesn't seek close contact with visitors when he plays with them. ** Middle if he won't play with visitors.*
58. Child largely ignores adults who visit the home. Finds his own activities more interesting **(3.00)**. *Low: Finds visitors quite interesting, even if he is a bit shy at first.*
66. Child easily grows fond of adults who visit his home and are friendly to him **(6.50)**. *Low: Doesn't grow fond of new people very easily.*
67. When the family has visitors, child wants them to pay a lot of attention to him **(4.50)**.
78. Child enjoys being hugged or held by people other than his parents and/or grandparents **(3.75)**.

(c) Alternative choices between social and non-social stimuli:

5. Child is more interested in people than in things **(6.00)**. *Low: More interested in things than people.*
16. Child prefers toys that are modeled after living things (e.g., dolls, stuffed animals) **(5.00)**. *Low: Prefers balls, blocks, pots and pans, etc.*
76. When given a choice, child would rather play with toys than with adults **(3.25)**. *Low: Would rather play with adults than toys.*

It appears that—similar to the Strange Situation—the AQS focuses much more on the social than on object-related behaviors. Still, it would be quite interesting to know more about the object-related behaviors as reported with the AQS. Currently, no studies focusing on exploratory or sociability aspects from the AQS are available. These would certainly be highly relevant for future research investigating the relationship between attachment and motivational concepts.

The Inhibition Perspective

Within the framework of behavioral inhibition, the focus is on self-regulatory capacities of the developing child itself. Kagan, Reznick, Clarke, Snidman, and Garcia Coll (1984) suggested that initial differences in the arousal system lead a certain percentage of the population to show specific reluctance, withdrawal, and anxiety when confronted with new objects, people, or situations. Kagan and his co-workers maintain that behavioral inhibition is a stable feature of the individual; others have suggested that the stability is more limited, and that the high correlations across age are a result of the extreme-group design employed by Kagan's research (Asendorpf, 1990). Behavioral inhibition is a concept that is rooted in the physiological makeup of the individual, a position that explains why issues of stability across development are of utmost importance. Some research has been devoted to establishing which parts of the autonomous nervous system actually negotiate behavioral inhibition (see Schölmerich, Broberg, & Lamb, in press). However, even within this physiologically based theory (Kagan, 1994), it is assumed that

> "further environmental conditions can modulate the behavioral profile; levels of motor attention and crying are not constant from day to day and daily experiences permit some children to learn to control their irritability and, later, their fear. It is even possible that experiences that reduce levels of uncertainty can alter the excitability of the limbic systems or change the density of receptors on neurons." (p. 35)

Negative Emotionality. Alternative conceptions of behavioral inhibition suggest that it is a component of a more general system regulating negative emotionality, generally discussed under the heading of temperamental factors (Rothbart, 1989). All authors in the field would agree that behavioral inhibition can be seen as part of the very basic human and subhuman regulatory capacities around the approach-avoidance dimension. Negative emotionality has been assessed from the newborn period onwards, most prominently in the Louisville Twin Study (Matheny, Riese, & Wilson, 1985; Riese, 1987). From the newborn assessments, irritability and resistance to soothing predicted negative emotional tone at 9 months, and irritability was still a predictor for signs of distress during a laboratory session at 24 months of age (Riese, 1987). There was, however, no stability in predictions based on the newborn period to assessments at either 12 or 18 months of age. It may be that the relationships are more apparent during times of greater developmental instability, as Riese (1987) suggests, but no conclusive evidence is available. For approach-avoidance, no stability information during early development is available.

While it has been shown that infants react to increasing levels of stimulation with looking away or head turning (McGuire & Turkewitz, 1979), the individual predisposition has not been investigated longitudinally. The approach-avoidance dimension, as originally described by Thomas and Chess (1977), is of high relevance for future motivational development, since it directly links to descriptions of adults' motivational tendencies like information seeking (Henderson, 1994), sensation seeking (Zuckerman, 1979), or exploration (Schölmerich, 1994).

Shyness and Sociability. Whereas approach-withdrawal tendencies are typically applied to objects or situations in the environment, social withdrawal may be considered to rely on the same regulatory mechanisms, with the objects being people. Shyness is only applicable to social situations (Jones, Briggs, & Smith, 1986). Kagan et al. (1984) included social withdrawal in their initial definition of behavioral inhibition as a tendency to show reluctance, withdrawal, and fearfulness especially when encountering novel situations, objects, or people. In their study of selected highly inhibited toddlers, Kagan, Reznick, Snidman, Gibbons, and Johnson (1988) found that many of them became shy and isolated school children. The long-term developmental outcomes of behavioral inhibition are discussed in Kagan (1994). The author reported that children initially (e.g., at two years of age) classified as inhibited tended to show few smiles during an interview performed at 12 to 14 years of age, produced very little spontaneous speech to the interviewer, and smiled less during an unsolvable task when compared with uninhibited children, and can thus be classified as relatively shy in comparison with the children originally classified as uninhibited.

Differences Between Social and Nonsocial Inhibition. It appears that inhibition towards objects and shyness show different long-term developmental trajectories, since specific and different coping mechanisms could be effective in dealing with different situations. For example, Asendorpf (1990) found situation-specific effects on the development of inhibition during childhood in assessing reactions to strangers and familiar people in different settings. Hoshi, Kusanagi, and Chen (1997) claim that object-related inhibition and social inhibition are independent even in toddlers, and Goldsmith (1996) found items related to more social aspects of fearful behavior to be independent of items indicating fear in nonsocial domains on the Toddler Behavioral Assessment Scale. This finding is in line with results from another study by Kochanska (1991), who also concluded that there may be two forms of inhibition, one a reaction to novelty in the social domain, and the other limited to the nonsocial environment. Other researchers, however, maintain that inhibition towards objects and towards people remain comparable (Andersson, 1999). The most interesting question here would be how the two tendencies influence each other, as expressed in the extreme levels of object-oriented behaviors of socially isolated children. No such research is currently available.

Positive Emotionality. Positive emotionality has received much less attention in the empirical research literature than negative emotionality. Such positive emotionality typically includes smiling, approach, and motor activity directed towards other people and objects. Infants approach objects with the same emotional signals as those they show when approaching social objects, hence the term sociability describes positive emotionality in social situations as shyness describes negative emotionality. Both positive and negative emotionality have implications for object contacts as well, as noted above. While approach behavior is associated with positive emotionality and avoidance with negative emotionality, we tend to think of approach-avoidance as end poles of one dimension (Thomas & Chess, 1977). This, however, seems to be problematic if one considers the empirical independence of positive and negative emotionality (Goldsmith & Campos, 1986; Haynie & Lamb, 1995). Several researchers have suggested separating approach tendencies from inhibition (Rothbart, 1988) or from withdrawal tendencies (Pien & Rothbart, 1980). Developmental stability of positive and negative emotional expressiveness seem comparable, at least over early development, both for observations of infants in standardized situations (Schölmerich et al., in press) as well as for maternal ratings on temperament scales (McDevitt & Carey, 1981). In addition, under fear induction the inhibited children show a decrease of memory performance, and prolonged response times in a Stroop test. However, no differences in intelligence could be identified (Kagan, 1994).

Persistence and Mastery Motivation. Persistence, a temperamental factor most likely relevant for performance indices, shows a rather limited stability over time (Thomas & Chess, 1977). This was also true within the first year of life (Schölmerich et al., in press). It may be that persistence is a motivational construct that is subject to extended environmental and socialization influences.

The more specific characteristics of children classified as inhibited, for example, in terms of curiosity, mastery motivation, or the tendency to explore novel objects in proximal or distal modalities, remain unknown. We can speculate, however, that certain areas of interest and distal or epistemic modalities are more likely to be selected by inhibited children than by uninhibited ones. No studies are available to support this position.

Curiosity, Fear, and Information Extraction. In a series of studies, Trudewind, Mackowiak, and Schneider (1999) have investigated the relationship between curiosity, fear, and information-extraction strategies in children 3 to 6 years old. In one study, a fear subscale from their instrument ELFRANA called social fear and shyness contributes to an explanation of variance in task performance (which indicated information extraction) independently of curiosity, albeit in the form of an interaction with other variables. Their measurement of fear (see items below) seems to be conceptually related to inhibition and shyness. The relative empirical independence of curiosity and fear poses challenges for the theory of behavioral inhibition, where one would expect curiosity to correlate negatively with fear. The subscale "social fear and shyness" consists of the following items [translated from German by the author]:

2. If a situation is new and unfamiliar, my child frequently feels uneasy.
9. Sometimes my child will be unable to speak when asked to say hello to an adult.
15. My child addresses unknown adults on his/her own.
21. If other children ask my child to come along and play, he/she will show reluctance in accepting the invitation.
26. My child hardly dares to ask other people for something.
35. If my child enters into new environments, he/she will hesitate for a while before looking around.
50. My child will only rarely approach other children on his/her own.
58. Whenever I visit an unknown house, my child will stay by my side.
65. Should my child be addressed by an unknown adult, he/she will hide behind me.

As with the AQS items, there is considerable measurement overlap of the concepts discussed in this chapter. Clearly, multi-method assessments of inhibition and shyness, curiosity, and fear are needed to find out how much of the relationships among the concepts are determined by measurement overlap.

Conclusion

Much can be gained from a combination of different perspectives in this challenging and promising area. Within inhibition theory, a somewhat mechanistic interpretation prevails, which also tends to acknowledge the potential modification of psychophysiological structures through experience and exposure to stimulation without ever investigating those effects with the necessary precision. Research on temperament, which traditionally includes approach-avoidance as an important dimension, has been overly concerned with issues of simple correlational stability over the years of childhood and beyond (Rothbart, 1989). Other influences and crossings in developmental pathways have not received sufficient attention to bring the available information to full fruit, even though models of this type exists in the area of shyness (Asendorpf, 1999). Finally, the attachment literature tends to view every aspect of development as a secondary process based on the quality of attachment resulting from patterns in mother-infant interactions, with only a few studies paying attention to individual differences at birth or continually existing differences in self-regulatory capacities. Grossmann et al. (1999) suggest "pay[ing] more attention to the full range of adaptive consequences of different attachment patterns, especially to consequences that can be understood in terms of exploration" (p. 760). Much could be gained if this suggestion would result in new conceptions of research in early development. Another limitation of most existing studies in both areas reviewed is that they employ designs illustrated in the three models above as type 1 or 2, where developmental outcomes are explained based on single concepts (Model 1) or combinations of several concepts (Model 2) without explicitly paying attention to the possible interactions. To understand the developmental dynamic inherent in the system under study, we should pay more attention to the full range of antecedents of motivational development.

References

Ainsworth, M. D. S. (1967). *Infancy in Uganda. Infant care and the growth of love.* Baltimore, MD: Johns Hopkins University Press.

Ainsworth, M. D. S. (1970). Attachment, exploration, and separation: Illustrated by the behavior of one-year-olds in a strange situation. *Child Development, 41,* 49–67.

Ainsworth, M. D. S. (1985). Patterns of infant-mother attachment: Antecedents and effects on development. *Bulletin of the New York Academy of Medicine, 61,* 771–791.

Ainsworth, M. D. S., Blehar, M. C., Waters, E., & Wall, S. (1978). *The strange situation: Observing patterns of attachment.* Hillsdale, NJ: Erlbaum.

Andersson, K. (1999). *Reactions to novelties: Developmental aspects.* Unpublished doctoral dissertation, Uppsala University, Uppsala, Sweden.

Asendorpf, J. B. (1990). The development of inhibition during childhood: Evidence for a two-factor model. *Developmental Psychology, 26,* 721–730.

Asendorpf, J. B. (1999). *Psychologie der Persönlichkeit* [The psychology of personality]. Berlin, Germany: Springer.

Bühler, K. (1919). *Abriß der geistigen Entwicklung des Kindes* [Overview on the mental development of the child]. Leipzig, Germany: Quelle & Meyer.

Frodi, A., Bridges, L., & Grolnick, W. (1985). Correlates of mastery-motivated behavior: A short-term longitudinal study of infants in their second year. *Child Development, 56,* 1291–1298.

Goldsmith, H. H. (1996). Studying temperament via construction of the Toddler Behavior Assessment Questionnaire. *Child Development, 67,* 218–235.

Goldsmith, H. H., & Campos, J. J. (1986). Fundamental issues in the study of early temperament: The Denver Twin Temperament Study. In M. E. Lamb, A. Brown, & B. Rogoff (Eds.), *Advances in developmental psychology* (pp. 231–283). Hillsdale, NJ: Erlbaum.

Grossmann, K. E., Grossmann, K., & Zimmermann, P. (1999). A wider view of attachment and exploration. In J. Cassidy & P. R. Schaver (Eds.), *Handbook of attachment. Theory, research, and clinical applications* (pp. 760–786). New York: The Guilford Press.

Halliday, M. S. (1966). Exploration and fear in the rat. *Symposia—Zoological Society of London, 18,* 45–59.

Harter, S. (1978). Effectance motivation reconsidered: Toward a developmental model. *Human Development, 21,* 34–64.

Harter, S. (1981). A model of mastery motivation in children: Individual differences and developmental change. *The Minnesota Symposium on Child Psychology* (Vol. 14, pp. 215–255). Hillsdale, NJ: Erlbaum.

Haynie, D. L., & Lamb, M. E. (1995). Positive and negative emotional expressiveness in 7-, 10-, and 13-month-old infants. *Infant Behavior and Development, 18,* 257–259.

Heckhausen, H. (1980). *Motivation und Handeln. Lehrbuch der Motivationspsychologie* [Motivation and action]. Berlin, Germany: Springer.

Henderson, B. (1994). Individual differences in experience-producing tendencies. In H. Keller, K. Schneider, & B. Henderson (Eds.), *Curiosity and exploration* (pp. 213–225). Berlin, Germany: Springer.

Hoppe-Graff, S., & Engel, I. (1996). *Entwicklungsmuster und Erwerbsprozesse früher Symbolkompetenzen* [Developmental patterns and acquisition processes in early symbolic competence]. Leipzig, Germany: Institute for Psychology, University of Leipzig (Abschlußbericht DFG-Projekt Ho 922/4-2).

Hoshi, N., Kusanagi, E., & Chen, S. J. (1997). Nyuji no kishitsuteki tokucho to siteno jodo hyoshyutsu ni okeru sutairu ha sonzai suruka [An individual style does not exist for different emotional expressions in laboratory observations of infants]. *Kyoiku Shinrigaku Kenkyu* [Japanese Journal of Educational Psychology], *45,* 96–104.

Jones, W. H., Briggs, S. R., & Smith, T. G. (1986). Shyness: Conceptualizations and measurement. *Journal for Personality and Social Psychology, 51,* 629–639.

Kagan, J. (1994). *Galen's prophecy: Temperament in human nature.* London: Free Association.

Kagan, J., Reznick, J. S., Clarke, C., Snidman, N., & Garcia Coll, C. (1984). Behavioral inhibition to the unfamiliar. *Child Development, 55,* 2212–2225.

Kagan, J., Reznick, J. S., Snidman, N., Gibbons, J., & Johnson, M. O. (1988). Childhood derivatives of inhibition and lack of inhibition towards the unfamiliar. *Child Development, 59,* 1580–1589.

Keller, H., Lohaus, A., Völker, S., Cappenberg, M., & Chasiotis, A. (1999). Temporal contingency as an independent component of parenting behavior. *Child Development, 70,* 474–485.

Keller, H., Schölmerich, A., Miranda, D., & Gauda, G. (1987). The development of exploratory behavior in the first four years of life. In D. Görlitz & W. F. Wohlwill (Eds.), *Curiosity, imagination, and play* (pp. 127–150). Hillsdale, NJ: Erlbaum.

Kochanska, G. (1991). Patterns of inhibition to the unfamiliar in children of normal and affectively ill mothers. *Child Development, 62,* 250–263.

Lamb, M. E. (1981). The development of social expectations in the first year of life. In M. E. Lamb & L. R. Sherrod (Eds.), *Infant social cognition: Empirical and theoretical considerations* (pp. 155–176). Hillsdale, NJ: Erlbaum.

Main, M., Kaplan, N., & Cassidy, J. (1985). Security in infancy, childhood, and adulthood: A move to the level of representation. In I. Bretherton & E. Waters (Eds.), Growing points of attachment theory and research. *Monographs of the Society for Research in Child Development, 50* (1–2, Serial No. 209) 66–104.

Main, M., & Solomon, J. (1986). Discovery of a new, insecure disorganized/disoriented attachment pattern. In M. Yogman & T. B. Brazelton (Eds.), *Affective development in infancy* (pp. 96–124). Norwood, NJ: Ablex.

Main, M., & Solomon, J. (1990). Procedures for identifying infants as disorganized/disoriented during the Ainsworth Strange Situation. In M. Greenberg, D. Cicchetti, & E. M. Cummings (Eds.), *Attachment in the preschool years* (pp. 121–160). Chicago, IL: University of Chicago Press.

Maslin, C. A., Bretherton, I., & Morgan, G. A. (1986, April). *The influence of attachment security and maternal scaffolding on toddler mastery motivation.* Paper presented at the International Conference on Infant Studies, Los Angeles, CA.

Maslin-Cole, C., & Spieker, S. J. (1990). Attachment as basis for independent motivation. In M. T. Greenberg, D. Cicchetti, & E. M. Cummings (Eds.), *Attachment in the preschool years: Theory, research, and intervention* (pp. 245–272). Chicago, IL: University of Chicago Press.

Matas, L., Arend, R. A., & Sroufe, L. A. (1978). Continuity of adaptation in the second year: The relationship between quality of attachment and later competence. *Child Development, 49,* 547–556.

Matheny, A. P., Riese, M. L., & Wilson, R. S. (1985). Rudiments of infant temperament: Newborn to nine months. *Developmental Psychology, 21,* 486–494.

McDevitt, S. C., & Carey, W. F. (1981). Stability of ratings vs. perception or temperament from early infancy to 1–3 years. *American Journal of Orthopsychiatry, 51,* 342–345.

McGuire, I., & Turkewitz, G. (1979). Approach-withdrawal theory and the study of infant development. In M. Bortner (Ed.), *Cognitive growth and development* (pp. 131–147). New York: Brunner & Mazel.

Pien, D., & Rothbart, M. K. (1980). Incongruity, humor, play, and self-regulation of arousal in young children. In A. Chapman & P. McGhee (Eds.), *Children's humor* (pp. 85–94). New York: Wiley.

Riese, M. L. (1987). Temperamental stability between the neonatal period and 24 months. *Developmental Psychology, 23,* 216–222.

Rothbart, M. K. (1988). Temperament and the development of inhibited approach. *Child Development, 59,* 1241–1250.

Rothbart, M. K. (1989). Temperament and development. In G. A. Kohnstamm, J. E. Bates, & M. K. Rothbart (Eds.), *Temperament in childhood* (pp. 187–247). Chichester, UK: Wiley.

Russel, P. A. (1973). Relationships between exploratory behaviour and fear: A review. *British Journal of Psychology, 64,* 417–433.

Schölmerich, A. (1994). The process and consequences of manipulative exploration. In H. Keller, K. Schneider, & B. Henderson (Eds.), *Curiosity and exploration* (pp. 241–257). Berlin, Germany: Springer.

Schölmerich, A., Broberg, A., & Lamb, M. E. (in press). Precursors of inhibition and shyness in the first year. In R. Crozier (Ed.), *Shyness.* London: Routledge.

Schölmerich, A., Lamb, M. E., Leyendecker, B., & Fracasso, M. P. (1997). Mother-infant teaching interactions and attachment security in Euro-American and Central-American immigrant families. *Infant Behavior and Development, 20,* 165–174.

Seifer, R., & Schiller, M. (1995). The role of parenting sensitivity, infant temperament, and dyadic interaction in attachment theory and assessment. In E. Waters, B. E. Vaughn, G. Posada, & K. Kondo-Ikemura (Eds.), Caregiving, cultural, and cognitive perspectives on secure-base behavior and working models. New growing points of attachment theory. *Monographs of the Society for Research in Child Development, 60* (2–3, Serial No. 244) 146–174.

Spieker, S. J., & Morisset, C. (1986, April). *Competence, persistence, and motivation: Relationships in structured and unstructured assessments of high-social-risk 13-months olds.* Paper presented at the International Conference on Infant Studies, Los Angeles, CA.

Sroufe, L. A. (1978). Attachment and the roots of competence. *Human Development, 1,* 50–57.

Thomas, A., & Chess, S. (1977). *Temperament and development.* New York: Brunner & Mazel.

Trudewind, C., Mackowiak, K., & Schneider, K. (1999). Neugier, Angst und kognitive Entwicklung [Curiosity, fear, and cognitive development]. In M. Jerusalem & R. Pekrun (Eds.), *Emotion, Motivation und Leistung* (pp. 105–126). Göttingen, Germany: Hogrefe.

Waters, E. (1987). *Attachment Q-set (version 3.0).* Stony Brook, NY: State University of New York at Stony Brook.

Waters, E., & Deane, K. E. (1985). Defining and assessing individual differences in attachment relationships: Q-methodology and the organization of behavior in infancy and early childhood. In I. Bretherton & E. Waters (Eds.), Growing points of attachment theory and research. *Monographs of the Society for Research in Child Development, 50* (1–2, Serial No. 209) 41–65.

White, R. W. (1959). Motivation reconsidered: The concept of competence. *Psychological Review, 66,* 297–333.

Zuckerman, M. (1979). *Sensation seeking: Beyond the optimal level of arousal.* Hillsdale, NJ: Erlbaum.

3 Activity and Motivation: A Plea for a Human Frame Motivation

Rolf Oerter

Introduction

In motivation psychology, specific motivational systems have been well described (Heckhausen, 1989) and their theoretical assumptions experimentally confirmed. Attribution theory of motivation (Kelley, 1972; Weiner, 1986), theory of volition (Gollwitzer, 1987; Kuhl, 1987), and the assumption of a rationally acting and, therefore, predictable person are widely used and accepted. All these approaches have in common that the specific motivation system is regulated by an actor who compares competing wishes, makes decisions, and controls her actions.

The assumption of an actor "behind" seems plausible and necessary but it gives rise to theoretical problems. The actor "behind" is a kind of homunculus in the brain who regulates consciously or unconsciously the whole psychic apparatus. This would mean that the acting individual is doubled. His functioning is explained by a miniaturized copy within the hierarchy of systems that are in permanent interaction with each other. There are two ways to deal with this problem. One is to view the actor "behind" as an illusion that emerges from our self-perception in spite of the fact that the coordination of subsystems works without a central regulation (Prinz, 1998). The second way is to accept the existence of the self as a central regulating and controlling entity (Cicchetti & Cohen, 1995; Mischel & Shoda, 1995). For both opinions a number of authors can be found defending their standpoint.

I emphasize in the following the assumption that human behavior and action is governed by an emergent autopoietic system that develops from birth on and is activated when the environment or internal systems demand coordinated and effective actions. Such a self-organizing system is postulated in quite different frameworks. Neurological research as well as psychological investigation and ethnological data with animals seems to suggest the idea of such a system that we call the self. Roland (1985) described, for example, neurological patterns for voluntary attention. Cicchetti and Cohen (1995) explained development as well as dysfunctioning and functioning of individuals by the emerging self as a central system. Gottlieb (1991) used such a system as an explanatory concept for different levels of organismic life, for example, molecular, subcellular, and cellular. In human ontogenesis, we observe from the very beginning a central organizing principle at work. Von Hofsten (1989) and Thelen et al. (1993) conclude from their observation of the development of grasping in infancy that grasping is a kind of problem solving for the whole organism and does not function only as the outcome of one or several subsystems. This view holds also for other progresses in motor development such as crawling and walking.

The assumption of such a self-organizing system does not imply that it always works consciously and that it is always active. It can be assumed that the self as a system is very complex and that only some of its activity is conscious while the majority of its work is not, because the working memory is very limited and the self as a system would not be very effective if all of its tasks were under conscious control. Therefore, the self-system can also function as a well-tuned interaction of a subsystem or an integration of those subsystems (see, e.g., Lewis, 1995; Prigogine & Stengers, 1981).

The Specific Situation of the Human Self-System

If we accept the existence of a super-ordered system, the question arises of what the special conditions for the human self-system are. The notion of "self" suggests that there is a conscious core of attention directed toward oneself. Human beings are aware of themselves as a center of activity and of their body (embodiment, see also Overton, 1998) living in an environment. Their ability to represent themselves and the world around them means that they are in charge of the world twice, first through immediate perception, and second, through representation that becomes independent from the organism's actual relation to the environment (the "world").

Taken together, the two aspects of the self, namely (1) the existence of a self-system that (2) represents the individual and the surrounding world, are responsible for a genuine human need. Imagine an organism that is able to represent itself and the environment a second time independently from an actual situation. This organism is aware of the future and able to undertake time travel into the future and into the past. Anticipating future events evokes the need to cope with uncertainty, which has to be reduced in order to manage anxiety and to remain capable of acting. One possibility to fulfill this need is to use experience from the past and to apply it to possible future events. To put it another way, the self steps into the future, moves into the past, and then travels with new luggage into the future again. Uncertainty, however, exists also in the present. The simultaneous representation of many options and the incomplete knowledge of their outcomes force the individual to explore permanently conditions and the conception of plans that should optimize the outcome of real action. This activity is predominant of all other actions. It serves the well-being of the individual as well as the community. The force that maintains this activity can be conceived of as the human frame motivation, a paramount motivation in which all other specific motivation like the need for affiliation, need for achievement, and even curiosity is embedded.

Fortunately, the individual is not alone with this intriguing but frightening situation. Representations of the world and of the self existing in the world are not solitary constructions but emerge from communication within the community where the individual lives. Culture and community provide frames for specific motivation systems to handle uncertainty of a high degree. This process leads to shared meanings about the world (Mead, 1934). These meanings are co-constructed and, therefore, offer security about the existence of the individual and of the world (Gergen, 1985; Mehan & Wood, 1975; Vygotski, 1978). Thus, for the analysis of the assumed specific human motivation system, we can follow two paths. One path is to look at the individual ontogenesis and to investigate the emergence of its frame motivation. The second path is to follow the development of human culture and to study how human societies have historically coped with uncertainty. Since I focus primarily on the first path, at least a few remarks about the frame motivation in culture should be made.

Religion as a Frame Motivation in Culture History

For 150,000 years cults of the dead have existed (Klix, 1980). This fact is a piece of evidence for religious activity. Religion plays a crucial role in all cultures up to the present. In modern societies religion seems to lose its importance. This development goes against our expectations insofar as we would predict that only societies that have a sufficient economic basis can afford religion. The contrary is true. In prehistorical times when whole societies suffered from starvation, cold, and sickness they showed intense and time-consuming religious practice. Some cultures were even ruined by their religious beliefs. From the standpoint of biological survival religious practices are unnecessary and even dangerous. Religious activity as a crucial part of cultures across time and region cannot be explained through the motivation system offered by psychology. Neither curiosity, pleasure, nor achievement are useful candidates for an explanation. However, the assumption of a general human frame motivation helps us to understand this strange behavior. Facing the situation of being conscious self-systems, human beings construct an explanatory framework of their existence in the world, thus gaining control over their environment in the present and the future. Furthermore, they cope with the knowledge that individual biological existence ends and, therefore, also ends self-consciousness and representation about the world. Religion was the paramount means to cope with life. Every action in life was regulated or co-regulated by religious beliefs. Religion as a frame motivation often ranged higher than biological needs. The necessary everyday activities of finding food, bringing up the next generation, and defending one's own territory were reinforced and secured by religious explanations. From this background, it seems reasonable to search also for frame motivations in individuals and to look for a motivation that is a priori and beyond specific motives.

Four Categories of Human Person-Environment Relationship

A frame motivation is always connected with reality construction and with the necessity to act intentionally in the environment. This specific human kind of relationship has been discussed by many authors who used fundamental categories for its description. Piaget (1976) introduced the concepts of assimilation and accommodation but was primarily interested in the way individuals recognize the world. Lewin (1936) used the term life-space when he described the person-environment relationship. Boesch (1980), taking a cultural perspective, preferred the concepts of subjectivization and objectivization. Last but not least, Vygotski (1978) and Leontjew (1977) described the relations between culture/society and individual with the terms reification and internalization. In the following, I synthesize these categories in order to combine the different perspectives taken by the authors.

The person-environment relationship has two directions, one from the person to the environment, and the other from the environment to the individual. The first direction is called reification because the acting person is producing objects or changing objects in the environment. This process is fundamental for the production of culture, it has to do with the construction of artifacts,

Table 1
The Combination of Four Basic Categories of Action Presenting Example From Adulthood (Table 1a) and Childhood (Table 1b)

	Subjectivization	*Objectivization*
Table 1a		
Internalization	Listening to music	Knowledge acquisition
Reification	Furnishing one's flat	Constructing a tool
Table 1b		
Internalization	Listening to a story	Pretend play
Reification	Exploring toys Naming of pictures	Constructing a puzzle; constructing a building with blocks

of norms for behavior, and of mental knowledge. In individual life, the person is able through reification to adapt her environment to her needs and goals.

The second direction, internalization, appropriates characteristics of the environment that are important for orientation and action. Internalization is mainly learning how to handle objects. This is especially important for the use of tools that are provided in a culture. Tools can be material objects, but language and meanings are also important human tools. On the whole, human learning and enculturation are the prototypes of internalization.

A second pair of concepts describing the person-environment relationship is subjectivization and objectivization. Subjectivization adapts the relationship between person and environment to the individual's needs and desires. Thus, the person establishes a centripetal goodness-of-fit between individual and environment. Objectification means an adaptation to objective characteristics of the environment. This implies a centrifugal goodness-of-fit.

The four categories are combined with each other. Table 1 presents examples for each of the four possible combinations separately for adults and children. The mutual exchange between person and environment through activity provides a reality construction in which the conscious self can achieve a basic feeling of security.

The need for constructing a reality in which one finds oneself emerges from the uncertainty of a self who is conscious of ambiguity and who has to cope with future events. Exchanges with the environment elicit basic emotions that are specifically human and connected with the conscious representation of the self and the world.Therefore, it is not pleasure that is the crucial emotion for human beings but security, safety, and familiarity.

Internalization, especially subjectivizing internalization, provides familiarity, the person feels at home in an environment that was adapted to individual needs. Reification provides the belief of external control over the environment, which in turn guarantees security.

Control as Frame Motivation

Control (Kanfer, 1975), self-causation (DeCharms, 1968), and self-efficacy (Bandura, 1994) are viewed as the most powerful motivating forces of human beings. They obviously belong to the human frame motivation. Our approach of reality construction via the four categories of action provides an explanatory framework for the crucial role of control in human activity. Control provides the feeling of security, the world becomes predictable and calculable. Through control the reduction of uncertainty can be efficiently achieved.

My argument is that control is an outcome of the more basic components of activity described above. It can be shown that these components produce the different forms of control discussed in the literature thus far and two further forms that are not mentioned.

Table 2 presents the relation between different forms of control as conceived by Heckhausen and Schulz (1995) and the four basic components of interaction between person and environment. Heckhausen and Schulz first take the distinction between primary and secondary control made by Rothbaum, Weisz, and Snyder (1982). Primary control involves attempts to change the world so that it fits the needs and desires of the individual. Secondary control refers to the attempt to fit with the world and to "flow with the current" (Heckhausen & Schulz, 1995, p. 285). Another distinction is made between

Table 2
Control as an Outcome of Four Basic Components of Person-Environment Interaction

	Reification: *Primary control*	*Appropriation:* *Secondary control*
Subjectivization	Illusionary	Illusionary Orienting control: subjective order
Objectivization	Veridical	Veridical Orienting control: objective order

illusory and veridical control. If control is based on valid accounts of reality, it is veridical. If control is not based on a kind of physical and social reality, it is illusory since the control belief is unrealistic. Nevertheless, both forms of control can be functional or dysfunctional. For example, a prayer is a type of illusory control but might be functional if a positive outcome is attributed to this action.

In Table 2 it is shown how the four basic components of interaction between individual and environment produce different forms of control. Reification produces primary control since reification changes the environment according to one's own goals and intentions. Internalization provides secondary control because through internalization the individual adapts subjectively or objectively to the environment. Subjectivization produces illusionary control because it does not consider objective features of reality. Objectivization provides veridical control since it takes aspects of reality into consideration that exist independently of one's own wishes and needs.

However, the fourfold combination shows an additional form of control, orienting control. Internalization of environmental characteristics acquires knowledge about the world and about oneself (through feedback from the social environment). "Knowledge is power": It provides orientation and order, which is also a form of control since the individual is capable of acting in a reasonable way.

As a conclusion, it seems appropriate to start with the frame motivation of constructing the reality and then find an orientation for this reality. Again, this is not only a task of solitary individuals but rather an outcome of shared activity.

Activity Theory and Frame Motivation

Vygotski (1978), and Leontjew (1977) argued that the basic human expression is neither behavior nor a mental process like thinking but activity understood as orientation in a world of objects (Leontjew, 1977, p. 23). Activities of individuals are embedded in a societal system of relations. While psychological concepts are mainly formal, that is, applicable to varying contents, activity is always defined by the relation between individual and environment in specific cultural contexts. Those contexts are, for example, playing, school learning, working in a firm, or doing chores for the family, to name a few. Mental processes like emotions, cognitions, and motives do not exist independently and abstractly in the human mind but are always part of specific activities. Therefore, we do not study isolated mental processes but rather look at human activities and analyze how thinking, planning, feeling, and action emerge from them.

Leontjew (1977) introduced a fruitful division of activity into three levels: operation, action, and activity. Operations, at the bottom level, are mostly automated processes that are acquired during development. They are needed for the performance of action. They are a *means* for action. Action, as the next highest level of the system, is defined as the conscious and intentional process of performance. Action is always directed toward a *goal.* The highest level of the system is called activity. It is the frame for the lower-level processes and provides the *motive* for becoming active and striving for a goal. However, the term "motive" does not mean a specific abstract term applicable to any content or goal but refers to the motivation for an object-related activity in a specific situation defined by culture. Therefore, the term "motive" can also be substituted for the concepts "motif" and "theme." Since activity is always embedded in concrete person-environment relations and activity is the expression of the individual as a whole, the personal biography including all experiences had thus far become part of the activity. Themes, issues, and motifs of life lie behind the concrete process of person-environment interaction. Thus, action theory provides a promising basis for frame motivation. Frame motivation turns out to be the "motive" or "motif" of activity. This motivation is the outcome not only of the specific person-environment interaction but also of the person's biography and of the sociocultural history of the situation.

At this point it becomes possible to link our previous view of frame motivation with action theory. The four basic components of person-environment interaction, reification-internalization, and objectivization-subjectivization describe activity at a very general level. The term "activity" is still correct in the above defined meaning, since it refers to interaction between a physical person and a material environment. In concrete situations such as play and school learning, more specific themes and "motifs" complete and overlie the general frame motivation. These themes are becoming autonomous in infancy and childhood, being accepted and loved by social partners, later coping with school, and—as a general theme—becoming adult.

From the perspective of activity theory, frame motivation has two sources: (1) the internalized experience and emotions of reality construction in different fields of life and (2) the generalized values, meanings, and affordances of the culture in which the individual lives. In the following, I focus on the first source of frame motivation but include occasionally the perspective of cultural/environmental components.

Examples of Frame Motivation in Child Development

The notion of frame motivation leads to a better understanding of motivational development in infancy and childhood. In the following, I present some examples and conclude with a more systematic perspective.

Attachment and Motivation

Attachment as a behavioral system has been widely studied in different cultures. As a main result, attachment behavior seems to emerge in every society around the age of one to one-and-a-half years (Waters, Vaughn, Posada, & Kondo-Ikemura, 1995). It is assumed that an internal working model is linked with attachment behavior. The internal working model is a sort of early representation of the self in the world, that is, it seems to be an early construction of reality. For the present state of the art see Waters et al. (1995).

Let us first consider the securely attached child (Type B, see Ainsworth, 1979). If the child could verbalize her view of reality, she might say: My world is secure. Whenever danger is arising, my mother (care person) is available. I can trust her thoroughly. The frame motivation emerging from this view is trust in the social and physical environment and the desire to explore it. In fact, the attachment system is linked with the exploration system. When the child feels securely attached, she begins to explore her environment. Whenever this environment shows threatening cues, the child again looks for attachment (Bowlby, 1969).

Let us now consider insecurely attached children. The Type-A child (insecure avoiding) would probably express her world view this way: In my environment, I cannot count on other persons. It is better to rely on objects rather than on persons. This internal working model fits especially for a subgroup of infants with A-type attachment who play quietly with toys during the absence of the mother and continue playing when the mother returns without taking notice of her. The frame motivation for the insecure avoiding type of attachment is to orient oneself in a world without relying on a significant person.

The insecure ambivalently attached infant (Type C) might express her world view thusly: There is a person who should only be here for me. But my mother is not reliably available. I love her but I hate her also. The frame motivation of the Type-C child could be to reduce insecurity by forcing the mother to stay with her all the time.

Since different types of attachment are also found in later years, people are able to describe their reality construction with regard to social partners (Wensauer, 1995; Zimmermann, Spangler, Schieche, & Becker-Stoll, 1995). Unfortunately, attachment representation is only measured by standardized interviews, while a subject's sophisticated reality construction can only be investigated by the subject's own free description with his private categories and explanations for reality. Nevertheless, we can assume different types of frame motivation also for adults showing one of the three main types of attachment representation.

Gaining Relative Independence

In the second and third year of life a child shows the need to achieve self-reliance. He is proud of performing alone without the assistance of others (Geppert & Heckhausen, 1990; Geppert & Küster, 1983). This tendency can be viewed as part of a frame motivation emerging from the growing self-experience. This frame motivation is manifested in the child's desire to become autonomous from his parents. Winnicott (1965) described this process as personalization reaching from relative dependency to relative independence. We observed the frame motivation of becoming relatively independent in children's play (Oerter, 1999). This motivation was symbolized as spatial removal and delimitation. For example, one boy of two years and five months takes a box, sits down, and pretends to be in a boat. He takes a little figure with him, claiming that he is swimming alone in the boat. Another child, two years six months, visiting his grandfather in the hospital enters the bathroom, closes the door, and turns off the light so that he is completely in the dark for a while. Then he comes out and smiles. Another child of about the same age creeps under the table and pulls the chair close to the table. He comments: "My flat is closed. I am in my house." He repeats the procedure, opens the "door" by pushing the chair away, and remarks "Now the door is open." Then he says "I am going inside," again pulling the chair close to the table and commenting "Now I am in my house."

Every child about the age of two-and-a-half to three years will show similar actions expressing the frame motivation of becoming independent from the parents but simultaneously maintaining the secure base of attachment to the caregiver. The spatial transformation of separation and delimitation through removal, fencing, walling, and so forth shows that the whole person and the whole world is included in the developmental theme of gaining relative independence.

The three examples presented above suggest that frame motivation and developmental task are related to each other. Whenever a developmental task becomes a central issue for the individual, it can gain the status of frame motivation. The concept of developmental task is related in a more general way to our approach to frame motivation insofar as it combines the internal component of the developing person with the external component of environment (Havighurst, 1953). Developmental tasks are also culturally defined. Here, the person-environment interaction becomes a challenge that demands the activity for a longer period of time.

However, developmental task and frame motivation are not the same. Frame motivation goes beyond developmental issues. It is—as I have already shown—the permanent and necessary need for orientation of a person who is conscious of herself and the environment and has to cope with reality in a different way from animals, though higher animals may have the roots of such a specific self-environment relationship. Frame motivation is first of all defined within the four components of interaction between individual and environment and is, during the course of development, more and more concerned with themes, issues, and challenges of life. As early as the 1960s researchers were aware of these frame motivations, when Thomae (1968), for instance, found so-called *Daseinsthematiken* (themes of existence) in interviews with adult subjects.

Frame Motivation in Everyday Life

If frame motivation influences our action, it must also be effective in everyday activities. Here, I examine three typical activities of modern life: traveling, sports, and divorce.

Traveling

Every year people spend billions of dollars on travel. From the traditional viewpoint of motivation psychology, traveling is caused by curiosity or interests. But there must be more involved than mere curiosity because the individual would not need to travel in order to acquire knowledge about foreign cultures. Mass media present visual information about foreign countries. In most cases, this information is broader and more precise, and the visual material is presented in a brilliant manner. Certainly, information from a medium is not satisfying for people who want to travel. However, in other domains individuals prefer virtual reality, as evidenced by the many hours some spend playing computer games. Obviously traveling provides experience that is not available through second-hand information. From the perspective of reality orientation, the person wants be with his body, that is, as a whole in the new environment. The frame motivation seems bifurcated. On the one hand, the person wants to flee from the usual environment into a new reality. On the other hand, the person wants to be in touch with the new reality as closely as possible. This tendency leads to the experience of fusion between individual and environment. The motivation of being not separated from the environment might be especially strong for individuals who grow up in a culture that strongly emphasize the unique properties of the person, thus maximizing the distance between individual and environment. Traveling provides an imagined or real expansion of reality, that is, a reality that is experienced by the person as a whole. At this point in the argument, the term "embodiment" should be mentioned, which was introduced by several authors (Overton, 1998). The concept of embodiment emphasizes the perspective that mental processes as well as action are not isolated from the body that carries these processes. Rather, experience is always linked with body sensations.

Sports

What kind of motivation is the basis for sports activities? Is it achievement motivation, the need for body movement, or the need for affiliation? Let us consider some typical modern sorts of sports: skiing, mountaineering, surfing, and hang-gliding. In all these cases, we can find a common frame motivation that has to do with an intense closeness to nature. Again, the fusion between individual and environment is the theme but now the fusion is of the individual and nature. Skiing and mountaineering provide immediate contact between person and soil (snow, rock). Simultaneously, the mastering of a difficult task mediates happiness and the well-known experience of flow (Csikszentmihalyi, 1975). Similarly, surfing and hang-gliding provide immediate contact with an "element," water/wind and air, respectively. The fusion with a natural medium that is usually not touched or seized is a unique experience not available in usual settings of life. From the perspective of frame motivation, the concept of flow receives a systematic position in person-environment interaction. The very specific experience of fusion of person and environment together with the loss of feeling of time and mastery of an activity in a specific setting becomes a frame motivation for the future, so that the individual wants to repeat this kind of interaction. However, flow seems not to be a secondary motivation but rather an outcome of a very basic form of relationship between person and environment. A prototype of a typical flow experience is children's play behavior (see Oerter, 1999).

Looking for Another Partner and Divorce

Research on divorce has explored many conditions that destabilize the family and especially marriage and partnership. Many of these variables are known: family history, economic situation, personality variables, and growing demands for a partnership in marriage. One condition that is frequently discussed by sociologists is individualism and self-realization. Popenoe (1988) introduced the term "family decline" to describe the growing rate of divorce and the decreasing readiness to invest time and energy in the family. Family decline is explained by the growing individualism and desire for self-realization in modern societies. In a more positive view, Shorter (1975) and Stone (1977) see the roots of modern family relations in the gradual rise in individualism during the last centuries.

Individualism and self-realization can be considered as a frame motivation in modern Western societies (see also Bellah, Madsen, Sullivan, Swidler, & Tipton, 1985). The sort of reality construction lying behind individualism is that people view themselves as the center of the world. Values, persons, and objects are evaluated according to their usefulness for reaching individual goals. Some have criticized the position of individualism as a cause for family decline (Skolnick, 1991; Stacey, 1991). However, individualism and self-realization may emphasize the frame motivation of living several lives and not only one life. If the reality in which a husband or a wife lives becomes boring, lacking any new perspective, one or both may yearn for a new life, that is, may intend to construct a new reality for him- or herself. Divorce and establishing a new relationship is in any case a seemingly new reality for the protagonist who takes this step. A person with a strong egocentric individualism wants to enjoy eventful times, that is, they want to expand their reality or—to put it another way—to live in many realities. This frame motivation is a modern construction; in past centuries the hope for a better reality was postponed to the life after death.

This more general aspect of reality expansion and/or multiplication of reality also fits our previous examples of traveling and sports. Traveling is above all (in most cases only illusionary) an expansion and multiplication of reality and suggests that one lives many lives instead of only one. Sports activities in different settings mediate in a similar way different realities.

Frame Motivation and Co-Construction

Frame motivation is rooted in the person's need for reality construction in order to achieve security and control. But reality construction is not a solitary task of the individual. Rather, it is an outcome of shared activity. One can approach this viewpoint from two directions, first, from our starting point of activity as a general or specific person-environment interaction. Therefore, activity is always fed by two sources, internal and external ones. It depends on the structure of the environment how activity is shaped. The environment in which the individual grows up has constraints and affordances that determine the person's reality construction. A tool like a hammer shapes the action of handling the tool. Affordances of a tool are combined with constraints. The hammer is useful for driving a nail into a board, but it functions appropriately only when one seizes it at the end of the handle, using the physical leverage. The examples of traveling and sports show how affordances and constraints in the environment shape behavior. The environmental affordances elicit frame motivation in that they mediate different types of control through reification and internalization (see Table 2). But affordances in the environment are co-constructions of members of the culture. Therefore, the first perspective taken here can be extended to a cultural point of view where specific affordances and constraints can be systematically ordered. We shall deal with the cultural perspective of co-construction in the last section.

Motivational Co-Construction Between Partners

The second direction of co-construction is to look at the interaction of two or more persons and to analyze how they achieve a shared motivation. Let us start with examples where shared motivation emerges from a concrete activity. This is the case in children's social play. When children play together, one frame motivation is to maintain companionship and play behavior. Whenever a conflict or a failure to coordinate actions occurs, children may try to overcome the disturbance by renouncing privileges they have claimed thus far. In these cases the frame motivation to maintain joyful play regulates shared activity on a higher level.

From play behavior a type of complementary frame motivation also seems to arise. Let us take the example of a nine-year-old girl playing a buy-and-sell game with a five-year-old girl. The older girl tries again and again to play this game with the younger partner, obviously enjoying teaching her the roles of buyer and seller. The younger girl enjoys learning from the older partner and imitating her behavior. Thus, we find a complementary frame motivation. The older partner wants to teach, that is, her frame motivation is to make the little girl like her. The younger girl wants to learn and to imitate, that is, she wants to become like the older girl. Such a co-constructed frame motivation can often be inferred. It arises whenever the relationship between partners is that between an expert and a novice.

Co-constructed frame motivation can be maintained over a long period of time. Consider the partnership in a marriage where a long-lasting goal regulates shared activity between both partners. A shared intended goal can be to start a business, to construct a house, to plan a journey, or to arrange a party. Shared goals and shared motivation can maintain relationships that otherwise would break. Again, we may also find complementary frame motivation for shared goals. One partner may engage only to maintain partnership, whereas the other partner feels committed to the goal itself. Complementary motivation is also present when for both people the goal itself is the object of endeavor, however, different accents are at work. In the case of constructing a house, one partner may focus more on the social advantages of living in a house, while the other partner may be more interested in the technical aspects of house construction. If we consider frame motivation at a higher level, we have to search for a more general theme of life that links two or more partners together. One of those themes can again be seen in the kind of attachment. Attachment types often show stability over the lifetime and even over generations. This phenomenon is better understood if one considers attachment as a co-construction between two partners, first between caregiver and child, later between parents and adolescents, and in adulthood between sexual partners. Co-constructions of attachment seem to be transmitted across time and across persons. Other forms of co-motivational construction over a long period of time can be shared exploration (expansion of reality), feeling familiar and at home (subjectivizing internalization), and mutual assistance in self-enhancement.

Cultural Roots of Frame Motivation

At the beginning of this article, I mentioned religion as a cultural reality construction that fulfills the need for orientation of individuals who have self-consciousness at their disposal. Religion might be the prototype for the shared construction of an existential frame motivation. In the following, I discuss some further outcomes of co-construction in modern culture that contribute to human frame motivation.

As already mentioned, individualism and the personal goal of self-realization are typical characteristics of modern societies. The frame motivation coming from individualism is to enjoy life for one's own sake, to achieve as many goals and objects as possible, and to gain control over the environment. I discussed already the desire for reality expansion and the desire to live several lives as possible outcomes of individualism.

Individualism in the culture develops persons who all consider themselves unique. As a consequence, people with such a self-concept feel more or less separated from the environment. Western naive epistemology considers the person as substantially different from the environment, while Eastern societies emphasize sameness of person and environment (Markus & Kitayama, 1991). The strict distinction between self and other and self and environment may cause a strong frame motivation for fusion of self and environment, as in the case of specific kinds of sports like surfing and hang-gliding, discussed above. Rheinberg (1991) found similar experiences reported by motorcyclists. They describe driving either as penetrating into the landscape or as internalization and absorption of landscape. Adolescents attend situations where the barriers between self and environment are diminished. Those opportunities are found in pop and rock concerts where the behavior of the masses is brought into line and shared feelings are predominant. However, the same behavior is shown in illiterate cultures during a feast. Therefore, the desire for collective emotions seems to be a universal frame motivation.

In combination with the need for fusion we find in Western cultures affordances for intense stimuli that are perceived through different sensory channels. In discos very loud acoustic stimuli are combined with colored blinking lights and rhythmic movement. The kind of experience resulting from such a stimulus combination is a holistic existential feeling combined probably with a strong feeling of fusion with the environment.

The intensity of stimuli is amplified by modern techniques and has shown a steady increase during the last five decades. This development seems to fit a human frame motivation of people in modern societies. If such a motivation would not exist, these affordances of intense stimuli would have already disappeared. The intensification of stimuli and the combination of intense stimuli of different modalities is present in many cultural settings. Mass media like television and magazines permanently try to exceed the presentation of yesterday. People are attracted by such affordances, but they would not be if there did not exist a strong motivation for intense stimuli. Since not all people are addicted, this phenomenon cannot be explained only by curiosity and/or attention to stimuli. With regard to the need for individualism and self-realization, an intensive experience of one's own self and its existence in a world of abundant affordances becomes an important frame motivation.

Finally, let us consider the cultural products of goods that are offered in affluence. The possession and use of industrial products has become the basis of modern economy. A flourishing economy is based on a steady increase in the production of goods. As a consequence, every member of an affluent society is surrounded by a huge amount of artifacts. Relations to those material objects change the definition of the self. The self is not only a system of traits and capabilities but also an entity that is defined by material objects (see, e.g., Habermas, 1996). The more a person becomes addicted to artifacts, the more strongly the self is defined by material objects. Thus, society constructs a frame motivation for the majority of its members that determines individual activity to a high degree. For the individual it seems undeniable to acquire important goods like a car, a computer, and a house. People spend the most time of their life gaining material objects.

The acquisition of material objects also means a reality expansion. Most artifacts are tools that can be used. The extension of action possibilities is at the same time an expansion of the individual's reality.

A certain class of artifacts provides a specific form of reality expansion. They mediate virtual worlds. In television, computer games, and books virtual realities are presented where the individual can participate either by imagining to be the hero of the story with whom the individual can identify or becoming an actor, as in computer games. The high attraction of these affordances fits the frame motivation of reality expansion. This kind of illusionary reality expansion is the counterpoint to traveling where the "real" world is explored. In both cases the same frame motivation seems to be at work.

A glance at our Western culture under the perspective of reality construction and reality experience shows that never in history have individuals had such a huge variety of action possibilities. Actually there are many realities available for each individual, while in former cultures only one rather constrained reality was provided. This circumstance might be the reason for the problem that a formal motivation theory without regard to content fails to understand everyday human behavior.

Summary and Conclusion

I have suggested that there is a level of motivation above specific motivational systems that emerges from the permanent interaction of a self-conscious person with the environment and from the necessity to orient in time and space in a world that is represented a second time within the individual independently from immediate perception. This level of motivation forms a frame motivation and can be derived from two theoretical perspectives. The first perspective deals with frame motivation as a process embedded in four basic components of person-environment interaction: reification, internalization, objectivization, and subjectivization. From this basic interaction the individual constructs (and co-constructs) reality. An important purpose of reality construction (world view) is to reduce insecurity and to achieve control. These needs form a general frame motivation of human beings.

The second perspective relates frame motivation to activity theory. Beyond the basic and general components of interaction, activity occurs as a long-lasting or an actual process in concrete settings. Following Leontjew (1977), three levels of activity can be distinguished: operation (fast and automated), action (conscious and goal-directed), and activity (motive or theme). The highest level corresponds with frame motivation. It is especially related to themes of life that lie behind specific goals and desires. An important stage of frame-motivation in infancy is the development of attachment where the infant elaborates an internal working model in which frame motivation of searching for security is the central force for behavior. The personal history of the development of frame motivation shapes an orientation system that is unique for each individual. Therefore, individuals have to be compared not only by quantitative dimensions but also on the basis of their reality construction and the life themes that result from their biography. Themes and issues as frame motivation can be identified and classified, similar to motives like achievement, affiliation, and curiosity. The main difference in classification consists in consideration of contents, that is, of person-environment relations that have become a part of the individual's experience. From the individual frame motivation, specific goals and motives get a systematic position within the whole self-system.

One aspect that was not discussed in this article should, finally, be addressed. Even though frame motivation results from self-consciousness and the conscious representation of reality, it is not fully available as declarative knowledge (Anderson, 1981). Life themes and also specific actual themes such as gaining a partner, earning money, interest in a movie emerge from a huge range of experience gathered during the life-course. Usually it is not possible to crystallize myriads of perceptions, representations, and experiences into a verbalized summary. The working memory with a very restricted space cannot represent the complete biography of one's life. Therefore, frame motivation works at least partially as an unconscious force. Methodologically, we have to look for procedures of measurement other than just asking questions. For children, play is an excellent medium to get information about themes that are actually at work (Oerter, 1999). The child uses mainly two ways to transform frame motivation into play behavior: (1) narrative transformation, and (2) spatial transformation. In narrative transformation, the theme is expressed through a story that is played by the child (pretend play, role play). Spatial transformation can be found with the child's constructive activity. The theme is expressed through spatial relation. Separation and autonomy, for example, are transformed into spatial arrangements. The child creeps under the table and "closes" the door by pulling the chair close to the table. Similarly, we should look for other types of expression and reification like drawing, painting, photography, and inventing stories.

The introduction of the idea of frame-motivation as a higher-order type of motivation does not question traditional motivation theory but tries to complete it and add a facet that explains the genuine human situation of a self-conscious individual in a world that can be represented independently from perception.

References

Ainsworth, M. D. S. (1979). *Attachment: Retrospect and prospect.* Presidential address to the Biennial Meeting of the Society for Research in Child Development, San Francisco.

Anderson, J. R. (1981). *Foundations of information integration theory.* New York: Academic Press.

Bandura, A. (1994). *Self-efficacy. The exercise of control.* New York: Freeman.

Bellah, R. N., Madsen, R., Sullivan, W. M., Swidler, A., & Tipton, S. M. (1985). *Individualism and commitment in American life.* Berkeley: University Press.

Boesch, E. E. (1980). *Kultur und Handlung. Einführung in die Kulturpsychologie* [Culture and action. Introduction to cultural psychology]. Stuttgart, Germany: Klett.

Bowlby, J. (1969). *Attachment and loss.* New York: Basic Books.

Cicchetti, D., & Cohen, D. J. (1995). Perspectives on developmental psychopathology. In D. Cicchetti & D. J. Cohen (Eds.), *Developmental psychopathology* (pp. 3–22). New York: Wiley.

Csikszentmihalyi, M. (1975). *Beyond boredom and anxiety.* San Francisco: Jossey-Bass.

DeCharms, R. (1968). *Personal causation.* New York: Academic Press.

Geppert, U., & Heckhausen, H. (1990). Ontogenese der Emotion [Ontogenesis of emotion]. In K. R. Scherer (Ed.), *Enzyklopädie der Psychologie, Teilband C/IV/3, Psychologie der Emotion* (pp. 115–213). Göttingen, Germany: Hogrefe.

Geppert, U., & Küster, U. (1983). The emergence of "wanting to do it oneself": A precursor of achievement motivation. *International Journal of Behavioral Development, 6,* 355–369.

Gergen, K. J. (1985). The social constructionist movement in modern psychology. *American Psychologist, 37,* 266–275.

Gollwitzer, P. M. (1987). The implementation of identity intentions: A motivational-volitional perspective on symbolic self-completion. In F. Halisch & J. Kuhl (Eds.), *Motivation, intention and volition* (pp. 349–369). Berlin, Germany: Springer.

Gottlieb, G. (1991). Experiential canalization of behavioral development: Theory. *Developmental Psychology, 27*(1), 4–13.

Habermas, T. (1996). *Geliebte Objekte. Symbole und Instrumente der Identitätsbildung* [Loved objects. Symbols and instruments of identity formation]. Berlin, Germany: de Gruyter.

Havighurst, R. J. (1953). *Human development and education.* New York: Longmans, Green.

Heckhausen, H. (1989). *Motivation und Handeln* [Motivation and action]. Berlin, Germany: Springer.

Heckhausen, J., & Schulz, R. (1995). A life-span theory of control. *Psychological Review, 102*(2), 284–304.

Hofsten, C. von (1989). Motor development as the development of systems: Comments on the special section. *Developmental Psychology, 25,* 950–953.

Kanfer, F. H. (1975). Self-management methods. In F. H. Kanfer & A. P. Goldstein (Eds.), *Helping people change* (pp. 52–98). New York: Pergamon Press.

Kelley, H. H. (1972). *Causal schemata and the attribution process.* New York: General Learning Press.

Klix, F. (1980). *Erwachendes Denken* [Emerging thought]. Berlin, Germany: VEB Deutscher Verlag der Wissenschaften.

Kuhl, J. (1987). Action control: The maintenance of motivational states. In F. Halisch & J. Kuhl (Eds.), *Motivation, intention and volition* (pp. 279–291). Berlin, Germany: Springer.

Leontjew, A. N. (1977). *Tätigkeit, Bewußtsein, Persönlichkeit* [Activity, consciousness, personality]. Stuttgart, Germany: Klett-Cotta.

Lewin, K. (1936). *Principles of topological psychology.* New York: McGraw-Hill.

Lewis, M. D. (1995). Cognition-emotion feedback and the self-organization of developmental paths. *Human Development, 38,* 71–102.

Markus, H. R., & Kitayama, S. (1991). Culture and the self: Implications for cognition, emotion, and motivation. *Psychological Review, 98,* 224–253.

Mead, G. H. (1934). *Mind, self, and society. From the standpoint of a social behaviorist.* Chicago, IL: University of Chicago Press.

Mehan, H., & Wood, H. (1975). *The reality of ethnomethodology.* New York: Wiley.

Mischel, W., & Shoda, Y. (1995). A cognitive-affective system theory of personality: Reconceptualizing situations, dispositions, dynamics, and invariance in personality structure. *Psychological Review, 102*(2), 246–268.

Oerter, R. (1999). *Psychologie des Spiels* [The psychology of play]. Weinheim, Germany: Psychologie Verlags Union.

Overton, W. F. (1998). Relational-developmental theory: A psychological perspective. In D. Görlitz, H. J. Harloff, G. Mey, & J. Valsiner (Eds.), *Children, cities, and psychological theories: Developing relationships* (pp. 315–335). Berlin, Germany: de Gruyter.

Piaget, J. (1976). *Die Äquilibration der kognitiven Strukturen* [Equilibration of cognitive structures]. Stuttgart, Germany: Klett.

Popenoe, D. (1988). *Disturbing the nest. Family change and decline in modern societies*. New York: Plenum Press.

Prigogine, I., & Stengers, I. (1981). *Dialog mit der Natur. Neue Wege naturwissenschaftlichen Denkens* [Dialogue with nature: New paths in the natural sciences]. München, Germany: Piper.

Prinz, W. (1998). Wille und Tat—und was dazwischen liegt [Will and act—and what is in between]. *Psychologische Rundschau, 49*(1), 29–30.

Rheinberg, F. (1991). Flow-Erleben beim Motorradfahren: Eine Erkundungsstudie zu einem besonderen Funktionszustand [Flow-experience when motorcycling: A study of a special human condition]. In R. Brendicke (Ed.), *Proceedings of the 1991 International Motorcycle Conference* (pp. 349–362). Bochum, Germany: Institut für Zweiradsicherheit.

Roland, P. E. (1985). Cortical organisation of voluntary behaviour in man. *Human Neurobiology, 4,* 155–167.

Rothbaum, F., Weisz, J. R., & Snyder, S. S. (1982). Changing the world and changing the self: A two-process model of perceived control. *Journal of Personality and Social Psychology, 42*(1), 5–37.

Shorter, E. (1975). *The making of the modern family.* New York: Sage.

Skolnick, A. (1991). *Embattled paradise. The American family in age of uncertainty.* New York: Plenum Press.

Stacey, J. (1991). Zurück zur postmodernen Familie. Geschlechterverhältnisse, Verwandtschaft und soziale Schicht im Silicon Valley [Back to the postmodern family: Gender relations, kinship, and social class in the Silicon Valley]. *Soziale Welt, 42,* 300–322.

Stone, L. (1977). *The family, sex and marriage in England 1500–1800.* New York: Harper & Row.

Thelen, E., Corbetta, D., Kamm, K., Spencer, J. P., Schneider, K., & Zernicke, R. F. (1993). The transition to reaching: Mapping, intention and intrinsic dynamics. *Child Development, 64,* 1058–1098.

Thomae, H. (1968). *Das Individuum und seine Welt. Eine Persönlichkeitstheorie* [The individual and its world: A theory of personality]. Göttingen, Germany: Hogrefe.

Vygotski, L. S. (1978). *Mind in society: The development of higher psychological processes.* Cambridge, MA: Harvard University Press.

Waters, E., Vaughn, B. E., Posada, G., & Kondo-Ikemura, K. (Eds.). (1995). Caregiving, cultural, and cognitive perspectives on secure-base behavior and working models. *Monographs of the Society for Research in Child Development, 244.*

Weiner, B. (1986). *An attribution theory of motivation and emotion.* New York: Springer.

Wensauer, M. (1995). Bindung, soziale Unterstützung und Zufriedenheit im höheren Erwachsenenalter [Attachment, social support, and satisfaction in late adulthood]. In G. Spangler & P. Zimmermann (Eds.), *Die Bindungstheorie. Grundlagen, Forschung und Anwendung* (pp. 232–248). Stuttgart: Klett-Cotta.

Winnicott, D. W. (1965). *The maturational process and the facilitating environment.* New York: International University Press.

Zimmermann, P., Spangler, G., Schieche, M., & Becker-Stoll, F. (1995). *Bindung im Lebenslauf: Determinanten, Kontinuität, Konsequenzen und künftige Perspektiven* [Attachment across the life span: Determinants, consequences, and future perspectives]. Stuttgart, Germany: Klett-Cotta.

PART TWO

Motivation, Emotion, and Interests in School Learning

4 Motivation and Self-Regulated Learning

Falko Rheinberg, Regina Vollmeyer, and Bruce D. Burns

Introduction

It is obvious that the acquisition and development of competence are strongly dependent on motivational factors. For this reason, questions regarding motivation have always been of great interest to psychologists and educationalists (e.g., Dewey, 1913; Fischer, 1912; Herbart, 1965; Lunk, 1926). At first, philosophical and speculative concepts dominated the approach to these questions (e.g., Herbart, 1965; Lunk, 1926). However, in the 1960s research on learning motivation took a more empirical orientation[1](e.g., Atkinson & Litwin, 1960; Gjesme, 1971; Isaacson, 1964; Mahone, 1960; for an overview, see Rand, 1987). In particular, the concept of achievement motivation—as described by McClelland, Atkinson, Clark, and Lowell (1953), Atkinson (1957), and Heckhausen (1963, 1969)—gained influence in educational psychology.

The earlier speculative theories did not anticipate a surprising problem discovered by empirical research in the 1960s: The influence of achievement motivation on learning outcomes was more difficult to demonstrate empirically than would be expected based on our naive everyday-life experience (for an overview, see Heckhausen, Schmalt, & Schneider, 1985; Rheinberg, 1996). Naive expectations were similarly confounded when other motivational concepts were examined, for example, individual interest (U. Schiefele, 1996). Even if we could reliably show a clear effect of motivation on the outcome of learning, it remains unclear as to how exactly motivation could influence the

---

[1] In Germany there existed much earlier an experimentally oriented research program into the impact of volitional processes on learning (i.e., Ach, 1905) and on level of aspiration (Hoppe, 1930). However, the program's impact on educational psychology remained small, although it did have some effect on other areas of psychology.

cognitive processes that lead to learning and the acquisition of competence (Rheinberg, Vollmeyer, & Rollett, 2000; U. Schiefele & Rheinberg, 1997).

Before we can know what to look for when searching for an empirical relationship between motivation and learning, it is necessary to construct a plausible theoretical model of the path by which motivation impacts learning. Only then will we know what variables to measure and what processes to examine. Without a model, we are in effect arbitrarily choosing what experiments to run without a firm basis for knowing what to expect. Therefore, it is not surprising that the proposed relationships have proved difficult to find. Such a model will be proposed for self-regulated learning in this chapter. First, we will describe the framework, and in doing so we will define learning motivation. Then, we will show how other motivational concepts could be explained in terms of the framework. Finally, the results of some initial empirical investigations based on this framework will be discussed.

The Conceptual Framework

Self-regulated learning (SRL) is central to the development of our theoretical framework for learning motivation. SRL is learning that is goal oriented, conscious, and not under a tutor's immediate control (Rheinberg et al., 2000). Examples of SRL are, trying to gain familiarity with a mathematical formula, practicing the correct pronunciation of a foreign language, studying for a pilot license, learning how to work with a computer, or practicing a piece for the piano. During SRL a tutor's immediate control and guidance is missing, so learning motivation should play a particularly important role. Figure 1 presents a framework that organizes the variables and processes that must be considered if we want to try to understand how motivation has an impact on learning.

Figure 1 consists of four sections. It begins with the fixed *antecedents* of a learning situation for a given person: the person (Box 1) and situation (Box 2) characteristics. The second section encompasses *aspects of current learning motivation* (Boxes 3 and 4). Such current motivation results from the interaction between the situation (Box 2) and person characteristics (Box 1). It has a certain strength and quality and—if strong enough—leads to learning behavior. The third section (Box 5) refers to the *mediating variables during learning* that affect the learning process. The final section is the learning outcome achieved from engaging in a specific learning behavior in a specific learning episode.

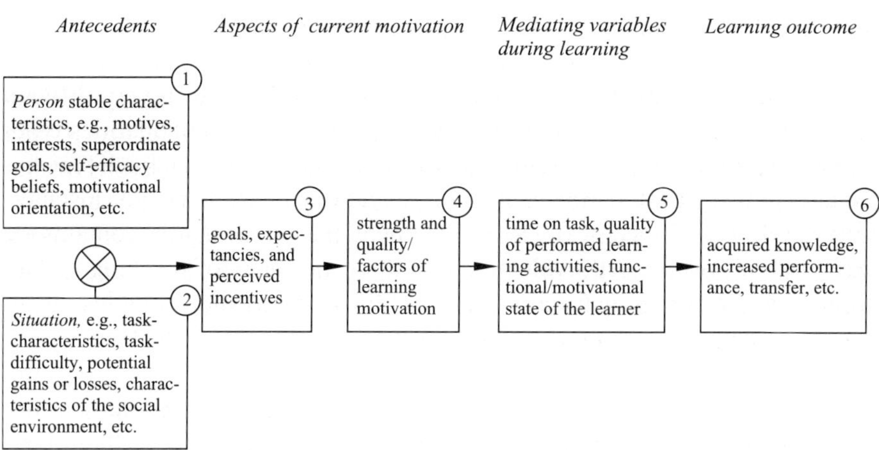

Figure 1. A framework for learning motivation and its effects on self-regulated learning.

We assume that motivated behavior is always a function of person *and* situation, similar to Lewin (1951). With regard to *person* characteristics we place into Box 1 motivational traits, such as competence-related motives (e.g., Atkinson, 1957; White, 1959), individual interests (Krapp, 1992), superordinate goals (Heckhausen, 1977), and similar variables that describe stable motivational characteristics of the person. With regard to *situation,* Box 2 encompasses task characteristics, such as the subject matter or the task's structure and difficulty. Box 2 also contains more general features of the learning situation, including the social setting (learning alone vs. learning within a group) and the potential gains and losses the learner could anticipate in the presented situation. Possible gains could be new information about one's own ability, good marks, learning about something one finds interesting, praise from relevant agents, and so on. Possible losses could be a feeling of not understanding a topic, bad grades, or blame from important people. Which aspects of Box 2 are most salient will depend on the situation.

However, Box 1 and Box 2 interact. Each salient aspect of the situation does not have equal power to influence learning motivation but instead depends on the learner's motivational traits (Box 1). Thus the impact of situation characteristics on the stimulation of a learner's motivation for SRL will vary. In particular, the interaction between person and situation characteristics influences goal setting, the learner's expectancies, and the incentives the person perceives as possible in this situation (Box 3). These variables in turn determine both the strength and quality/type of learning motivation (Box 4). For example, students may study a text because they are very interested in the topic described in the text, they may enjoy the challenge of a very difficult task, or they may anticipate praise from others. These different qualities/types of learning motivation correspond to different motives (Box 1). Each type has a characteristic constellation of incentives and/or expectancies. For instance, motivation related specifically to achievement, that is, *challenge,* contains the incentive of positive self-evaluation and the expectancy of reaching a challenging goal by one's own action; interest-related motivation contains the incentive to be in close contact with an appreciated object or topic (see exposition in this Chapter).

The next step in developing the model is to ask how, in detail, do motivational variables influence learning and how can we understand the impact they can have on the learning outcome? As learning motivation per se cannot produce any learning outcome, we propose that there must be variables that mediate the influence learning motivation may have on learning (Box 5). In the case of SRL, in which the learner has numerous degrees of freedom for how to learn, we assume that *time on task* and the *mode of learning activity* are clearly relevant mediating variables. A further mediating variable may be the learner's *functional state* during learning. This variable refers to the learner's physiological and psychological activation and concentration during learning. Last but not least, we think that the learner's *motivational state* during learning mediates the effects that the initial learning motivation (i.e., the motivation that led the person to start learning) has on the learning outcome. As the initial learning motivation may change considerably during a long learning period, it is not tautological to regard motivational state during learning as a mediating variable for the impact of initial motivation on learning outcome. Learning outcome (Box 6) marks the end of the chain of processes presented in Figure 1.

Taking into account the number of intervening processes between the person's motivational characteristics (Box 1) and the learning outcome (Box 6), it is not surprising that the contents of these two boxes turn out to be only weakly correlated. Therefore, when attempting to understand the effect of motivation on learning, correlational analyses between such distantly related variables will not reveal much. Instead it is necessary to study functionally closely related variables in a research program that examines every single step of the framework specified in Figure 1.

An Expanded Cognitive Model of Motivation to Learn

As already discussed, learning motivation results from the interaction between person (Box 1) and situation (Box 2). Trait-like person characteristics, such as motives, affect the perception of the situation as well as the development of the expectancies and incentives from consequences that can result from a person's action in a specific situation (Box 3). Expectancies and incentives are variables that were studied by "classical" motivation psychology (see Heckhausen, 1991; Rheinberg, 2000). However, the key question is how, in detail, the variables in Box 3 interact in order to affect the strength and the quality of the resulting learning motivation (Box 4). To deal with this question successfully we need a specific model of the processes within Box 3 that specifies the relations between the perceived situation expectancies and incentives.

To explain learning motivation, traditionally *expectancy × value* models have been used (Feather, 1982). These models usually consider only a single type of expectancy and a single type of incentive, that is, value. However, especially when studying learning motivation in everyday life, these simple models need to be expanded, because more than one type of expectancy and incentive is important in all but the simplest learning situations. As an example, let us consider a person who is aiming to pass the written exam to obtain a pilot's license. This person may be almost certain of passing the exam. This represents a form of expectancy. In addition, successfully passing the exam may have a certain incentive value. This incentive value develops from the anticipated consequences of passing the exam. In our example of the pilot's license, one such consequence may be being allowed to start taking flying lessons. Other consequences may be the satisfaction of having managed a difficult task, or gaining prestige in the eyes of peers, and so on. People may differ in how positively they evaluate such consequences, and in how likely they think the consequences will flow from passing such exams. Expectancy regarding the likelihood of the consequences is separate from the expectancy related to being able to manage the task successfully: The latter expectancy relates to how likely the outcome is and depends on one's own action. The former relates to how likely desirable consequences are to flow from obtaining the outcome and depends on relation structures that are established in a given situation. We have to consider such consequence- versus outcome-related expectancies when we try to understand the incentive value of an action-outcome or when we try to influence an outcome value by manipulating the situation. However, the simpler models would either lump both expectancies

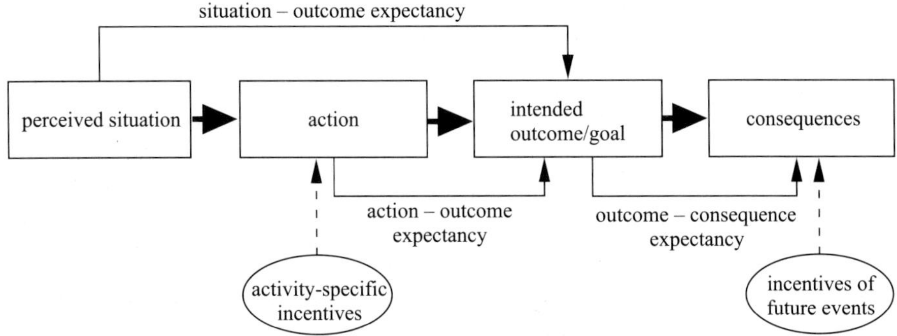

Figure 2. A modified version of the Expanded Motivation Model (Heckhausen & Rheinberg, 1980; Rheinberg, 1989).

into one variable or only consider one of them. To analyze learning motivation in complex everyday life situations, as in our example, Heckhausen and Rheinberg (1980) proposed the *Expanded Motivation Model* (EMM). Figure 2 shows the model's structure in Rheinberg's (1989) final version of it.

The EMM expands Box 3 of Figure 1 in order to explain the derivation of a specific person's learning motivation and its strength and quality (Box 4) in a specific learning episode. This learning motivation subsequently produces behavior, but the derivation processes operate on *anticipated* learning behavior and what the learner believes to be the outcomes and consequences of that behavior. The model subdivides this process into four interacting elements: the perceived situation, the action being considered, the intended outcome/goal of that action, and consequences that may flow from attaining the intended goal. In the pilot's license example used above, let us assume that this person has set a date for the pilot practical test. In the model, this is the current *situation* with all of its perceived options for actions, and positive and negative expectancies. Although the passed test is the *intended outcome/goal,* the model also takes into account the anticipated consequences of failing the test. As already discussed, the intended outcome may have various *consequences,* for example: the chance to fly alone, gain in self-determination, pride in passing a test, gain in mobility, heightened prestige in the eyes of peers, and so on. The most critical element is the *action* because it is the current learning motivation to perform a specific action that we want to study. For each possible action that the person believes could improve his or her skill at the tasks necessary to pass the test, the model can derive a motivational strength (see Heckhausen et al., 1985). For the budding pilot, these actions could be reading several books or memorizing the necessary theoretical knowledge.

To derive the motivational strength for each learning activity, we first have to know the characteristics of the consequences of the activities' outcome: The learner's estimation of the *likelihood* that a hoped-for consequence will result from reaching the intended goal (e.g., from receiving the pilot's license), and the *value* of each of these consequences. Such values represent the *incentives from future events,* an input to the consequences element in Figure 2. These two aspects of consequences are independent: High value does not necessarily imply high likelihood of obtaining that consequence. For example, it may be highly likely that the new pilot will gain the consequence of prestige in the eyes of his or her peers; however, this consequence may have only a moderate incentive-value. On the other hand, gaining the consequence of being allowed to fly an airplane alone will have a high incentive-value but may be less than certain unless one owns a plane, as it is unlikely that other people will lend their planes to a new pilot. The likelihood that an outcome produces a consequence is the *outcome→consequence expectancy,* which is also called *instrumentality* (Heckhausen, 1991; Heckhausen & Rheinberg, 1980).

In parallel to the attractive consequences of a positive outcome, the person may take into account the negative incentives of the consequences of failing to reach the intended goal, for example, feeling oneself to be a failure, loss of prestige, the costs of repeating the exam, and so on. Depending on the person and the situation, either the positive consequences of a success or the negative consequences of a failure can have greater weight in the person's mind (see Heckhausen et al., 1985).

Independent of the consequence-related expectancies people can vary in their certainty that an action will increase the probability of passing the exam. This *action→outcome expectancy* is the same concept as *probability of success,* a concept known from the traditional research on level of aspiration and achievement motivation (Atkinson, 1957). This expectancy can be very high ("If I practice enough, I'm sure to pass the exam"), or it can be very low ("Even if I practice a lot, I won't pass the exam").

As well as these *outcome→consequence* and *action→outcome expectancies* there is a third one: the *situation→outcome expectancy.* It relates to the perceived likelihood that the situation will lead to the desired outcome without the expenditure of effort (e.g., "I already can fly so well that without any further practice I will pass the exam").

The EMM predicts that the motivational strength for a learning activity will be sufficiently high for the action to be performed if the following four criteria are met: (1) consequences have a sufficiently high incentive; (2) such consequences seem highly likely to result from the intended outcome (high *outcome→consequence expectancy*); (3) the outcome is strongly dependent on learning (high *action→outcome expectancy*); and, (4) the outcome does not already flow from the current situation (low *situation→outcome expectancy*). In a series of studies on students preparing for a test or an exam, this model successfully predicted learning motivation when these four conditions were fulfilled (Heckhausen & Rheinberg, 1980; Rheinberg, 1989). However, these studies also showed that the learning activity itself was an important incentive, separate from the incentive derived from the anticipated consequences. For example, learning by heart may be a highly aversive activity for some students, whereas learning by discussing a topic with others may be highly attractive.

In our example of the person studying for a pilot's license, the practical training of flying a flight simulator may be more attractive than learning the facts about motors and rules about how to fly and maintain an airplane. Rheinberg (1989) added these *activity-specific incentives* to the original model, as can be seen in Figure 2. Thus, the model can be described as not only consequence centered (i.e., action focused on consequences) but also as incorporating a hedonistic component (i.e., enjoying a pleasant activity or finishing an aversive activity as quickly as possible). Taking these activity-specific incentives into account helped to improve the predictive goodness of the model (Rheinberg, 1989).

Exposition: The Expanded Motivation Model and Other Concepts of Learning Motivation

Depending on which incentives are uppermost, and therefore, which expectancies become more or less important, different aspects of learning motivation become most salient in Box 4 of the framework in Figure 1. In previous research on learning motivation, other theories of the motivation to learn have focused on various characteristic constellations of specific incentives and expectancies. The generality of the EMM gives it a high potential for incorporating other well-known theories as special cases that can be characterized in terms of the EMM. In the following exposition we will briefly attempt such integration.

Achievement Motivation

The classical *achievement motivation* theory, especially as reformulated by Heckhausen (1972, 1975), defines achievement motivation as "a person's striving to improve his or her competence (or maintain it on the highest possible level) in all those activities where a person has committed himself or herself to a standard of excellence" (Heckhausen, 1965, p. 603). The incentive lies in the self-evaluation of one's own competence (pride or shame after success or failure, respectively). The classical achievement motivation theory defines two dimensions of achievement-related motivation—namely *hope for success* and *fear of failure*—which differ in terms of goal preference (realistic vs. too simple or too difficult goals) and how strongly success or failure is an incentive.

In the EMM, achievement motivation can be conceptualized as the extent to which the learner has a tendency to perform an action that produces a desired consequence via an intended outcome. With regard to achievement motivation, these consequences are the experience of pride in one's own competence or the minimization of shame. Other consequences such as the praise or admiration of other people, prestige, material gain, and so on, may also be important incentives for achievement. However, these kinds of incentives are not relevant to achievement motivation as it is conceptualized by Atkinson (1957) or Heckhausen (1963, 1967). The topic in which the learner is acquiring competence is also irrelevant. Critical are only that people feel committed to a standard of excellence and to improving their competence.

The difference in goal preference discussed above (hope for success vs. fear of failure) leads to differences in the expectancies specified by the EMM. Specifically, people with high hope for success prefer situations (learning or otherwise), in which they experience high *action→outcome* and low *situation→outcome* expectancies that result from realistic goal setting. However, people with high fear of failure do not have this preference and may even show the reversed tendency (Heckhausen et al., 1985). Their preferences lead people with high hope for success, in combination with their preferred attribution strategy (internal attribution of success, unstable attribution of failure), to experience the positive incentive of success (i.e., pride as a consequence of success) as outweighing the negative incentive of failure (i.e., shame as a consequence of failure). Thus, they approach an achievement situation with a positive perspective. Therefore, people with high hope for success are attracted to such situations. In contrast, for people with high scores on fear of failure, the negative consequences of failure outweigh the positive incentives of success. Thus, they tend to avoid achievement situations because for them the net effect of doing nothing outweighs the perceived consequences of trying to learn. Such behavior is ultimately counterproductive as eventually the learner may be faced with situations in which assessment and evaluation cannot be avoided.

Motive Modification Programs

These differences in the goal-setting, expectancies, and incentives people feel in achievement situations have led to the development of *motive modification programs* (Krug & Hanel, 1976; Rheinberg & Fries, 1998; Weßling-Lünnemann, 1985). These programs have tried to influence the students' goal setting so that the *action→outcome expectancy* is experienced as higher than the *situation→outcome expectancy.* Furthermore, these programs attempt to increase causal self-attribution of success to create higher positive self-evaluation after success (i.e., strengthening the *outcome→consequence expectancy* for positive self-evaluation). More generally, these programs aim to improve all expectancy variables identified by the EMM, as well as the positive consequences of self-evaluation (pride following success). These theory-based programs have been successful in practice (for an overview see Heckhausen & Krug, 1982).

Similarly, in his *origin training,* DeCharms (1976) tries to increase the learner's experience of positive personal causation (i.e., making himself or herself a positive *origin* of action and outcome) by supporting the *action→outcome expectancy.* This training strengthens the learner's tendency to attribute outcomes to one's own actions.

Individual Reference-Norm Orientation

Other programs that try to affect learning via variables that are part of the EMM, are those that aim to support an *individual reference-norm orientation* in school classes (Rheinberg, 1974, 1980; Rheinberg & Krug, 1999; for an English summary see Heckhausen et al., 1985). In contrast to the programs just discussed, programs for individual reference-norm orientation change the teachers' approach. Teachers learn to evaluate students' current performance in comparison to their original state (i.e., create individual reference norms). Furthermore, teachers learn to tailor task difficulty to fit each student's own competence level. Both interventions seek to create learning situations in which students can experience high *action→outcome* and low *situation→outcome expectancies,* and in which success leads to positive self-evaluative emotions. Students know that their performance will not be compared *inter*individually with those of other learners (i.e., social reference norm), but instead compared with their own previous performance *intra*individually (i.e., individual reference norm). So the consequent self-evaluative emotions are not linked with stable differences in ability. Instead these emotions should be linked to the changes in competence for each individual learner. Several intervention programs have successfully used this training concept (for an overview see Rheinberg & Krug, 1999).

Motivational Orientation

The concept of reference-norm orientation focuses on teachers and their particular instructional techniques. These programs were developed in Germany in the 1970s (Rheinberg, 1974, 1980; for an English summary see Rheinberg, 1983). Later on, Dweck and Leggett (1988) and Nicholls (1984) independently developed the concept of *motivational orientation.* These concepts have their roots in studies of learned helplessness (Dweck, 1975) and in developmental psychology (Nicholls, 1978). However, motivational orientation is not regarded as a property of the teachers' approach but is instead a property of learners who are distinguished with respect to the kinds of goals they strive for. If they strive for *learning goals* then they have the goal to acquire competence and to do better than they did before (an individual reference norm). As these students consider ability to be something that can be developed, success gives them feedback that they are on the right track. Even failure does not bother them because they believe that with additional learning they can improve their abilities. In contrast, if students strive for *performance goals* then their aim is to demonstrate to others their own abilities and superiority (a social reference norm), presumably through using their own high ability. However, if they believe themselves to have low ability, they will want to avoid situations in which their learning outcomes are assessed and evaluated. Failures give them a great deal of trouble as they believe that abilities are stable over time and that additional learning will not lead to improvement. Unlike students with a learning goal orientation, failure thus leads to performance impairment (Elliot & Dweck, 1988; Stiensmeier-Pelster & Schlangen, 1996; for further differentiation see Elliot & Church, 1997).

In the EMM, the crucial distinction between performance and learning goal orientations lies in the consequences, as well as in the *outcome→consequence expectancies* (i.e., instrumentality). Social consequences are particularly important for learners with a high performance goal-orientation especially, as the *evaluation of others* has high positive and negative incentives for them. If self-evaluated ability is high, then attractive situations are those that provide opportunities for actions that can be used instrumentally to demonstrate one's own high ability (high *outcome→consequence expectancy* for evaluations by others). If self-evaluated ability is low, then such situations are instead avoided by learners with a high performance goal-orientation because failure is especially threatening.

Differences in the belief that abilities can be improved by learning lead to differences in the *action→outcome expectancy,* especially for learners experiencing performance failure. Learners with a learning goal orientation believe they can increase their ability through learning; therefore, they generally have a high *action→outcome expectancy* for their learning activities. However, for learners with a performance goal orientation and a low evaluation of their ability the *action→outcome expectancies* are low following performance failure, because the learners do not believe that they can improve their stable abilities through learning activities.

Interest

Whereas all concepts discussed so far involve variables representing both incentive and expectancy in the EMM, the *pedagogical theory of interest* (Krapp, 1992, 1999; Prenzel, 1988; H. Schiefele, Haußer, & Schneider, 1979) refers mainly to the incentive variables of the EMM. In the pedagogical theory *individual interest* (as a personality trait) is defined as "an individual's relatively enduring predisposition to attend to and engage a class of objects" (Renninger, Hoffmann, & Krapp, 1998, p. 11). (The term *object* was used by Renninger et al. in a very abstract way. It refers to topics and even activities, as well as what would be conventionally called "objects." For a critical discussion of this issue, see Rheinberg, 1998.) As defined this way, interest has two kinds of incentive components: a cognitive and an affective component. The first is called *value-related valence* and refers to the personal significance of an object (similar to task value beliefs, Eccles, 1983; Pintrich & Schunk, 1996). The second is called *feeling-related valence.* It refers to positive affective states while engaging in interest-based activity (Krapp, 1999).

The cognitive component of interest-based learning focuses on the typical attraction and guidance provided by a specific object or topic: A learner wants to acquire knowledge and different perspectives on an object through learning because this object has a high significance for the self (Krapp, 1999). In the EMM this motivation type represents a way of learning in which outcomes are desirable because, as a consequence, a person gains a deeper understanding of a highly valued object. Through learning, the object of interest is integrated step-by-step into the person's knowledge and value structures. Thus interest-motivated learning is a special form of learning based on consequences.

Although there is a cognitive valence component (*value-related valence*) to interest-based learning, this type of learning also has an affective valence component (*feeling-related valence*): Mere consideration or interaction with the object of interest results in positive emotions and feelings during learning. In the EMM this affective valence can be represented by the *activity-specific incentives*[2] (see Figure 2). Thus the activity of interest-based learning itself is attractive—independent of the outcome and consequences. However, this is only true as long as learners are occupied with the specific object of their interest.

Perhaps the existence of positive activity-specific incentives during learning explains why researchers into interest have ignored outcome-related expectancies. It appears to us that expectancies do not play an important role in the pedagogical theory of interest. Instead incentives and valences are all that is considered necessary for motivating learning.

Self-Efficacy

The opposite is true for the concept of *self-efficacy* (Bandura, 1977, 1997): This concept considers only the expectancies and ignores incentives. Originally, Bandura divided what the EMM refers to as *action→outcome expectancy* into two components: (1) the *outcome expectancy* ("a person's estimate that a given behavior will lead to certain outcomes" Bandura, 1977, p. 193) and the *efficacy expectancy,* which he called *self-efficacy* ("... the conviction

[2] We do not consider a possible differentiation between object- and activity-specific incentives in this article, but see Rheinberg (1998, p. 133) and U. Schiefele and Rheinberg (1997, p. 225).

that one can successfully execute the behavior required to produce the outcomes" Bandura, 1977, p. 193). Both expectancies determine what traditionally is called *probability of success:* the actor's subjective probability that he or she is able to produce a certain outcome (Atkinson, 1957; Lewin, Dembo, Festinger, & Sears, 1944).

Thus, self-efficacy expectancy and outcome expectancy were presented as important, and theoretically novel, components of a well-known expectancy concept. However, a close reading of Bandura's research on self-efficacy and learning (e.g., Bandura & Schunk, 1981; Bandura & Wood, 1989) reveals that in learning situations he simply measures the traditional probability of success but calls it self-efficacy expectancy. Therefore, Kirsch (1985) titles his criticism "Old wine with new labels." This gap between Bandura's theory and his operationalization of self-efficacy has attracted some criticism (e.g., Eastman & Marziller, 1984; Meyer, 1984; Rheinberg, 2000), despite the concept's popularity.

In terms of the EMM, self-efficacy—as operationalized by Bandura and Schunk (1981) and Bandura and Wood (1989)—is just the *action→outcome expectancy.* Further, by using the EMM as a theoretical guideline, another critical issue emerges: The self-efficacy concept does not include any incentive component. Therefore, this concept is applicable only to situations in which no participant has any doubt that the potential outcomes are of high incentive value. However, in most realistic situations the learner has a degree of uncertainty as to whether the potential outcome is sufficiently valuable. In such cases, the *action→outcome expectancy* would provide an insufficient basis for determining learning motivation.

Intrinsic Motivation

Finally, the popular distinction between *intrinsic* and *extrinsic motivation* can be reconstructed in the EMM. The problem with this distinction has been that different theorists have given it inconsistent definitions (see Heckhausen & Rheinberg, 1980; Krapp, 1999; Rheinberg, 2000; U. Schiefele & Köller, 1998). All definitions have in common that *intrinsic* denotes a kind of motivation coming from *within* whereas *extrinsic* means a kind of motivation coming from *without* (Heckhausen, 1991). However, there are considerable differences among definitions as to what "within" and "without" refers to (Dyer & Parker, 1975). Sometimes "within" versus "without" refers to the perceived *locus of the determination of behavior* (DeCharms, 1968; Deci &

Ryan, 1987). According to this definition people are intrinsically motivated if they feel *self-determined,* that is, they perceive themselves as causes of their own behavior rather than subject to forces or rewards outside themselves. The latter would be a case of extrinsic motivation. However, DeCharms himself (1976) criticized equating intrinsic motivation with the perception of personal causation. Thus, we do not discuss this conception here.

There are other quite different conceptions of intrinsic motivation (Heckhausen, 1991). Most of them focus on the distinction between "within" and "without" on the components of an action sequence: *action, outcome,* and *consequences*. However, there are considerable differences in the way this is done. Using the EMM as a framework it becomes possible to differentiate between these conceptions in a theoretically meaningful way. Thus, we can determine which kind of incentives and expectancies the different conceptions of intrinsic motivation implicitly include.

First, we can consider a very restrictive definition of intrinsic motivation that includes only behavior that is performed exclusively for the sake of the activity itself (Deci, 1998; McReynolds, 1971; Pekrun, 1993). All actions in pursuit of the relevant end states or goals are called extrinsic. Thus, "within" refers to the *action,* and "without" are *outcomes* and *consequences.* A good example is a person who eats a delicious meal despite not feeling hungry. In this situation the outcome (i.e., being overfed) and the consequence (i.e., feeling bad for hours) are even disliked. The relevant incentive for such consumption is without doubt anchored in the activity itself.

At first glance, this activity-based conception of intrinsic motivation seems to be identical with the conception of *activity-specific incentives* in the EMM (see Figure 2). However, a deeper analysis reveals that this is not true in all cases because many activities that are done for their own sake require an outcome that is a goal. Their goals are integral to the action as they enable and regulate the activity. This is especially true for productive and artistic activities as well as hill climbing, hiking, or many games. If people enjoy the tension of winning or losing a game then the game needs an outcome, even though this outcome has no incentive itself. As soon as the outcome is reached, people start a new game. Thus, this second conception of intrinsic motivation includes the outcome if the activity-specific incentives cannot be gained without it (Rheinberg, 2000). However, motivation that primarily arises from outcome consequences is defined as extrinsic. In sum, this second conception regards "within" as *action plus outcome* and "without" as *consequences*.

Heckhausen (1991) proposed a third conception. It includes all three components of an action sequence (*action, outcome,* and *consequences*) as parts of intrinsic motivation as long as all three components belong to the same *theme* (in the sense of Murray, 1938). An example of such intrinsically motivated learning would be when a person is engaging in learning (i.e., action) to reach a self-set standard of excellence that indicates an acquisition of a new competence (i.e., outcome), about which one will be proud (i.e., internal consequence). In such learning, action, outcome, and consequence belong to the same theme, that is, the development of competence that is *naturally* linked with a specific affect (pride as a *natural incentive,* Weinberger & McClelland, 1990). In this example, consequence-oriented learning would be called extrinsically motivated if the relevant consequence belonged to a different theme than the activity and its intended outcome, for instance, acquisition of a new competence that allows one to reach a powerful position, or help other people. Increasing power or helping other people are not naturally linked with an increase of competence and pride. Instead, they belong to different systems of motives and affects and thus, could be reached in some way other than by gaining competence (Weinberger & McClelland, 1990). In sum, this conception of intrinsic motivation relates "within" to the *theme* to which action, outcome, and consequence belong.

Projecting these three different conceptions of *intrinsic motivation* onto the structure of the EMM reveals that these concepts differ with respect to the extent they include the model's elements: action, outcome, and consequence. Thus, it is evident that the same term *intrinsic* denotes quite different motivational phenomena: from simple pleasure-seeking activities like eating rich food to quite complex and deliberate actions aimed at achieving anticipated consequences. With the help of the EMM we are able to specify which type of expectancies and incentives we have to assess if we want to predict the different phenomena that are labeled with the same term *intrinsic motivation.* Moreover, we can specify recommendations to someone who plans to foster a type of motivation called *intrinsic.*

Motivation and Learning Activity

Assessing Current Motivation to Learn

As the previous exposition demonstrates, theories of learning motivation differ with regard to the question of which expectancy and incentive variables of the EMM they include and model. Setting different theoretical emphasis seems quite meaningful because—depending on the situation and person—

components of learning motivation that differ in quality can be influential. Therefore, each component needs to be described, theoretically modeled, and specifically measured. Different theories can be seen as carrying out the role of specifying the details of different components. Personality-oriented motivation researchers, for example, McClelland (1951, 1985) or Atkinson (1958, 1983), follow the strategy of studying single types of motivation such as achievement or power motivation. They then measure these motives as personality traits that affect behavior in a broad spectrum of situations. Such a research strategy extends our knowledge about the structure and nature of motivational traits (e.g., motives or individual interests). However, research that is less focused on personality traits as such, but more oriented toward *processes* (especially with regard to how specific motivation components affect learning) tries to measure directly specific motivation components in specific learning situations (Rheinberg, Vollmeyer, & Burns, 2000; Vollmeyer & Rheinberg, 1998). When using this research strategy, all motivation components—expectancies, fears, positive and negative incentives—are measured that may play an essential role in the specific learning situation. To discover the underlying structures, factor or cluster analysis can be used to help find the essential dimensions for these motivation components. If this analysis is successful then it will be possible to conduct research with empirically derived factors representing current *learning motivation* instead of stable motives.

By following this research strategy, learning motivation (in Box 4 in Figure 1) need no longer be a vague concept based on the interaction between person and situation. Instead, it can be conceptualized as a variable that is directly measured by gathering learners' conscious responses to relevant questions.[3]

The advantage of being able to measure learning motivation directly is that it removes the need to speculate as to whether in a specific learning situation a particular personality trait, for example, motive, was activated or not. Instead the already-activated motivation could be measured and directly plugged into Box 4 in Figure 1. Of course, a new problem arises now: Because the indicators of learning motivation can vary between situations, any measure must be specific to the situation. In contrast, stable personality traits can be measured in the same way regardless of the situation.

---

[3] The problem of conscious self-attributed versus unconscious implicit motives (McClelland, Koestner, & Weinberger, 1989), cannot be discussed here.

Table 1
Example Items for the Motivational Factors With Factor Loadings

	Factor loading
Probability of success	
I probably will manage to do this task.	.72
I think I am up to the difficulty of this task.	.70
I think I won't do well at that task.	–.68
Challenge	
I am eager to see how I will perform in the task.	.83
This task is a real challenge for me.	.70
If I can do this task, I will feel proud of myself.	.68
Fear	
It would be embarrassing to fail at this task.	.87
I'm afraid I will make a fool out of myself.	.84
I feel under pressure to do the task well.	.71
Interest	
While doing this task I will enjoy playing the role of a scientist.	.80
I would work on this task even in my free time.	.67
I like riddles and puzzles.	.60

The idea of measuring factors of current learning motivation was embraced by Vollmeyer and Rheinberg (1998), who studied self-regulated learning of a computer task. In a learning phase the participants' task was to learn how a complex linear system works. To discover the system's rules, participants could change the inputs to the system in a more or less systematic way (*strategy systematicity*): By observing the resultant changes to the outputs, learners could induce the rules governing the system. To increase the complexity of the system it included a decay; that is, the system changed its state even if the inputs were kept constant. In an application phase participants had to reach goal states for the system (see Vollmeyer, Burns, & Holyoak, 1996; Vollmeyer, Rollett, & Rheinberg, 1997, 1998).

A questionnaire specific to this learning situation (QCM, Questionnaire of Current Motivation) was used to collect responses to a diverse set of items reflecting different motivation components (e.g., expectancies, perceived consequences, incentives). After several studies with these items, four dimensions of current motivation to learn emerged. Table 1 shows these factors with example items (Vollmeyer, 2000).

The four factors were identified through factor analysis, but each was based on a theoretically distinct concept. The probability of success stands for the *action→outcome expectancy* of the EMM. The motivational factor *challenge* measures to what extent learners interpret the situation as a test of their own abilities—in terms of the EMM that means whether the situation is instrumental to evaluating one's own competence (*outcome→consequence expectancy*). In Lazarus and Folkman's (1984) stress model, challenge is assigned only positive emotions like enthusiasm or exhilaration from mastering a new situation. However, our data show that some people develop fear because they believe they will fail in situations that they perceive as a challenge, because the situation is a test of their own competence. Therefore, the QCM treats challenge as neutral but allows the positive or negative connotation to be measured by other factors. Independent of the factor challenge was the affective component *fear*. This factor covers negative incentives coming from self- and other's evaluation. The final factor we identified reflected the value-related valence for the task's topic. This factor fits to the concept of *interest* discussed above.

However, correlational analyses by Rheinberg and Vollmeyer (in press) showed that interest and challenge were not completely independent (they share about 25% common variance). Rheinberg and Vollmeyer replicated this result in several studies with a variety of tasks. This empirical relationship between challenge and interest is theoretically plausible as individual interests tend to develop in areas in which people can satisfy their need to experience competence (Deci, 1998; Krapp, 1992). This experience of competence is only possible if a situation is challenging (Deci, 1998). Therefore, theoretically it would be predicted that the motivation components of challenge and interest will have a medium-sized empirical relationship, despite that they refer to theoretically distinct concepts (achievement motivation vs. preference for a specific object or activity).

From Motivation to Learning Outcome

Although most people are convinced that learning motivation affects learning outcome, little is known about what the mediating processes for this effect are (Rheinberg, 1996; U. Schiefele & Rheinberg, 1997). For example, it is known that for measures of topic interest and the outcomes from studying text, a common variance of nine percent is found on average (U. Schiefele, 1996). However, it was not clear how this effect is mediated. In a series of studies with a variety of mediating variables U. Schiefele (1996) found no replicable effects of possible mediating variables. Highly interested learners read the text differently (e.g., experienced flow) and did different things (e.g., had more elaborative processes) than uninterested readers. However, these and the other mediating variables studied had no effect on the learning outcome. Thus, the proposed mediating variables failed to be validated. Only a single finding of an effect of the mediating variable *activation while reading* was found, but it could not be replicated (U. Schiefele, 1996). Thus, it is unclear whether or not activation mediates motivational effects on learning.

In summary, surprisingly little is known about how the effects of motivation on learning are mediated. This is even more surprising given that self-regulated learning processes have been the subject of much theorizing and empirical study (e.g., Boekarts, Pintrich, & Zeidner, 2000; Pintrich & DeGroot, 1990; Zimmerman & Schunk, 1989).

As discussed above, we have proposed a framework that describes how learning motivation affects learning and learning outcome via three different variables (see Box 5, Figure 1): (a) *time on task,* (b) *quality of the learning activity,* and (c) *functional/motivational state* of the learner during the course of the learning period. Using the framework in Figure 1 we assume that the variables in Box 5 mediate the influence that the motivational factors (Box 4) have on the learning outcome (Box 6). We have already published results applying this framework to the task we discussed above; that is, learning to control a complex computer simulated system (Vollmeyer & Rheinberg, 1998; Vollmeyer, Rheinberg, & Burns, 1998; Vollmeyer, Rollett, & Rheinberg, 1997) .

That there is an effect of *time on task* on learning outcomes has long been known in educational psychology (e.g., Bloom, 1968; Carroll, 1963). Nevertheless, when studying time on task with shorter but more constrained tasks (as compared to those used in school settings) difficulties may arise: Learners with high abilities may quickly reach a high level of achievement, at which point they have the necessary competence to control a system or to solve a problem. Once they have attained competence they stop their self-regulated learning, leaving learners who need longer to reach this competence level to increase their time on task. So poor but sufficiently motivated learners may work longer but reach the same knowledge level as learners with high ability. Therefore, when comparing the learners *inter*individually (social reference norm) there is no reason to expect an effect of the mediating variable time on task: Good learners simply do not need much time, and poor learners with sufficient motivation work longer. Both reach the same competence level. However, when comparing the learner's *intra*individual performance (individual reference norm) it was clear that time on task increased each learner's com-

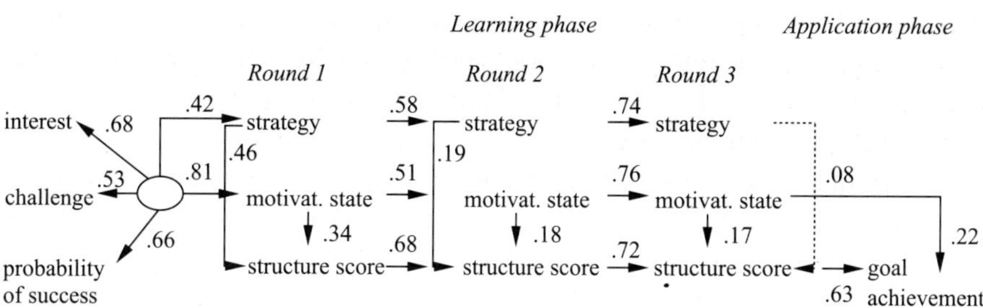

Figure 3. Path analysis for the cognitive-motivational process model.

petence (Vollmeyer & Rheinberg, 2000). An individual learns more by spending more time on a task, but this effect is obscured when we compare across individuals with their different abilities and approaches.

The second mediating variable is *quality of learning activity.* Which learning activities will be considered by the learner depends critically on the task's demands. For our task of controlling a complex system, we already knew that *strategy systematicity* plays a crucial role (Vollmeyer, et al., 1996). Indeed, Vollmeyer, Rollett, and Rheinberg (1998) showed that strategy systematicity mediates the effect of initial learning motivation on learning outcome: With increasing learning motivation, strategy systematicity increases, which then in turn has a positive effect on knowledge acquisition.

The third mediating variable we proposed is the motivational state. As pointed out above, it is not trivial to conceptualize motivational state as a mediating variable for learning motivation, because initial motivation can change during a learning episode (Vollmeyer & Rheinberg, 1998). Figure 3 depicts a path analysis reported in Vollmeyer (2000) that shows how this mediator and strategy systematicity can be integrated into one empirically derived model. This model demonstrates the importance of *motivational state during learning.*

The data for this model was collected in a study in which participants had to learn a system like that described above. Before they started working with the system their initial motivation was measured using the QCM to determine the levels of the motivational factors of interest, challenge, probability of success, and fear. Only fear had no effect on the learning process. A high initial motivation led to a more systematic strategy and a higher motivational state during learning. As we interrupted the learning process three times, we were able to study how variables develop and interact over time. Thus, we found that more systematic strategies helped knowledge acquisition, but also a higher motivational state led to better learning. Finally, when participants had to apply their knowledge, not only did high knowledge help performance, but so did high motivational state.

Currently, we know little about the hypothesized mediator *functional state,* although we would like to measure it directly. A first attempt showed that self-rating for *concentration* during the task mediated motivational effects on performance (Vollmeyer & Rheinberg, 1998). In the future, we will attempt to develop measures that assess concentration and other functional state variables more directly.

Prospects and Constraints

Our theoretical cognitive motivational process model for learning motivation has been empirically supported in several replications (Vollmeyer et al., 1997, 1998). For a specific task it is possible to construct mediating paths for how motivational factors influence learning outcome that are theoretically derived and empirically supported. Although we have initial results, this is only the beginning of a research program.

At this point, the model can only be considered predictive for individual and self-regulated learning activities in a specific computer task, because so far this is the only task we have applied it to. We are now studying different tasks and learning situations. When using different tasks, different mediating variables will probably emerge as most effective. In particular, we expect to require new indicators for both the nature and achievement level of learning activity. Different knowledge will be acquired and different strategies used for different tasks, so appropriate measures must be tailored to the specific characteristics of the task.

In addition, attention has to be paid to the fact that this research program only considers the final three components of the framework described in Figure 1 (Boxes 4–6). If we find solid enough empirical results for these components, then the next task is to test the whole model—starting with Boxes 1 and 2. However, this task creates a practical problem, because given the number of variables and paths between variables, testing the whole model would require a huge number of participants for the statistical tests to have sufficient power. Thus, we prefer to take a smaller step first, which is to investigate the left part of Figure 1 using the computer learning task we have already used. For this purpose we need to design new experiments that can trace the path from the person and situation interaction (Boxes 1 and 2) through to the current learning motivation (Box 4). This will be our next step.

Despite the complexity of our framework, we have not taken into consideration three important aspects of learning. This places constraints on the generality of our framework. First, we have examined motivational variables, but we did not model the effect of *volitional processes* (Heckhausen, 1991; Kuhl, 1998). These volitional processes might have especially strong effects on variables in Box 5 of our framework, because some of the mediators in Box 5 may be controlled voluntarily (e.g., time on task). It would be possible to integrate volitional variables, but for reasons of clarity we have not done this yet. In the long run, doing so would be desirable.

The second constraint is that we have looked at only one type of learning: self-regulated, goal-directed learning. This learning type only applies when people decide they want to improve at something through a learning activity that they regulate themselves. Learning controlled completely by another, such as a tutor who dictates goals and strategies and then gives feedback, is not encompassed by the model. The same is true for learning processes that happen without intention because they are not the focus of one's attention (i.e., incidental and implicit learning).

A third constraint is that long-term changes in the learner's personal characteristics are not included in the model. Such changes could result from the learning outcome and the experience of learning. To take those changes into account in the framework shown in Figure 1, it would be possible to build in feedback loops, in particular connecting the learning outcome (Box 6) to the person (Box 1). Additionally, we could speculate about the person's learning and development in general. This is not our intention. For the moment we consider it most useful to pursue empirical studies that demonstrate the way motivation affects learning.

Acknowledgments

This research was supported by DFG Grant Vo 514/5 to R. Vollmeyer and F. Rheinberg and by DFG Grant Rh 14/3 to F. Rheinberg.

References

Ach, N. (1905). *Über die Willenstätigkeit und das Denken* [On volitional activity and thinking]. Göttingen, Germany: Vandenhoeck und Ruprecht.

Atkinson, J. W. (1957). Motivational determinants of risk-taking behavior. *Psychological Review, 64,* 359–372.

Atkinson, J. W. (1958). *Motives in fantasy, action, and society.* Princeton, NJ: Van Nostrand.

Atkinson, J. W. (1983). *Personality, motivation, and action.* New York: Praeger.

Atkinson, J. W., & Litwin, G. H. (1960). Achievement motive and test anxiety conceived as motive to approach success and motive to avoid failure. *Journal of Abnormal and Social Psychology, 60,* 52–63.

Bandura, A. (1977). Self-efficacy: Toward a unifying theory of behavior change. *Psychological Review, 84,* 191–215.

Bandura, A. (1997). *Self-efficacy: The exercise of control.* New York: Freeman.

Bandura, A., & Schunk, D.H. (1981). Cultivating competence, self-efficacy and intrinsic interest through proximal self-motivation. *Journal of Personality and Social Psychology, 41,* 586–598.

Bandura, A., & Wood, R. (1989). Effect of perceived controllability and performance standards on self-regulation of complex decision making. *Journal of Personality and Social Psychology, 56,* 805–814.

Bloom, B. S. (1968). *Learning for mastery.* Evaluation comment, University of California, Los Angeles.

Boekaerts, M., Pintrich, P. R., & Zeidner, M. (Eds.). (2000). *Handbook of self-regulation.* San Diego, CA: Academic Press.

Carroll, J. B. (1963). A model of school learning. *Teachers college record, 64,* 723–733.

DeCharms, R. (1968). *Personal causation.* New York: Academic Press.

DeCharms, R. (1976). *Enhancing motivation: Change in the classroom.* New York: Irvington.

Deci, E. L. (1998). The relation of interest to motivation and human needs—the self-determination theory viewpoint. In L. Hoffmann, A. Krapp, K. A. Renniger, & J. Baumert (Eds.), *Interest and learning* (pp. 146–164). Kiel, Germany: IPN.

Deci, E. L., & Ryan, R. M. (1987). The support of autonomy and the control of behavior. *Journal of Personality and Social Psychology, 53,* 1024–1034.

Dewey, J. (1913). *Interest and effort in education.* Boston, MA: Riverside Press.

Dweck, C. S. (1975). The role of expectations and attributions in the alleviation of learned helplessness. *Journal of Personality and Social Psychology, 31,* 674–685.

Dweck, C. S., & Leggett, F. L. (1988). A social-cognitive approach to motivation and personality. *Psychological Review, 95,* 256–273.

Dyer, L., & Parker, D. F. (1975). Classifying outcomes in work motivation research: An examination of the intrinsic-extrinsic dichotomy. *Journal of Applied Psychology, 60,* 455–458.

Eastman, C., & Marziller, J. S. (1984). Theoretical and methodical difficulties in Bandura's self-efficacy theory. *Cognitive Therapy and Research, 8,* 213–229.

Eccles, J. (1983). Expectancies, values and academic behaviors. In K. W. Spence (Ed.), *Achievement and achievement motives* (pp. 75–146). San Francisco: Freeman.

Elliot, A. J., & Church, M. A. (1997). A hierarchical model of approach and avoidance achievement motivation. *Journal of Personality and Social Psychology, 72,* 218–232.

Elliot, A. J., & Dweck, C. S. (1988). Goals: An approach to motivation and achievement. *Journal of Personality and Social Psychology, 54,* 5–12.

Feather, N. T. (1982). *Expectations and actions: Expectancy-value models in psychology.* Hillsdale, NJ: Erlbaum.

Fischer, A. (1912). Über die Faulheit [On laziness]. *Zeitschrift für pädagogische Psychologie und experimentelle Pädagogik, 8,* 507–516.

Gjesme, T. (1971). Motive to achieve success and motive to avoid failure in relation to school performance for pupils of different abiltity levels. *Scandinavian Journal of Educational Research, 15,* 81–99.

Heckhausen, H. (1963). *Hoffnung und Furcht in der Leistungsmotivation* [Hope and fear in achievement motivation]. Meisenheim, Germany: Hain.

Heckhausen, H. (1965). Leistungsmotivation [Achievement motivation]. In H. Thomae (Ed.), *Handbuch der Psychologie, Bd. 2: Motivation* (pp. 602–702). Göttingen, Germany: Hogrefe.

Heckhausen, H. (1967). *The anatomy of achievement motivation.* New York: Academic Press.

Heckhausen, H. (1969). Förderung der Lernmotivierung und der intellektuellen Tüchtigkeiten [Fostering learning motivation and intellectual abilities]. In H. Roth (Ed.), *Begabung und Lernen* (pp. 193–228). Stuttgart, Germany: Klett.

Heckhausen, H. (1972). Die Interaktion der Sozialisationsvariablen in der Genese des Leistungsmotivs [The interaction of socialization variables in the achievement motives development]. In C. F. Graumann (Ed.), *Handbuch der Psychologie* (Vol. 7/2, pp. 955–1019). Göttingen, Germany: Hogrefe.

Heckhausen, H. (1975). Fear of failure as a self-reinforcing motive system. In I.G. Sarason & C. Spielberger (Eds.), *Stress and anxiety* (pp. 117–128). Washington, DC: Hemisphere.

Heckhausen, H. (1977). Achievement motivation and its constructs: A cognitive model. *Motivation and Emotion, 1,* 283–329.

Heckhausen, H. (1991). *Motivation and action.* Berlin: Springer.

Heckhausen, H., & Krug, S. (1982). Motive modification. In A. J. Stewart (Ed.), *Motivation and society* (pp. 274–318). San Francisco: Jossey-Bass.

Heckhausen, H., & Rheinberg, F. (1980). Lernmotivation im Unterricht, erneut betrachtet [Learning motivation in classes reconsidered]. *Unterrichtswissenschaft, 8,* 7–47.

Heckhausen, H., Schmalt, H.-D., & Schneider, K. (1985). *Achievement motivation in perspective.* New York: Academic Press.

Herbart, J. F. (1965). Allgemeine Pädagogik, aus dem Zweck der Erziehung abgeleitet [General pedagogics, deduced from the purpose of education]. In J. F. Herbart (Ed.), *Pädagogische Schriften* [Educational scripts] (pp. 9–155). Düsseldorf, Germany: Küpper.

Hoppe, F. (1930). Untersuchungen zur Handlungs- und Affektpsychologie, IX. Erfolg und Mißerfolg [Studies on action and affect psychology, IX. Success and failure]. *Psychologische Forschung, 14,* 1–63.

Isaacson, R. L. (1964). Relation between n-achievement, test anxiety and curricular choices. *Journal of Abnormal and Social Psychology, 68,* 447–452.

Kirsch, J. (1985). Self-efficacy and expectancy: Old wine with new labels. *Journal of Personality and Social Psychology, 49,* 824–830.

Krapp, A. (1992). Das Interessenkonstrukt. Bestimmungsmerkmale der Interessenhandlung und des individuellen Interesses aus der Sicht einer Person-Gegenstands-Konzeption

[The interest construct]. In A. Krapp & M. Prenzel (Eds.), *Interesse, Lernen, Leistung* (pp. 297–330). Münster, Germany: Aschendorff.

Krapp, A. (1999). Intrinsische Lernmotivation und Interesse [Intrinsic learning motivation and interest]. *Zeitschrift für Pädagogik, 45,* 387–406.

Krug, S., & Hanel, J. (1976). Motivänderung: Erprobung eines theoriegeleiteten Trainingsprogrammes [Motive modification: Evaluation of a training program]. *Zeitschrift für Entwicklungspsychologie und Pädagogische Psychologie, 8,* 274–287.

Kuhl, J. (1998). Decomposing self-regulation and self-control: The volitional component inventory. In H. Heckhausen & C. S. Dweck (Eds.), *Motivation and self-regulation across the life span* (pp. 15–49). Cambridge, UK: Cambridge University Press.

Lazarus, R. S., & Folkman, S. (1984). *Stress, appraisal and coping.* New York: Springer.

Lewin, K. (1951). *Field theory in social science.* Chicago, IL: University of Chicago Press.

Lewin, K., Dembo, T., Festinger, L., & Sears, P. S. (1944). Level of aspiration. In J. M. V. Hunt (Ed.), *Personality and the behavior disorders* (Vol.: 1, pp. 333–378). New York: Ronald.

Lunk, G. (1926). *Das Interesse* [The interest]. Leipzig, Germany: Klinkhardt.

Mahone, C.H. (1960). Fear of failure and unrealistic vocational aspiration. *Journal of Abnormal and Social Psychology, 60,* 253–261.

McClelland, D.C. (1951). *Personality.* New York: Holt, Rinehart and Winston.

McClelland, D.C. (1985). *Human motivation.* Glenview, IL: Scott, Foresman & Co.

McClelland, D. C., Atkinson, J. W., Clark, R. A., & Lowell, E. L. (1953). *The achievement motive.* New York: Appleton-Century-Crofts.

McClelland, D.C., Koestner, R., & Weinberg, J. (1989). How do self-attributed and implicit motives differ? *Psychological Review, 96,* 690–702.

McReynolds, P. (1971). The nature and assessment of intrinsic motivation. In P. McReynolds (Ed.), *Advances in psychological assessment.* Palo Alto, CA: Science and Behavior Books.

Meyer, W.-U. (1984). *Das Konzept von der eigenen Begabung* [The concept of one's own ability]. Stuttgart, Germany: Huber.

Murray, H. A. (1938). *Explorations in personality.* New York: Oxford University Press.

Nicholls, J. G. (1978). The development of the concepts of effort and ability, perception of attainment, and the understanding that difficult tasks require more ability. *Child Development, 49,* 800–814.

Nicholls, J. G. (1984). Achievement motivation: Conceptions of ability, subjective experience, task choice, and performance. *Psychological Review, 91,* 328–346.

Pekrun, R. (1993). Entwicklung von schulischer Aufgabenmotivation in der Sekundarstufe: Ein erwartungswert-theoretischer Ansatz [Development of academic task motivation in secondary school: An expectancy-value approach]. *Zeitschrift für Pädagogische Psychologie, 7,* 87–98.

Pintrich, P. R., & Schunk, D.H. (1996). *Motivation in education. Theory, research and applications.* Englewood Cliffs, NJ: Prentice Hall.

Pintrich, P. R., & DeGroot, E. V. (1990). Motivational and self-regulated learning components of classroom academic performance. *Journal of Educational Psychology, 82,* 33–40.

Prenzel, M. (1988). *Die Wirkungsweise von Interesse* [How interest works]. Opladen, Germany: Westdeutscher Verlag.

Rand, P. (1987). Research on achievement motivation in school and college. In F. Halisch & J. Kuhl (Eds.), *Motivation intention and volition* (pp. 215–232). Berlin, Germany: Springer.

Renninger, K. A., Hoffmann, L., & Krapp, A. (1998). Interest and gender: Issues of development and learning. In L. Hoffmann, A. Krapp, K. A. Renninger, & J. Baumert (Eds.), *Interest and learning* (pp. 9–24). Kiel, Germany: IPN.

Rheinberg, F. (1974). *Kognitive Zwischenprozesse bei der Verarbeitung von Informationen über Schülerleistungen—Versuch einer Lehrertypologie* [Mediating cognitions when processing information on students' performance—A typology of teachers]. Arbeitsbericht der Arbeitseinheit Motivation und Entwicklung, Psychologisches Institut der Universität Bochum, Germany.

Rheinberg, F. (1980). *Leistungsbewertung und Lernmotivation* [Achievement evaluation and motivation to learn]. Göttingen, Germany: Hogrefe.

Rheinberg, F. (1983). Achievement evaluation: A fundamental difference and its motivational consequences. *Studies in Educational Evaluation, 9,* 185–194.

Rheinberg, F. (1989). *Zweck und Tätigkeit* [Purpose and action]. Göttingen, Germany: Hogrefe.

Rheinberg, F. (1996). Von der Lernmotivation zur Lernleistung. Was liegt dazwischen? [From motivation to learn to learning outcome. What's between both?] In J. Möller & O. Köller (Eds.), *Emotion, Kognition und Schulleistung* [Emotion, cognition, and academic achievement] (pp. 23–51). Weinheim, Germany: PVU.

Rheinberg, F. (1998). Theory of interest and research on motivation to learn. In L. Hoffmann, A. Krapp, K.A. Renninger, & J. Baumert (Eds.), *Interest and learning* (pp. 126–145). Kiel, Germany: IPN.

Rheinberg, F. (2000). *Motivation* [Motivation] (3rd ed.). Stuttgart, Germany: Kohlhammer.

Rheinberg, F., & Fries, S. (1998). Förderung der Lernmotivation: Ansatzpunkte, Strategien und Effekte [Promotion of learning motivation: Approaches, strategies, and effects]. *Psychologie in Erziehung und Unterricht, 3,* 168–184.

Rheinberg, F., & Krug, S. (1999). *Motivationsförderung im Schulalltag* [Fostering motivation at school] (2nd ed.). Göttingen, Germany: Hogrefe.

Rheinberg, F., & Vollmeyer, R. (in press). Sachinteresse und leistungsthematische Herausforderung—zwei verschiedenartige Motivationskomponenten und ihr Zusammenwirken beim Lernen [Content-related interest and achievement challenges—two different components of motivation and their joint influence]. In K. P. Wild & U. Schiefele (Eds.), *Lernumgebung, Lernmotivation und Lernverhalten* [Learning environment, learning motivation, and learning behavior]. Münster, Germany: Waxmann.

Rheinberg, F., Vollmeyer, R., & Burns, B. D. (2000). *FAM: Ein Fragebogen zur Erfassung aktueller Motivation in Lern- und Leistungssituationen* [QCM: A questionnaire to assess current motivation in learning situations]. Manuscript in preparation.

Rheinberg, F., Vollmeyer, R., & Rollett, W. (2000). Motivation and action in self-regulated learning. In M. Boekaerts, P. R. Pintrich, & M. Zeidner (Eds.), *Handbook of self-regulation: Theory, research, and application* (pp. 503–529). San Diego, CA: Academic Press.

Schiefele, H., Haußer, K., & Schneider, G. (1979). "Interesse" als Ziel und Weg der Erziehung. Überlegungen zu einem vernachlässigten pädagogischen Konzept [Interest as goal and way of education]. *Zeitschrift für Pädagogik, 25,* 1–20.

Schiefele, U. (1996). *Motivation und Lernen mit Texten* [Motivation and text learning]. Göttingen, Germany: Hogrefe.

Schiefele, U., & Köller, O. (1998). Intrinsische und extrinsische Motivation [Intrinsic and extrinsic motivation]. In D. H. Rost (Ed.), *Handwörterbuch Pädagogische Psychologie* (pp. 193–197). Weinheim, Germany: PVU.

Schiefele, U., & Rheinberg, F. (1997). Motivation and knowledge acquisition: Searching for mediating processes. In P. Pintrich & M. L. Maehr (Eds.), *Advances in motivation and achievement* (pp. 251–302). Greenwich, CT: JAI Press.

Stiensmeier-Pelster, J., & Schlangen, B. (1996). Erlernte Hilflosigkeit und Leistung [Learned helplessness and performance]. In J. Möller & O. Köller (Eds.), *Emotionen, Kognitionen und Schulleistung* (pp. 69–90). Weinheim, Germany: Psychologie Verlags Union.

Vollmeyer, R. (2000.). *Motivational effects when learning a complex system.* Manuscript in preparation.

Vollmeyer, R., Burns, B. D., & Holyoak, K. J. (1996). The impact of goal specificity on strategy use and the acquisition of problem structure. *Cognitive Science, 20,* 75–100.

Vollmeyer, R., & Rheinberg, F. (1998). Motivationale Einflüsse auf Erwerb und Anwendung von Wissen in einem computersimulierten System [Motivational influences on the acquisition and application of knowledge in a simulated system]. *Zeitschrift für Pädagogische Psychologie, 12,* 11–23.

Vollmeyer, R., & Rheinberg, F. (2000). Does motivation affect learning via persistence? *Learning and Instruction, 10.*

Vollmeyer, R., Rheinberg, F., & Burns, B. D. (1998). Goals, strategies, and motivation. In M. A. Gernsbacher & S. J. Derry (Eds.), *Proceedings of the Twentieht Annual Conference of the Cognitive Science Society* (pp. 1090–1095). Hillsdale, NJ: Erlbaum.

Vollmeyer, R., Rollett, W., & Rheinberg, F. (1997). How motivation affects learning. In M. G. Shafto & P. Langley (Eds.), *Proceedings of the nineteenth annual conference of the cognitive science society* (pp. 796–801). Mahwah, NJ: Erlbaum.

Vollmeyer, R., Rollett, W., & Rheinberg, F. (1998). Motivation and learning in a complex system. In P. Nenniger, R. S. Jäger, A. Frey, & M. Wosnitza (Eds.), *Advances in motivation* (pp. 53–67). Landau, Germany: Verlag für Empirische Pädagogik.

Weinberger, J., & McClelland, D. C. (1990). Cognitive versus traditional motivational models. In E. Higgins & R. M. Sorrentino (Eds.), *Handbook of motivation and cognition: Foundations of social behavior* (pp. 562–597). New York: Guilford Press.

Weßling-Lünnemann, G. (1985). *Motivationsförderung im Unterricht* [Fostering motivation in classes]. Göttingen, Germany: Hogrefe.

White, R. W. (1959). Motivation reconsidered: The concept of competence. *Psychological Review, 66,* 297–333.

Zimmerman, B. J., & Schunk, D. H. (1989). *Self-regulated learning and academic achievement. Theory, research, and practice.* New York: Springer.

Motivational Psychology of Human Development – J. Heckhausen (Editor)

5 Interest and Human Development During Adolescence: An Educational-Psychological Approach

Andreas Krapp

Far into the 20th century educational psychological research has dealt very intensively with the interaction of motivation, learning, and personality development. The scientific discussion was based on relatively broad dynamic conceptions of the personality, and the concept of interest was often taken into account to describe the motivational components (e.g., Dewey, 1913; Kerschensteiner, 1926; Rubinstein, 1958; cf. Berlyne, 1949; Lunk, 1926, 1927; Prenzel, 1988, p. 20ff.). A major emphasis of the discussions dealt with the question of how the personality adapts to the given environmental conditions in the course of a person's life, at the same time establishing an individualized pattern of motivational and cognitive structures.

In the second half of the century, these kinds of questions, however, became less important due to the growing influence of new theoretical and methodological paradigms (e.g., behaviorism, methodological orientation of empirical research according to the principles of critical rationalism). Instead of the empirically less easily accessible question of how the "self" emerges as a central structure of personality, modern educational-psychological research has preferred to analyze seemingly more immediate problems which are also more easily studied on an empirical basis, for example, the relative importance of motivational factors for the explanation and prediction of academic achievement (cf. contributions in Section 3 of this volume) or the development of an achievement-related "self-concept" (Helmke, 1992).

In recent years, however, a reversal in trend can be recognized: Several authors have rediscovered the concepts and ideas of the early (phenomenological) theories of personality and develop new methods for measuring these concepts (e.g., Fend, 1994). A further indicator is the increasing interest in theories and studies on "personal goals" (e.g., Brunstein & Maier, 1996; Gollwitzer, 1993). Unlike the formal concept of "goal orientations" (Elliott & Dweck, 1988; cf. Köller, Chap. 6, this volume), this research line deals more with the contents or "object" of an individual's personal goals and their influence on general aspects of personality development.

New lines of research on motivation have picked up similar ideas, especially in the area of educational psychology. Typical examples are new approaches to "interest-research," which have received more and more recognition in the last few years (Hoffmann, Krapp, Renninger, & Baumert, 1998; Krapp & Prenzel, 1992; Renninger, Hidi, & Krapp, 1992; U. Schiefele, 1991, 1996; Todt, 1978). This line of motivation research is also concerned with the influence of motivation on learning and academic achievement (Krapp, Hidi, & Renninger, 1992; U. Schiefele, Krapp, & Winteler, 1992), however, unlike many other motivation theories in the domain of educational psychology, topics that relate to the complex interrelations of (content-related) motivation, learning, and individual development are explicitly included (Hoffmann et al., 1998; Renninger et al., 1992; Todt, 1985).

This chapter presents some typical theoretical and empirical approaches within this field of educational-psychological research. In the first section, the *"person-object conception of interest"* (POI) will be outlined. It has been rather influential in different educational contexts, and quite a few research programs now refer to this concept. Following this, theoretical considerations and empirical results about the complex interrelations between dispositional (high-ranking) interests of a person and his or her personality development during adolescence will be discussed. Here two aspects are taken into account: (1) the role of interests in preparing and realizing decisions about educational and professional careers; and (2) the question of how the development of interests can be described and explained.

A Person-Object Conception of Interest (POI)

The basic ideas about the development of POI can be traced back to considerations of H. Schiefele on the development of a genuinely educationally oriented theory of motivation (H. Schiefele, 1974, 1981; H. Schiefele, Haußer, & Schneider, 1979; H. Schiefele, Krapp, Prenzel, Heiland, & Kasten, 1983). Such a theory was expected to be able to make explicit statements about how an individual develops preferences for specific subjects or contents of learning, that is, how the development of content specificity in learning motivation can be explained. Besides, motivational phenomena should not only be discussed with respect to academic achievement and the prediction of interindividual differences in learning but also with respect to the emergence of central motivational dispositions that are stabilized during adolescence and have a growing influence on the direction of an individual's life-long development.

The Interest Construct

Both earlier and more recent concepts of interest are, as a rule, based on a person-object concept that interprets the psychological phenomena of learning and development as a (permanent) interchange between a person and his or her social and objective environment. In accordance with ideas of Lewin (1936), Nuttin (1984), Oerter (1995), Deci and Ryan (1985, 1991), Renninger (1992), and many others, it is postulated that the individual, as a potential source of action, and the environment as the object of action, constitute a bipolar unit. Therefore, the interest construct is conceptualized as a relational concept.

An interest represents or describes a specific relationship between a person and an object in his or her "life-space" (*Lebensraum;* cf. Lewin, 1936), which can be characterized by a series of features more closely (see below). With a view to the processes of (intentional) learning and the development of the personality, the person's "epistemic interests" play an especially centralized role. They induce a person to be interested in certain object areas more intensively than others and to acquire new knowledge and competencies related to these areas. It is important to recognize that an "object of interest" can refer to a concrete thing, a topic, a subject matter, an abstract idea, or any other content of the cognitively represented life-space (Krapp & Fink, 1992; Prenzel, 1988, 1992). All these "objects" are represented cognitively, that is, the person has an object-specific knowledge, which differentiates increasingly (see below).

Two Levels of Analysis

Interests can be examined and reconstructed theoretically on two analysis levels. At the first level, research is concerned with the processes and states during concrete interactions between a person and his or her object of interest. In this case, the analysis focuses on the description and explanation of interest-triggered actions. Krapp et al. (1992) have proposed a conceptual model that differentiates between two prototype kinds of motivational states based on interest. An "actualized individual interest," on the one hand, is the realization of an already established personal interest in a concrete situation. In the terminology of Csikszentmihalyi and Rathunde (1998), this experiential state is called "undivided interest." A "situational interest," on the other hand, is primarily created by conditions or incentives of the learning situation. This is called "interestingness" in the vernacular (Hidi, 1990; cf. Hidi & Berndorff, 1998). A situational interest can be the initial state of a longer lasting "real" interest.

At the second level of analysis, interest is seen as a more or less lasting motivational characteristic of the person. An interest-oriented "person-object-relationship" represents a content-specific motivational disposition (motive). Thus, at the first level of analysis, interest is interpreted as a motivational process or *state,* and at the second level as some kind of *trait.*

From a development theory perspective, both analysis levels are important. While at the first level processes are primarily studied that are responsible for the dynamics of the developmental course, the "crystallized" results or effect of the developmentally relevant processes and events are studied at the second level.

Characteristics of the Interest Construct

Independent of whether interest is examined on the level of the current processes or on the level of the dispositional structures of the individual, the specificity of this concept can be more closely characterized by a series of theoretically derived features. A first, general characteristic previously mentioned is the *content or object specificity.* In contrast to most other motivational constructs, especially in modern educational psychology, which are first of all concerned with formal aspects of the motivational conditions of learning, that is, with the general principles of the emergence of intentions and goals and their effects on learning and achievement (see above), the concept of interest explicitly adheres to the motivational meaning of the content of a learning goal or the quality of the objects of interest. Interests are, moreover, characterized by a pattern of formal characteristics that also show clear differences to the neighboring motivational constructs (cf. the appropriate chapters in Section 3 of this volume).

A central criterion is the *close combination of value-oriented and emotional components.* POI assumes that a person shows a high subjective esteem for the objects and actions in his or her areas of interest. These have the quality of personal significance, and in an emotional reference it is postulated that a person likes to deal with them. Interest-triggered actions produce mainly positively experienced emotions. This also applies to situations that require a high degree of effort. Dewey (1913) has already characterized the interest as an "undivided activity," in which no contradiction is experienced between the cognitive rational assessment of the personally experienced importance of an action and positive emotional evaluations of the activity itself (cf. also Rathunde, 1993, 1998). This is one of the reasons why an interest-based action (e.g., knowledge acquisition in the area of interest) has the quality of "intrinsic motivation."

From the POI perspective, this kind of experiential quality is the result of the very basic developmental principle of *identification.* Relating to similar ideas in self-determination theory (Deci, 1992; Deci & Ryan, 1985), it is postulated that a person experiences the realization of an interest as "intrinsically motivated" as he or she has—at least in the concrete situation—totally identified with the contents and tasks related to this interest. Even if the activity is strenuous or exhausting, the person has the impression of doing exactly what he or she wants to do in this situation. According to POI, an interest-determined action corresponds to the criterion of "self-intentionality."

In addition to the content specificity and the emotional and value-related features discussed up to now, further characteristics can be used to describe the specific theoretical meaning of the interest construct. On the one hand, they concern the level of differentiation of the cognitive representations related to an individual's interest (interest-specific knowledge) and on the other hand the readiness for activation and change at the initiation and realization of interest-oriented actions. Empirical studies have shown that a person acquires relatively differentiated knowledge in the content areas of his or her interests (Renninger, 1992; Tobias, 1994) and that a learning motivation based on interest leads to a relatively high level of academic achievement (U. Schiefele, Krapp, & Schreyer, 1993; U. Schiefele, Krapp, & Winteler, 1992). Taking this into account, several authors use the amount of available knowledge (in connection with value-oriented indicators) as the empirical (and theoretical) indicator of interest. Renninger (1998), for example, characterizes the personal interests of children "as those classes of objects, events, or ideas for which students have both more knowledge and more value (stronger positive feelings) than they have about other such classes" (p. 230). In this definition, the amount of knowledge is used primarily as a comparison criterion to identify those person-object relations of a child that fulfill the theoretical criteria of an interest with high probability. In theoretical and empirical studies on the influence of interest on learning, however, it would not be meaningful to include the postulated effects of interest-based activities in the operational definition of this construct. Therefore, U. Schiefele (1991, 1996) and Krapp (1992, 1999) have argued that this cognitive aspect might be appropriate for the identification of interest with small children whose knowledge acquisition is mainly interest determined, but not for a definition of interests in general.

Two further (cognitive) characteristics are of a more general nature. They also seem to be important because they allow a relatively clear separation of the interest concept from other motivational concepts frequently used in motivation research (e.g., a positive attitude). First, there is the relatively high readiness to activate a dispositional interest in situations that allow a lot of leeway. In situations that leave a person free to decide what to do and/or how to perform a task, there is a high probability that the person turns toward his or her current interests. The stronger the interest, the fewer incentives for the initiation of an interest-thematic action the person needs. Second, interests are signified by a high readiness to test and acquire new things, to learn and assume new knowledge, and to enlarge the competencies related to this domain. This implies that the person has comparatively differentiated, metacognitive knowledge opportunities for learning and development, which play an important role in the planning and execution of (future) interest-related actions. A highly interested person knows what he or she does not know yet but would like to know and be capable of doing in the future. Prenzel (1988, p. 159ff.) refers to this as knowledge about "inherent object engagements" that goes beyond the domain of already executed interest-related actions. This trend to develop and improve further the pattern of interest-related competencies is an essential indicator for the current dynamics and "liveliness" of a current interest. If this trend disappears completely, one would no longer speak of interest; rather it would be an indicator of the fact that the person has given up this interest.

Summarizing, we can say that the concept of interest is defined as a particular person-object relationship, which can be studied and theoretically reconstructed both on the level of concrete interactions or engagements and on the level of dispositional individual structures. Essential (formal) characteristics refer to specific value- and feeling-related qualities (personal significance and positive emotional experiences during interest-based actions) and the "intrinsic quality," which is based on a high level of identification with the object of interest, furthermore, interest is characterized by a high readiness for activation and change.

Interest as a Condition and Result of Developmental Processes

If one looks at a person's interests from a developmental perspective, many theoretical and empirical implications concerning the above-mentioned interdependence of the changing structure of a person's longer lasting interests and the individual course of personality development can be discovered. In the following, we will look at both sides of this interrelationship, referring particularly to theoretical considerations and research approaches about the development during adolescence, namely, (1) studies about the role of interests for planning and realizing satisfactory educational and/or professional careers; (2) typical developmental changes of male and female interests during adolescence; and (3) theoretical considerations and empirical studies concerning the functional principles of interest development.

Interests and Mastering Developmental Tasks During Adolescence

Under the present social conditions the process of planning and realizing a subjectively satisfactory course of education and a rewarding professional career is one of the most important developmental tasks faced during adolescence. Empirical findings show that development in adulthood depends to an important degree on the way the problems connected with these developmental tasks are mastered (Häfeli, Kraft, & Schallberger, 1988; Hoff, 1994; Kohn & Schooler, 1983)—besides other factors that result from objective demands in the family and on the job.

The search for a suitable profession is connected to the earlier decisions on one's course of education, the educational and academic degrees attained, and the more or less explicitly recognized experiences an individual has had in the different educational settings. Therefore, in many cases the choice of occupation is a long-lasting and sometimes painful procedure. This is to a large degree due to the fact that all these decisions are closely connected with the young person's developing identity and the necessity to establish a realistic self-concept (Gottfredson, 1981; Seifert, 1989).

In the context of questions related to these problems, results on the role of interests in planning and realizing these decisions seem to be instructive. Studies from different research approaches show that topic interests that relate to the contents of school or college subjects have a significant impact on the choice and realization of the educational as well as the professional career. In educational settings where a student can choose among different courses the decisions are made on the very basis of an individual's actual pattern of interests and not so much with respect to (extrinsic) advantages. Contrary to common opinion, German students at the upper secondary level *(Orientierungsstufe)* make their choice of subjects much more strongly according to their topic-related interests and other intrinsic criteria than according to a rational cost-benefit calculation (e.g., the probability of receiving relatively good grades with a minimum of effort; Roeder, 1989; Roeder & Gruehn, 1996).

This similarly applies to the choice of a student's major subjects in college. In representative surveys conducted every few years exploring the conditions of studying at German Fachhochschulen and universities, beside many other aspects, the central motives for selecting an academic program and/or a specific major have regularly been taken into account (Bargel, Framheim-Peisert, & Sandberger, 1989). The results show that subject-related individual interests play the most important role in all these decisions. Indicators of extrinsic motives, such as expected income or the chances of finding a good job, are obviously subordinate. This remarkable tendency to consider first of all one's own topic-related interests when making such important decisions about future living conditions is most evident with students of linguistics, cultural studies, and social sciences. In addition, female students seem to be more strongly influenced by their interests than male students. Finally, it seems important to recognize that the general picture has been rather stable over the years.

Even considering that data gained from retrospective survey studies will show a tendency to overestimate the actual significance of interests, one can conclude from these and other research findings that adolescents' decisions about the contents and directions of their educational training is to a high degree influenced by the topic-related interests they have developed in the preceding years (Krapp, 1997).

Studies that specifically explore the influence of interests with respect to vocational choice provide comparable results: In retrospective interviews as well as in prospective (longitudinal) studies, individual interests are given considerable weight in making vocation-related decisions (Bergmann, 1992). However, there are considerable differences in the degree of the significance of interest-related aspects depending on the occupational field/domain, and the standard qualification level of the job. In this context, one also has to consider the fact that there are a large number of professional fields that require only simple tasks and hardly allow the realization and differentiation of any profound individual interest (Kohn & Schooler, 1983). Thus, it can be assumed that a successful fit between an individual's pattern of interests and the requirements of a profession is more likely the higher the level of aspiration or the more sophisticated the tasks of a profession are perceived to be, and the better the profile of demands matches the individual's interests and abilities.

This hypothesis is supported by results from a qualitative study by Drottz-Sjöberg (1989) with graduate students in the field of science. Answering the question of why they decided to continue their studies at this level, all subjects referred to arguments that correspond to the central criteria of a "genuine" or "undivided" interest in the sense of POI and Csikszentmihalyi and Rathunde's (1998) theoretical approach, respectively: for example, to learn and to work on tasks that are enjoyable and that provide the opportunity to develop one's competencies regardless of whether this will result in a direct payoff in one's vocational career.

Studies by Csikszentmihalyi and colleagues with talented adolescents and renowned artists and scientists provide further evidence for the validity of this assumption. In the "creativity in later life study" (Csikszentmihalyi & Rathunde, 1998), exceptionally creative and successful people were asked to describe and explain the conditions and processes in their lives that allowed them to reach this extraordinary level of success. According to Rathunde (1993, 1998), all subjects reported experiences that very clearly can be interpreted as the life-long realization of an "undivided interest." The results from the longitudinal study with talented adolescents (Rathunde, 1993; Rathunde & Csikszentmihalyi, 1993) show that individuals who report more undivided interest in areas in which they are talented during high school are much more strongly committed to these domains and show a higher readiness for professional training in a related field (e.g., to major in their talent area in college).

On the other hand, these results also indicate an effect in the opposite direction: The newly acquired knowledge and abilities, the broad variety of topic-specific stimulations during educational and vocational training, and learning experiences induced by parents, teachers, or peers are strong developmental incentives for the expansion and reorganization of the pattern of individual interests.

Typical Changes of Interests During Adolescence

The relation between a person's interests and the way of mastering current development tasks at a specific stage of development is not at all unidirectional; rather, there is a reciprocal relationship. Growing into a new phase of development includes facing new requirements and new possibilities of person-environment interaction, which brings about an expansion and differentiation of already existing interests and sometimes leads to the complete reorganization of the individual's structure of personal interests. This is the case both within and outside academic and professional training.

A typical example is the well-known fact that with the beginning of puberty we can often observe dramatic changes in an individual's personal interests. In part this is a result of the general tendency in adolescence to adapt the contents and pattern of interests to the gender role stereotype (Hannover, 1998; Todt, 1985). Young people try to establish a clearly defined and "visible" self-concept that fits the requirements of his or her view of a desirable gender role without any doubt. As a consequence, during early adolescence already existing interests are newly evaluated under this perspective and eventually rigidly eliminated if they do not seem to be in accordance with the gender-role stereotype.

As a consequence, boys and girls develop different interest patterns in school-related areas as well as in leisure activities. H. Schiefele and Stocker (1990), for example, examined the development of interest in reading (interest in literature) at the upper secondary level and found significant gender differences with respect to preferred topics in leisure-time reading. Boys read far more books and other texts on science and technology; girls, on the other hand, more often read journals and books on history, society, foreign countries, and travel. This is in accordance with results from many different cross-sectional and longitudinal studies on the development of subject-matter interests in secondary school. Although there is a general decline in the average degree of the student's school-related interests, rather marked differences can be observed between the developmental trajectories of boys and girls: In subject areas that are labeled as "typically male" (e.g., mathematics, physics, and chemistry), the average interest of girls declines strongly, especially at the level of secondary school.

In more recent interest research, there have been a relatively large number of studies on the question of gender-typical developmental trends with regard to school-related interest areas. Findings from studies using different populations of students—also on a level of international comparison—show that (the average) interest in the contents of the curriculum decreases continuously during the whole period of secondary school with both boys and girls. There are, however, notable gender differences in the developmental trajectories that become more salient during secondary level I (i.e., grades 6 to 10). It became clear, for example, that the average interest in mathematics and the classical natural sciences (physics, chemistry) declines far more strongly with girls than with boys. However, there are considerable topic-specific differences. In some areas, there are even contrary trends.

In more recent studies on the moderating influence of contents and thematic areas on the course of interest development in the area of physics, Häußler and Hoffmann (1998) were able to show that the intensity of girls' interest depends, among other factors, on whether subject contents relate to topics that they view as important and interesting with respect to their female gender role. If, for example, topics that relate to the human body (e.g., functioning of the heart) are covered during physics lessons, girls find them at least as interesting as boys do. These findings, at the same time, can be interpreted as an empirical proof for the validity of the theoretical principle of content- or object-specificity of interests mentioned above.

Moreover, in a pilot project conducted in several German secondary schools, it could be shown that these findings can be used for improving lessons in the natural sciences (Hoffmann & Häußler, 1998). In connection with other reform measures, a significant increase in interest in physics and a considerable improvement in performance could be achieved by adapting the physics curriculum to girls' gender-specific interests. The boys' learning and performance were not impaired by this. Prenzel, Eitel, Holzbach, Schoenheinz, and Schweiberer (1993) found a similarly positive effect of a curricular revision on interest development with students of medicine in the area of surgery training.

Research Approaches and Theoretical Concepts for Explaining Interest Development

Despite the implied diversity, a differentiated description of developmental changes in the area of an individual's interests is a relatively simple research task. The question on how to *explain* the process of developmental changes is a far more difficult one. The impulse for changes comes from different directions, and there are a large number of hypothetical factors that can be used to explain different aspects of development. Since a complete description and/or explanation of interest development cannot be stated as a realistic goal of research, more specific questions that can be of greater or lesser importance with regard to educational considerations and actions have to be defined.

One research goal that is highly preferred by actual educational psychological approaches to motivation is directed to the explanation of *interindivid-*

ual differences. For example, on the basis of correlational data the relative importance of family- and/or school-related factors for predicting and explaining interindividual differences in specific areas of interest has been assessed. Findings from this line of research have shown that only a small amount of variance can be explained by school-related predictors. The influence of parents and peers seems to be much stronger (Gardner, 1998; Todt, 1978). These results have sometimes been interpreted as if school hardly had any influence on the stimulation and maintenance of school interests (Todt, 1978; Travers, 1978). However, such a far-reaching inference is not justified. On the one hand, the positive experiences with curricular intervention studies mentioned above prove the contrary. On the other hand, one has to take into consideration that estimates of the explained portions of variance gained from correlational data do not provide a valid indicator of the functional importance of these variables with regard to an individual's intraindividual course of development (Valsiner, 1986).

Yet studies that analyze the course of development explicitly on the level of intraindividual changes on a longitudinal base instead of analyzing it on the level of interindividual differences are comparatively rare. Among the studies that attempt to explore the development of interests on this level of analysis over a longer period of time are those of Gisbert (1995, in press). One of her central research goals was to explore the developmental conditions and effects of women's interest in mathematics, which, as a rule, do not fit into women's recognition of an appropriate gender role. Using a casuistic research approach, she reconstructed the women's individual courses of development from childhood to mid-adulthood and tried to identify those conditions and experiences that—from a subjective point of view—had an influence on the emergence and further development of the women's "atypical" interests.

There is some evidence that the first contact with this specific object of interest is often mediated by a male attachment figure in the family (e.g., father). In later periods during school and at university, the quality of social relationships to persons who share the same interest seems to play an important role with regard to maintenance and continuity of interest. Furthermore, the women report severe problems in finding a profession that allows them to integrate their interest-related goals and activities with their own gender role in a harmonious way.

The findings from casuistic studies naturally can only be used for generating hypotheses and not for validating theoretical assumptions. In this field, a large amount of research has yet to be done. This holds true not only for the necessity of testing hypotheses drawn from qualitative findings in further studies; the development of theoretical models for the description and explanation of the psychological processes responsible for interest genesis is at least as equally important.

Prenzel (1988, 1992) has developed a model that postulates a series of specific emotional and cognitive processes that continually accompany the course of actions to describe and explain the "selective persistence" of epistemic interests. Normally, the acting person is not aware of these processes because they do not take place on the level of conscious-reflexive information processing. They instead take place on the level of unconscious or subconscious experiential states that can be understood as components of a largely autonomous system of control and feedback. In his "functional model of interest genesis" Krapp (1998) also assumes that the control of single-interest actions and, on a long-term basis, the control of interest development take place on at least two different functional levels of information processing: first, on the level of conscious-reflexive information processing, which typically concerns the process of goal clarification and intention formation; and second, on the level of subconscious information processing, which mainly concerns the continuous process of evaluating the course and refers to a great extent to emotional (feeling-related) factors.

In our theoretical models and considerations on interest genesis, subconscious experiences and emotionally controlled qualities of experience play an important role in addition to the consciously rational processes of longer-term goal decisions. In interest development, cognitive-rational processes are also important, for example, in deciding on special educational and professional careers. Thus, however, only one side of the coin becomes central, namely, the development of an intention, that is, a principal readiness to look at a new potential area of interest. The other side of the coin is the problem of a continual maintenance of the chosen goals and a longer-term identification with the tasks and topic areas connected with this. As stated above, this is a central precondition for the development and stabilization of an interest-controlled "PO relation." With the conceptual "tools" of the traditional expectancy-value models that are primarily concerned with the cognitive-rational factors of intention formation, these phenomena cannot be described and explained comprehensively. As do many other approaches in modern motivation research, POI assumes that additional concepts and theoretical ideas have to be considered to be able to provide an adequate picture of these not directly observable emotional factors of action control.

Following Deci and Ryan's (1985, 1991) self-determination theory (SDT) and other process-oriented concepts of motivational action control (e.g., Boekaerts, 1996; Epstein, 1990; Nuttin, 1984), POI postulates a regulation system working partly autonomously beside or "beneath" the system of conscious-cognitive control. Informational processes on this level occur mostly without conscious-reflexive control. We experience the mechanisms and feedback processes as specific qualities of experience accompanying actions with a specific emotional "tinge."

Traditional approaches in the field of cognitive psychology have attempted to describe and explain the conscious-cognitive components of the regulation system. Thus, a great number of theories, concepts, and empirical findings refer to this level of action control. In contrast, the subconscious and/or emotional factors have been explored only sporadically and rarely with a view to the postulated interactions between the two subsystems. Theoretical considerations can, therefore, only be speculative or hypothetical at the moment.

In recent research approaches of POI we have tried to specify those emotional experiences that play a function in interest development on the basis of the concept of "basic psychological needs." According to Nuttin's (1984) relational theory of behavioral dynamics and theory of self-determination (Deci & Ryan, 1985, 1991; Ryan, 1995), it is assumed that living organisms are naturally endowed with a system of primary, that is, innate basic biological and psychological needs. During ontogenesis, these needs become more and more integrated into the increasingly complex systems of behavior control. Their basic efficacy, however, is not canceled by this.

Besides the rather clearly defined system of primary biological needs, a less clearly definable system of primary psychological needs is postulated. Based on SDT (Deci, 1998; Ryan, 1995), three qualitatively different needs can be distinguished within this system, namely, competence, self-determination, and social relatedness. Just as the fulfillment of basic biological needs is a natural necessity, sufficient fulfillment of the three psychological needs is a necessary requirement for optimal functioning of the psychological system (Deci & Ryan, 1985; Nuttin, 1984; Ryan, 1995). According to Nuttin's (1984) theory, the basic needs have to be understood as a holistically functioning system that provides continual signals about the functional effectivity of the current person-environment interactions.

In the context of processes that control the course of interest development, these need-related qualities of experience are very important, especially as they provide permanent, emotional feedback on the micro-level of behavior regulation and thus contribute to the emergence of object-related preferences or aversions. It is postulated that a person will only engage continuously in a certain topic area if he or she assesses it, on the basis of rational considerations, as sufficiently important (value-related valency) and if he or she experiences the course of interactions on the whole as positive and emotionally satisfactory (Krapp, 1999; see also Deci, 1992, 1998).

There are a number of findings that corroborate these theoretical suppositions empirically. The majority of these studies were carried out with students and young adults in vocational settings (Kleinmann, Straka, & Hinz, 1998; Prenzel, Kramer, & Drechsel, 1998). We are currently studying the conditions and processes of interest genesis in the context of vocational education on the basis of longitudinal study. Here, especially the mechanisms of need-related qualities of experience are studied by using both quantitative and qualitative methods (Lewalter, Krapp, Schreyer, & Wild, 1998; Wild & Krapp, 1996; Wild, Krapp, Schreyer, & Lewalter, 1998). The test sample consisted of 117 trainees from the insurance business. The quantitative analyses are based on data from questionnaires and ESM (Experience Sampling Method) studies and observational techniques. The qualitative analyses are based on retrospective interviews with a smaller number of randomly chosen subjects from the main study. Both in the quantitative as well as in the qualitative analyses, statistically significant relations between the occurrence of positive need-related experience and different indicators of interest development could be observed in the retrospective interviews. For example, 76% of the 49 subjects who were interviewed at the end of the first year refer to competence, and 65% refer to relatedness as a reason for interest development. Only 35% mention the experience of autonomy. If we look at the results at the end of the second year ($n = 71$) we have almost the same picture, except that the influence of autonomy seems to be a little higher (Lewalter et al., 1998). Although the results from different research approaches differ in several important aspects, they seem to support the overall hypothesis. We find substantial empirical relations between indicators of need-related experiences and indicators of the emergence and stabilization of longer-lasting interests.

References

Bargel, T., Framheim-Peisert, G., & Sandberger, J. U. (1989). *Studienerfahrungen und studentische Orientierungen in den 80er Jahren. Trends und Stabilitäten* [Experiences from studying and study-related orientations of students in the 80s. Trends and stabilities]. Bonn, Germany: Bock.

Bergmann, C. (1992). Schulisch-berufliche Interessen als Determinanten der Studien- bzw. Berufswahl und -bewältigung. Eine Überprüfung des Modells von Holland [School and vocation-related interests as determinants of the student's choice and mastery of major or career. An examination of Holland's model]. In A. Krapp & M. Prenzel (Eds.), *Interesse, Lernen, Leistung. Neuere Ansätze einer pädagogisch-psychologischen Interessenforschung* (pp. 195–220). Münster, Germany: Aschendorff.

Berlyne, D. E. (1949). Interest as a psychological concept. *British Journal of Psychology, 39,* 184–195.

Boekaerts, M. (1996). Personality and the psychology of learning. *European Journal of Personality, 10,* 377–404.

Brunstein, J. C., & Maier, G. W. (1996). Persönliche Ziele: Ein Überblick zum Stand der Forschung [Personal goals. An overview of current research]. *Psychologische Rundschau, 47,* 146–160.

Csikszentmihalyi, M., & Rathunde, K. (1998). The development of the person: An experiential perspective on the ontogenesis of psychological complexity. In W. Damon (Editor-in-chief) & R. M. Lerner (Vol. Ed.), *Handbook of Child Psychology: Vol. 1. Theoretical models of human development* (5th ed., pp. 635–684). New York: Wiley.

Deci, E. L. (1992). The relation of interest to the motivation of behavior: A self-determination theory perspective. In K. A. Renninger, S. Hidi, & A. Krapp (Eds.), *The role of interest in learning and development* (pp. 43–47). Hillsdale, NJ: Erlbaum.

Deci, E. L. (1998). The relation of interest to motivation and human needs—the self-determination theory viewpoint. In L. Hoffmann, A. Krapp, K. A. Renninger, & J. Baumert (Eds.), *Interest and learning. Proceedings of the Seeon-Conference on Interest and Gender* (pp. 146–162). Kiel, Germany: IPN.

Deci, E. L., & Ryan, R. M. (1985). *Intrinsic motivation and self-determination in human behavior.* New York: Plenum Press.

Deci, E. L., & Ryan, R. M. (1991). A motivational approach to self: Integration in personality. In R. Dienstbier (Ed.), *Nebraska Symposium on Motivation: Vol. 38. Perspectives on motivation* (pp. 237–288). Lincoln: University of Nebraska Press.

Dewey, J. (1913). *Interest and effort in education.* Boston: Riverside Press.

Drottz-Sjöberg, B. M. (1989). Interest in science education and research: A study of graduate students. *Göteborg Psychological Reports, 19*(4), 1–33.

Elliott, E. S., & Dweck, C. S. (1988). Goals: An approach to motivation and achievement. *Journal of Personality and Social Psychology, 54,* 5–12.

Epstein, S. (1990). Cognitive-experiential self theory: Implications for developmental psychology. In M. Gunnar & L. A. Sroufe (Eds.), *Minnesota Symposia on Child Psychology: Self processes and development* (Vol. 23, pp. 79–123). Hillsdale, NJ: Erlbaum.

Fend, H. (1994). *Die Entdeckung des Selbst und die Verarbeitung der Pubertät* [The discovery of the self and the dealing with puberty]. Göttingen, Germany: Huber.

Gardner, P. L. (1998). The development of males' and females' interest in science and technology. In L. Hoffmann, A. Krapp, K. A. Renninger, & J. Baumert (Eds.), *Interest and learning. Proceedings of the Seeon-Conference on Interest and Gender* (pp. 41–57). Kiel, Germany: IPN.

Gisbert, K. (1995). *Frauenuntypische Bildungsbiographien: Diplom-Mathematikerinnen* [Educational biographies untypical for women: Graduated mathematicians]. Frankfurt a.M., Germany: Lang.

Gisbert, K. (in press). *Geschlechtsidentität und Fachinteresse. Psychologisch-biographische Analysen geschlechtstypischer und -untypischer Studienwahlen.* [Gender identity and subject interest. Psychological-biographical analyses of gender-typical and -untypical choices of university subjects]. Frankfurt a.M., Germany: Lang.

Gollwitzer, P. M. (1993). Goal achievement: The role of intentions. In W. Stroebe & M. Hewstone (Eds.), *European Review of Social Psychology, 4,* 141–185.

Gottfredson, L. S. (1981). Circumscription and compromise: A developmental theory of occupational aspirations. *Journal of Counseling Psychology, 28* (Monograph No. 6), 545–579.

Häfeli, K., Kraft, U. & Schallberger, U. (Eds.). (1988). *Berufsausbildung und Persönlichkeitsentwicklung* [Professional education and the development of personality]. Bern, Switzerland: Huber.

Häußler, P., & Hoffmann, L. (1998). Chancengleichheit für Mädchen im Physikunterricht—Ergebnisse eines erweiterten BLK-Modellversuchs [Equality of opportunity for girls in physics lessons—Results from an intervention study]. *Zeitschrift für Didaktik der Naturwissenschaften, 4,* 51–67.

Hannover, B. (1998). The development of self-concept and interests. In L. Hoffmann, A. Krapp, K. A. Renninger, & J. Baumert (Eds.), *Interest and learning. Proceedings of the Seeon-Conference on Interest and Gender* (pp. 105–125). Kiel, Germany: IPN.

Helmke, A. (1992). *Selbstvertrauen und schulische Leistung* [Self-confidence and scholastic achievement]. Göttingen, Germany: Hogrefe.

Hidi, S. (1990). Interest and its contribution as a mental resource for learning. *Review of Educational Research, 60,* 549–571.

Hidi, S., & Berndorff, D. (1998). Situational interest and learning. In L. Hoffmann, A. Krapp, K. A. Renninger, & J. Baumert (Eds.), *Interest and learning. Proceedings of the Seeon-Conference on Interest and Gender* (pp. 74–90). Kiel, Germany: IPN.

Hoff, E.-H. (1994). Arbeit und Sozialisation [Work and socialization]. In K. A. Schneewind (Ed.), *Psychologie der Erziehung und Sozialisation. Enzyklopädie der Psychologie (D/I/1)* (pp. 525–552). Göttingen, Germany: Hogrefe.

Hoffmann, L., & Häußler, P. (1998). An intervention project promoting girls' and boys' interest in physics. In L. Hoffmann, A. Krapp, K. A. Renninger, & J. Baumert (Eds.), *Interest and learning. Proceedings of the Seeon-Conference on Interest and Gender* (pp. 301–316). Kiel, Germany: IPN.

Hoffmann, L., Krapp, A., Renninger, A., & Baumert, J. (Eds.). (1998). *Interest and learning. Proceedings of the Seeon-Conference on Interest and Gender.* Kiel, Germany: IPN.

Kerschensteiner, G. (1926). *Theorie der Bildung* [Theory of education]. Leipzig, Germany: Teubner.

Kleinmann, M., Straka, G. A., & Hinz, I. M. (1998). Motivation und selbstgesteuertes Lernen im Beruf [Motivation and self-regulated learning at work]. In J. Abel & C. Tarnai (Eds.), *Pädagogisch-psychologische Interessenforschung in Studium und Beruf* (pp. 95–109). Münster, Germany: Waxmann.

Kohn, M. L., & Schooler, C. (1983). *Work and personality. An inquiry into the impact of social stratification.* Norwood, MA: Ablex.

Krapp, A. (1992). Das Interessenkonstrukt. Bestimmungsmerkmale der Interessenhandlung und des individuellen Interesses aus der Sicht einer Person-Gegenstands-Konzeption [The interest construct. Characteristics of individual interests and interest-related actions from the perspective of a person-object conception]. In A. Krapp & M. Prenzel (Eds.),

Interesse, Lernen, Leistung. Neuere Ansätze einer pädagogisch-psychologischen Interessenforschung (pp. 297–329). Münster, Germany: Aschendorff.

Krapp, A. (1997). Interesse und Studium [Interest and academic education]. In H. Gruber & A. Renkl (Eds.), *Wege zum Können. Determinanten des Kompetenzerwerbs* (pp. 45–58). Bern, Switzerland: Huber.

Krapp, A. (1998). Entwicklung und Förderung von Interessen im Unterricht [Development and promotion of interest in instruction]. *Psychologie in Erziehung und Unterricht, 45,* 186–203.

Krapp, A. (1999). Interest, motivation and learning: An educational-psychological perspective. *European Journal of Psychology in Education, 14,* 23–40.

Krapp, A., & Fink, B. (1992). The development and function of interests during the critical transition from home to preschool. In K. A. Renninger, S. Hidi, & A. Krapp (Eds.), *The role of interest in learning and development* (pp. 397–429). Hillsdale, NJ: Erlbaum.

Krapp, A., Hidi, S., & Renninger, K. A. (1992). Interest, learning and development. In K. A. Renninger, S. Hidi, & A. Krapp (Eds.), *The role of interest in learning and development* (pp. 3–25). Hillsdale, NJ: Erlbaum.

Krapp, A., & Prenzel, M. (Eds.). (1992). *Interesse, Lernen, Leistung. Neuere Ansätze einer pädagogisch-psychologischen Interessenforschung* [Interest, learning, achievement. Recent approaches of educational-psychological interest research]. Münster, Germany: Aschendorff.

Lewalter, D., Krapp, A., Schreyer, I., & Wild, K.-P. (1998). Die Bedeutsamkeit des Erlebens von Kompetenz, Autonomie und sozialer Eingebundenheit für die Entwicklung berufsspezifischer Interessen [The importance of experiencing competence, autonomy, and social relatedness for the development of vocation-related interests]. In K. Beck & R. Dubs (Eds.), *Kompetenzentwicklung in der Berufserziehung—Kognitive, motivationale und moralische Dimensionen kaufmännischer Qualifizierungsprozesse* (pp. 143–168). Stuttgart, Germany: Steiner.

Lewin, K. (1936). *Principles of topological psychology.* New York: McGraw-Hill.

Lunk, G. (1926). *Das Interesse: Bd.1. Historisch-kritischer Teil* [Interest: Vol. 1. History]. Leipzig, Germany: Klinkhardt.

Lunk, G. (1927). *Das Interesse: Bd. 2. Philosophisch-pädagogischer Teil* [Interest: Vol. 2. Philosophical-educational approaches]. Leipzig, Germany: Klinkhardt.

Nuttin, J. (1984). *Motivation, planning, and action.* Hillsdale, NJ: Erlbaum.

Oerter, R. (1995). Motivation und Handlungssteuerung [Motivation and action regulation]. In R. Oerter & L. Montada (Eds.), *Entwicklungspsychologie* (pp. 758–822). Munich, Germany: PVU.

Prenzel, M. (1988). *Die Wirkungsweise von Interesse. Ein Erklärungsversuch aus pädagogischer Sicht* [Functioning of interest. An explanatory approach from an educational point of view]. Opladen, Germany: Westdeutscher Verlag.

Prenzel. M. (1992). Selective persistence of interest. In K. A. Renninger, S. Hidi, & A. Krapp (Eds.), *The role of interest in learning and development* (pp. 71–98). Hillsdale, NJ: Erlbaum.

Prenzel, M., Eitel, F., Holzbach, R., Schoenheinz, R.-J., & Schweiberer, L. (1993). Lernmotivation im studentischen Unterricht in der Chirurgie [Motivation to learn in surgery courses]. *Zeitschrift für Pädagogische Psychologie, 7,* 125–137.

Prenzel, M., Kramer, K., & Drechsel, B. (1998). Changes in learning motivation and interest in vocational education: Halfway through the study. In L. Hoffmann, A. Krapp, K. A. Renninger, & J. Baumert (Eds.), *Interest and learning. Proceedings of the Seeon-Conference on Interest and Gender* (pp. 430–440). Kiel, Germany: IPN.

Rathunde, K. (1993). The experience of interest: A theoretical and empirical look at its role in adolescent talent development. In M. Maehr & P. R. Pintrich (Eds.), *Advances in motivation and achievement* (Vol. 8, pp. 59–98). London: Jai Press.

Rathunde, K. (1998). Undivided and abiding interest: Comparisons across studies of talented adolescents and creative adults. In L. Hoffmann, A. Krapp, K. A. Renninger, & J. Baumert (Eds.), *Interest and learning. Proceedings of the Seeon-Conference on Interest and Gender* (pp. 367–376). Kiel, Germany: IPN.

Rathunde, K., & Csikszentmihalyi, M. (1993). Undivided interest and the growth of talent: A longitudinal study of adolescents. *Journal of Youth and Adolescence, 22,* 1–21.

Renninger, K. A. (1992). Individual interest and development: Implications for theory and practice. In K. A. Renninger, S. Hidi, & A. Krapp (Eds.), *The role of interest in learning and development* (pp. 361–395). Hillsdale, NJ: Erlbaum.

Renninger, K. A. (1998). The role of individual interest(s) and gender in learning: An overview of research on preschool and elementary school-aged children/students. In L. Hoffmann, A. Krapp, K. A. Renninger, & J. Baumert (Eds.), *Interest and learning. Proceedings of the Seeon-Conference on Interest and Gender* (pp. 165–174). Kiel, Germany: IPN.

Renninger, K. A., Hidi, S., & Krapp, A. (Eds.). (1992). *The role of interest in learning and development.* Hillsdale, NJ: Erlbaum.

Roeder, P. M. (1989). Bildungsreform und Bildungsforschung: Das Beispiel der gymnasialen Oberstufe [Reform and research in education: The example of senior high school]. *Empirische Pädagogik, 3,* 119–142.

Roeder, P. M., & Gruehn, S. (1996). Kurswahlen in der Gymnasialen Oberstufe—Fächerspektrum und Kurswahlmotive [The choice of advanced level courses in upper secondary school]. *Zeitschrift für Pädagogik, 42,* 497–518.

Rubinstein, S. (1958). *Grundlagen der Allgemeinen Psychologie* [Basics of general psychology]. Berlin, Germany: Verlag Volk und Wissen. (Original Russian work published 1935)

Ryan, R. M. (1995). Psychological needs and the facilitation of integrative process. *Journal of Personality, 63*(3), 397–427.

Schiefele, H. (1974). *Lernmotivation und Motivlernen* [Motivation to learn and learning of motives]. Munich, Germany: Ehrenwirth.

Schiefele, H. (1981). Interesse [Interest]. In H. Schiefele & A. Krapp (Eds.), *Handlexikon zur Pädagogischen Psychologie* (pp. 192–196). Munich, Germany: Ehrenwirth.

Schiefele, H., Hausser, K., & Schneider, G. (1979). "Interesse" als Ziel und Weg der Erziehung. Überlegungen zu einem vernachlässigten pädagogischen Konzept [Interest as an aim and path in education. Considerations on a neglected educational concept]. *Zeitschrift für Pädagogik, 25,* 1–20.

Schiefele, H., Krapp, A., Prenzel, M., Heiland, A., & Kasten, H. (1983, August). *Principles of an educational theory of interest.* Paper presented at the 7th Meeting of the International Society for the Study of Behavioral Development, Munich, Germany.

Schiefele, H., & Stocker, K. (1990). *Literaturinteresse* [Interest in literature]. Weinheim, Germany: Beltz.

Schiefele, U. (1991). Interest, learning and motivation. *Educational Psychologist, 26*(2 & 3), 299–323.

Schiefele, U. (1996). *Motivation und Lernen mit Texten* [Motivation and learning with texts]. Göttingen, Germany: Hogrefe.

Schiefele, U., Krapp, A., & Schreyer, I. (1993). Metaanalyse des Zusammenhangs von Interesse und schulischer Leistung [Meta-analysis of the relation between interest and scholastic achievement]. *Zeitschrift für Entwicklungspsychologie und Pädagogische Psychologie, 25,* 120–148.

Schiefele, U., Krapp, A., & Winteler, A. (1992). Interest as a predictor of academic achievement: A meta-analysis of research. In K. A. Renninger, S. Hidi, & A. Krapp (Eds.), *The role of interest in learning and development* (pp. 183–212). Hillsdale, NJ: Erlbaum.

Seifert, K. H. (1989). Berufliche Entwicklung und berufliche Sozialisation [Vocational development and vocational socialization]. In E. Roth (Ed.), *Organisationspsychologie. Enzyklopädie der Psychologie* (pp. 608–630). Göttingen, Germany: Hogrefe.

Tobias, S. (1994). Interest, prior knowledge, and learning. *Review of Educational Research, 64*(1), 37–54.

Todt, E. (1978). *Das Interesse* [Interest]. Bern, Switzerland: Huber.

Todt, E. (1985). Elements of a theory of science interests. In M. Lehrke, L. Hoffmann, & P. L. Gardner (Eds.), *Interests in science and technology* (pp. 59–69). Kiel, Germany: IPN.

Travers, R. M. W. (1978). *Children's interests.* Kalamazoo: Michigan University, College of Education.

Valsiner, J. (1986). Between groups and individuals. Psychologists' and laypersons' interpretations of correlational findings. In J. Valsiner (Ed.), *The individual subject and scientific psychology* (pp. 113–151). New York: Plenum Press.

Wild, K.-P., & Krapp, A. (1996). Die Qualität subjektiven Erlebens in schulischen und betrieblichen Lernumwelten. Untersuchungen mit der Erlebens Stichproben Methode [The quality of emotional experiences in vocational and company learning environments. Studies with the experience-sampling method]. *Unterrichtswissenschaft, 24,* 195–216.

Wild, K.-P., Krapp, A., Schreyer, I., & Lewalter, D. (1998). The development of interest and motivational orientations: Gender differences in vocational education. In L. Hoffmann, A. Krapp, K. A. Renninger, & J. Baumert (Eds.), *Interest and learning. Proceedings of the Seeon-Conference on Interest and Gender* (pp. 441–454). Kiel, Germany: IPN.

Motivational Psychology of Human Development – J. Heckhausen (Editor)

6 Goal Orientations: Their Impact on Academic Learning and Their Development During Early Adolescence

Olaf Köller

There is plenty of evidence that superordinate individual goals have a major influence on behavior in academic contexts (Ablard & Lipschultz, 1998; Ames, 1992; Ames & Archer, 1988; Dweck & Leggett, 1988; Elliot & Harakiewicz, 1996; Elliott & Dweck, 1988; Nicholls, 1984, 1992; Thorkildson & Nicholls, 1998). A review of the recent literature reveals that there is much agreement in this field about the two kinds of goal orientation, although different authors use different labels. Dweck and Leggett (1988) label the two categories *learning goals* and *performance goals;* Ames and Archer (1988) use the terms *mastery* and *performance goal orientation;* and Nicholls (1984, 1992) proposes the concepts of *task orientation* and *ego orientation.*

Among all of these terms, the first type of goal orientation refers to preoccupation with the mastery of new skills and knowledge. Students who have this type of goal orientation are concerned with increasing their own competence. Achievement or learning behavior is usually intrinsically initiated. The second type of goal orientation refers to preoccupation with performance and social comparison. People preferring this goal orientation are concerned with securing favorable judgments of their competence. Thus, achievement behavior of this type is usually extrinsically initiated.

Some researchers (e.g., Elliot & Harakiewicz, 1996; Middleton & Midgley, 1997) have proposed two different types of performance goal orientation: *performance-approach goal orientation* and *performance-avoid goal orientation.* Students with high performance-avoid goal orientation are typically concerned with avoiding the demonstration of lack of ability, while students with high performance-approach goal orientation strive to demonstrate their high ability. This conception of performance goal orientation refers directly to the traditional distinction of approach and avoidance tendencies in motivational psychology (e.g., Atkinson, 1957; Heckhausen, 1991).

In this chapter, three key issues of goal theory are emphasized: first, the question of whether goal orientations reflect quantitatively or qualitatively different categories of a construct; second, the impact of goal orientations on academic achievement; and third, as the most important issue of this chapter, the development of goal orientations during early adolescence.

Goal Orientations: Qualitative or Quantitative Constructs?

Several authors mentioned above treat both kinds of goal orientation theoretically as types or, in the sense of Meehl (1992), as "taxa." Experimental studies (e.g., Elliott & Dweck, 1988) in which performance and learning goal orientations were manipulated by an experimenter support this view of qualitative differences between both types of goal orientation. Ames (1987; see also Ames & Ames, 1984) as well as Middleton and Midgley (1997) have argued that goal theory is a qualitative rather than a quantitative conception of motivation. Ames and Ames (1984) stated:

> Motivation, however, can also be conceptualized as a qualitative variable that represents different value or goal orientations, different ways of processing or attending to information, and different cognitions about one's performance. (p. 535)

However, when measuring goal orientations as personal characteristics and reporting results, authors often refer to a trait conception and correlate the different scale scores with other variables (e.g., Anderman & Anderman, 1999; Anderman & Midgley, 1997; Duda & Nicholls, 1992; Nicholls, Patashnick, & Nolen, 1985; Stipek & Gralinski, 1996; Thorkildson & Nicholls, 1998).

From a theoretical point of view, it seems to be more consistent to refer to a typological conceptualization in the sense of Meehl (1992) or Gangestad and Snyder (1985). Starting with the work of Ames and Archer (1988), a series of studies has been conducted in which goal orientations were treated as categories of a typological variable. These researchers administered a questionnaire containing scales on ego and on task orientation to students attending a junior high school for academically advanced students. Since the scales were uncorrelated, the authors argued that people can score high or low on both scales (see also Nicholls, 1992), and they divided the whole sample by means of a median-split into four types with different goal orientations: (a) high ego and high task, (b) high ego and low task, (c) low ego and high task, and (d) low ego and low task. Only types (b) and (c) corresponded to the different orientations stated in previous goal theories. The same procedure was used in studies by Meece and Holt (1993) and Bouffard, Boisvert, Vezeau, and Larouche (1995), while Pintrich and Garcia (1991) extended the splitting procedure by dividing each scale into three parts, resulting in nine different types.

Problems with this approach arise because the number of different goal orientations is always determined by the splitting procedure. Alternative grouping methods, for example, cluster analyses or mixture distribution models, were applied in studies by Seifert (1995, 1996, 1997) and Köller (1998a, 1998b). Seifert (1995, 1996) analyzed data sets of n = 79 fifth graders and identified three different clusters: one ego-oriented, one task-oriented, and one indifferent cluster, the last group consisting of people with similar scores on both goal orientation scales. Köller (1998a, 1998b) analyzed a large sample of n = 1,941 seventh graders by means of mixture distribution models and identified three classes as well. In addition to one ego-oriented and one task-oriented class, Köller (1998a, 1998b) also found an indifferent class scoring similarly on ego- and task-orientation items. Furthermore, Köller (1998a) showed that treating goal orientations qualitatively has more predictive power for academic learning than treating them quantitatively. In sum, it seems to be more consistent with existing goal theories to conceptualize goal orientations qualitatively. The studies by Seifert and Köller show that the theoretical distinction of ego and task orientation can be empirically supported by different types of typological analyses. Nevertheless, studies treating goal orientations quantitatively often reveal similar results to those conceptualizing them qualitatively (e.g., Bouffard et al., 1995).

Goal Orientations and Achievement

Several researchers (e.g., Ablard & Lipschultz, 1998; Albaili, 1998; Biggs, 1985; Bouffard et al., 1995; Dweck, 1998; Fisher & Ford, 1998; Ford, Smith, Weissbein, Gully, & Salas, 1998) have suggested that the type of goal orientation affects cognitive functioning and the level of commitment to learning. Learning goals (task orientation) should thus promote effort, task motivation, and an adequate use of learning strategies in order to master the material to be learned. In contrast, performance goals (ego orientation) should be detrimental to task engagement and thus knowledge acquisition. Correlational studies, however, show only small or moderate associations between grades and goal orientations. Wolters, Yu, and Pintrich (1996) reported coefficients of $r = .13$ (performance goal orientation) and r = .14 (learning goal orientation) for eighth graders at the end of the school year. Based upon path-analytic findings in a sample of university students, Albaili (1998) reported direct paths both from learning goal orientation ($\beta = .22$) and from performance goal orientation ($\beta = -.20$) to grade point averages (GPAs).

Most researchers agree that the effect of goal orientation on academic performance is more or less totally mediated by motivational variables and learning strategies, so that direct effects of goal orientation on academic outcomes are quite rare (but see Albaili, 1998). In particular, Dweck (1986; see also Dweck & Leggett, 1988; Elliott & Dweck, 1988) has theoretically and empirically elaborated differences in the attribution styles of students with performance and learning goal orientations, suggesting that a maladaptive attributional pattern of performance goal-oriented students with low self-concept of ability is responsible for their failure in performance and learning situations. Concerning the relationship between goal orientation and effort, Fisher and Ford (1998; see also Ford et al., 1998) found that performance goal orientation had negative correlations with effort indicators, while the coefficients were positive for learning goal orientation. Regarding learning strategies, Meece, Blumenfeld, and Hoyle (1988) found that elementary school students with learning goal orientation were more likely to report engaging in self-regulated activities such as the use of cognitive strategies, planning, monitoring, and help seeking. Other studies (e.g., Albaili, 1998; Bouffard et al., 1995; Nolen, 1988; Pintrich & DeGroot, 1990; Pintrich & Garcia, 1991) have shown that students with learning goals (task orientation) are more likely to report deeper processing strategies such as planning, comprehension monitoring, and regulation. Concerning performance goal orientation (ego orientation), studies (e.g., Albaili, 1998; Bouffard et al., 1995; Fisher & Ford, 1998) have shown that it is positively related to surface strategies (Entwistle, 1988), such as rehearsal.

Although most of these studies underline the influence of goal orientation via attributional styles, effort, and learning strategies on achievement, there is still a lack of longitudinal studies in the school setting that investigate the impact of different goals on learning over time. In a longitudinal study of cognitive and motivational development of German adolescents (BIJU study; Köller, 1998a, 1998b), knowledge acquisition in English and mathematics was regressed on different types of goal orientation (ego-oriented vs. task-oriented vs. indifferent). Standardized achievement tests for both subjects were administered at the beginning, middle, and end of grade 7. Goal orientations were conceptualized as qualitatively different motivational characteristics of students. The sample contained seventh graders from different types of sec-

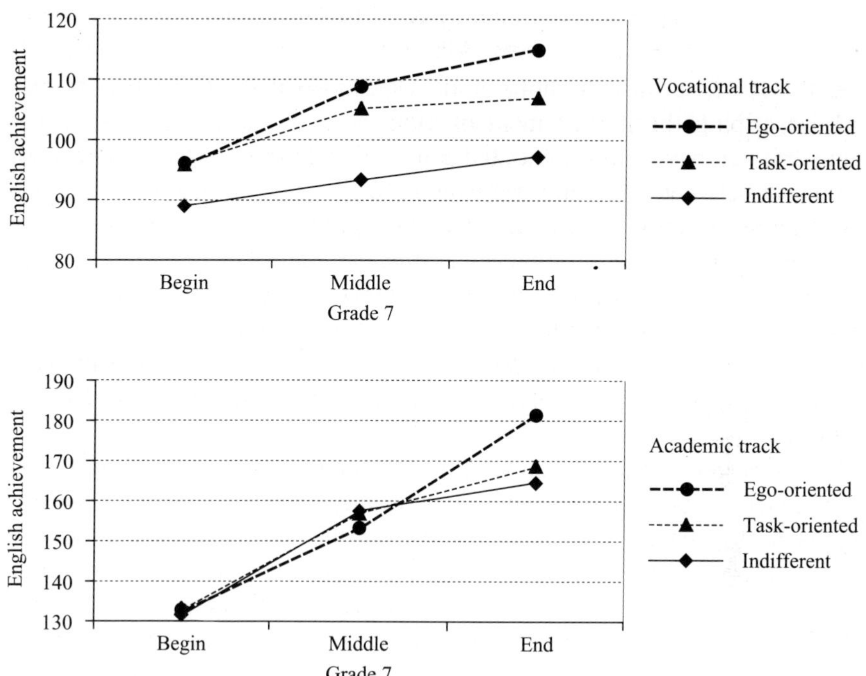

Figure 1. Development of English achievement in grade 7 by school track and type of goal orientation.

ondary schools. Due to the tracked system of German secondary schools, the sample was divided into students attending the vocational track and students attending the academic track. Figure 1 provides the findings for English, which were similar to those for mathematics. Achievement scores were constructed by means of procedures based on Item Response Theory and rescaled so that there was a mean of $M = 100$ and a standard deviation of $SD = 30$ in the whole sample at the first measurement point.

Differences in initial achievement (beginning of grade 7) among the three groups were only reliable in the vocational track. In both tracks, however, ego-oriented students had the smallest achievement gains over one year. Multilevel growth curve modeling revealed that the differences between the three groups' learning rates were statistically significant, thus providing evidence that goal orientations are important predictors of academic learning both in a numerical and in a verbal domain (see Köller, 1998a, for details of the analyses).

The Development of Goal Orientations

Nicholls (1984; see also Nicholls et al., 1985) provided a theoretical framework describing the development of goal orientations. He suggested that young children have undifferentiated concepts of ability and therefore cannot distinguish between effort and ability. A child who tries hard, in this view, has a high degree of ability. Furthermore, achievement or performance is usually compared with prior performance, that is, an individual reference norm (Heckhausen, 1991) or the tendency for temporal comparisons (Albert, 1977), respectively, dominates. Standards of excellence are always internal, and successes are defined by doing better than the last time. The internal drive is to increase competencies. Children in this developmental stage are task oriented.

As they get older, children learn to understand ability and effort as distinct concepts, that is, they develop a more differentiated concept of ability. High performance achieved with low effort indicates higher ability than the same performance level reached with high effort. Furthermore, the children learn to compare their own performances with those of others (peers, parents, etc.), which indicates a change from an individual to a social reference norm (cf. Heckhausen, 1991). Ability is always assessed with respect to social criteria, that is, high ability means outperforming peers and low ability means doing worse than peers. Success is defined by demonstrating high ability to others or by hiding incompetence. Children or adolescents in this developmental stage are ego oriented.

Problems with Nicholls' theory, however, include (a) the question of whether the change from task to ego orientation is more or less inevitable, and (b) lack of concrete predictions regarding at which age or developmental stage children's conceptions of ability become more differentiated. Referring to the second problem, research and theories on the development of social comparisons (Ruble, Feldman, & Boggiano, 1976; Suls, 1986) have shown that children at the age of 7 are able to conduct social comparisons and to assess their own ability on the basis of these comparisons. Although this research suggests that changes from task to ego orientation might be observable in elementary school, empirical work on students' goal orientations (e.g., Seifert, 1995, 1996), has shown that task orientation still dominates in grade 5, corresponding to an age of 10 or 11 years. In Seifert's cluster-analytic findings, only 8 percent of the students were classified as ego oriented.

Other authors have suggested that it is not the age but the transition from elementary to secondary school that is associated with the decline in intrinsic motivation and learning goal orientation (e.g., Eccles & Midgley, 1989; Wigfield, Eccles, & Pintrich, 1996). Anderman and Midgley (1997; see also Anderman & Anderman, 1999) reported a decline in task orientation and an increase in ego orientation from grade 5 (elementary school) to grade 6 (junior high school). Young (1997) found in a sample of $n = 316$ students a substantial decline in task orientation in English and mathematics from grade 6 to grade 7, while at the same time extrinsic goal orientation increased. In my own studies (see above; see also Köller, 1998a; Köller, Baumert, & Rost, 1998), I found that more than 50 percent of seventh-grade students favored performance goals. Analyses on the development of motivational orientation in grade 7 revealed that the increase of the number of ego-oriented students was an ongoing process, while the frequency of task-oriented students decreased (see Figure 2). This process, however, was the same in the vocational and academic racks of junior high school.

Explanations of this process at the transition to junior high school concern the question of whether it is caused by the physiological and psychological changes in puberty or whether it is determined by the changing academic environments. During the early adolescent years, children experience biolog-

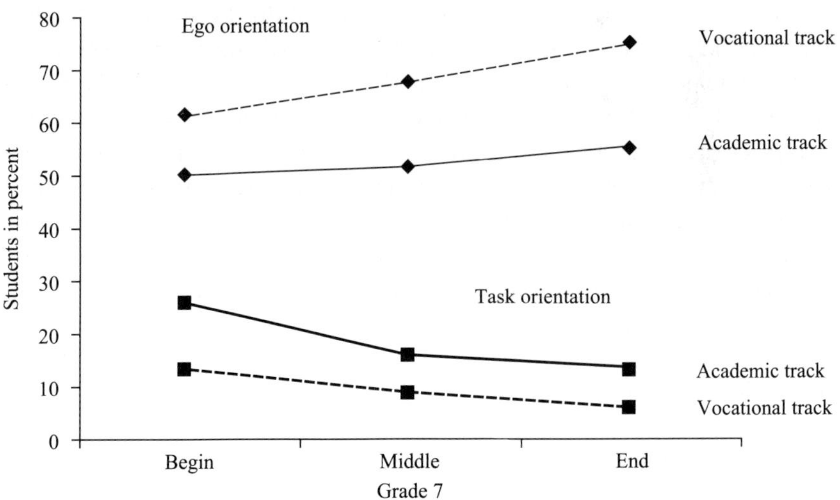

Figure 2. Development of ego and task orientation from the beginning of grade 7 to the end of grade 7 ($n = 1{,}731$).

ical and social changes associated with puberty, while they more or less simultaneously change from primary to secondary school, such that the time of biological changes coincides with changes in the school environment (cf. Simmons & Blyth, 1987; Simmons, Blyth, van Cleaves, & Bush, 1979). The developmental "stage-environment fit" model proposed by Eccles and colleagues (e.g., Eccles, Midgley, Wigfield, Buchanan et al., 1993; Eccles & Midgley, 1989; Wigfield et al., 1996) posits that negative effects on students' motivation are to be expected when they are in environments that do not fit well with their needs. Exposure to developmentally appropriate environments would facilitate both motivation and cognitive growth. With respect to the instructional setting, Hunt (1975)

> (...) suggested that teachers need to provide the optimal level of structure for children's current level of maturity while at the same time providing a sufficiently challenging environment to pull the children along a developmental path toward higher levels of cognitive and social maturity (Wigfield et al., 1996, p. 161).

Particularly in the field of goal orientations, research by Ames and Archer (1988; see also Anderman & Anderman, 1999; Anderman & Maehr, 1994; Anderman & Midgley, 1997) suggests that students' perceptions of the goal structures in their classrooms influence their adoption of goal orientations. When teachers emphasize improvement, effort, and learning for intrinsic reasons, students are likely to adopt personal learning goals; in contrast, when teachers emphasize grades, ability differences, and outperforming classmates, students are likely to adopt personal performance goals (see experimental intervention studies by Krampen, 1987, and Rheinberg, 1980). Goals within classrooms differ substantially between primary and secondary school: Competitive goal structures become more prominent in secondary schools. The substantial impact of classroom goals on the individual development of goal orientations is well known. Anderman and Anderman (1999), for example, investigated changes in goal orientations from grade 5 to grade 6, caused by perceived class goal orientations. Students were asked whether their teachers preferred performance goals (example item: "Our teachers tell us how we compare to other students") or learning goals (example item: "Our teachers think mistakes are okay as long as we are learning").[1] Regression analyses revealed that the perceived classroom goal structure predicted changes in individual goal orientations, that is, classroom learning goal orientation had a positive effect on change in individual learning goal orientation while, at the

---

[1] Example items are taken from Anderman and Anderman (1999, p. 35).

same time, classroom performance goal orientation had a positive effect on individual performance orientation.

Young (1997) conducted a similar study investigating changes in individual goal orientations from grade 6 to grade 7. Regarding the impact of perceived class goal orientations on the change in individual goals, the findings were highly congruent with those of Anderman and Anderman (1999). Limitations of both studies, as well as other investigations on this topic (e.g., Ames & Archer, 1988), are that they (a) only focused on students' assessments of the instructional context, ignoring the "real," objective context beyond individual perceptions, and (b) were restricted to teachers' goals, not considering the cooperative or competitive goal orientations of the classmates and their impact on changes in individual goal orientations.

Therefore, in the BIJU study, 2,524 students from 153 classes were analyzed to predict changes in goal orientations over one school year with individual goals, perceived cooperation and competitiveness of the classmates, and "real" cooperation and competitiveness measures of the class. At the beginning and the end of grade 7, students filled out a questionnaire on individual goal orientations. Furthermore, a questionnaire on the classroom climate was administered at the end of the school year containing items on the cooperation and competitiveness of the students within the class. The items of the goal orientations scales were adopted from the Motivational Orientation Scales (MOS) by Nicholls, Patashnick, and Nolen (1985). Items were prefaced with the heading "I feel most satisfied in school if—." Example items were "I am the only one who knows the right answer" (ego orientation) and "The tasks require many considerations and reflections" (task orientation). Reliabilities (Cronbach's alpha) of both scales were above .77. Cooperation and competitiveness of the classmates were each measured with four items. Example items were for competitiveness "Some students in our classroom always try to outperform others" (1 = totally disagree, 4 = totally agree) and for cooperation "If a student has problems, the classmates help him or her immediately." Internal consistencies were above .70. To separate effects of the perceived classroom environment and the "real environment" on changes in goal orientations, I used both the individual scores of the cooperation and competitiveness scales and their class averages as predictors of ego and task orientation at the end of grade 7. While cooperation and competitiveness at the individual level represent students' perceptions of the classroom environment, the collectively aggregated scores of these measures at classroom level reflect measures of the environment (see Bryk & Raudenbush, 1992, for details about analyzing context effects). Because the characteristics of individuals

Table 1
Findings of Multilevel Analyses Predicting Individual Change in Goal Orientations (Standardized Regression Coefficients)

	Dependent variable	
	Ego orientation at the end of grade 7	*Task orientation at the end of grade 7*
Predictors		
Ego orientation at the beginning of grade 7	.34***	.02
Task orientation at the beginning of grade 7	–.03	.28***
Perceived competiveness within the class	.25***	.14***
Competiveness (class average)	.01	.00
Perceived cooperation within the class	.03	.22***
Cooperation (class average)	.03	.22***
R^2	.19	.15

Notes. R^2: explained variance; *** p < .002.

and classes were to be analyzed simultaneously, we conducted multilevel analyses on the basis of the hierarchical linear modeling approach (HLM) by Bryk and Raudenbush (1992). Table 1 shows the HLM findings. All regressions coefficients are standardized.

Beyond the stability coefficient of $\beta = .34$, only the perceived competitiveness of the classmates predicted ego orientation at the end of grade 7. Concerning task orientation, both the perceived classroom climate as well as the "real" climate predicted task orientation at the end of grade 7, that is, students who assessed their classmates as cooperative ($\beta = .22$) as well as those belonging to a class of cooperative classmates ($\beta = .22$) had higher task orientation at the end of grade 7. Surprisingly, students perceiving their classmates as very competitive developed higher task orientations. In general, the findings show quite clearly that the classroom climate in terms of perceived and "real" goals of the students substantially influences the development of goal orientations, suggesting that task orientation increases in cooperative settings while ego orientation increases in competitive settings.

Conclusion

There is obviously a strong tendency in early adolescence to change individual goal orientations from learning to performance goals, although the latter tend to have negative effects on academic learning. This change in goal orientations, however, is fostered by developmental changes as well as changes in the academic environment. Developmental changes render social comparison and thus performance goals available. Whether this less adaptive goal orientation prevails in adolescents' approach to school achievement critically depends on the instructional setting in their classrooms. Thus, teachers could use their influence to provide and learning environment, in which cooperation among students is enhanced and feedback is given in a way that increases learning orientation (task orientation). The typical climate of junior high schools focusing more on competition and highlighting the role of grades for achievement feedback is thus counter-productive for students' motivational development.

References

Ablard, K. E., & Lipschultz, R. E. (1998). Self-regulated learning in high achieving students: Relations to advanced reasoning, achievement goals, and gender. *Journal of Educational Psychology, 90,* 94–101.

Albaili, M. A. (1998). Goal orientations, cognitive strategies, and academic achievement among United Arab Emirates college students. *Educational Psychology, 18,* 195–203.

Albert, S. (1977). Temporal comparison theory. *Psychological Review, 84,* 485–503.

Ames, C. (1987). The enhancement of students' motivation. In M. L. Maehr, P. R. Pintrich, D. E. Bartz, M. Steinkamp, J. G. Nicholls, D. A. Kleiber, & C. Ames (Eds.), *Advances in motivation and achievement: Enhancing motivation* (Vol. 5, pp. 123–148). Greenwich, CT: JAI Press.

Ames, C. (1992). Classrooms: Goals, structures, and student motivation. *Journal of Educational Psychology, 84,* 261–271.

Ames, C., & Ames, R. (1984). Systems of student and teacher motivation: Toward a qualitative definition. *Journal of Educational Psychology, 76,* 535–556.

Ames, C., & Archer, J. (1988). Achievement goals in the classroom: Students' learning strategies and motivation processes. *Journal of Educational Psychology, 80,* 260–267.

Anderman, E. M., & Maehr, M. L. (1994). Motivation and schooling in the middle grades. *Review of Educational Research, 64,* 287–309.

Anderman, E. M., & Midgley, C. (1997). Changes in achievement goal orientations, perceived academic competence, and grades across the transition to middle-level schools. *Contemporary Educational Psychology, 22,* 269–298.

Anderman, L. H., & Anderman, E. M. (1999). Social predictors of changes in students' achievement goal orientations. *Contemporary Educational Psychology, 24,* 21–37.

Atkinson, J. W. (1957). Motivational determinants of risk-taking behavior. *Psychological Review, 6,* 359–372.

Biggs, J. B. (1985). The role of metalearning in study processes. *British Journal of Educational Psychology, 55,* 185–212.

Bouffard, T., Boisvert, J., Vezeau, C., & Larouche, C. (1995). The impact of goal orientation on self-regulation and performance among college students. *British Journal of Educational Psychology, 65,* 317–329.

Bryk, A. S., & Raudenbush, S. W. (1992). *Hierarchical linear models: Applications and data analysis methods.* Newbury Park, CA: Sage.

Duda, J. L., & Nicholls, J. G. (1992). Dimensions of achievement motivation in schoolwork and sport. *Journal of Educational Psychology, 84,* 290–299.

Dweck, C. S. (1986). Motivational processes affecting learning. *American Psychologist, 41,* 1040–1048.

Dweck, C. S. (1998). The development of early self-conceptions: Their relevance for motivational processes. In J. Heckhausen & C. S. Dweck (Eds.), *Motivation and self-regulation across the life span* (pp. 257–280). New York: Cambridge University Press.

Dweck, C. S., & Leggett, E. L. (1988). A social-cognitive approach to motivation and personality. *Psychological Review, 95,* 256–273.

Eccles, J. S., & Midgley, C. (1989). Stage/environment fit: Developmentally appropriate classrooms for early adolescents. In R. E. Ames & C. Ames (Eds.), *Research on motivation in education* (Vol. 3, pp. 139–186). New York: Academic Press.

Eccles, J. S., Midgley, C., Wigfield, A., Buchanan, C. M., et al. (1993). Development during adolescence: The impact of stage environment fit on young adolescents' experiences in schools and in families. *American Psychologist, 48,* 90–101.

Elliot, A. J., & Harakiewicz, J. M. (1996). Approach and avoidance achievement goals and intrinsic motivation: A mediational analysis. *Journal of Personality and Social Psychology, 70,* 461–475.

Elliott, E. S., & Dweck, C. S. (1988). Goals: An approach to motivation and achievement. *Journal of Personality and Social Psychology, 54,* 5–12.

Entwistle, N. J. (1988). Motivational factors in students' approaches to learning. In R. R. Schmeck (Ed.), *Learning strategies and learning styles* (pp. 21–52). New York: Plenum.

Fisher, S. L., & Ford, J. K. (1998). Differential effects of learner effort and goal orientation on two learner outcomes. *Personnel Psychology, 51,* 397–420.

Ford, J. K., Smith, E. M., Weissbein, D. A., Gully, S. M., & Salas, E. (1998). Relationships of goal orientation, metacognitive activity, and practice strategies with learning outcomes and transfer. *Journal of Applied Psychology, 83,* 218–233.

Gangestad, S., & Snyder, M. (1985). "To carve nature at its joints": On the existence of discrete classes in personality. *Psychological Review, 92,* 317–349.

Heckhausen, H. (1991). *Motivation and action.* New York: Springer.

Hunt, D. E. (1975). Person-environment interaction: A challenge found wanting before it was tried. *Review of Educational Research, 45,* 209–230.

Köller, O. (1998a). *Zielorientierungen und schulisches Lernen* [Goal orientations and academic learning]. Münster, Germany: Waxmann.

Köller, O. (1998b). Different aspects of learning motivation: The impact of interest and goal orientation on scholastic learning. In L. Hoffmann, A. Krapp, K. A. Renninger, & J. Baumert (Eds.), *Interest and learning* (pp. 317–326). Kiel, Germany: IPN.

Köller, O., Baumert, J., & Rost, J. (1998). Zielorientierungen: Ihr typologischer Charakter und ihre Entwicklung im frühen Jugendalter [Goal orientations: Their typological character and their development during early adolescence]. *Zeitschrift für Entwicklungspsychologie und Pädagogische Psychologie, 30,* 128–138.

Krampen, G. (1987). Differential effects of teacher comments. *Journal of Educational Psychology, 79,* 137–146.

Meece, J. L., Blumenfeld, P. C., & Hoyle, R. H. (1988). Students' goal orientations and cognitive engagement in classroom activities. *Journal of Educational Psychology, 80,* 514–523.

Meece, J. L., & Holt, K. (1993). A pattern analysis of students' achievement goals. *Journal of Educational Psychology, 85,* 582–590.

Meehl, P. E. (1992). Factors and taxa, traits and types, differences of degree and differences in kind. *Journal of Personality, 60,* 117–174.

Middleton, M. J., & Midgley, C. (1997). Avoiding the demonstration of lack of ability: An underexplored aspect of goal theory. *Journal of Educational Psychology, 89,* 710–718.

Nicholls, J. G. (1984). Achievement motivation: Conceptions of ability, subjective experience, task choice, and performance. *Psychological Review, 91,* 328–346.

Nicholls, J. G. (1992). Students as educational theorists. In D. H. Schunk & J. L. Meece (Eds.), *Students' perceptions in the classroom* (pp. 267–287). Hillsdale, NJ: Erlbaum.

Nicholls, J. G., Patashnick, M., & Nolen, S. B. (1985). Adolescents' theories of education. *Journal of Educational Psychology, 77,* 683–692.

Nolen, S. B. (1988). Reasons for studying: Motivational orientations and study strategies. *Cognition and Instruction, 5,* 269–287.

Pintrich, P. R., & De Groot, E. V. (1990). Motivational and self-regulated learning components of classroom academic performance. *Journal of Educational Psychology, 82,* 33–40.

Pintrich, P. R., & Garcia, T. (1991). Student goal orientation and self-regulation in the college classroom. In M. L. Maehr & P. R. Pintrich (Eds.), *Advances in motivation and achievement: Vol. 7. Goals and self-regulatory processes* (pp. 371–402). Greenwich, CT: JAI Press.

Rheinberg, F. (1980). *Leistungsbewertung und Lernmotivation* [Achievement feedback and learning motivation]. Göttingen, Germany: Hogrefe.

Ruble, D. N., Feldman, N. S., & Boggiano, A. K. (1976). Social comparison between young children in achievement situations. *Developmental Psychology, 12,* 192–197.

Seifert, T. L. (1995). Characteristics of ego- and task-oriented students: A comparison of two methodologies. *British Journal of Educational Psychology, 65,* 125–138.

Seifert, T. L. (1996). The stability of goal orientations in grade five students: Comparison of two methodologies. *British Journal of Educational Psychology, 66,* 73–82.

Seifert, T. L. (1997). Academic goals and emotions: Results of a structural equation model and a cluster analysis. *British Journal of Educational Psychology, 67,* 323–338.

Simmons, R. G., & Blyth, D. A. (1987). *Moving into adolescence: The impact of pubertal change and school context.* Hawthorne, NY: de Gruyter.

Simmons, R. G., Blyth, D. A., van Cleaves, E. F., & Bush, D. (1979). Entry into early adolescence: The impact of school structure, puberty, and early dating on self-esteem. *American Sociological Review, 38,* 553–568.

Stipek, D. J., & Gralinski, J. H. (1996). Children's beliefs about intelligence and school performance. *Journal of Educational Psychology, 88,* 397–407.

Suls, J. (1986). Comparison processes in relative deprivation: A life-span analysis. In J. M. Olson, C. P. Herman, & M. P. Zanna (Eds.), *The Ontario symposium* (Vol. 4, pp. 95–116). Hillsdale, NJ: Erlbaum.

Thorkildsen, T. A., & Nicholls, J. G. (1998). Fifth graders' achievement orientations and beliefs: Individual and classroom differences. *Journal of Educational Psychology, 90,* 179–201.

Wigfield, A., Eccles, J. S., & Pintrich, P. R. (1996). Development between the ages of 11 and 25. In D. C. Berliner & R. C. Calfee (Eds.), *Handbook of educational psychology* (pp. 148–185). New York: Macmillan.

Wolters, C. A., Yu, S. L., & Pintrich, P. R. (1996). The relation between goal orientation and students' motivational beliefs and self-regulated learning. *Learning and Individual Differences, 8,* 211–238.

Young, A. J. (1997). I think, therefore I'm motivated: The relations among cognitive strategy use, motivational orientation and classroom perceptions over time. *Learning and Individual Differences, 9,* 249–283.

2000 Elsevier Science B.V.

7 A Social-Cognitive, Control-Value Theory of Achievement Emotions

Reinhard Pekrun

Emotions may be important for human learning, development, achievement, and health. Therefore, since the beginning of the 1980s, personality, social, and developmental psychology have been researching human emotions more intensively than ever. However, in spite of this boom of basic emotion research, applied fields like educational, organizational, and work psychology have neglected emotions until recently (cf. Pekrun & Frese, 1992). As a result, we still lack knowledge today about achievement-related emotions, their impact on learning and performance, and their development and antecedents.

One major exception is research on students' test anxiety. Since Mandler's and Sarason's pioneering research titled "A study of anxiety and learning" (Mandler & Sarason, 1952), more than 1,000 empirical studies on this single achievement emotion have been published. Results of these studies have consistently shown the following (Hembree, 1988; Zeidner, 1998; Pekrun, in press): (a) Test anxiety is frequently experienced by school and university students around the world. (b) Typically, this emotion develops during the preschool and elementary years. In secondary and post-secondary years, average test anxiety values tend to be more or less stable in North American and European student populations. Nevertheless, there may be individual changes, thus indicating developmental plasticity beyond the elementary years. (c) Test anxiety is correlated with a number of social-environmental factors including negative achievement feedback, pressure for achievement and high achievement expectancies by parents and teachers, punishment following failures, and competition within classrooms. (d) Test anxiety interferes with task-focused attention and, therefore, tends to impair performance at complex and difficult tasks, and to correlate negatively with academic achievement at school and university.

A second notable exception is research into attributional antecedents of achievement-contingent emotions. This research has demonstrated that specific emotions following success and failure (e.g., pride and shame) may depend on the subject's appraisal of the causes of success or failure, and on perceived properties of causes like stability, internality, and controllability (cf. Weiner, 1985, 1994).

With the exception of test anxiety and attributional studies, our knowledge about achievement-related emotions is limited. This applies to negative emotions beyond anxiety (achievement-related anger, hopelessness, shame, boredom, contempt, etc.) as well as to positive emotions (like enjoyment of learning, hope for success, pride, relief, or admiration). Therefore, our research group at Regensburg started a program of research into achievement and academic emotions a number of years ago (cf. Pekrun & Hofmann, 1999). This program involves a sequence of research steps including the following: (1) exploratory analyses of frequencies, structures, and phenomenology of achievement-related emotions in different populations (e.g., Pekrun, 1992a); (2) construction of diagnostic measures (e.g., Academic Emotions Questionnaire, cf. Pekrun, Titz, Molfenter, & Ingrisch, 1999); (3) analysis of the functions of achievement emotions for learning, achievement, health, and personality development (e.g., Pekrun, Hochstadt, & Kramer, 1996; Pekrun, Molfenter, Titz, Ingrisch, & Perry, 2000; Perry, Hladkyi, Pekrun, & Pelletier, 2000); (4) analysis of development and antecedents; (5) applied studies on optimization, prevention, and therapy of achievement-related emotions.

The present contribution focuses on antecedents and development of achievement emotions. After giving an overview of the domain of achievement-related emotions, a social-cognitive theory of achievement emotions and their development will be outlined, and exemplary, preliminary evidence pertaining to this theory will be presented. This evidence pertains to academic emotions experienced in school and university settings, but the theory is applicable to emotions in other domains of human achievement as well (e.g., work and sports, cf. Pekrun & Frese, 1992).

Achievement Emotions: Definition and Relevance of the Domain

Generally, *emotions* may be regarded as systems of interrelated psychological processes including the following: (a) an activation of subsystems of subcortical brain systems (mainly the limbic system) which is subjectively experienced as emotional feelings (affective component of emotions, e.g., uneasy, nervous feelings in anxiety); (b) emotion-specific cognitions (e.g., threat-related worries in anxiety); (c) emotion-specific motivational tendencies (goals, wishes, and intentions, like wishes to avoid a situation in anxiety); (d) emotion-specific physiological processes (e.g., activation); (e) emotion-specific expressive behavior (cf. Scherer, 1984; Pekrun, 1988). The affective component may be regarded as a necessary defining constituent of the term "emotion." Other components may typically be present in full-blown emotions like intense joy or anger, but they may also be lacking (e.g., in low-intensity emotions and in dissociative clinical states).

Component definitions of emotion imply that *motivation* may be part of an emotion on condition that it is affectively colored and emotionally "hot." Another implication is that emotions may be important ingredients of *interest* as defined by educational interest researchers (cf. Krapp, this volume). Specifically, positive emotions directed toward an object or an activity may be regarded as facets of an individual's interest in this object or activity. However, in addition to emotion, cognitive appraisals referring to intrinsic or instrumental values of the object/activity may also be important elements of interest, implying that the construct of interest may be conceptualized as reaching beyond emotion by comprising both emotional and nonemotional facets.

The domain of *achievement emotions* may be defined in both broad and narrow ways. Broadly, an emotion may be regarded as an achievement emotion if it relates to an activity or outcome of an activity which is evaluated by the subject according to some external or internal standard of quality. Examples for activity-related achievement emotions are enjoyment of learning or boredom; examples for outcome-related achievement emotions are hope for success or shame about failure. In a more narrow way, the domain may definitionally be restricted to emotions relating to achievement outcomes (i.e., success and failure). In the present theory, a broader conception of achievement emotions is favored. Such a conception allows us to deal in integrated ways both with emotions relating to achievement activities, and with emotions relating to success and failure outcomes of such activities.

As emotions in general, achievement emotions may be classified according to their valence (positive, negative, or neutral), to their contextual frame of reference (individual or social), and to their time reference (concurrent, prospective, or retrospective). Concurrent, activity-related achievement emotions refer to the process of performing an achievement-related activity, whereas retrospective and prospective achievement emotions pertain to past and future achievement-related activities or their outcomes (like success and failure). Some examples are given in Table 1.

Theoretically, any kind of human emotions may be experienced when performing achievement activities or thinking of own or others' success and

Table 1
Classification of Achievement Emotions: Examples

		Positive	*Negative*
	Concurrent	Enjoyment of learning	Boredom
Self-related	*Prospective*	Hope for success Anticipatory joy	Anxiety Hopelessness
	Retrospective	Joy after success Relief Pride	Sadness Disappointment Shame/guilt
Social		Gratitude Empathy Admiration Sympathy/love	Anger Envy Contempt Antipathy/hate

failure. This even applies to emotions normally tied to quite different categories of events like, for example, disgust. However, depending on cultural, situational, and individual conditions, some achievement emotions may be experienced more frequently than others. In our exploratory interview studies, achievement emotions reported frequently by school and university students were joy, hope, relief, pride, anger, anxiety, boredom, and dissatisfaction. In both school and university students, achievement-related anxiety proved to be the one emotion reported most often. Anxiety was reported not only for exams and tests (test anxiety), but for situations of being in class or learning at home as well (class-related and learning-related anxiety). Typically, anxiety accounted for 15 to 20 percent of the emotional episodes reported (e.g., Pekrun, 1992a; Holzwarth, 1997). Such findings corroborate assumptions about the pervasiveness of anxiety at school and university, as well as the importance of research into achievement-related anxiety. However, they also imply that more than 80 percent of our students' emotional life is made up of other emotions, including not only negative emotions, but a number of positive emotions as well.

Beyond just being experienced frequently, achievement emotions also proved to be relevant for students' motivation, learning, and achievement. Again, this applied not only to the well-researched emotion of test anxiety, but also to a great variety of emotions beyond anxiety. Findings from our studies imply that activating positive emotions like enjoyment of learning and hope for success may exert positive effects on motivation to learn, the use of flexible learning strategies, task-focused attention, and resulting achievement. Deactivating negative emotions like boredom and hopelessness seem to be detrimental for motivation, learning, and achievement. Activating negative emotions like anxiety and anger, however, may well exert ambivalent effects (e.g., anxiety may reduce interest and intrinsic motivation, but may at the same time strengthen extrinsic motivation to invest effort in order to avoid failures). Overall, emotions like enjoyment of learning, boredom, and hopelessness proved to exert stronger effects on learning and achievement than the well-researched emotion of test anxiety, implying that test anxiety should not necessarily be regarded as the most important achievement-related emotion experienced by school and university students (cf. Pekrun, 1992b; Pekrun & Hofmann, 1999).

Since achievement emotions seem to be both frequent and relevant, an analysis of their antecedents and development may be worthwhile both from scientific and applied perspectives. Such an analysis may be regarded as a precondition for designing suitable methods of intervention fostering achievement-related emotional life and, by implication, learning, achievement, health, and personality development.

Control-Value Theory of Achievement Emotions: Basic Assumptions

Emotion Formation

Generally, it may be assumed that human emotions may be induced and modulated in a number of different ways. Five important mechanisms may be the following.

Genetically Based Emotions. Human beings are capable of experiencing emotions early in life. In the early stages of development, an induction of emotions may primarily be based on inherited, hard-wired cognitive schemata, and may be triggered by schema-congruent perceptions (such as in fear of heights, fear of snakes or spiders, or enjoyment of fulfilling basic physiological needs). Furthermore, genetical dispositions may predispose an individual to experience specific emotions more or less frequently and more or less intensively, thus contributing to interindividual differences of emotional experiences.

Neurophysiologically Mediated Emotions. Emotions are probably also triggered by basic neurochemical mechanisms (e.g., in psychopathological depressive states).

Conditioned Emotions. Neuropsychological evidence implies that emotions may be produced by early conditioning establishing direct links between situational perceptions and subcortical, limbic emotional reactions (cf. LeDoux, 1995).

Cognitively Mediated Emotions. Emotions may be induced by cognitive appraisals of present, past, or future situations. This type of emotion induction has been addressed by appraisal theories of emotions and has been researched intensively over the past four decades (Roseman, Antoniou, & Jose, 1996).

Habitualized Emotions. Cognitive mediation of emotions implies that situational perceptions do not trigger an emotion directly, but have to be appraised cognitively before being able to do so. It may be assumed, however, that cognitive mediation of emotions may become proceduralized in recurring situations (cf. Pekrun, 1988). In similar ways as with any proceduralization of cognitive skills, this process may basically comprise three stages: (a) automatization of declarative cognitive appraisals; (b) stepwise compilation of these appraisals; (c) final short-circuiting of perception and emotion via formation of procedural schemata linking perception and emotion in direct ways. Such schemata may still include declarative appraisal structures which, however, need no longer play a causal role in triggering the emotion. An example would be recurring anxiety of math exams experienced by a school student, which may become proceduralized in such a way that the mere announcement of a math test is sufficient to induce anxiety, implying that any calculation of probabilities and consequences of failure is no longer necessary for anxiety to be induced.

Genetically based and subcortically conditioned emotions may primarily be important early in life, and neurophysiologically mediated emotions in psychopathological states. In contrast, cognitively mediated and habitualized emotions may be assumed to be important across the life span and in a variety of situations, including situations mediating socio-cultural influences on emotional development. Specifically, concerning achievement emotions, genetical, neurophysiological, or subcortical conditioning mechanisms may be less important since standards of quality defining achievement are socio-culturally constructed, thus rendering processes of cognitive mediation a central status.

Therefore, control-value theory of achievement emotions addresses cognitively mediated emotions, and by implication, habitualized emotions, as well as social influences on the development of such emotions. It builds on a more general model of cognitively mediated, reflective types of human motivation and emotion (Pekrun, 1988, 1992c). In doing so, the theory transfers assumptions from motivational expectancy-value theories to the domain of emotions, and enlarges these assumptions in such ways that future-related as well as retrospective and concurrent emotions can be addressed.

Control-Related and Value-Related Cognitions

For all kinds of prospective as well as retrospective and concurrent achievement emotions, the theory postulates that two types of cognitions may be central: (a) control-related cognitions, and (b) value appraisals.

Control-Related Cognitions. "Control" is used here as a generic term denoting causal, functional, and conditional relationships. Control-related cognitions thus refer to subjective appraisals of any type of cause-effect relations, functional relations between variables, or relations between antecedent variables and consequences. Examples are future-related causal expectancies and retrospective or concurrent causal attributions. Control-related cognitions may focus on cause-effect relationships, but they may also more indirectly refer to control by appraising the conditional side of control relations. One important type of cognitions of this latter category is self-appraisals of one's own competences (e.g., self-concepts of abilities, self-efficacy expectancies).

Concerning causal expectancies, control-value theory borrows conceptually from Heinz Heckhausen's theory of achievement motivation and Bandura's conception of self-efficacy expectations (cf. Heckhausen, 1977; Bandura, 1986). Building on concepts of these theories, three different types of expectancies may be differentiated (for details, see Pekrun, 1988, 1992c): (a) situation-outcome expectancies referring to relations between situations and situational outcomes which may be expected on condition that no own action is undertaken (e.g., appraisals of the probability of getting a bad grade at an exam if one does not prepare for the exam); (b) action-control expectancies appraising possibilities to initiate and perform suitable actions (e.g., the expectation to be able to prepare for an exam by investing effort and concentration); (c) action-outcome expectancies pertaining to the consequences of action (e.g., the expectation to get a good mark resulting from preparation). The term "action" is used in a broad way here (also referring to, e.g., motivated cognitive processes), implying that action-control and action-outcome expectancies may embrace both primary and secondary subjective control (cf. Heckhausen & Schulz, 1995).

Value Cognitions. Situations, actions, and outcomes may have intrinsic or extrinsic values for an individual. Intrinsic values refer to inherent properties of the situation, action, or outcome. Extrinsic values pertain to being instrumental for the attainment of other valuable outcomes. For example, good grades may be intrinsically valent for a student who is intrinsically motivated to achieve, and of instrumental value for another student who focuses on their functions for getting a good job. Extrinsic, instrumental values may depend on the intrinsic values of the outcomes to which they relate, and on the expectancy that these outcomes can be attained.

The Impact of Control and Value Cognitions on Achievement Emotions

Control-value theory postulates that control- and value-related cognitions are of primary importance for achievement emotions. More specifically, it may be assumed that any type of achievement emotion depends on value appraisals, and that most of them also depend on control-related cognitions (cf. also Patrick, Skinner, & Connell, 1993). This may be assumed for prospective, retrospective, and concurrent achievement emotions, including both self-related and social achievement emotions. Concerning habitualized emotions, control and value appraisals need not factually be present, but may have produced these emotions in the first place when the process of habitualization started. For some more important emotions, the following may be assumed.

Prospective emotions. Primary examples for future-related achievement emotions are hope, anticipatory joy, anxiety, and hopelessness relating to future achievement activities and their outcomes. For such emotions to arise, both expectancies and value appraisals of activities/outcomes may be assumed to be necessary. For example, anxiety of failures will arise on condition that failures are expected with some subjective probability, and that these failures are sufficiently important to the subject. In similar ways as postulated by traditional expectancy-value theories for the domain of motivation, this implies combinations of expectancy and value appraisals which follow multiplicative types of rules. Expectancies relating to achievement activities and outcomes may be based on causal situation-outcome, action-control, and action-outcome expectancies, value appraisals on both intrinsic and instrumental valences of activities and outcomes (for details and formalizations of these assumptions, cf. Pekrun, 1988, 1992c).

Positive anticipatory emotions may arise when values are positive, negative emotions when values are negative. When value appraisals are ambivalent, both positive and negative emotions may be triggered (e.g., when an exam is simultaneously inducing hope for positively valued success and fear of negatively valued failure). In addition, the type of emotion induced may depend on the subjective probabilities implied by expectancies. Concerning positively valued activities/outcomes, anticipatory joy may be induced by high subjective probabilities, hope by medium probabilities implying uncertainty, and hopelessness by low or zero probabilities. As for negatively valued activities/outcomes, anxiety may be produced by medium probabilities (uncertainty about failures and/or their consequences), and subjective certainty may induce hopelessness. Such a view implies that hopelessness may be caused both by subjective certainty about upcoming failure, and by certainty about the nonattainment of success (which, subjectively, may or may not be defined as failure, implying that these two cases of hopelessness should be separated logically).

Retrospective Emotions. Examples for retrospective achievement emotions are joy, pride, sadness, and shame. Whereas expectancies may be assumed to be central for future-related emotions, retrospective emotions are based on recollections of past achievement activities and outcomes. In addition to being remembered, however, these activities/outcomes have to be valued in order to induce emotional feelings, implying that both recollections and value appraisals may be necessary conditions for the induction of such emotions. It follows that there is some structural similarity between the mechanisms of future-related and of retrospective emotions: Both of them are based on time-related cognitions (expectancies, recollections), on the one hand, and value-related cognitions, on the other. There is an important difference, however: Whereas the quality of future-related emotions may depend on subjective probabilities of the events they relate to, past events are sure events, at least in most cases. In retrospective emotions, perceived causes of an event may determine the quality of an emotion (in addition to its values), instead of probabilities of the event.

Retrospective joy or sadness about past achievement activities or outcomes, however, may arise independently of causal perceptions (attribution-independent emotions). In contrast, pride and shame may depend on internal attributions relating past achievement to factors like effort or competence, and social emotions like gratitude and anger on external attributions (Weiner, 1985, 1994).

Concurrent Emotions. The two most important concurrent, activity-related achievement emotions are enjoyment and boredom. Enjoyment and boredom may be assumed to depend on subjective competences and the perceived amount of control over task performance. Specifically, enjoyment may be induced if demands are challenging, but can nevertheless be met, implying that control is difficult to achieve, but is attainable in spite of challenging demands. Boredom, on the other hand, may be triggered when control is either very high (as implied by low demands and tasks which are too easy), or when it is too low (high demands and tasks which are too difficult). The latter condition may simultaneously lead to anticipations of failure inducing anxiety or hopelessness, thus giving rise to mixed emotional states consisting of activity-related boredom and prospective anxiety/hopelessness, or to oscillations between these different low-control emotions.

Empirical Evidence

Evidence pertaining to some of these assumptions may be found in test anxiety research and in attributional studies. In a number of investigations, test anxiety correlated positively with students' failure expectancies and negatively with their academic self-concepts of ability (cf. Hembree, 1988; Zeidner, 1998). Corroborating control-value assumptions, our own cross-sectional and longitudinal studies have shown that failure expectancies, effort-control expectancies, and values of achievement may be regarded as important antecedents of test anxiety in school and university students (cf. Pekrun, 1991, 1992c). These studies had been based on an expectancy-value theory of anxiety (EVTA; Pekrun, 1992c) which is consistent with the more general control-value framework presented here. Concerning retrospective emotions following success and failure, research on attributional antecedents has shown that such emotions may, in fact, be linked in specific ways to causal attributions of success and failure (Weiner, 1985, 1994).

Beyond test anxiety and attributional studies, empirical knowledge on individual antecedents of achievement emotions is limited. Some evidence on the relevance of control- and value-related cognitions for achievement emotions beyond test anxiety has been gathered in a recent cross-sectional study involving a sample of N = 1.867 German secondary school students (grades 5–13, n = 823/1.044 boys/girls; cf. Jacob, 1996). The primary aim of the study was to construct and validate self-report scales for assessing such emotions, but measures of antecedent variables were included as well. Emotions addressed were test-related joy, anger, anxiety, shame, and hopelessness (27/27/28/29/28 items; α = .91/.93/.95/.95/.95; sample items: "I enjoy writing tests at school"; "Having to prepare for tests at school makes me angry"; "The day before an exam I am very nervous"; "I feel ashamed when the teacher asks questions I can't answer"; "I feel hopeless when taking an exam at school"). Parts of the scale on test anxiety are based on Sarason's Reactions-to-Tests Questionnaire (Sarason, 1984). Each scale consists of four subscales relating to affective, cognitive, motivational, and physiological emotion components.

Two scales pertaining to control-related academic cognitions were included in this study (academic self-concept of ability and general self-esteem; 9/8 items; α = .85/.82), as well as two scales on value-related cognitions (value of academic achievement, self-exerted pressure for achievement; 7/7 items; α = .81/.61; sample items: "It is very important for me to get good grades"; "I always think I should achieve more at school").

Table 2 shows the correlations between these control- and value-related variables and students' test emotions. Academic self-concept and general self-esteem were positively related to enjoyment of tests, and negatively related to all four negative test emotions. The two value-related variables, on the other hand, correlated positively with both positive and negative test emotions. In line with assumptions of control-value theory, this pattern of correlations implies that control-related cognitions are important for the quality of emotions (positive vs. negative), whereas high values of achievement may generally lead to increased achievement-related emotionality including both positive and negative emotions. Similar results have been found for achievement emotions in university students (cf. Pekrun & Hofmann, 1999).

Table 2
Self-Concepts, Achievement Values, and Students' Test-Related Emotions

Emotion	*Self-concept of ability*	*General self-esteem*	*Value of achievement*	*Achievement pressure (self)*
Enjoyment	.44	.22	.28	.31
Anger	–.37	–.43	.21	.25
Anxiety	–.36	–.44	.39	.39
Shame	–.27	–.47	.41	.39
Hopelessness	–.49	–.59	.32	.34

$p < .01$ for $r > .06$.

Developmental Implications: Social Influences on Achievement Emotions

Control-related and value-related cognitions may be regarded as proximal antecedents of achievement emotions that mediate the influence of social factors located in environments like family, school, university, and the workplace. This implies that those social factors may be assumed to be influential that affect individual control cognitions andvalues in the first place. A large number of more or less distant features of social and cultural environments may be assumed to do so. All those factors may be relevant which (a) define success and failure, their situational conditions, probabilities, and values, (b) set boundary conditions and values for performing achievement activities, and/or (c) affect individual antecedents of achievement activities and outcomes (e.g., competences), thus influencing control and subjective values. The following groups of variables may be of primary importance (see Figure 1; for more specific assumptions on job-related factors, cf. Pekrun & Frese, 1992).

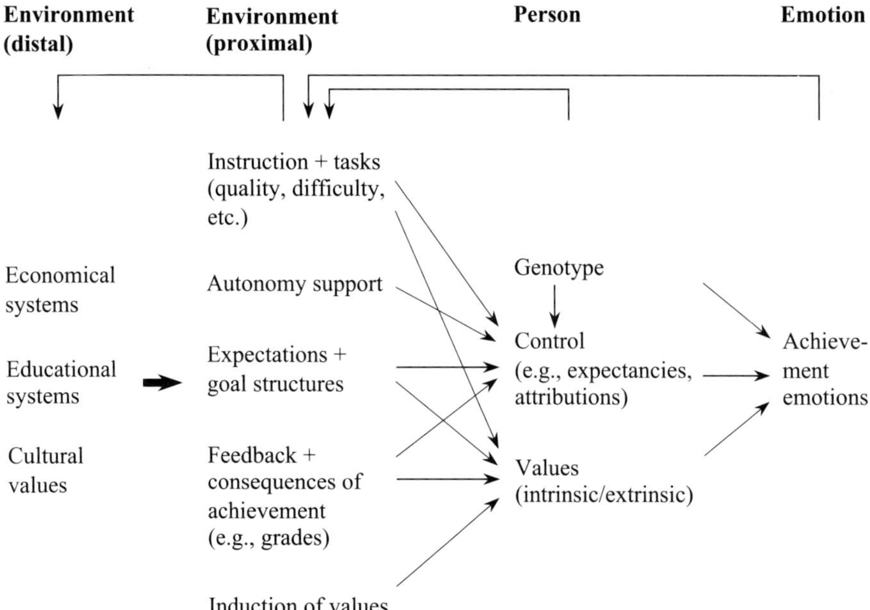

Figure 1. Control-value theory of achievement emotions: Basic assumptions

Proximal Social Antecedents

Instruction. Individual competences built up by instructional methods used in family, school, universities, and the workplace may underly the formation of control- und competence-related self-appraisals and, therefore, of achievement emotions. This applies both to direct instruction and to indirect methods of instruction like creating stimulating learning environments, providing suitable learning materials, and giving emotional, informational, and material support for learning. In addition, attending high-quality instruction may be enjoyable for students. Such enjoyment may generalize to related activities of learning and achieving. Quality instruction may thus contribute to positive intrinsic values of achievement activities and, therefore, to the long-term development of activity-related positive emotions. The converse may hold for low-quality instruction producing boredom.

Tasks. Learning-related and job-related tasks and standards of quality for task completion may play specific roles in building up control-related cognitions and values. Above all, this applies to the difficulty and complexity of tasks and to criteria defining successful task completion. These features of tasks contribute to success and failure, and may therefore be critical for the development of success- and failure-related emotions like prospective enjoyment, anxiety, and hopelessness, or retrospective pride and shame. Furthermore, task demands are important for the development of activity-related emotions like enjoyment of learning and boredom which may be dependent on demand/competence ratios.

Autonomy Support Versus Control. Some level of autonomy is a necessary condition for any self-regulation of learning and work activities. On condition that individual capabilities to regulate own activities are sufficiently high, autonomy support can be assumed to be beneficial for the development of competences and competence-related emotions (cf. Deci & Ryan, 1985; Weinert & Helmke, 1995). In addition, although autonomy may imply greater demands for investing effort, it may foster enjoyment of learning and performing since it may provide chances for fine-tuning self-defined elements of tasks and task performance according to the profile of available competences. Finally, autonomy may be beneficial for the development of those emotions that depend on internal causal attributions of activities and outcomes. This may apply to the experience of "flow" (Csikszentmihalyi, 1975) and to flow-related enjoyment of performing activities, as well as to achievement-contingent emotions like pride and shame (Weiner, 1985).

Expectancies and Goal Structures. Achievement expectancies of significant others imply social definitions of success and failure as well as more or less implicit information about the value of achievement. Achievement expectancies have traditionally been regarded as primary agents of children's achievement-related development and their status career over the life course by sociologists (cf. Seginer, 1983). High expectations may convey messages about high values of achievement, along with restricted definitions of success. If the individual accepts these messages, any type of achievement-contingent emotions may be intensified. Furthermore, the implied reduction of success expectancies may increase negative prospective achievement emotions like anxiety and hopelessness.

In educational institutions, companies, and other types of professional organizations, achievement expectancies and criteria for success and failure may be defined by institutional goal structures. Three important types of goal structures are the following (cf. Johnson & Johnson, 1974): (a) competitive structures implying negative contingencies of success probabilities in different individuals (success in some individuals implies failure in others); (b) cooperative structures implying positive contingencies (individual success is dependent on others' success or the success of a group); and (c) individualistic structures implying independence of success probabilities in different individuals. Furthermore, hybrid mixtures of these structures are typical of many settings (e.g., mixtures of between-group competition and within-group cooperation like in market economies; cf. Covington, 1992). Such goal structures may be important for the development of self-related achievement emotions, as well as for social achievement emotions like admiration, empathy, contempt, or envy.

For example, competitive goal structures, related interindividually referenced norms for achievement, and resulting competitive climate imply both limitations for chances of being successful and high values of being more successful than others, which may lead both to reduced success expectancies and to high values of achievement in many individuals. Such a combination of appraisals may in turn foster hope for and pride of success in high-achieving students, and anxiety and shame of failure in low-achieving students. At the same time, such a structure may increase those emotions which are tied to upward and downward social comparisons (like admiration and contempt).

Feedback and Consequences of Achievement. Success and failure feedback may situationally produce achievement-contingent emotions (joy, disappointment, pride, shame, etc.). Beyond situational effects, on condition that feedback is accepted by the individual and attributed accordingly, it may underlie the formation of competence and control appraisals and, therefore, the long-term development of success- and failure-related emotions. Cumulative feedback of success may foster positive emotions like success-related hope and pride, whereas cumulative negative feedback may lead to the development of negative prospective and retrospective emotions like test anxiety, shame about failures, and hopelessness.

Beyond feedback, consequences of achievement may produce expectancies of achievement-following outcomes and, therefore, extrinsic values of achievement underlying prospective emotions like hope for career success or fear of punishment. This may apply to social reactions (like praise and punishment by parents, teachers, or supervisors), financial consequences (e.g., increase or decrease of one's salary), career consequences across the life course, and so on.

It may be assumed that emotions produced by feedback and consequences of achievement can generalize, implying that they can contribute to activity-related emotions. For example, joy about success at learning may gradually induce intrinsic enjoyment of learning (via mechanisms of classical conditioning and internalization). On the other hand, negative emotions following failure may lead to subjective devaluation of learning and achievement (as one strategy of coping with the emotional consequences of failure), thus contributing to aversion and boredom.

Induction of Values. As outlined above, achievement-related values may be transmitted by autonomy support which stimulates flow experiences and internal attributions of success, by expectancies of significant others and related goal structures, and by instrumental functions of achievement for the attainment of distal outcomes. However, values may also be socialized in more direct ways. This applies to extrinsic as well as to intrinsic values of achievement-related activities and outcomes. Some important mechanisms may be the following: (a) Information about values may be given directly (e.g., by informing a student about the career consequences of failure at school). (b) Values may be modeled, implying that values conveyed by the behavior of significant others may be adopted. One mechanism of such modeling may be emotion contagion. For example, listening to an instructor who herself is enthusiastic about the material may induce enjoyment of a lesson in students via emotion contagion. This implies that achievement-related enthusiasm in parents, teachers, peers, and supervisors may be beneficial for the development of achievement emotions. (c) Values may be transmitted by creating learning and work environments which are stimulating (e.g., by providing cognitive challenge) and meaningful to the individual (e.g., "authentic" environments and tasks relating to a students' everyday life). (d) Finally, achievement values may be fostered by environments allowing the fulfillment of needs which themselves are not achievement-related. For example, this may apply to environments serving needs for social relatedness when performing tasks (cf. also Krapp, Chap. 5, this volume).

Distal Social Antecedents

Using Bronfenbrenner's (1979) terms, proximal social antecedents like those described above are primarily located in the individual's social microsystems. Such microsystems are themselves dependent on subsystems of the society in which they are embedded (work environments depend to some extent on the organization of a society's economy, school environments on the structure of school systems, etc.). These systems themselves are interrelated and dependent on larger systems of cultural norms and values. One implication is that the development of achievement emotions may systematically differ between school systems, economical systems, societies, and cultures. For example, achievement emotions may differ between societies having market economies and societies characterized by alternative types of economies, or between traditional competitive types of school systems and alternative schools. However, it should be noted that relations between social systems at different levels (culture, society, subsystems of society, immediate social environment of an individual) may be far from being isomorphic. This implies that differences may be more dependent on immediate environments than on larger systems, and that differences between societies and cultures may be different from what might be expected theoretically when deducing assumptions at the level of macrosystems.

Feedback Mechanisms and Genetical Influences

In addition to being affected by social-cognitive influences, the development of achievement emotions may be characterized by reciprocal causation implying that individuals act in response to their developmental environments. For example, instructional behavior and support by a teacher may affect students' achievement emotions, but the teacher's behavior may be shaped according to students' emotional and nonemotional classroom behavior, and by their achievement. Such reciprocal causation may involve complex feedback mechanisms of negative and positive types. Furthermore, beyond social influences, the development of achievement emotions may be assumed to depend to some degree on genetical factors and on genotype-environment interactions that influence individual differences in primary emotions and, by implication, individual differences in related achievement emotions (like enjoyment, anxiety, or anger in academic settings).

Empirical Evidence

Evidence on all of the different social mechanisms described above is largely lacking. Again, research on test anxiety is one major exception. In line with the above assumptions, studies have consistently shown that test anxiety correlates positively with environmental factors including the following (cf. Zeidner, 1998): (a) cumulative feedback of failure; (b) punishment after failure by parents and teachers; (c) high expectancies and pressure for achievement by parents and teachers; and (d) competition within classrooms. Social support by parents, teachers, and peers, however, tends to be uncorrelated with test anxiety. One possible explanation is that achievement-related support may play an ambivalent role by serving multiple functions: alleviating anxiety, but simultaneously implying messages of control and pressure for achievement. Another possibility is that anxiety and support are linked by reciprocal causation and negative feedback loops, implying that support reduces anxiety, but is provoked by anxiety in the first place, thus producing overall correlations near zero.

Results of the above study on test-related emotions in school students (Jacob, 1996) give some correlational evidence for social antecedents of a number of different achievement emotions. This study included measures for student perceptions of (a) teacher enthusiasm, (b) pressure for achievement by teachers and parents, (c) positive reinforcement after success, punishment after failure, and support after failure by teachers and parents, and (d) competition within the classroom. In line with the above assumptions deduced from control-value theory, teacher enthusiasm, positive reinforcement for success, and support after failure correlated positively with students' enjoyment (cf. Table 3). As in previous studies, correlations of support with anxiety and other negative emotions were near zero. Punishment after failure, on the other hand, was correlated positively with anger, anxiety, shame, and hopelessness. Finally, pressure for achievement and competition within the classroom corre-

Table 3
Social Environments and Students' Test-Related Emotions

	Joy	*Anger*	*Anxiety*	*Shame*	*Hopelessness*
Enthusiasm					
Teachers	.35	–.22	.01	.13	–.11
Pressure for achievement					
Teachers	.15	.38	.25	.34	.36
Parents	.12	.36	.26	.30	.34
Competition					
Classroom	.19	.29	.23	.36	.28
Positive reinforcement					
Teachers	.39	–.08	.01	.10	–.06
Parents	.30	–.04	.13	.13	.00
Punishment					
Teachers	.01	.38	.19	.26	.31
Parents	.04	.36	.24	.28	.33
Support after failure					
Teachers	.36	–.12	–.02	.09	–.09
Parents	.33	–.05	.09	.16	–.02

$p < .01$ for $r > .06$.

late positively with the negative emotions, but they also tended to relate positively to enjoyment. This may be due to the value-inducing functions of achievement expectancies and competitive behavior of significant others which may intensify not only negative achievement emotions, but positive emotions as well.

In sum, this pattern of relations is in line with the assumptions formulated above. However, the causal mechanisms underlying these correlations cannot be inferred from cross-sectional evidence of this type. Specifically, as argued above, feedback effects of achievement emotions on the environment may play a role here, in addition to social influences on the development of emotions. Feedback loops implied by such reciprocal causation have been investigated in a small number of longitudinal studies on relations between test anxiety and achievement. Results imply that both directions of causality may, in fact, play a developmental role (negative achievement feedback inducing test anxiety, and test anxiety in turn impairing achievement and, therefore, contributing to negative achievement feedback; cf. Meece, Wigfield, & Eccles, 1990; Pekrun, 1991, 1992c).

Conclusions

In this chapter, basic assumptions of a control-value theory of achievement emotions have been presented, and preliminary correlational evidence on some of these assumptions has been discussed. Beyond addressing individual antecedents of achievement emotions, control-value theory may be used as a framework for identifying and constructing social environments that nurture achievement-related emotional life and, thereby, learning, achievement, development, and health. The model is part of the larger family of social-cognitive theories of human development, thus being connected to cognitive models of social influences on motivation. As outlined above, it also relates to educational interest theory, since positive emotions directed toward achievement activities may be regarded as constituents of individual and situational interest in such activities. Furthermore, activity-related achievement emotions may be regarded as important elements of experiences of "flow" when performing such activities. One implication of this latter connection is that it might be worthwhile to disentangle different elements of flow experiences and analyze their interrelations instead of just relying on their holistic character, which flow research seems to have favored to do up-to-date.

Control-value theory focuses on antecedents and development of achievement emotions. However, beyond unidirectional perspectives on emotional development, achievement emotions may themselves be important causes for individual development. Achievement situations are ubiquituous in our global, economically oriented cultures, and they are highly relevant for most individuals because of their functions for education, occupation, and life courses, which implies that achievement emotions may be a primary category of human emotions today. They may be assumed to influence achievement-related motivation, strategies of learning, and resulting academic and occupational achievement. Furthermore, they may influence the formation of self-concepts and identity in the achievement domain and beyond. Finally, like emotions in general, achievement emotions may be assumed to be important factors in psychosomatic health. All of this implies that future research should invest more effort in addressing the full range of this multifaceted domain.

References

Bandura, A. (1986). *Social foundations of thought and action.* Englewood Cliffs, NJ: Prentice Hall.

Bronfenbrenner, U. (1979). *The ecology of human development.* Cambridge, MA: Harvard University Press.

Covington, M. V. (1992). *Making the grade: A self-worth perspective on motivation and school reform.* New York: Cambridge University Press.

Csikszentmihalyi, M. (1975). *Beyond boredom and anxiety.* San Francisco: Jossey-Bass.

Deci, E. L., & Ryan, R. M. (1985). *Intrinsic motivation and self-determination in human behavior.* New York: Plenum Press.

Heckhausen, H. (1977). Achievement motivation and its constructs: A cognitive model. *Motivation and Emotion, 1,* 283–329.

Heckhausen, J., & Schulz, R. (1995). A life-span theory of control. *Psychological Review, 102,* 284–304.

Hembree, R. (1988). Correlates, causes, effects, and treatment of test anxiety. *Review of Educational Research, 58,* 47–77.

Holzwarth, A. (1997). *Prüfungsemotionen bei Schülern: Eine explorative Interviewstudie* [Test emotions in school students: An exploratory interview study]. Unpublished master's thesis, University of Regensburg, Germany.

Jacob, B. (1996). *Leistungsemotionen bei Schülern* [Achievement emotions in school students]. Unpublished master's thesis, University of Regensburg, Germany.

Johnson, D. W., & Johnson, R. T. (1974). Instructional goal structure: Cooperative, competitive or individualistic. *Review of Educational Research, 4,* 213–240.

LeDoux, J. E. (1995). Emotion: Clues from the brain. *Annual Review of Psychology, 46,* 209–235.

Mandler, G., & Sarason, S. B. (1952). A study of anxiety and learning. *Journal of Abnormal and Social Psychology, 47,* 166–173.

Meece, J. L., Wigfield, A., & Eccles, J. (1990). Predictors of math anxiety and its influence on young adolescents' course enrollment intentions and performance in mathematics. *Journal of Educational Psychology, 82,* 60–70.

Patrick, B. C., Skinner, E. A., & Connell, J. P. (1993). What motivates children's behavior and emotion? Joint effects of perceived control and autonomy in the academic domain. *Journal of Personality and Social Psychology, 65,* 781–791.

Pekrun, R. (1988). *Emotion, Motivation und Persönlichkeit* [Emotion, motivation and personality]. München, Germany: Psychologie Verlags Union.

Pekrun, R. (1991). Prüfungsangst und Schulleistung: Eine Längsschnittanalyse [Test anxiety and school achievement: A longitudinal analysis]. *Zeitschrift für Pädagogische Psychologie, 5,* 99–109.

Pekrun, R. (1992a). Kognition und Emotion in studienbezogenen Lern- und Leistungssituationen: Explorative Analysen [Cognition and emotion in academic situations of learning and achievement: Exploratory analyses]. *Unterrichtswissenschaft, 20,* 308–324.

Pekrun, R. (1992b). The impact of emotions on learning and achievement: Towards a theory of cognitive/motivational mediators. *Applied Psychology: An International Review, 41,* 359–376.

Pekrun, R. (1992c). Expectancy-value theory of anxiety: Overview and implications. In D. G. Forgays, T. Sosnowski, & K. Wrzesniewski (Eds.), *Anxiety: Recent developments in self-appraisal, psychophysiological and health research* (pp. 23–41). Washington, DC: Hemisphere.

Pekrun, R. (in press). Test anxiety and academic achievement. In F. E. Weinert (Section Ed.), *International encyclopedia of the social and behavioral sciences. Section education.* Oxford, UK: Elsevier Science.

Pekrun, R., & Frese, M. (1992). Emotions in work and achievement. In C. L. Cooper & I. T. Robertson (Eds.), *International review of industrial and organizational psychology* (Vol. 7, pp. 153–200). Chichester, UK: Wiley.

Pekrun, R., Hochstadt, M., & Kramer, K. (1996). Prüfungsemotionen, Lernen und Leistung [Test emotions, learning and achievement]. In C. Spiel, U. Kastner-Koller, & P. Deimann (Eds.), *Motivation und Lernen aus der Perspektive lebenslanger Entwicklung* (pp. 151–161). Münster, Germany: Waxmann.

Pekrun, R., & Hofmann, H. (1999). Lern- und Leistungsemotionen: Erste Befunde eines Forschungsprogramms [Emotions in learning and achievement: First results of a program of research]. In M. Jerusalem & R. Pekrun (Eds.), *Emotion, Motivation und Leistung* (pp. 247–267). Göttingen, Germany: Hogrefe.

Pekrun, R., Molfenter, S., Titz, W., Ingrisch, M., & Perry, P. (2000, April). *Emotion, motivation, and self-regulated learning in university students: Longitudinal studies.* Paper presented at the annual meeting of the American Educational Research Association, New Orleans, LA.

Pekrun, R., Titz, W., Molfenter, S., & Ingrisch, M. (1999, April). *Developing concepts and measures of students' academic emotions: The 24 Academic Emotions Questionnaire.* Paper presented at the annual meeting of the American Educational Research Association, Montreal, Canada.

Perry, R., Hladkyi, S., Pekrun, R., & Pelletier, S. (2000). *Academic control and action control in college students: A longitudinal study of self-regulation.* Manuscript submitted for publication.

Roseman, I., Antoniou, A. A., & Jose, P. E. (1996). Appraisal determinants of emotions: Constructing a more accurate and comprehensive theory. *Cognition and Emotion, 10,* 241–277.

Sarason, I. G. (1984). Stress, anxiety, and cognitive interference: Reactions to tests. *Journal of Personality and Social Psychology, 44,* 929–938.

Scherer, K. R. (1984). On the nature and function of emotion: A component process approach. In K. R. Scherer & P. Ekman (Eds.), *Approaches to emotion* (pp. 293–317). Hillsdale, NJ: Erlbaum.

Seginer, R. (1983). Parents' educational expectations and children's academic achievement: A literature review. *Merrill-Palmer Quarterly, 29,* 1–23.

Weiner, B. (1985). An attributional theory of achievement motivation and emotion. *Psychological Review, 92,* 548–573.

Weiner, B. (1994). Integrating social and personal theories of achievement striving. *Review of Educational Research, 64,* 557–573.

Weinert, F. E., & Helmke, A. (1995). Learning from wise mother nature or big brother instructor: The wrong choice as seen from an educational perspective. *Educational Psychologist, 30,* 135–142.

Zeidner, M. (1998). *Test anxiety: The state of the art.* New York: Plenum Press.

Motivational Psychology of Human Development – J. Heckhausen (Editor)

8 Training in Empirical Research Methods: Analysis of Problems and Intervention From a Motivational Perspective

Robin Stark and Heinz Mandl

In several disciplines of the social sciences the prescribed courses of studies demand a strenuous training in empirical research methods and in statistics that comprises several semesters. During the semesters before the mid-studies' exams, the obligatory seminars and lectures on empirical research methods and on statistics, plus additionally offered tutorials, encompass a considerable part of the curriculum in psychology. Unfortunately, there is no exaggeration in viewing the training in research methods in the social sciences as a markedly problematic subject. The no-pass rates of the exams that are far above the failing rates in other obligatory subjects make this sufficiently clear. The titles alone of quite a number of publications reveal that we are dealing with an *emotional* problem as well, which we may assume is not the least aspect responsible for the low performance in exams: Schulmeister (1983) published a volume called *The fear of statistics,* which compiles a number of empirical studies on the problem of teaching and learning about statistics in the domain of psychology. Gruber and Renkl (1996) even speak of "nightmares of the students of social sciences." There is also talk of the *negative attitude* of students toward empirical research methods (Gruber et al., 1995).

The studies cited point repeatedly to *motivational* problems on the part of the students, too. The analyses and the empirical studies of motivational problems in the context of training in research methods that have been completed up to now do not, however, do justice to the great significance that adverse motivational learning prerequisites have, according to our own teaching experience and according to the reports of our colleagues.

The question here, from the perspective of instructional psychology, is why especially the training in empirical research methods is such a large-scale problem for the students. It should be clear that mono-causal explanations such as assuming that it is the students' fear when confronted with mathematical challenges or their adverse motivational learning prerequisites alone that turn training in research methods into a problem subject do not address the complexity of the phenomenon. As there are no studies yet in which a differentiated model for the explanation of the problems in question has been developed, we begin by illustrating "isolated" findings and then discuss their relation to other explanatory dimensions. In addition to viewing cognitive learning prerequisites we focus on *motivational* aspects and students' attitudes toward empirical research methods.

Then we develop a multi-dimensional, heuristic model for the description and explanation of the problems at hand and present an innovative instructional approach for the training in empirical research methods. This approach, which is based on different principles of situated learning, primarily aims at fostering topic-specific motivation.

Dimensions to Explain Problems Regarding Training in Empirical Research Methods

Next we will list variables that can explain problems concerning the training in empirical research methods. We interrelate them and bring them to bear on the students' learning behavior and their learning successes.

Cognitive Learning Prerequisites

One explanation for the problems we consider here is that students lack cognitive learning prerequisites and especially prior mathematical knowledge (Webel, 1983). Schulmeister and Birkhan (1983) investigated this hypothesis in an empirical study, which conceptually followed Piaget's theory of cognitive development. The authors came to the conclusion that even among students it is only a minority who master operations on the formal-abstractive level. An important condition—the competent use of mathematical formulae—can thus not be regarded as given.

According to findings of Kettler (1998), students would rather deal with those types of tasks that necessitate calculations and algorithms that merely demand the operative use of mathematical symbols but not their understanding. For example, students often simply insert the appropriate values into the formulae for the calculation of the correlation coefficient. Open tasks, which demand processes of understanding, are solved incorrectly, or, if the situation permits, left out completely. Many students do not manage to conceive a relation between that which they are calculating and that which the calculation means. Similar to what happens in other science courses, students obviously seem to develop "compartmentalizations" (Mandl, Gruber, & Renkl, 1993): From the point of view of many students, the "world" of mathematics or of statistics seems to be barely related to everyday reality and its problems, if at all. In addition, it could be shown that even the definitions of important terms like "variable" are being memorized but not really understood. The use of symbols also quite often presents students with distinctive difficulties (Kettler, 1998). Many authors regard the understanding of symbols as an important condition for the competent use of formulae (e.g., Wagenschein, 1965). According to Herscovics and Bergeron (1983), deficiencies in this area preclude the attainment of the mental level of formalization that forms an essential condition for processes of understanding in mathematics.

Our own experiences with training in empirical research methods point in the same direction. We can, therefore, assume that many students lack cognitive learning prerequisites that would enable them to profit from the training and especially to cope with mathematical demands that traditionally are inherent in this kind of training.

We assume that low topic-specific learning prerequisites are largely due to an (auto-) selective process. Many of the students in social sciences imagine that their chosen discipline will at last offer them an area "free" of mathematics (Gruber & Renkl, 1996)—an assumption that, as a rule, has to be falsified within the first semester.

Emotional Aspects

Against this background and keeping in mind the fact that in the social sciences training in empirical research methods is compulsory and quite often serves as an instrument for selecting students (Schulmeister, 1983), it is hardly surprising that many students develop topic-specific fear (Gruber, 1994). Quite a few of the students are likely to have already had negative experiences with respect to mathematical demands during their school time, which are reinforced when such experiences are repeated (Gruber et al., 1995; Kettler, 1998). "Horror stories" concerning the level of difficulty of the subject and of the exams, which are quite often spread by students in higher semesters (Renkl, 1994), do their part to increase the unease or fear felt by many students. At Munich University there is additional pressure on the training in empirical research methods because of a special regulation: One of the conditions for admittance to the exam is the certificate for Latin, the "Latinum." If students do not have this certificate they can compensate by attaining the result of "good" (roughly the equivalent of grade "B") in their training, a mark that is composed of a number of grades. This regulation forms learning conditions that have negative effects on emotional aspects in general and that, given a corresponding disposition on the part of the students, may add to the development of topic-specific exam nerves.

Fear is often accompanied by worries about one's own lack of competence and about a possible failing, and it leads to broodings that are totally irrelevant to the task at hand, which in turn can dramatically reduce the task-related attention (Pekrun & Schiefele, 1996). We can also assume that fear tends to have a negative effect on learning behavior: It rather inhibits a deeper processing of information and it favors a superficial, passive processing. Since positive and negative emotions are incompatible, at least on the upper intensity level, we can further assume that negative emotions like fear have an adverse effect on motivational aspects like intrinsic motivation and interest and on self-efficacy beliefs. There may also be undesired effects on the students' topic-specific attitudes. There is, however, as yet only little supporting data for these assumptions (see Pekrun, 1988; Pintrich, McKeachie, Yu, & Hofer, 1995).

We also assume reciprocal relations between fear and learning success. Longitudinally we see not only the (negative) effect of fear on learning performance but also the effects of (low) learning performance on the development of fear (Pekrun, 1991).

Motivational Aspects

In the face of the undisputed importance of motivational aspects, especially with regard to the attainment of transferable knowledge and to a learning behavior conducive to this aim (Schiefele, Krapp, & Schreyer, 1993), we consider motivational aspects as absolutely decisive factors in the context of the problem at hand. The reasons cited by teachers and students for the problems regarding training in research methods are that it is largely an extrinsic learning motivation that dominates the students (Webel, 1983), and that students' interest in methodical course contents is rather weak.

To verify these pessimistic motivational explanations empirically we had students of pedagogics at Munich University answer a rating scale focusing on various motivational aspects (Henninger & Balk, 2000). According to the early results, we can state that the responding students were, on the whole, hardly intrinsically motivated to deal with empirical research methods. In addition, learners hardly seemed to experience themselves as self-determined, which as a rule also coincides with undesired motivational effects (Deci & Ryan, 1993). In accordance with the motivational explanations of problems concerning the training in research methods reported by Webel (1983), the compulsory status of the series of lectures made extrinsic motivation the dominant one: Many students simply attended the course because they needed their graded papers to be allowed to pursue their course of studies, not because they found dealing with empirical research methods enriching or the knowledge imparted in the lectures interesting.

Since the lectures evaluated with respect to motivational aspects were already being presented in a problem-oriented way, so that "frightening" mathematical-statistical contents were less dominant—at least when compared to traditional seminars and lectures—we had expected rather more positive motivational results. Unfortunately, there are no findings on the motivational situation of students who complete a *traditional* training in research methods, for example, in psychology, in which mathematical and statistical demands play a much larger part.

In addition to the presumably negative effects of low cognitive learning prerequisites and of topic-specific negative emotions, negative motivational effects must also be referred back to adverse conditions of the instructional setting. The compulsory status of training alone creates conditions that may not "only" have negative effects on aspects of the motivational value components such as, for example, intrinsic motivation. Aspects of the motivational expectancy components (e.g., self-efficacy beliefs) will also be affected negatively. This situation is further exacerbated by additional adverse conditions of the instructional setting, such as the large number of participants (at Munich University about 180 students). This is presumably true not only of the training at Munich University, but of the training in empirical research methods for social scientists in general (Webel, 1983).

Against the background of the empirically validated relation between motivation and interest on one hand, and learning behavior and learning success on the other (Hidi & Anderson, 1992; Schiefele et al., 1993; Schiefele & Schreyer, 1994), the learning conditions realized in the context of the training in empirical research methods are not the best. There is much room for instructional innovations.

Just as with fear and lack of success we also assume *reciprocal* influences between motivation and learning success. Since we can also assume a reciprocal relationship between fear and aspects of motivation, as well as between aspects of the different motivational components (Stark, Gruber, & Mandl, 1998), it is difficult to explain the conditions and the consequences of certain motivational findings and clearly separate one from the other. The as yet somewhat speculative assumptions stated here have to be investigated in a longitudinal study. There are currently only a few findings in this area (see, e.g., Gruber & Renkl, 1996).

Students' Attitudes Toward Empirical Research Methods

The findings and considerations described so far make us assume that students of the social sciences have rather negative attitudes toward empirical research methods and the corresponding training (Gruber et al., 1995). Especially when planning innovative measures to overcome the problem under consideration, it is important to know to what extent negative attitudes have developed as a result of (fairly recent) negative training experiences, say, as a consequence of insufficient exam performance, and to what extent they can already be identified before there are any topic-specific experiences.

To answer this question, students of pedagogics (roughly $n = 50$) who were novices regarding this topic were questioned in written form on the weaknesses and limits of empirical research methods. In this study, we focused on the *cognitive* dimension of attitudes. We expected that novices, not having any personal experiences with empirical research methods, would predominantly evince diffuse, little-differentiated concepts. The concepts verbalized by the students were subsumed under different categories (see Table 1).

We could identify concepts that referred to the sampling in empirical studies and to the resulting problems of generalizing findings. A second category of concepts referred to problems of quantification in empirical studies and to the necessary reduction of complexity in these studies in general. A third category of concepts made the subjectivity of and the possibility of manipulating statistical findings an issue and focused on related problems of data protection. A fourth category encompassed concepts that saw a problem in the lack of reference to the "real world" or the lack of orientation by practically relevant questions on the part of empirical studies.

The results of this open questioning reveal that students can verbalize concepts that point to a *critical* attitude even at the beginning of a course in research methods. The students' concepts were very heterogeneous in their sophistication and precision. The scope ranged from little-elaborated, often

Table 1
Students' Attitudes Concerning the Weaknesses and Limits of Empirical Research Methods

Problems in sampling and generalization
"Observations and questions generally take only a part of the population into consideration."
"Surveys never concern the current situation."
"Empirical research is influenced by the choice of respondents."
"There is far too much generalization."

Problems related to quantification and complexity-reduction
"The individual is not taken into account."
"Results show only an average view of things."
"Figures do not do justice to the many human possibilities."
"Mathematics does not reach far enough where people are concerned."
"A person's behavior can never be absolutely predicted."

Subjectivity of statistical results and the problem of data manipulation
"No one can have an insight into what a researcher does with the data."
"Possibility of data manipulation"
"Do not trust in statistics which you have not manipulated yourself."
"It leads to an undesired intrusion into privacy."
"There is no sufficient data protection."
"Anonymity often not guaranteed"

Lack of reference to practice, lack of relevance
"Often uninteresting or even irrelevant questions are investigated."
"Too little reference to issues with practical relevance"
"Often they investigate topics which have little to do with practical problems."

diffuse, and not always understandable (pre-)judgments to considerations that—in a more elaborated form, of course—can also be found in theoretical studies on qualitative social research. Specific concepts that focused on the problems of quantification and on the reduction of complexity showed an unexpected sophistication. The students questioned here were, therefore, largely not "naive" novices. On the whole only a few concepts could be rated as way beyond the reasonable; most could—given the appropriate level of sophistication and precision—be reconstructed as serious criticism of certain characteristics of empirical research. It also became clear that for most of the students, empirical research methods and statistics or quantitative data processing are the same.

On the basis of the concepts verbalized we assume that students may have a critical, but not necessarily a *negative* attitude toward empirical research methods. This difference is by no means trivial. When the students were asked to reflect on the strengths and opportunities of empirical research methods, we also could identify many—in part—quite elaborated concepts. According to Windisch (1983), the students' criticisms of empirical research methods often appear together with the opinion that an intensive analysis of the underlying principles of research methods is necessary. The frequently formulated desire to criticize empirical research methods does not necessarily result in an unwillingness to study the corresponding contents intensely. We assume that any critical attitudes that become negative ones are linked to unfavorable motivational states and learning behavior, and that these attitudes primarily begin to develop after the students have had negative experiences in the course of their own training in research methods. Top among these negative experiences are certainly failures in exams, which frequently occur in this subject. Negative experiences also occur when the students find a confirmation of their suspicions regarding the lack of practical relevance of empirical research methods while attending lectures or seminars. According to a study by Gruber et al. (1995), this seems to be the case quite frequently. Since the acceptance of the course contents and the engagement students of pedagogics show very strongly depend on the perceived practical relevance of the corresponding topics, we expect not *only* negative attitudes, but also negative motivational effects and little effort to learn. What becomes apparent here is a grave problem in the coordination of curriculum topics and students' interests and career plans. Traditional training in social sciences aims at a later scientific career whereas the students for some reason or another clearly prefer job profiles outside the context of science.

A Multi-Dimensional Model and Consequences for Future Research

It became apparent that the problems under consideration here have multiple causes and that mono-causal explanations, therefore, necessarily fail. As a main dimension, we consider conditions of the instructional setting (see Figure 1). In addition to the exam regulations, these conditions comprise the curriculum, which generally is oriented toward (experimental) research, and the form of lecturing, dictated by the large number of students. This context dimension is connected with cognitive, motivational, and emotional characteristics and attitudes on the part of the learners and with learning behavior and learning performance. With respect to the cognitive, motivational, and emotional dimensions, we differentiate between learner characteristics in the sense of dispositions and actualized aspects of cognition, motivation, and emotion (Pekrun & Schiefele, 1996) that become manifest in concrete learn-

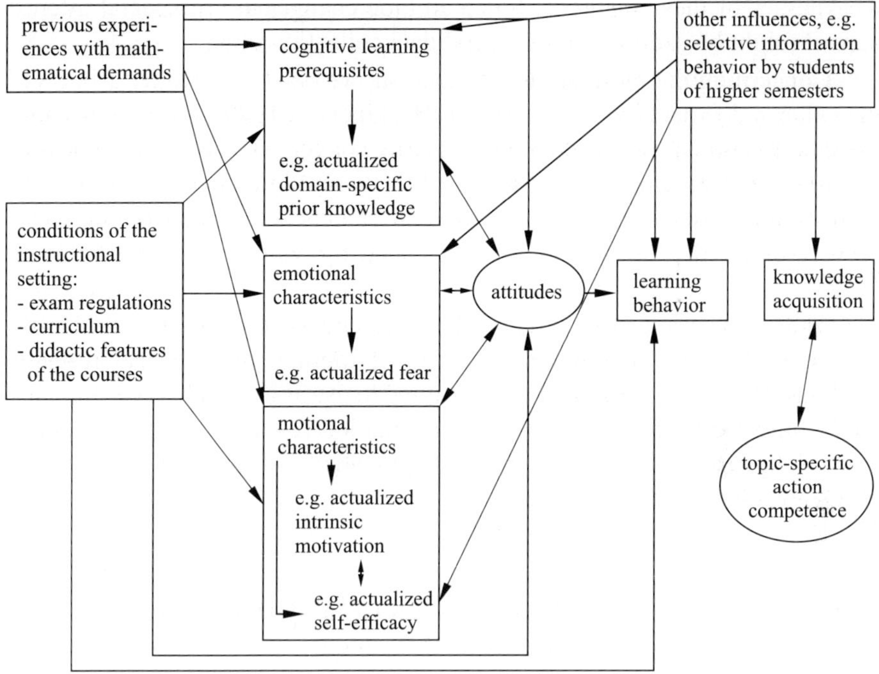

Figure 1. Model for the description and explanation of problems concerning the training in empirical research methods.

ing situations. Thus, we are dealing with a complex system of interrelations that is marked by the reciprocal relations of various dimensions and that has not yet been analyzed in a systematic manner.

The relations shown in the model (see Figure 1) seem plausible, but they have not yet been empirically confirmed. The present studies must, therefore, be supplemented by a longitudinal research approach in which cognitive, motivational, and emotional variables should be integrated in multiple ways. Independent variables that have been surveyed *before* the beginning of the training should be operationalized in a more distal and global manner (but without giving up the topic-specific orientation). Additionally, they should be operationalized in a proximal, situation- and task-specific way and registered as dependent variables.

Furthermore, students' attitudes toward empirical research methods should be analyzed, for example, by questioning them about the strengths and weaknesses of these methods. Since attitude changes are of special interest here, it might be useful to plan several data collection times.

Concerning the motivational dimension, we need to consider aspects of the value and expectancy components (Heckhausen, 1989), not least because these motivational aspects do not necessarily converge (Stark et al., 1998). To identify the motivational processes as directly and immediately as possible, there should also be repeated short measurements *during* the training. This process-oriented procedure is recommended by Vollmeyer and Rheinberg (1997).

The research approach described here can be used in the context of a formative evaluation (Henninger, in press) of training in empirical research methods. However, our model is not limited to use as a tool for systematically analyzing specific problems or doing evaluation research in this domain. It can also have a heuristic function when innovative instructional measures are to be developed and implemented.

Innovative Training in Empirical Research Methods: Overcoming Motivational Problems

Theoretical Reflections

The first attempts at innovation in the context of training in empirical research methods for students of pedagogics at Munich University were initiated by Gruber and Renkl (Gruber, 1994; Gruber et al., 1995; Gruber & Renkl, 1996; Renkl, 1994).

The most important innovations consist in *didactic measures* that concern all parts of the training in research methods—especially the series of lectures offered over two semesters, the exams, the training of the tutors, and finally, all of the instructional measures implemented to give added support to the students (see below). A further important innovation was the implementation of a virtual tutorial accompanying the lectures (Lerche, 1999) that supplements the hitherto traditional tutorials. The innovations, therefore, tackle the central aspects of (alterable) conditions regarding the instructional setting (see Figure 1). The exam regulations and the large number of participants that necessitates teaching by lectures have to be regarded as constraints that can hardly be altered. The number of lessons within a semester and the personnel resources (lecturers, tutors) are additional constraints.

The instructional approach directly aims at motivational effects. That is, motivation is conceived as a kind of catalyst for changes that will positively affect other dimensions of the model as well. In this sense we assume there will be positive effects on emotional aspects and also on domain-specific attitudes. In addition, we expect positive effects with regard to learning behavior and learning success.

The overriding instructional aim of our approach is to foster *action competence* in the area of empirical research methods. The students should be capable of understanding and of critically judging scientific literature, especially with respect to the research methods described there. Additionally, they should be able to deduce research questions and hypotheses from various research problems and to develop simple research designs. Moreover, they should know which statistical procedures have to be employed to answer these research questions and test the hypotheses deduced. Finally, with the guidance of the lecturers and tutors they have to cope with a "real" research task: They have to plan and carry out a simple empirical study and interpret and document the results in different ways according to (eased) scientific standards. This research task and the problem-oriented tests represent the most important indicators of action competence. A further indicator that informs us about the *development* of action competence is the quality of answers given by students to problems implemented in the virtual tutorial.

Our instructional approach is theoretically embedded in different approaches of situated learning, especially in the *anchored instruction* approach (Cognition and Technology Group at Vanderbilt, 1992). We implemented the design principles of this approach in multiple ways. In addition, we also refer back to the *cognitive apprenticeship* approach (Collins, Brown, & Newman, 1989). We also draw on the *random access* approach and the *cognitive flexibility* theory (Spiro, Feltovich, Jacobson, & Coulson, 1991).

Description of the Innovative Measures and of Their Potential Effects on Motivation

The contents of the method lecture series are presented in a consistently problem-oriented way. To render this possible, the curriculum had to be "slimmed down": A problem-oriented presentation of a lecture is significantly more time-consuming than more traditional forms of teaching. In addition, this form of imparting the subject matter pushes mathematical and statistical issues more into the background. If the topic is, for example, variance analysis, the lecture does not begin with definitions and formulae for the breaking down of variances but with a relevant and authentic research problem. We construct a problem scenario that cannot be solved by the procedures dealt with in the course so far and, consequently, make it necessary to employ variance analysis. Of course, this teaching procedure does not preclude the presentation of formulae for statistical parameters or test statistics and so forth. We do not avoid such topics if they actually support the understanding of a procedure. As opposed to traditional training in psychology, however, this kind of subject matter is not dealt with merely for its own sake.

As a rule, the research problems and questions selected can be viewed as complex, at least from the students' perspective. Therefore, the topics to be learned by the students are embedded in a meaningful context, so that the relevance and the functional nature of the knowledge to be acquired is made clear. We try to demonstrate that the problems dealt with and the resulting findings are by no means "merely" of academic interest. On the contrary, they are supposed to be interesting for the majority of the students.

For the virtual tutorial we have implemented a narrative format for presenting problems. In additicn, we employ other design principles of situated learning. We introduce as narrators and "heroes" two students of pedagogics who fight their way through the "jungle" of empirical research methods and who struggle with problems of understanding and with identifying their own misconceptions. With these two protagonists we try to make possible a certain kind of identification with the job of coping with research problems. The expected predominance of extrinsic motivation can then be replaced by primarily intrinsically motivated coping processes. Identification processes should also be enhanced by the research task, which confronts the students with a "real" research problem. The students build teams of cooperating "scientists" and are systematically prepared to work on this problem by the two models in the virtual tutorial.

With the help of the narrative problem presentation realized, especially in the virtual tutorial, we specifically try to address the students' curiosity motive (Berlyne, 1960). The learners' curiosity for problems and for possible solutions is raised through the two "student-scientist" models. The additional principle of embedded data, which is consistently employed in the virtual tutorial, should also contribute to an increase in the students' curiosity. The problems are selected in such a way that while the learners are dealing with them they should gain the impression that they do not as yet have sufficient information to arrive at a satisfactory solution. The discrepancy between actual knowledge and the knowledge necessary to solve the problems is also meant to encourage close attention to the contents of the lectures needed for working effectively on the problems. Ideally, the narrative format and the principle of embedded data, in connection with the use of relatively complex problems, will raise even intellectual or epistemological curiosity (Berlyne, 1960). This kind of curiosity is to be understood as a special case of situational interest (Schiefele, 1996). Learners with epistemological curiosity are characterized by their eagerness to acquire more knowledge to understand problems better and to deal with them more effectively; they develop a kind of urge for research and they aspire to understanding. Epistemological curiosity is fostered by surprise, doubt, bewilderment or uncertainty, and helplessness, as well as through confrontation with incompatible information. It is very likely that some of these conflict-generating variables regularly become active in the context of our training.

The implementation of the design principles described so far aims at fostering interest and topic-related intrinsic motivation (Krapp, 1999). However, by altering didactic features of the training, we not "only" try to increase topic-related but also activity-related intrinsic motivation (Schiefele, 1996). Within the virtual tutorial and in the context of the research task, the students are over and again immersed in problem situations that they define themselves (principle of the generative learning format) and that they consequently want to overcome. Therefore, we assume that such learning activities as, for example, the search for solution-relevant information, will be undertaken primarily for their own sake and not only because the students feel obliged to engage in them.

The narrative format, the generative format, and the principle of embedded data could even help to have intrinsically motivated activities accompanied by flow-like sensations (Csikszentmihalyi, 1985). A necessary condition for flow that is extremely conducive to learning is the adjustment of task difficulty to the learners' abilities. When learners are in flow, they are totally wrapped up in the activities they perform in connection with the problem they work on. In these motivationally ideal states there are no self-directed reflections like self-doubt, which generally interfere with learning activities. Thus, flow is also incompatible with unease or fear. However, when low cognitive learning prerequisites are given, it is more likely instructors will overtax the learners than induce flow by presenting complex problems. This problem leads to the central topic of additional instructional support, which will be dealt with in detail below.

The motivational concepts considered up to now can be subsumed under the motivational value component. In the following we will deal with potential instructional effects that concern aspects of the motivational expectancy component. The complexity of the problems presented in the lectures and the students' research task makes most of the learning activities assume the character of a challenge (Lepper & Malone, 1987). By presenting complex, nontrivial problem situations, the students are given the opportunity to experience a step-by-step improvement of their own competence. They are given the chance to experience making progress in mastering relevant problems. Hereby, motives that are related to the effectiveness of the learners (White, 1959), their competence, and their performance are addressed. If the complexity of the problem and the students' abilities are suited to each other in such a way that the learners are really successful, a situation emerges in which beliefs of self-efficacy (Bandura, 1986), feelings of autonomy and control (DeCharms, 1976), and, ideally, flow states (Csikszentmihalyi, 1985) are fostered. The learners' self-efficacy beliefs are important both for the acceptability of performance targets and for the persistence in the learning effort (Schunk, 1991). The latter is especially relevant in view of the long time the students have to devote to the training in empirical research methods.

The principle of the generative learning format should promote the effect on self-efficacy aimed at here, since it explicitly prompts learners to become active, to get involved and take matters in hand by themselves. Compared to traditional forms of training in research methods, our training, which is "reformed" according to various principles of situated learning, aims at inducing a learning and mastery orientation rather than a performance orientation (Dweck, 1991). This goal is also to be attained by implementing cooperative learning.

To succeed in matching the problems' degree of complexity with the students' abilities and to render possible the positive effects of the instructional innovations described above we implement a wide range of additional supportive measures. Many problems that result from traditional training in empirical research methods are very likely due to a systematic overtaxing of the students. Overtaxing the learners does not just prevent them from experiencing flow. As a consequence, it also keeps them from reaching motivational states that are very "precious" with respect to both motivation and cognition.

The lecture format inevitably affords only limited possibilities of student support. The support here consists mainly of making all of the transparencies shown during the lectures available to the students in the form of copies before each lecture. Additionally, students are invited to pose questions. To probe into the students' understanding of central concepts, we also direct questions at the students and give detailed feedback.

The virtual tutorial offers an extensive "support package." The students are systematically prepared for the written exams and for their research task through assignments they have to work through on a weekly basis. The task forums of the tutorial are supervised by experienced tutors. The students cope with the assignments and the research task cooperatively. The implementation of cooperative learning and problem solving also aims at positive motivational effects. The feeling of belonging to a group is an important condition for intrinsic motivation, according to Deci and Ryan (1993). To prevent problems of communication and cooperation from undermining potentially motivational advantages, tutors are instructed in dealing especially with these types of problems, which are not at all trivial in the context under consideration (Renkl, Gruber, & Mandl, 1996). During the weeks before the exams traditional tutorials are offered that are prepared together with the lecturers. The instructional support the tutors give in various contexts is based primarily on principles and strategies of the *cognitive apprenticeship* approach (Collins et al., 1989).

Outlook

The motivational effects that we hope to attain through our instructional approach have not as yet been systematically investigated. Evaluation data gathered in the past have not been fully analyzed, especially with respect to motivational aspects. However, regarding the overriding aim of our training—fostering action competence—we can report positive results even now. The majority of the students reached sufficient or better results in the last exams; only very few students failed. The same is true for the research tasks. The poster presentation of the results of the research task reached a professional level in several teams of "scientists." It is to be stressed here that these successes were in no way achieved through a systematic lowering of standards. As far as the application of empirical research methods on relevant scientific questions and thus the *understanding* of central concepts and procedures was concerned, the demands were even higher than in exam papers written in traditional courses. To complete the final research task, the students had to evaluate lectures and seminars, that is, empirical surveys had to be planned, carried out, analyzed, and documented in various ways. The demands of this task are by no means trivial even for more advanced students.

The virtual tutorial, too, shows promising evaluation results (Lerche & Mandl, 1999). For example, the participants felt that they were better prepared for the exams, which can be regarded as progress, especially in view of the widespread emotional problems described above.

To expect that all the problems we described can be overcome successfully by implementing our instructional approach would be naive. Many constraints (e.g., the large number of participants, the very few lecturers and tutors, low cognitive learning prerequisites) that cannot be eliminated or lessened by our approach will continue to have negative effects on successful learning. However, if adverse conditions of the instructional setting and other variables that threaten learning success can at least be partly compensated for by the instructional approach described, we have gained a lot indeed.

References

Bandura, A. (1986). *Social foundations of thought and action: A social cognitive theory.* Englewood Cliffs, NJ: Prentice Hall.

Berlyne, D. E. (1960). *Conflict, arousal and curiosity.* New York: McGraw-Hill.

Cognition and Technology Group at Vanderbilt. (1992). The Jasper series as an example of anchored-instruction: Theory, program description, and assessment data. *Educational Psychologist, 27,* 291–315.

Collins, A., Brown, J. S., & Newman, S. E. (1989). Cognitive apprenticeship: Teaching the crafts of reading, writing and mathematics. In L. B. Resnick (Ed.), *Knowing, learning, and instruction. Essays in honour of Robert Glaser* (pp. 453–494). Hillsdale, NJ: Erlbaum.

Csikszentmihalyi, M. (1985). *Das Flow-Erlebnis* [The flow-experience]. Stuttgart, Germany: Klett-Cotta.

DeCharms, R. (1976). *Enhancing motivation.* New York: Irvington.

Deci, E. L., & Ryan, R. M. (1993). Die Selbstbestimmungstheorie der Motivation und ihre Bedeutung für die Pädagogik [The self-determination theory of motivation and its importance for pedagogics]. *Zeitschrift für Pädagogik, 39,* 223–238.

Dweck, C. S. (1991). Self-theories and goals: Their role in motivation, personality, and development. In R. A. Dienstbier (Ed.), *Nebraska Symposium on Motivation: Vol. 38. Perspectives on motivation* (pp. 199–235). Lincoln, NE: University of Nebraska Press.

Gruber, H. (1994). Klausurangst, subjektive Verstehenseinschätzung und Prüfungsleistung von Pädagogikstudenten in der Methodenausbildung [Exam nerves, subjective evaluations of understanding and exam performance students of pedagogics show in the context of training in empirical research methods]. In R. Olechowski & B. Rollett (Eds.), *Theorie und Praxis. Aspekte empirisch-pädagogischer Forschung—quantitative und qualitative Methoden* [Theory and practice. Aspects of empirical research in pedagogics—quantitative and qualitative methods] (pp. 184–189). Frankfurt a.M., Germany: Lang.

Gruber, H., Balk, M., Dreyer, A., Kaiser, U., Schätz, U., Stumpf, L., & Völkmann, U. (1995). *"Mein Leben mit dem Methodenkurs"—Analyse von StudentInnenwünschen und Möglichkeiten zu deren Umsetzung* ["My life with the course in methods"— students' wishes and possibilities to realize them] (Research Rep. No. 62). Munich, Germany: Ludwig Maximilians University, Chair of Educational Psychology and Pedagogics.

Gruber, H., & Renkl, A. (1996). Alpträume sozialwissenschaftlicher Studierender: Empirische Methoden und Statistik [Nightmares of students of the social sciences. Empirical research methods and statistics]. In J. Lompscher & H. Mandl (Eds.), *Lehr- und Lernprobleme im Studium. Bedingungen und Veränderungsmöglichkeiten* [Teaching and learning problems of students. Conditions and intervention] (pp. 118–130). Bern, Switzerland: Huber.

Heckhausen, H. (1989). *Motivation und Handeln* [Motivation and behavior]. Heidelberg, Germany: Springer.

Henninger, M. (in press). Evaluation: Diagnose oder Therapie [Evaluation: diagnosis or therapy]. In C. Harteis, H. Heid, & S. Kraft (Eds.), *Kompendium Weiterbildung—Aspekte und Perspektiven betrieblicher Personal- und Organisationsentwicklung* [Compendium of further training—aspects and perspectives of personnel and organizational development]. Opladen, Germany: Leske + Budrich.

Henninger, M., & Balk, M. (2000). *Motivationale Implikationen von Evaluation* [Motivational implications of evaluation]. Manuscript in preparation.

Herscovics, N., & Bergeron, J. C. (1983). Models of understanding. *Zentralblatt für Didaktik der Mathematik, 15,* 75–83.

Hidi, S., & Anderson, V. (1992). Situational interest and its impacts on reading and expository writing. In K. A. Renninger, S. Hidi, & A. Krapp (Eds.), *The role of interest in learning and development* (pp. 215–238). Hillsdale, NJ: Erlbaum.

Kettler, M. (1998). *Der Symbolschock. Ein zentrales Lernproblem im mathematisch-naturwissenschaftlichen Unterricht* [The symbol shock. A central learning problem in mathematics and science instruction]. Frankfurt a.M., Germany: Lang.

Krapp, A. (1999). Intrinsische Lernmotivation und Interesse. Forschungsansätze und konzeptuelle Überlegungen [Intrinsic learning motivation and interest. Research approaches and conceptual considerations]. *Zeitschrift für Pädagogik, 43,* 387–405.

Lepper, M. R., & Malone, T. W. (1987). Intrinsic motivation and instructional effectiveness in computer-based education. In R. E. Snow & M. J. Farr (Eds.), *Aptitude, learning, and instruction: Vol. 3. Conative and affective process analyses* (pp. 255–285). Hillsdale, NJ: Erlbaum.

Lerche, T. (1999). *Konzeption und Durchführung eines virtuellen Tutoriums für den Methodenkurs* [Conceptualizing and realizing a virtual tutorial for training in empirical research methods]. Unpublished master's thesis, Ludwig Maximilians University, Munich, Germany.

Lerche, T., & Mandl, H. (1999). *ViT: Das virtuelle Tutorium für den Methodenkurs. Konzeption und Realisierung einer internetbasierten Lernumgebung* [ViT: The virtual tutorial for the course in research methods. Conceptualizing and realizing an internet-based learning environment] (Practice Rep. No. 16). Munich, Germany: Ludwig Maximilians University, Chair of Educational Psychology and Pedagogics.

Mandl, H., Gruber, H., & Renkl, A. (1993). Lernen im Physikunterricht—Brückenschlag zwischen wissenschaftlicher Theorie und menschlichen Erfahrungen [Learning physics at school—bridging scientific theory and human experiences]. In Deutsche Physikalische Gesellschaft e.V./Fachverband Didaktik der Physik (Ed.), *Didaktik der Physik* [Didactics in physics] (pp. 21–36). Esslingen, Germany: Deutsche Physikalische Gesellschaft.

Pekrun, R. (1988). *Emotion, Motivation und Persönlichkeit* [Emotion, motivation and personality]. Munich, Germany: Psychologie Verlags Union.

Pekrun, R. (1991). Prüfungsangst und Schulleistung: Eine Längsschnittanalyse [Exam nerves and performance at school. A longitudinal study]. *Zeitschrift für Pädagogische Psychologie, 5,* 99–109.

Pekrun, R., & Schiefele, U. (1996). Emotions- und motivationspsychologische Bedingungen der Lernleistung [Emotional and motivational conditions of learning performance]. In F. E. Weinert (Ed.), *Enzyklopädie der Psychologie: D/I/2. Psychologie des Lernens und der Instruktion* [Encyclopedia of psychology. Psychology of learning and instruction] (pp. 153–180). Göttingen, Germany: Hogrefe.

Pintrich, P. R., McKeachie, W. J., Yu, S. L., & Hofer, B. K. (1995, August). *The role of motivation and self-regulated learning in math and science classrooms.* Paper presented at the 6th European Conference for Research on Learning and Instruction (EARLI), Nijmegen, The Netherlands.

Renkl, A. (1994). Wer hat Angst vorm Methodenkurs? Eine empirische Studie zum Streßerleben von Pädagogikstudenten in der Methodenausbildung [Who is afraid of the training in research methods? An empirical study of stress students of pedagogics experience when learning methods]. In R. Olechowski & B. Rollett (Eds.), *Theorie und Praxis. Aspekte empirisch-pädagogischer Forschung—quantitative und qualitative Methoden* [Theory and practice. Aspects of empirical research in pedagogics—quantitative and qualitative methods] (pp. 178–183). Frankfurt a.M., Germany: Lang.

Renkl, A., Gruber, H., & Mandl, A. (1996). Kooperatives problemorientiertes Lernen in der Hochschule [Cooperative, problem-oriented learning at university]. In J. Lompscher & H. Mandl (Eds.), *Lehr- und Lernprobleme im Studium. Bedingungen und Veränderungsmöglichkeiten* [Teaching and learning problems of students. Conditions and intervention] (pp. 131–147). Bern, Switzerland: Huber.

Schiefele, U. (1996). *Motivation und Lernen mit Texten* [Motivation and learning with texts]. Göttingen, Germany: Hogrefe.

Schiefele, U., Krapp, A., & Schreyer, I. (1993). Metaanalyse des Zusammenhangs von Interesse und schulischer Leistung [The correlation between interest and school performance. A meta-analysis]. *Zeitschrift für Entwicklungspsychologie und Pädagogische Psychologie, 25,* 120–148.

Schiefele, U., & Schreyer, I. (1994). Intrinsische Lernmotivation und Lernen [Intrinsic motivation and learning]. *Zeitschrift für Pädagogische Psychologie, 8,* 1–13.

Schulmeister, R. (Ed.). (1983). *Angst vor Statistik. Empirische Untersuchungen zum Problem des Statistik-Lehrens und Lernens* [Fear of statistics. Empirical studies concerning the problem of teaching and learning statistics]. Hamburg, Germany: Arbeitsgemeinschaft für Hochschuldidaktik.

Schulmeister, R., & Birkhan, G. (1983). Untersuchung kognitiver Probleme beim Erlernen von Statistik: Denkniveaus und kognitive Komplexität [Investigating cognitive problems in statistics-learning. Thinking levels and cognitive complexity]. In R. Schulmeister (Ed.), *Angst vor Statistik. Empirische Untersuchungen zum Problem des Statistik-Lehrens und Lernens* [Fear of statistics. Empirical studies concerning the problem of teaching and learning statistics] (pp. 27–44). Hamburg, Germany: Arbeitsgemeinschaft für Hochschuldidaktik.

Schunk, D. H. (1991). Self-efficacy and academic motivation. *Educational Psychologist, 26,* 207–231.

Spiro, R. J., Feltovich, P. J., Jacobson, M. J., & Coulson, R. L. (1991). Cognitive flexibility, constructivism, and hypertext: Random-access instruction for advanced knowledge acquisition in ill-structured domains. *Educational Technology, 31*(5), 24–33.

Stark, R., Gruber, H., & Mandl, H. (1998). Motivationale und kognitive Passungsprobleme beim komplexen situierten Lernen [Motivational and cognitive problems of fit in complex situated learning]. *Psychologie in Erziehung und Unterricht, 45,* 202–215.

Vollmeyer, R., & Rheinberg, F. (1997). Motivationale Einflüsse auf Erwerb und Anwendung von Wissen in einem computersimulierten System [Motivational effects on knowledge acquisition and application in a computer-simulated system]. *Zeitschrift für Pädagogische Psychologie, 11,* 125–144.

Wagenschein, M. (1965). *Ursprüngliches Verstehen und exaktes Denken* [Original understanding and precise thinking]. Stuttgart, Germany: Klett.

Webel, R. (1983). Die institutionellen Bedingungen für die Methodenreform am Fachbereich Psychologie der Universität Hamburg [Institutional conditions for a reform of teaching research methods at the department of psychology at Hamburg University]. In R. Schulmeister (Ed.), *Angst vor Statistik. Empirische Untersuchungen zum Problem des Statistik-Lehrens und Lernens* [Fear of statistics. Empirical studies concerning the problem of teaching and learning statistics] (pp. 5–16). Hamburg, Germany: Arbeitsgemeinschaft für Hochschuldidaktik.

White, R. W. (1959). Motivation reconsidered: The concept of competence. *Psychological Review, 66,* 297–333.

Windisch, A. (1983). Studentische Veranstaltungskritik in Statistik-Kursen [Students' criticism of courses in statistics]. In R. Schulmeister (Ed.), *Angst vor Statistik. Empirische Untersuchungen zum Problem des Statistik-Lehrens und Lernens* [Fear of statistics. Empirical studies concerning the problem of teaching and learning statistics] (pp. 187–207). Hamburg, Germany: Arbeitsgemeinschaft für Hochschuldidaktik.

PART THREE

Motives, Goals, and Developmental Tasks as Organizers of Developmental Regulation

Motivational Psychology of Human Development – J. Heckhausen (Editor)

9 A Theory of Self-Development: Affective Fixation and the STAR Model of Personality Disorders and Related Styles

Julius Kuhl

People differ in their patterns of social interaction. Some are open toward other people and easily make contact, even with strangers. Others prefer to keep even friends at a distance, tending to be reserved, distrustful, or even negativistic. Another contrast relates to the degree of assertiveness: Some people impose their needs and goals on almost everybody, whereas others are considerate, easily give in, and comply with social expectations. Personality research is confronted with the challenge of examining relationships between personality and the expected behavioral consequences with more and more refined empirical methods. In addition to this big task of exploring the behavioral effects of personality differences, there is a second challenge—one that has received less attention in modern personality research—concerning understanding the development of individual differences. It is theory driven and can be illustrated by questions like these: How can we *explain* individual differences between outgoing and reserved or between assertive and considerate individuals? How can we explain the impact parental behavior has on children's personality development? How does parental behavior affect basic trust and autonomy, the two dimensions that seem to be so significant for the development of later social adjustment? There are different schools of personality that offer quite different answers to such questions. Some approaches attribute the personality differences mentioned to rather simple mechanisms such as *temperament,* for example, to the level of arousal or to the mood that is characteristic of a person (e.g., Cloninger, 1987; Eysenck, 1967). Other approaches refer to more complex processes such as the beliefs and cognitive schemas an individual has developed about the external world or about his or her own inner world (Deci & Ryan, 1991; Rogers, 1961). The latter set of beliefs, that is, beliefs that relate to an individual's inner world, to his or her feelings, preferences, values, and so forth, is called a person's *self.*

In the first part of this chapter, I delineate my theory of personality systems interactions (PSI theory) that integrates opposing theories of personality within a coherent framework. In the second part, I explore the developmental implications of this theory: In what ways can PSI theory help us investigate the interface between developmental mechanisms and personality functioning? Finally, some experimental findings are discussed that test central assumptions and illustrate the type of explanation suggested by PSI theory.

The Theory of Personality Systems Interactions

My PSI theory proposes to explain how cognitive schemas associated with various personality styles or disorders (Beck & Freeman, 1990) can develop early in infancy even though the cognitive functions necessary to form higher order cognition, such as paranoid, schizoid, narcissistic, or other beliefs, are not yet developed (Steinmetz, 1994). This explanation is compatible with developmental research showing that *affective learning* plays a major role during early development. On the basis of mutual expression of emotional states which is characteristic of mother-child interactions during the first months of life (affective sharing), the infant develops certain affective dispositions (e.g., a high or low sensitivity for positive affect). PSI theory's solution to the developmental paradox (i.e., the problem of how cognitive bias can develop at an age when the relevant cognitive system is not yet available) looks at the impact *affective learning* during early infancy has on the accessibility of higher order cognitive systems that develop much later. The preponderance of affective processes in early mother-infant interactions is unquestionable. PSI theory explains the cognitive beliefs and the styles of information processing developing later in life on the basis of characteristic *interactions* among affective and cognitive systems. For example, PSI theory claims that a preference for analytical thinking that is characteristic of reserved people develops later in life as a result of an inhibition of positive affect acquired early in life.

Four Cognitive Macrosystems

The causal link between early affective learning and later cognitive styles can be described by two assumptions that explain how positive and negative affects modulate four cognitive systems. The four cognitive macrosystems postulated by PSI theory are (1) a system based on analytical, explicit knowledge including explicit representations of intentions (intention memory), (2) a system based on holistic, implicit knowledge consisting of an extended associative network of alternative actions or alternative semantic connotations compatible with a goal or a message, respectively (extension memory), (3) a system consisting of intuitively controllable action routines (genetically prepared sensorimotor schemas that can be developed through learning), and (4) a system that supports explicit recognition of objects (i.e., any cognition or emotion that can be recognized when encountered repeatedly, albeit in a different context). The latter (elementary) system presumably emphasizes objects that create a discrepancy with expectations or wishes generated by the two higher order systems (i.e., thinking and feeling).

Activation of Macrosystems Through Positive and Negative Affects

PSI theory focuses on the determinants of the interactions among these systems. For example, analytical thinking and explicit intentions require some decoupling of thought from action. But how do thinking and intentionality make contact with systems controlling the performance of intended actions (i.e., intuitive behavior control systems)? The first modulation assumption identifies positive affect as a crucial factor establishing the connection between thought and action and the memory system representing explicit intentions (Kuhl & Kazén, 1999) after a period during which explicit thought has been decoupled from immediate enactment in order to compare possible action alternatives when solving a problem or preparing a new action plan:

First modulation assumption: Upregulation of low positive affect (i.e., restoring positive affect after it has been dampened in a difficult situation) activates the connectivity between intention memory and an *intuitive* type of sensorimotor processing *(intuitive behavior control, or IBC);* on the other hand, continuing inhibition of positive affect (e.g., in difficult or frustrating situations) activates intention memory and analytical thinking (supporting it) while shutting off explicit intentions from behavioral expression, that is, from the IBC system.

Another interaction described by PSI theory relates to the connectivity between feeling and discrepancy-sensitive object recognition, that is, recognition of "irrelevant" objects from the internal or external world (i.e., objects like a distracting, unwanted sound or visual input or a distracting, currently unwanted emotion). Holistic feeling that supports the implicit representation of a general idea of one's current goal or self-interest (i.e., an extended associative network of potential action outcomes that are compatible with one's needs, values, or other self-representations) requires some inhibition of thoughts and emotions that are not compatible with the current goal or self-related concern (i.e., thoughts and emotions that stem from the discrepancy-sensitive object recognition system). On the other hand, sometimes "distracting" information must be processed, for example, when it relates to an imminent danger that has to be coped with. The second modulation assumption identifies negative affect as the crucial process modulating the interaction between holistic feeling and discrepancy-sensitive object recognition:

Second modulation assumption: Downregulation of negative affect (i.e., reducing negative affect after it has been aroused in a stressful situation) facilitates the accessibility of an integrative (high-inferential) holistic and implicit (i.e., not necessarily conscious) form of information processing *(feeling)* and its inhibitory impact on discrepant (e.g., unwanted or irrelevant) elementary sensory processes such as recognition of objects in the external or internal world *(sensation and object perception)* including isolated affects; on the other hand, negative affect that cannot be downregulated inhibits this mechanism of selective inattention to unwanted information ("repression") and facilitates recognition of unexpected or unwanted objects.

These two affect-cognition modulation assumptions form the core of PSI theory. They spell out the modulatory impact of changes in positive and negative affect on the connectivity among four cognitive macrosystems. This is how the two modulation assumptions work: Inhibition of positive affect [A(+)] typically associated with frustration increases the activation of analytical thinking, including its most important motivational component, *intention memory.* This system configuration facilitates *persistence* because it supports the maintenance of an uncompleted intention in memory and because it inhibits performance of premature impulses that jeopardize enactment of the active intention. The release of inhibition of positive affect through generation of positive affect (A+) activates the connection between intention memory and the system that supports control of intuitive behavior programs, resulting in efficient enactment of intended actions *(volitional facilitation).* Empirical support for this first modulation assumption can be found in studies that show that focusing on the difficulties associated with an intention (presumably dampening positive affect) combined with a subsequent focus on the positive affect associated with goal attainment (e.g., separate from a difficult partner) leads to a higher rate of enactment than focusing on the difficulties or focusing on the positive value of goal attainment alone (Oettingen, 1997). On a microanalytical level, release of inhibited positive affect supposedly associated with loading intention memory with a difficult intention through experimental induction of positive affect resulted in volitional facilitation in a recent series of studies: The well-known Stroop interference effect (delayed response times under experimental conditions when participants were asked to name the color of the ink in which an incongruent color word was typed) could be removed simply by presenting positive words as warning signals before presentation of incongruent color words (Kuhl & Kazén, 1999).

Motivational Determinants of Affect

Where does the positive affect that facilitates volitional action (i.e., the connectivity between intention memory and the intuitive behavior control system) come from? PSI theory differentiates between stimulus-bound and self-generated affect: The energy for initiating an intended action can come from the situation encountered (e.g., finding the solution of a difficult problem, encountering a good opportunity for enacting an intention, receiving an encouragement from another person, etc.) or it can be self-generated through a volitional process called *self-motivation.*[1] On a deeper level of analysis, PSI theory relates the antecedents of positive affect to basic needs of the organism. Positive affect signals the potential of a situation encountered to satisfy a basic need, such as competence or achievement, relatedness or affiliation, or autonomy or power (McClelland, 1985; Ryan, 1995; Winter, 1996). The motivational basis of affect is especially important because it implies that the modulatory impact of positive affect on the interaction of intention memory and the IBC system is a function of the content of the predominant need or motive aroused in a particular situation. Specifically, positive affect associated with achievement and power motives should be more likely to facilitate the coupling between intention memory and behavior control because those motives are typically aroused when some difficulty has to be overcome (Heckhausen, 1991; McClelland, 1985). On the level of affect, difficult situations can be described in terms of inhibition of positive affect because the positive affect associated with a desired goal state is delayed until goal attainment. Without an initial period of inhibited positive affect, intention memory would not be activated (according to the first modulation assumption) and (subsequent) positive affect could not connect intention memory with the behavior control sys-

[1] The personality construct *prospective action orientation* describes a dispositional determinant of self-motivation (Kuhl & Beckmann, 1994).

tem (i.e., intention memory cannot be connected with another system unless it has been activated in the first place). This formal derivation from PSI theory is important because it predicts that positive affect associated with affiliative content does not facilitate the performance of difficult intentions.

According to the second modulation assumption, negative affect (A–) inhibits the selectivity that integrated self-representations and holistic feeling can exert on "irrelevant" object perception, whereas active downregulation of negative affect [A(–)] increases the impact of the integrated self and feeling systems on discrepant or irrelevant object perceptions; that is, downregulation of negative affect facilitates inhibition of unwanted and irrelevant thoughts, emotions, or distractors in the external world). This is to say that people who cannot downregulate their negative emotionality in stressful situations have problems behaving according to integrated self-representations, that is, they should have problems showing self-determined, intrinsically motivated behavior (Deci & Ryan, 1991): They tend to be distracted by internal or external "objects" (single thoughts, affects, incentives) from a holistic overview of the entire system of needs and values defining their selves (e.g., striving for money or sex disregarding other needs of their own or others, or ruminating about a single thought or affect even if this is in conflict with some of their current needs and intentions). The assumption that, compared to positive states, negative affect is associated with lower performance of holistic tasks was recently confirmed in a study on summation priming (Bolte, 1999). On the other hand, people who have access to a differentiated and well-developed self-system should be able to keep negative affect at a moderate level even in stressful situations by activating relevant self-representational knowledge. This assumption, which follows from the reversal of the second modulation assumption, has been confirmed in studies that show that participants who have a differentiated self (e.g., who describe themselves with many rather than only a few concepts) are better able to reduce subjective stress and symptoms associated with it (e.g., physical illness, depression) than participants having simple ("compartmentalized") self-representations (Linville, 1987; Showers & Kling, 1996).

The Integrated Self as a Functional System Based Upon Holistic Feeling

It is not common in personality theory to relate the self to a "real" (i.e., neurobiological) system: When we talk about the most integrated aspects of a person (i.e., the self), we hesitate to use functional language. However, in recent years, there has been an increasing amount of evidence suggesting that "autonoetic" information, that is, holistic information about one's own emotions, needs, experiences, attitudes, and so forth, is integrated by a specialized system of the brain that is probably located in the prefrontal parts (Wheeler, Stuss, & Tulving, 1997). The implicit basis of this memory system seems to be located in the right prefrontal cortex (Ivanitzky, 1994; Knight & Grabowecky, 1995). Implicit memory forms an unconscious (or "preconscious") background from which the contents of conscious awareness can be constructed (Baars, 1988). To the extent that negative affect interacts with self-representations (second modulation assumption), one would expect the right prefrontal hemisphere to be affected in negative emotional states. To the extent that the right prefrontal parts of the brain are involved in the construction and retrieval of integrated self-representations and to the extent that activation of self-representations facilitates affect regulation (e.g., "downregulation" of excessive amounts of negative affect), this part of the brain should be activated when people are exposed to threatening situations. Davidson (1993) discusses several studies that demonstrate a decrease in alpha activity of the EEG (which is interpreted as an index of brain activation) at electrode positions located at the right prefrontal cortex when negative mood states are reported or induced experimentally. According to the second modulation assumption, activation of the self-system through the shift from negative affect to its downregulation should turn into an inhibition of this system when the self is not well-developed or when its (inhibitory) pathways toward affect-generating systems are inhibited. Consistent with this prediction, we found that state-oriented people (i.e., individuals whose self-system—or whose holistic feeling system in general—is too weak under stress to inhibit unwanted rumination about aversive events) show EEG indices of inhibition rather than activation at prefrontal electrodes when exposed to words reminding them of painful life events (Haschke & Kuhl, 1994; Rosahl, Tennigkeit, Kuhl, & Haschke, 1993).

In addition to resolving the personality-development paradox, the modulation assumptions integrate the two divergent types of personality theory: Theories emphasizing temperament can be reconciled with theories emphasizing complex cognitive processing and self-development by specifying the way temperament, that is, basic characteristics of arousal and affect, modulate the relative activation of several cognitive systems such as analytical and explicit cognition *(thinking)* or holistic and implicit cognition *(feeling)*. For example, people who acquire a positive basic mood and a high sensitivity for reward early in life tend to become sociable people later in life because, according to the first modulation assumption, positive affect activates *intuitive programs* that are prerequisites for satisfying social interactions (Papoušek & Papoušek, 1987).

This example illustrates how PSI theory explains the various ways individuals learn to satisfy their needs (cf. McClelland, 1985; Ryan, 1995): The need to form close and friendly relationships with other people (i.e., the need for affiliation, attachment, or relatedness) can be satisfied through intimate interactions with others only if it becomes associated with a positive affective disposition (A+) early in life because otherwise the intuitive programs necessary for this type of interaction would not be easily accessible. On the other hand, the need for competence and achievement should be more dependent on the ability to tolerate phases of reduced (inhibited) positive affect [A(+)] that are typical of difficult situations and that are the prerequisite for accessing analytical thinking and problem-solving operations, according to the first modulation assumption. In short, the way needs and social motives are expressed in behavior heavily depends on the affective dispositions associated with them. Satisfaction of both achievement-related and affiliative needs would require *emotional flexibility,* that is, the ability to switch from positive to negative affective states and vice versa, depending on the current motivational state and the incentives available in the environment.

Functional Characteristics of Four Cognitive Macrosystems

Let us have a closer look at PSI theory to see how the concepts introduced in the preceding section can be described in more detail and how the two modulation assumptions can help answer some of the questions I raised. PSI theory is not limited to specifying assumptions about the effect positive and negative affects have on the interaction of the four cognitive systems. It also specifies the functional characteristics of these cognitive systems (Kuhl, 2000). In this brief summary, I can only provide a global outline of the four cognitive systems. Each of these systems has been investigated extensively in experimental psychology, albeit in separate areas of research. According to my review of this literature, two systems, that is, thinking and feeling, support high-level cognitive processing. The two other systems relate to low-level (i.e., elementary) processing: One low-level system controls behavioral output ranging from habit formation to intuitive behavior control. The second low-level system supports sensory processing from elementary sensation to object perception (OP), that is, recognition of objects and their classification into discrete categories that can be labeled with a verbal descriptor. The onto- and phylogenetic sequence of the development of these four systems is assumed to be as follows: (1) IBC, (2) OP, (3) feeling, and (4) thinking. During the first weeks of life, behavior is controlled primarily by intuitive sensorimotor schemas (Berthental & Pinto, 1993; Daniel & Lee, 1990), whereas OP starts developing at about the eighth month of life, or even earlier, depending on the method used to assess labeling of objects and object permanence (Gopnik & Meltzoff, 1986; Schaffer & Emerson, 1964).

Holistic forms of integrating perceived objects into extended experiences that we describe by the term feeling develop during the second and third years of life. An example of this form of cognitive representation is reflected in the first memories of personal episodes experienced, for example, when parents start explaining to their children how pictures in the family album are related to episodes experienced earlier (Neisser, 1989). The conscious part of episodic memories heavily depends on an unconscious context (Baars, 1988) that can be described in terms of extended networks of associations describing the many elements of each particular episode. We can compare this associative context to a landscape that combines many isolated objects into an integrated representation. Because the unconscious basis of consciously remembered parts of episodes is based on an extended network of many sensory elements, I call the memory system supporting this type of integrated representation *extension memory.* The last stage mentioned relates to the development of analytical thinking (Piaget, 1952). It includes more and more refined forms of planning and problem solving. An important memory system supporting planning and problem solving is called *intention memory:* When a child cannot reach a goal by simply performing available behavioral routines (e.g., when he or she cannot get a toy out of a locked box), the ability to find a solution to the problem heavily depends on the ability to keep the intended action in mind until a solution is found.

The term extension memory contrasts meaningfully with the term intention memory: Whereas an intention puts the organism into "tension" until the intention has been performed or canceled (Lewin, 1936), access to extension memory depends on relaxation, that is, it depends on the extent to which the tension associated with negative emotionality can be released. According to the second modulation assumption, the downregulation of negative affect (which is tantamount to relaxation) is the prerequisite of access to extension memory, feeling, and integrated self-representations supported by this system. The term extension memory describes both the cognitive and the emotional characteristic of the holistic system. It not only conveys the affective precondition for being able to access this form of memory (i.e., taking the organism "out of tension": ex-tension) but also expresses the crucial cognitive feature of this type of memory: It provides an *extended* network of even remote associations connected with an object perceived or an action considered.

Self-Regulation and Feeling

According to PSI theory, feeling differs from low-level intuitive behavior control not only in its contents (i.e., integrated representations of single object perceptions from external and internal environments rather than sensorimotor schemas) but also in its capacity to support central regulation of affective states. A nice illustration of the stronger connection between right hemispheric systems and subcortical affect-generating systems is an experiment in which a presentation of a video movie in the left visual field (by controlling for eye movements), which created a right hemispheric advantage, elicited considerably more changes in blood pressure and other autonomic indices than a presentation with a left hemispheric advantage (Wittling, 1990). The stronger connectedness of right hemispheric processing with physiological concomitants of affect makes right hemispheric implicit feeling a strong candidate for the functional locus of the self-regulation of affect. Specifically, according to this assumption, integrated implicit self-representations, irrespective of whether they are correctly reflected in explicit (left hemispheric) self-concepts, should have an impact on affect regulation, for instance, on the individual's ability to keep up his or her motivation even under difficult conditions ("self-motivation") and to "downregulate" negative affect in stressful situations ("self-relaxation").

Empirical evidence for this postulated relationship between implicit self-representations and affect regulation are available. For example, Linville (1987) found that people characterized by high self-complexity (i.e., who used many adjectives for describing themselves) were better able to downregulate stress experiences as reflected in subjective ratings and physiological concomitants of the stress reaction such as depressive symptoms and frequent infections (Sapolsky, 1992). Activating the feeling system, that is, activating configurational knowledge including integrated self-representations, seems to activate systems that are directly involved in the regulation of affect. The role of the hippocampus in reducing the concentration of stress hormones is corroborated by neurophysiological data (Sapolsky, 1992). Since self-development is based on configurational knowledge, especially episodic memories of one's own feelings and motivations experienced in a variety of situations, it can be expected to be an important prerequisite for the development of the self-regulation of positive and negative affect that forms the basis for intrinsic motivation for self-determined action (Deci & Ryan, 1991) and for self-regulated coping with stressful life events (Kuhl & Fuhrmann, 1998).

Self-Development and Personality Types

How do the modulation assumptions explain personality development, for example, why some people are outgoing whereas others are reserved and distrustful? In accordance with Gray's (1987) and Cloninger's (1987) theories, PSI theory attributes sociability to an increased sensitivity for reward and positive affect. In contrast to Gray's and other theories that focus on *temperament,* PSI theory also explains the *cognitive* concomitants of reserved personality styles and their pathological analogs, such as schizoid, paranoid, or negativistic personality disorders: Why are these styles and disorders associated with an analytical cognitive style and distrustful cognitive beliefs? According to the first modulation assumption, inhibition of positive affect that is characteristic of reserved styles facilitates analytical thinking and impairs access to intuitive programs. I already mentioned that easy access to intuitive programs is especially crucial for social interactions. Figure 1 describes the STAR model of personality types, which illustrates assumptions about affective dispositions associated with each type and about the cognitive styles resulting from each affective disposition, according to the two modulation assumptions.[2]

The distrustful or paranoid style is a good example that illustrates the relationship between the STAR model and PSI theory. According to the STAR model, this personality style is based on a disposition toward inhibition of positive affect [A(+)] combined with a disposition toward downregulation of negative affect [A(–)]. According to the first modulation assumption of PSI theory, inhibited positive affect is associated with increased activation of explicit intentions combined with volitional inhibition, that is, with an inhibition

[2] STAR is an acronym for the words: spatial, temporal, acceptance, rejection, which summarize basic features of the model: *Spatial* relates to the parallel-holistic characteristics of cognitive systems (feeling, extension memory, and intuitive-behavior control), *temporal* to sequential characteristic of analytical processing (i.e., thinking and object perception), *acceptance* and *rejection* to the modulatory basis of those cognitive systems (i.e., positive and negative affects, which lead to acceptance or rejection, respectively).

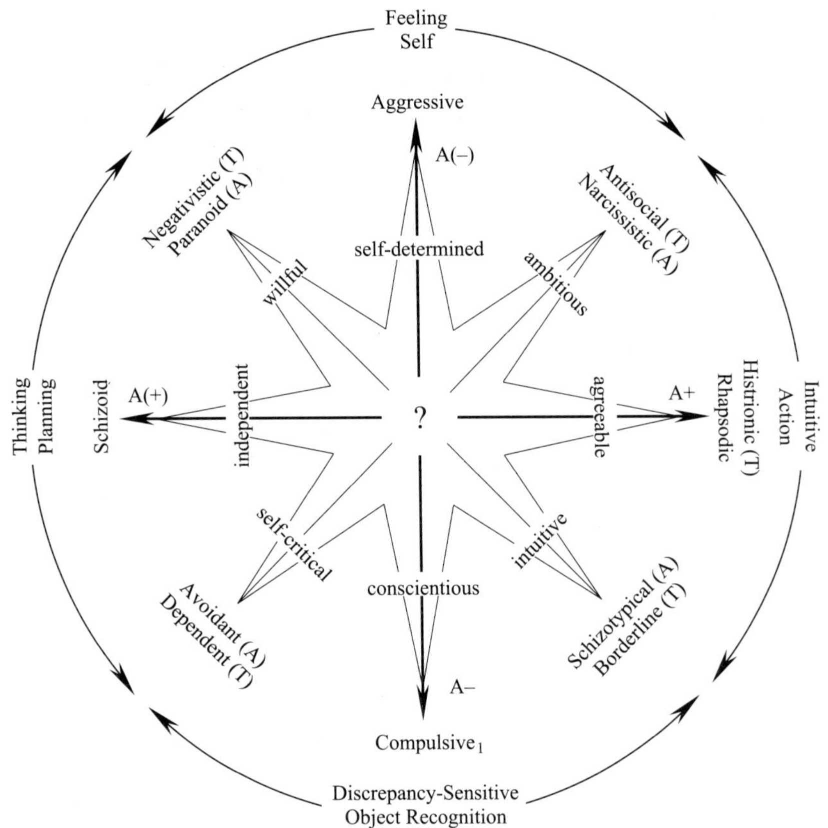

Figure 1. The STAR model describes each personality disorder (outer circle: aggressive, antisocial, etc.) and each nonpathological style (inner circle: self-determined, ambitious, etc.) in terms of a configuration of affective and cognitive systems [A+ = dispositional sensitivity for positive affect; A(+) = dispositional inhibition of A+; A– = dispositional sensitivity for negative affect; A(–) = dispositional inhibition of A–]. Compulsive$_1$ refers to the system configuration that is most frequently associated with compulsive disorders, according to the model (other system configurations are possible, e.g., compulsive$_2$ at the schizoid pole).

of the enactment of those intentions. Because of the dispositionally facilitated downregulation of negative affect, access to integrated self-representations should be facilitated. On the basis of this system configuration, distrustful beliefs can now be explained: Volitional inhibition results in frequent failures to enact intentions combined with a tendency to externalize those failures because of the strong activation of self-representations that lead to weak activation (or "repression") of discrepant, self-critical perceptions. The two modulation assumptions explain why paranoid personality is characterized by a (mis-)attribution to the bad intentions and impeding behaviors of others of personal deficits concerning the enactment of intentions.

The system configurations that are associated with various personality styles and disorders, according to the STAR model, are heuristic hypotheses meant to stimulate future research. At the University of Osnabrück, my colleagues and I have begun to develop methods for assessing the various components of hypothesized system configurations (i.e., affective dispositions and accessibility of each of the four cognitive macrosystems). In one study that focused on distrustful and paranoid styles, empirical evidence was obtained for two functional components that presumably characterize those styles: low tolerance for negative affect and increased self-assertiveness. According to these two characteristics, it was hypothesized that mothers who have high scores on a scale that assesses distrustful and paranoid styles should treat their babies in a "self-assertive" rather than "child-sensitive" way, especially when their babies were in a negative mood during a face-to-face interaction that was video taped. Exaggerated self-assertiveness was operationalized by an observational index of *intrusiveness* (e.g., enforcing the mother's intention to have the baby smile even if the baby provides signals of tiredness or overstimulation). Regression models predicting intrusive maternal behavior on the basis of paranoid style, negative mood, and the interaction between the two predictors yielded a significant effect for the interaction term only (Scheffer, Keller, Völker, & Kuhl, 1998). This is to say that paranoid mothers who have happy, well-tempered babies do not display this intrusive behavior. According to PSI theory and the STAR model, intrusive behavior occurs in paranoid personalities only when negative signals (eliciting fear or other negative affects) are encountered and downregulated: Intrusive behavior is explained, then, as a result of a tendency to downregulate negative affect (aroused by the baby's negative mood) immediately, which results, according to the second modulation assumption, in a strong activation of self-representations that render it difficult to be sensitive to the child's needs.

Personality Types Related to Affective Sharing

Emotional expression, affective sharing, and the dynamics of eye contact are examples of social behaviors that cannot easily be performed unless access to intuitive behavior control is facilitated by positive affect. This implication of the first modulation assumption explains the common experience that positive mood is indispensable for successful social interaction: It is difficult to plan or consciously control one's emotional expressions during social interaction without losing authenticity. A histrionic personality disorder (as characterized by dramatization of emotions and an exaggerated need to be in the focus of attention) exemplifies an extreme case of exaggerated reliance on emotional contagion and other intuitive programs for social interaction combined with an inhibition of planning and analytical thinking (Figure 1). On the other hand, to the extent that affective sharing based on emotional contagion is inhibited in reserved styles and corresponding personality disorders such as schizoid, paranoid, and negativistic personality types (Figure 1), critical cognitive beliefs are likely to develop for the simple reason that reserved people cannot be filled easily with enthusiasm for activities proposed by their interactional partners: Without the capacity for emotional contagion they are likely to stay at an emotional distance and perceive others as potential intruders into their own emotional autonomy. Moreover, according to the first modulation assumption, a histrionic personality should be associated with an inhibition of the impact of thinking on volitional control of action (due to a dispositional fixation on positive affect). Consistent with this derivation, histrionic patients showed a dominance of the right over the left hemisphere of the brain (Smokler & Shevrin, 1979).

The predictions concerning emotional contagion were recently confirmed in a study by Gunsch (1996) who explored the determinants of subjective relationship satisfaction among couples (married or not). Personality styles constructed as nonpathological analogs to classical personality disorders (Figure 1) were assessed with a new personality questionnaire (Kuhl & Kazén, 1997). Compared to participants scoring low on scales assessing reserved styles (i.e., styles associated with inhibited positive affect, according to Figure 1), high scorers had significantly lower indices of emotional contagion as operationalized by the change in ratings of the attractiveness of various leisure activities after an attentional shift to the preferences of the respective partner was induced.

Personality Types Related to Emotional Autonomy

In addition to individual differences regarding trust and emotional contagion, there is a second category of personality styles and personality disorders relating to emotional autonomy. Why do some people need "symbiotic" relationships, that is, partners who are not allowed to have their own emotions because they are needed as external regulators of the other partner's emotions? An answer to this question can be derived from the second modulation assumption. As illustrated by the vertical axis of the STAR model (Figure 1), personality types associated with a disposition to experience undampened, high levels of negative affect (A–) in stressful situations are self-critical, loyal, impulsive, and conscientious types as well as pathological exaggerations of these styles such as avoidant, dependent, compulsive, and borderline personality disorders (Figure 1). According to PSI theory, these personality styles and disorders are associated with an increased sensitivity for negative affect elicited in stressful situations. As a result, individuals with these styles are expected to have problems developing or accessing integrated self-representations and other components of holistic feeling. I have outlined a model of the developmental conditions leading to an impairment of the ability to downregulate negative affect on the basis of self-representations activated in stressful situations (Kuhl, in press; Kuhl & Völker, 1998).

The Systems Conditioning Assumption

According to this model, the capacity of the self-system to downregulate negative affect develops in a way that can be seen in analogy to the development of conditioned responses: In classical conditioning, an association is formed between a conditioned stimulus (CS), for example, Pavlov's bell, and a response (CR), for example, salivation elicited by an unconditioned stimulus such as a piece of meat (UCS). This CS-CR association is formed if the CS precedes the UCS several times within an optimal time window (e.g., < 800 msec). According to the *systems conditioning model* (Kuhl, 2000), a similar development of an associative pathway can develop between entire *systems,* provided the activation of one system is followed by the activation of another system frequently enough within a critical time window (e.g., < 800 msec). Applied to the case of self-regulated emotional coping, this model assumes that children whose caretakers respond to their negative self-expressions promptly with behaviors that help downregulate negative affect like feelings of pain or insecurity (e.g., by soothing, handling, or having body contact) develop an association between the activation of the self-system (CS) that occurs to express negative affect and the downregulation of negative affect that is elicited by the caretaker's behavior (UCS). The stronger this associative pathway between the self-system and the (externally elicited) downregulation of negative affect becomes, the more grows the capacity of the child to become independent of an external caretaker and downregulate negative affect in stressful situations through the activation of the self-system that naturally occurs to express negative affect grows. This developmental step can be called *emotional autonomy.*

Results from Gunsch's study are consistent with the systems conditioning model (Table 1): Most personality styles associated with elevated negative affect according to the STAR model (Figure 1) correlated significantly with a scale that assesses a preference for "symbiotic" interactions with their close partners (Gunsch, 1996). Items on this scale describe the wish that one's partner should always be prepared to respond to one's emotional needs and should have little or no emotional autonomy of his or her own (e.g., he or she should always be happy because the partner's positive mood is needed to regulate one's own emotion). According to PSI theory, symbiotic preferences associated with the personality styles mentioned (i.e., those in the lower quadrants of Figure 1) can be attributed to an impaired ability to downregulate negative affect on the basis of the activation of the self that naturally occurs whenever a negative affect needs to be expressed. It should be noted that symbiotic needs are expected only if a dispositional sensitivity for negative affect cannot be coped with, either by content-specific coping through activation of relevant self-representational knowledge or through ignoring (rather than dealing with) negative affect by activating other systems such as behavior control (e.g., avoiding confrontation with aversive experiences through overactivity), thinking (e.g., intellectualization), or positive affect (e.g., denial or extenuation).

Consistent with this application of PSI theory, four of the low and insignificant correlations in Table 1 relate to personality styles that are associated with positive affect, according to the STAR model: intuitive ("schizotypical"), self-determined ("antisocial"), agreeable ("histrionic"), and ambitious ("narcissistic"). These four groups should be able to cope with negative affect through evading into positive affect (i.e., neurobiologically speaking, activating the mesolimbic dopaminergic system). In a similar way, conscientious ("compulsive") individuals should be able to reduce negative affect through activating behavioral routines (i.e., activating the nigrostriatal dopaminergic system), whereas reserved ("schizoid") individuals should be able to avoid negative affect through activating analytical thinking (i.e., activating the left hemisphere, which has reduced access to emotional processes: Wittling, 1990). Each of these systems has little access to negative emotionality. Activating any of these systems to reduce negative affect is tantamount to employing an "immature," stress-avoidant defense mechanism, according to psychoanalytic terminology, because the individual escapes rather than deals actively with the threatening or painful experience (e.g., by integrating it into the self-system, by finding ways to protect oneself against it or by finding some meaning in it in terms of its positive associations with personal values, needs, or other self-aspects).

According to PSI theory, avoiding negative experiences through extenuation, intellectualization, or overactivity is associated with a high initial, but low final stability along a continuum of increasing stress: Negative affect can be avoided up to a critical stress intensity only and overwhelms the system if stress intensity grows beyond that critical point. The insignificant correlations between need for symbiotic relationships and the stress-avoidant types can be attributed to the delicate level of stability that can be accomplished through threat-avoidant defense mechanisms: The stress-avoidant types (i.e., ST, CP, SZ, AS, HI, and NA in Table 1) do not need external control of their emotions (i.e., through a partner in a symbiotic relationship) as long as their level of life

Table 1
Personality and Need for Symbiotic Relationships. Correlations Between Symbiotic Dependency (Emotional Autonomy Scale) and Scales From the Personality Styles and Disorder Inventory (Kuhl & Kazén, 1997)

Styles associated with low downregulation of negative affect[a] (A–)		*Styles associated with avoidance or quick down-regulation of negative affect[a] [A(–)]*	
Intuitive / ST[b]	.01	Distrustful / PN	–.38*
Impulsive / BL	.50**	Reserved / SZ	.22
Self-critical / AV	.37*	Self-determined / AS	.01
Loyal / DT	.43**	Agreeable / HI	–.10
Conscientious / CP	.25	Ambitious / NA	.30
Calm / DP	.53**	Critical / NT	.44**

[a] according to the STAR model of personality styles and disorders (Figure 1)
[b] abbreviations of personality disorders corresponding with personality styles, according to the STAR model: ST = schizotypical; BL = borderline; AV = avoidant; DT = dependent; CP = compulsive; DP = depressive; PN = paranoid; SZ = schizoid; AS = antisocial; HI = histrionic; NA = narcissistic; NT = negativistic. * $p < .05$; ** $p < .01$.

stress remains below the critical stress intensity. According to this interpretation, the low correlations of stress-avoidant types are composed of two subgroups, one having negative correlations between personality scores and need for symbiosis (i.e., stress-avoidant individuals exposed to low or moderate degrees of life stress) and the other characterized by a positive correlation between personality scores and need for symbiosis (i.e., stress-avoidant individuals exposed to high degrees of life stress). Self-regulatory competence or efficiency is considered another moderator of positive versus negative correlations between need for symbiosis and affective dispositions associated with various personality styles: Positive correlations are expected for people having low self-regulatory efficiency (e.g., state-oriented individuals: Kuhl & Beckmann, 1994) whereas negative correlations are expected for individuals having efficient self-regulation. Evidence concerning this hypothesis is discussed at the end of this chapter.

Among the personality styles considered, distrustful ("paranoid") styles seem to be best equipped to cope with negative experiences themselves rather than through their partners (Table 1). According to the STAR model (Figure 1), these people have facilitated access to their self-system and they are likely to use this system for coping with negative affect because they do not have the option to "escape into positive affect," an option that antisocial and narcissistic personalities have (who also have facilitated access to self-representations, according to the STAR model). This interpretation was confirmed in the study in which mothers' personality styles were related to their interactional styles with their 3-month-old babies (Scheffer, Keller, Völker, & Kuhl, 1998). As mentioned earlier, intrusive behavior (e.g., imposing "friendly" behavior like smiling or eye contact on an overstimulated baby) was significantly predicted by the interaction between distrustful ("paranoid") style of the mother and a negative mood of the baby. In other words, mothers leaning toward a paranoid style acted in an overly self-centered way (i.e., maintaining their own interactional intentions even if the child needed rest) provided the child was in a negative mood. This is exactly what is expected on the basis of the second modulation assumption and the position of the paranoid style in the STAR model (Figure 1): The strong dispositional tendency to downregulate negative affect [A(–)] through activation of relevant self-representations combined with an inability to escape into alternative coping mechanisms [A(+)] prevents escaping into positive affect. This should lead to excessive activation of self-determined intentions, especially when the negative mood of the child activates this coping style. Another finding of this study is consistent with the position of histrionic styles in the STAR model: Maternal warmth was significantly predicted by the interaction between histrionic style and positive mood of the baby (i.e., histrionic mothers displayed warm behavior only if their babies were in a positive mood).

Interaction of Affective-Cognitive Styles and Self-Regulatory Dispositions

A final point concerns the adaptiveness of personality styles. I have used pathological labels in conjunction with nonpathological analogs (e.g., distrustful and "paranoid") throughout this chapter to emphasize the common functional basis of personality disorders and corresponding nonpathological styles in terms of affective dispositions and the configuration of cognitive macrosystems resulting from them. This juxtapositioning of personality styles and disorders highlights the difficulty of specifying the criteria for transition from style to disorder. According to a common view adopted in the Diagnostic Statistical Manual (American Psychiatric Association, 1994), a style turns into a disorder if its affective and cognitive characteristics exceed a critical intensity and extensity. For example, when a distrustful person starts distrusting even his or her spouse without any objective reason, one might be inclined to diagnose a disorder. PSI theory emphasizes another criterion: A personality style characterized by high sensitivity at one or two poles of the two basic affective dimensions becomes pathological if it is associated with an inability to change that affective state through appropriate self-regulatory mechanisms. Even a high sensitivity for high or low (positive or negative) affect does not lock the system into one configuration of the four macrosystems as long as self-regulation of affect is intact. In this case, a strong affective sensitivity can even be a perfect precondition for healthy self-development because, in combination with self-regulated affective change, it supports the two essential elements of a developing self, namely, (1) accommodation to self-discrepant experiences and (2) assimilation ("integration") of novel experiences into a developing self-system. For example, a strong sensitivity for negative affect should facilitate the *perception* of isolated experiences that do not fit into existing self-representations (i.e., that are unexpected, unwanted, conflicting, threatening, painful, etc.) and subsequent downregulation of negative affect should help integrate such new experiences into a coherent self-representational system.

This prediction was corroborated in a recent study in which a significant positive relationship was obtained between projective measures of self-determined satisfaction of basic needs for relatedness, competence, and autonomy (intrinsic motivation) and the scores for related personality styles (Figure 2): People who had high scores on the impulsiveness-borderline scale of the Personality-Styles-and-Disorders-Inventory (PSSI: Kuhl & Kazén, 1997) had higher scores on measures of intrinsic (anxiety free) motivation for relatedness ("intimacy") than participants who scored low on the "borderline" scale, provided an index of healthy self-regulatory development was above average (Scheffer, 2000). This index was derived from a scale of perceived interpersonal reciprocity (e.g., "I have experienced a good balance of giving and receiving in my life"; Chasiotis, 1998). Interpersonal reciprocity (i.e., the mirroring of self-expressions through responsive behavior of significant others) is a prerequisite for the development of self-regulatory competence, according to psychoanalytical theory (Kohut, 1985) as well as according to the systems conditioning model of PSI theory. Similar results were obtained for measures of intrinsic achievement motivation (flow) and intrinsic power motivation (prosocial leadership). The independent-schizoid style showed a significant positive relationship with intrinsic achievement motivation in a subgroup that was characterized by high perceived reciprocity of social relations in their biography (as an index of benign conditions for the development of self-regulation) whereas a considerably smaller positive relationship was observed within the low-reciprocity group (Figure 2). Finally, the positive relationship between the willful-paranoid style obtained in the high reciprocity group turned into a negative relationship within the low-reciprocity group. The fact that each of the three styles mentioned in Figure 2 relates to a different need (i.e., need for affiliation, achievement, or power) suggests that the styles and disorders differ on more than the affective and cognitive dimensions described in Figure 1: Intuitive or borderline-like styles seem to have a close link to affiliative needs, independent or schizoid styles seem to be associated with achievement needs, and willful or paranoid styles seem to have a strong connection with power-related needs.

The theoretical and practical relevance of these findings can hardly be overestimated: Pathological labels like *neuroticism* or *borderline* are unwarranted descriptors of styles associated with an elevated sensitivity for punishment and negative affect until self-regulatory functions have been assessed and found to be deficient. This is tantamount to saying that exactly those personality functions whose impairment is most relevant for the development of neurotic symptoms (i.e., self-regulatory functions) are usually not assessed in clinical practice. One reason for this situation has been the lack of standardized instruments for the assessment of self-regulation. This situation has

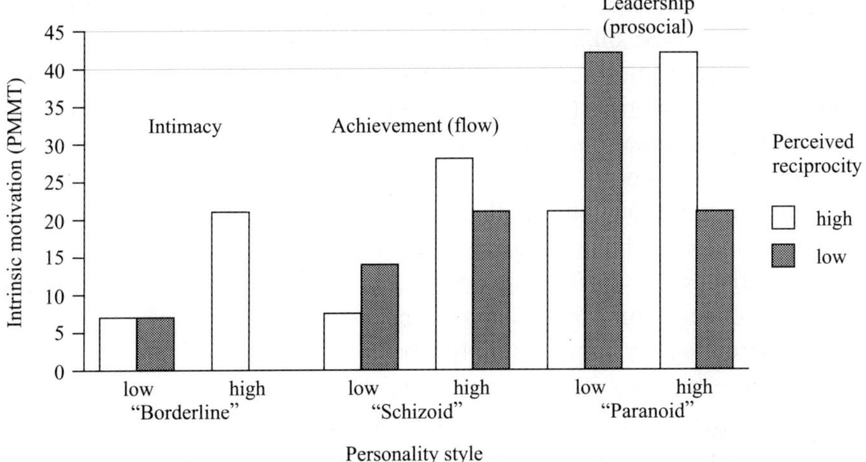

Figure 2. Projective indices of anxiety-free motivation for intimate relationships (intimacy), intrinsic achievement motivation (flow), and prosocial power motivation (leadership) as a function of various personality style associated with high or low affective sensitivity (nonpathological analogs of three personality disorders) and an index of self-regulatory competency (perceived reciprocity) (PMMT refers to the projective multi-motive test by Kuhl & Scheffer, 1999).

changed: We have developed nonreactive methods to assess self-regulatory competence (Kuhl & Kraska, 1989, 1992) as well as self-report scales that assess more than 30 functional components of self-regulatory competencies and their efficient use under stressful conditions (Kuhl & Fuhrmann, 1998).

Conclusions

What conclusions can be drawn from the foregoing analysis? Which personality style is most adaptive? At first glance, one might speculate that styles characterized by high positive or low (i.e., downregulated) negative affect are more adaptive than styles associated with low positive or high negative emotionality. However, the theory does not make this prediction. On the basis of the two modulation assumptions, it is easy to see that to be able to use each of the four cognitive systems, the most adaptive personality is the one that can switch between high and low positive and between high and low negative affect, according to the situational requirements encountered. *Emotional flexibility* is the precondition for cognitive flexibility. People who have to be in a positive mood all the time (e.g., rhapsodic or histrionic: Figure 1) are likely to have problems in situations that require careful planning and delay of gratification (e.g., when saving money for some purpose), according to the first modulation assumption. On the other hand, people who have to downregulate negative emotions all the time might have problems inhibiting their self-representations whenever this is needed, for example, when one has to comply with moral or legal rules even against one's own decisions, when one is in need of other people's help, or simply when one is trying to form a loyal and stable relationship that includes a certain dependency upon one's partner. When the self-system is always active and downregulating negative emotions all the time (e.g., in narcissistic, antisocial, or paranoid personality disorders), this system may appear very powerful, but it has few opportunities to accommodate, that is, to integrate new experiences into existing self-representations. This derivation from PSI theory describes the theory's basic view on self-development: The ability to develop the self-system across the life span critically depends on the capacity for self-regulated emotional change *(emotional dialectics),* that is, the ability actively to control switches of attention from positive to negative sides of objects and people encountered (Kuhl, 2000). This ability depends on the intactness and the level of maturation of the self-system.

The developmental conditions for healthy self-development can be related to unconditional positive regard (Rogers, 1961) for a child and to the "mirroring" of self-expressions (Kohut, 1985), that is, prompt and appropriate responses to the child's expressions of positive states (e.g., interests) or negative states (e.g., distress). The systems conditioning model was proposed to demonstrate that theoretical treatment of these developmental conditions need no longer be confined to phenomenological and humanistic theories of personality. The functional basis of self-development can be explained by generalizing the features of classical conditioning to the contiguity of activation of psychological systems. Future research may focus on examining the potential the theory and findings I reported have for assessing the role of self-development in training and therapy: A promising line of research would be to examine the degree to which over- or undersensitivity for positive or negative affect with the imbalance of cognitive systems resulting from it can be remedied if the conditions for healthy self-development that have been lacking during childhood or adolescence are offered later, no matter whether they consist of a mirroring therapist or a loving person who is able to facilitate self-expression and to respond to the affected individual in a prompt and appropriate way.

References

American Psychiatric Association. (1994). *Diagnostic and statistical manual of mental disorders* (4th rev. ed.). Washington, DC: American Psychiatric Association.

Baars, B. J. (1988). *A cognitive theory of consciousness.* Cambridge, UK: Cambridge University Press.

Beck, A. T., & Freeman, A. (1990). *Cognitive therapy of personality disorders.* New York: Guilford Press.

Berthental, B. I., & Pinto, J. (1993). Dynamical constraints in the perception and production of human movements. In E. Thelen & L. Smith (Eds.), *Dynamical systems in development* (Vol. 2, pp. 209–239).Cambridge, MA: Bradford Books.

Bolte, A. (1999). *Intuition und Emotion: Einflüsse von Stimmungen auf semantische Aktivierung und implizite Urteilsprozesse* [Intuition and emotion: Mood effects on semantic activation and implicit judgment]. Unpublished doctoral dissertation, University of Osnabrück, Germany.

Chasiotis, A. (1998). *Zur intergenerationellen Bedeutung des Kindheitskontextes für die somatische, psychologische und reproduktive Individualentwicklung. Untersuchungen zur evolutionären Entwicklungspsychologie der Lebensspanne* [On the cross-generational significance of childhood contexts for somatic, psychological and reproductive ontogenesis: Studies on evolutionary life-span development]. Unpublished doctoral dissertation, University of Osnabrück, Germany.

Cloninger, C. R. (1987). A systematic method for clinical description and classification of personality variants. *Archives of General Psychiatry, 44,* 573–587.

Daniel, B. M., & Lee, D. (1990). Development of looking with head and eyes. *Journal of Experimental Child Psychology, 50,* 200–216.

Davidson, R. J. (1993). Cerebral asymmetry and emotion: Conceptual and methodological conundrums. *Cognition and Emotion, 7,* 115–138.

Deci, E. L., & Ryan, R. M. (1991). A motivational approach to self: Integration in personality. In E. Dienstbier (Ed.), *Nebraska Symposium on Motivation 1990* (pp. 237–288). Lincoln, NE: University of Nebraska Press.

Eysenck, H. J. (1967). *The biological basis of personality.* Springfield, IL: Charles C. Thomas.

Gopnik, A., & Meltzoff, A. N. (1986). Relations between semantic and cognitive development in the one-word stage: The specificity hypothesis. *Child Development, 58,* 1523–1531.

Gray, J. A. (1987). *The psychology of fear and stress* (2nd ed.). Cambridge, UK: Cambridge University Press.

Gunsch, D. (1996). *Selbstbestimmung und Persönlichkeitsstile in Zweierbeziehungen* [Self-determination and personality styles in dyadic relationships]. Unpublished diploma thesis, University of Osnabrück, Germany.

Haschke, R., & Kuhl, J. (1994). Action control and slow potential shifts. In *Proceedings of the 41st International Congress of Aviation and Space Medicine* (pp. 207–210). Bologna, Italy: Monduzzi.

Heckhausen, H. (1991). *Motivation and action.* Berlin, Germany: Springer.

Ivanitzky, A. M. (1994). Interaction foci, informational synthesis and mental processes. *Neuroscience and Behavioral Physiology, 24,* 239–246.

Kohut, H. (1985). *Self psychology and the humanities.* New York: Norton.

Knight, R. T., & Grabowecky, M. (1995). Escape from linear time: Prefrontal cortex and conscious experience. In M. S. Gazzaniga (Ed.), *The cognitive neurosciences* (pp. 1357–1371). Cambridge, MA: MIT Press.

Kuhl, J. (2000). A functional-design approach to motivation and volition: The dynamics of personality systems interactions. In M. Boekaerts, P. R. Pintrich, & M. Zeidner (Eds.), *Self-regulation: Directions and challenges for future research* (pp. 111–169). New York: Academic Press.

Kuhl, J., & Beckmann, J. (1994). *Volition and personality: Action versus state orientation.* Göttingen, Germany: Hogrefe.

Kuhl, J., & Fuhrmann, A. (1998). Decomposing self-regulation and self-control: The volitional components inventory. In J. Heckhausen & C. S. Dweck (Eds.), *Life span perspectives on motivation and control* (pp. 15–49). Hillsdale, NJ: Erlbaum.

Kuhl, J., & Kazén, M. (1997). *Persönlichkeits-Stil-und-Störungs-Inventar (PSSI): Handanweisung* [Personality Styles and Disorders Questionnaire]. Göttingen, Germany: Hogrefe.

Kuhl, J., & Kazén, M. (1999). Volitional facilitation of difficult intentions: Joint activation of intention memory and positive affect removes Stroop interference. *Journal of Experimental Psychology: General, 128,* 382–399.

Kuhl, J., & Kraska, K. (1989). Self-regulation and metamotivation: Computational mechanisms, development, and assessment. In R. Kanfer, P. L. Ackerman, & R. Cudeck (Eds.), *Abilities, motivation, and methodology: The Minnesota Symposium on individual differences* (pp.343–368). Hillsdale, NJ: Erlbaum.

Kuhl, J., & Kraska, K. (1992). *Der Selbstregulations- und Konzentrationstest für Kinder (SRKT-K)* [Self-regulation and concentration test for children: SRTC]. Göttingen, Germany: Hogrefe.

Kuhl, J., & Scheffer, D. (1999). *Projektiver Multi-Motiv-Test (PMMT): Auswertungsmanual* [Projective multi-motive test: Scoring manual]. Unpublished paper, University of Osnabrück, Germany.

Kuhl, J., & Völker, S. (1998). Persönlichkeit und Entwicklung [Personality and development]. In H. Keller, (Ed.), *Lehrbuch der Entwicklungspsychologie* [Textbook of developmental psychology] (pp. 207–240). Bern, Switzerland: Huber.

Lewin, K. (1936). *Principles of topological psychology.* New York: McGraw-Hill.

Linville, P. W. (1987). Self-complexity as a cognitive buffer against stress-related illness and depression. *Journal of Personality and Social Psychology, 52,* 663–676.

McClelland, D. C. (1985). *Human motivation.* Glenview, IL: Scott, Foresman & Co.

Neisser, U. (1989). Five kinds of self-knowledge. *Philosophical Psychology, 1,* 35–59.

Oettingen, G. (1997). *Psychologie des Zukunftsdenkens* [The psychology of future orientation]. Göttingen, Germany: Hogrefe.

Papoušek, H., & Papoušek, M. (1987). Intuitive parenting: A dialectic counterpart to the infant's integrative competence. In J. D. Osofsky (Ed.), *Handbook of infant development* (2nd ed., pp. 669–720). New York: Wiley.

Piaget, J. (1952). *The origins of intelligence in children.* New York: Norton.

Rogers, C. R. (1961). *On becoming a person: A therapist's view of psychotherapy.* Boston, MA: Houghton Mifflin.

Rosahl, S. K., Tennigkeit, M., Kuhl, J., & Haschke, R. (1993). Handlungskontrolle und langsame Hirnpotentiale: Untersuchungen zum Einfluß subjektiv kritischer Wörter (Erste Ergebnisse) [Action control and slow brain potential shifts: Experiments on the impact of subjectively critical words (preliminary results)]. *Zeitschrift für Medizinische Psychologie, 2,* 1–8.

Ryan, R. (1995). Psychological needs and the facilitation of integrative processes. *Journal of Personality, 63,* 397–427.

Sapolsky, R. M. (1992). *Stress, the aging brain, and the mechanism of neuron death.* Cambridge, MA: MIT Press.

Schaffer, H. R., & Emerson, P. E. (1964). The development of social attachments in infancy. *Monographs of the Society for Research in Child Development, 29* (3, Serial No. 94).

Scheffer, D. (2000). *Implizite Motive: Entwicklungskontexte und modulierende Mechanismen* [Implicit motives: Developmental contexts and modulating mechanisms]. Unpublished dissertation, University of Osnabrück, Germany.

Scheffer, D., Keller, H., Völker, S., & Kuhl, J. (1998). *Personality and parenting: Differential sensitivity to positive and negative affect and components of parenting in early mother-infant exchange.* Manuscript submitted for publication.

Showers, C. J., & Kling, K. C. (1996). Organization of self-knowledge: Implications for recovery from sad mood. *Journal of Personality and Social Psychology, 70,* 578–590.

Smokler, I. A., & Shevrin, H. (1979). Cerebral lateralization and personality style. *Archives of General Psychiatry, 36,* 949–954.

Squire, L. R. (1992). Memory and the hippocampus: A synthesis from findings with rats, monkeys, and humans. *Psychological Review, 99,* 195–231.

Steinmetz, J. (1994). Brain substrates of emotion and temperament. In J. E. Bates & T. D. Wachs (Eds.), *Temperament: Individual differences at the interface of biology and behavior* (pp. 17–46). Washington, DC: American Psychological Association.

Wheeler, M. A., Stuss, D. T., & Tulving, E. (1997). Toward a theory of episodic memory: The frontal lobes and autonoetic consciousness. *Psychological Bulletin, 121,* 331–354.

Winter, D. G. (1996). *Personality: Analysis and interpretation of lives.* New York: McGraw-Hill.

Wittling, W. (1990). Psychophysiological correlates of human brain asymmetry: Blood pressure changes during lateralized presentation of an emotionally laden film. *Neuropsychologia, 28,* 457–470.

10 Developmental Regulation Across the Life Span: An Action-Phase Model of Engagement and Disengagement With Developmental Goals

Jutta Heckhausen

The active role of the individual in regulating development has become a topic of great interest in lifespan developmental research, ever since Lerner and Busch-Rossnagel published their seminal book on "individuals as producers of their own development" (Lerner & Busch-Rossnagel, 1981). However, earlier approaches to this phenomenon often addressed more passive contributions of the individual to his or her own developmental course, by way of investigating the role of temperament, attractiveness, gender, and other variables as elicitors of more or less promotive socialization behavior of primary caregivers (exemplar chapters from Lerner & Busch-Rossnagel, 1981). More recently, truly agentic influences of the individual have received more focal attention, especially from action- or control-theoretical perspectives (Brandtstädter & Lerner, 1999; Nurmi, 1992; Nurmi, Pulliainen, & Salmela-Aro, 1992; Schulz & Heckhausen, 1996; see review in Heckhausen, 1999a; Heckhausen & Schulz, 1999a, 1999b).

In this context, the effect of three systems of influence on development can be conceptualized as a transaction. Biological factors of maturation and aging set the stage for what is possible in terms of genotypical potential and constraints at any given age during the life course. The system of influence based on society involves age-graded norms and the institutions regulating development and life-course transitions such as school entry, retirement, and remarriage potential. The individual operates vis-à-vis these systems of influence not merely as a passive recipient, but as an active agent using opportunities provided by biological changes and societal institutions. Thus, it is the individual who brings to bear the biological and societal influences by reflecting them in his or her age-graded engagement and disengagement with developmental goals.

Developmental Regulation via Cycles of Engagement and Disengagement With Developmental Goals

In this chapter, an action-theoretical conception of developmental regulation is proposed. This conception integrates the life-span theory of control (Heckhausen, 1999a; Heckhausen & Schulz, 1995; Schulz & Heckhausen, 1996) with the Rubicon model of action phases (Heckhausen, 1991; Heckhausen & Gollwitzer, 1987). According to this conception, individuals' attempts to regulate their own development are organized in terms of engaging with or disengaging from developmental goals (Heckhausen, 1999a). Thus, developmental regulation is structured in phases of action representing increasing levels of engagement with a goal, and then disengagement when the goal seems no longer attainable. This focus on specific developmental goals allows the individual to invest resources selectively in a specific goal pursuit for a particular period of his or her life time rather than spreading resources thinly among too many goals pursued simultaneously.

Age-Graded Sequencing of Opportunities for Attaining Developmental Goals Across the Life Span

Given that sequential and age-structured investment in particular developmental goals is most adaptive, the question arises of when the best time for activating engagement with a particular goal has come. In this regard, the individual is scaffolded in his or her active shaping of the life course by age-graded structures of waxing and waning opportunities to achieve certain developmental goals. Figure 1 illustrates such a sequence of increasing and decreasing opportunities for a set of developmental goals across the adult life span. The goals range from graduating from school and finding an occupation to building a pension fund and being a grandparent. Each of these goals has ideal timing periods, when opportunities are at a maximum.

For any given developmental goal the waxing and waning of opportunities has important implications for the individual's investment in goal pursuit. The dark grey area in Figure 2 shows the required investment at increasing, maximum, and declining opportunities. During the increasing phase, goal pursuit is not urgent, because there is so much time left to reach the goal that it can easily be postponed. At maximum opportunities the individual can swim with the stream of conducive conditions and thus does not have to invest much energy in pursuing the goal. However, when opportunities decline and

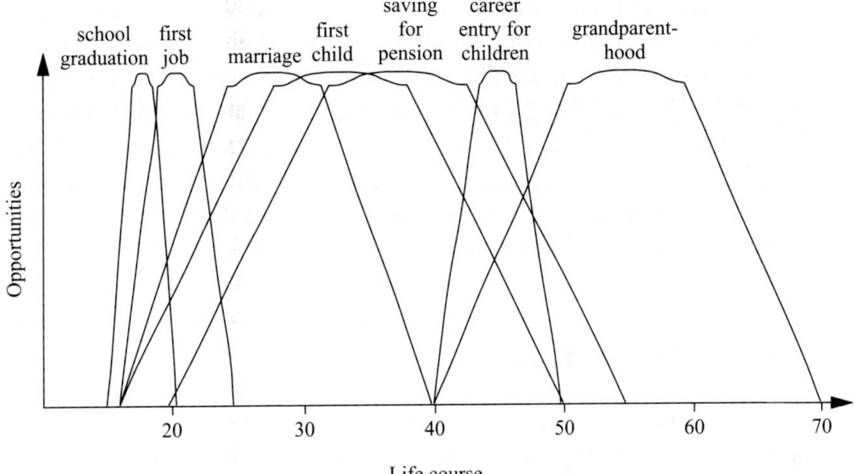

Figure 1. Age-graded sequencing of opportunity curves for different developmental goals (hypothetical).

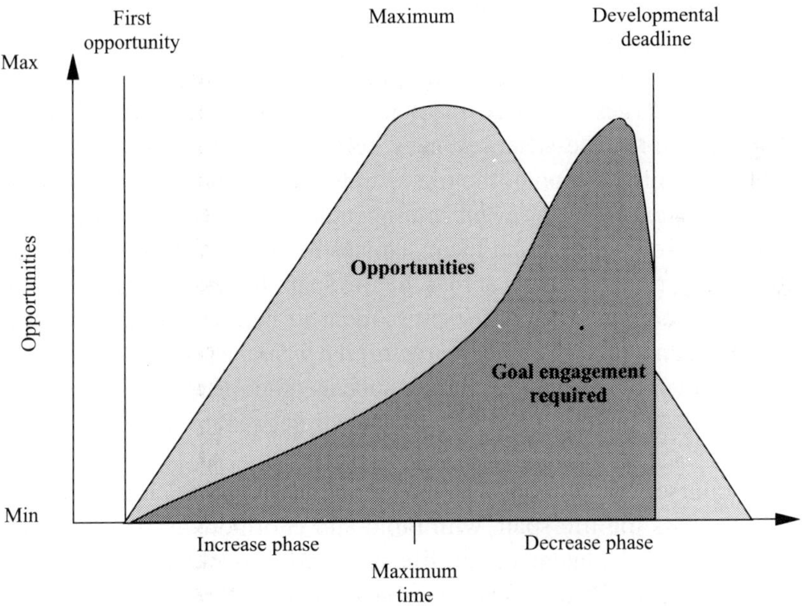

Figure 2. Age-graded opportunity structure for developmental goals.

approach a low-level threshold, goal pursuit becomes urgent and also has to come up against less favorable conditions. This is when individuals need to invest more resources to attain the goal before opportunities decline below a critical level. This critical point is conceptualized as the "developmental deadline." Passing the deadline is associated—at least in the perception of the individual involved in this situation—with exceedingly low levels of controllability of goal attainment and often also prohibitively high costs in terms of behavioral investment (Heckhausen, 1999a; Wrosch & Heckhausen, in press). Therefore, once the deadline is passed the individual should disengage from the goal to prevent wasting energy in a futile goal pursuit, and to avoid negative consequences for emotional balance and self-esteem.

Primary and Secondary Control in Goal Engagement and Disengagement

The behavioral and motivational processes involved in goal engagement and disengagement can be conceptualized in the framework of the life-span theory of control (Heckhausen & Schulz, 1995, 1999a; Schulz & Heckhausen, 1996). This theory distinguishes between primary and secondary control striving (see Table 1). *Primary control striving* is directed at the external world and serves to produce direct effects of behavior in the environment. In contrast, *secondary control striving* is directed at the internal world of the individual and serves to focus, maintain, or expand motivational resources, such as hope for success, self-efficacy, self-esteem, or emotional balance.

The core proposition of the life-span theory of control is that individuals strive to produce behavior-event contingencies and thus exert primary control over the environment around them. This primary control striving is a human universal and remains stable across the life span. It can take the form of *selective primary control,* that is, the investment of behavioral resources such as time, effort, and energy, or of *compensatory primary control,* which refers to the recruitment of external resources, such as other people's help or technical aids. Both these kinds of primary control strategies are involved in goal engagement.

Of course, the potential to realize primary control undergoes radical changes across the life span, with rapid and enormous growth in childhood and adolescence, a plateau in mid-life, and gradual decline in old age. The age and domain-related variations in primary control potential as well as the requirement to be selective in focusing one's resources for particular primary control goals calls for processes that regulate the motivational investment.

Table 1
Two-Dimensional Model of Primary/Secondary Control and Selection/Compensation (adapted from Heckhausen & Schulz, 1993)

	Selection	*Compensation*
Primary control	*Selective primary control* Investment of internal resources: effort, time, abilities, activity-inherent skills	*Compensatory primary control* Use of external resources: technical aids, other people's assistance, activity-external skills
Secondary control	*Selective secondary control* Metavolition: enhancement of goal commitment, remaining focused in order to avoid distractions	*Compensatory secondary control* Buffering negative effects of failure: goal change, strategic social comparison, or strategic causal attribution

These are secondary control processes, one selective and one compensatory. *Selective secondary control* is directed at focusing motivational resources on a chosen goal (selective secondary control) by enhancing the perceived value of the chosen goal and devaluing alternative goals, by increasing the perceived sense of control over attaining the goal, or by vividly anticipating positive self-reinforcement associated with achieving the goal. Along with the primary control strategies, selective secondary control is involved in goal engagement. In contrast, *compensatory secondary control* facilitates goal disengagement and serves the function of protecting motivational resources against damage after an experience of failure or control loss. This is done by disengaging from the futile goal and by protecting self-efficacy, self-esteem, and emotional balance by means such as self-serving attributions and downward social comparisons.

These four kinds of control strategies are not adaptive in and of themselves but only in relation to the appropriate structure of opportunities to engage in or disengage from a goal. For instance, selective primary and selective secondary control may be erroneously invested, when the opportunities for realizing a goal have faded away. An example is a 30-year-old who fails to disengage from the goal of becoming a world-class track-and-field athlete. Compensatory secondary control, on the other hand, may be activated prematurely, when favorable opportunities for achieving a goal are still abundant. A fourth grader, for instance, would be ill-advised to give up educational goals because of temporary difficulties in school.

It thus becomes clear that the activation and deactivation of control strategies has to be regulated by a higher-order mechanism that selects appropriate goals to strive for on the basis of the age-graded opportunity structure for the respective goals. In our model of developmental regulation we have included optimization as this higher-order mechanism of goal selection (Heckhausen, 1999a; Schulz & Heckhausen, 1996). In accordance with the core proposition of our theory about the functional primacy of primary control striving, the criterion for adaptive goal choice is whether primary control potential is optimized across life domains and on a long-term lifespan-encompassing basis. The example of investing in a career as a superathlete is a case in point. Such an investment in achieving world-class performance in a highly select domain of functioning typically is very risky, because of its high criterion of success. In addition, it has very detrimental effects on other domains (e.g., education, social relationships) and yields direct payoffs only for a very narrow time window of the life span. Thus, investing in a career to become a world-class athlete is adaptive in terms of promoting long-term and cross-domain primary control only in rare cases of very exceptional ability and training conditions, which would help to transfer the payoffs of success in the select domain to other important life domains and to the life course after the peak performance is no longer attainable. It is important to contrast this criterion of primary control potential with other criteria of adaptive functioning, which are based on subjective indicators (see, e.g., Baltes & Baltes, 1980; Diener, 1999; Ryff & Keyes, 1995). Subjective and psychological well-being is in our view only a proximate mediator of adaptive functioning, rather than its ultimate reason. As Frijda (1988) argues, positive affect habituates swiftly and gives way to further strivings for positive change. Individuals do not rest on their laurels for very long but quickly get used to a success and then move on to higher aspirations. This system of emotional and motivational functioning promotes a maximum investment in primary control, rather than optimized positive affect. Our motivational system is not aimed at happiness but geared towards expanding and maintaining primary control potential.

Specifically, the control model of developmental regulation identifies three core principles of optimization, which should, in the adaptive case, guide goal selection. The first principle is *age-appropriateness;* it implies that goals should be selected in accordance with the opportunities available in a given developmental ecology at a specific age. The second principle of optimization is *optimized trade-off relations;* and it states that goals should be selected to minimize negative consequences for other domains of functioning, to provide long-term primary control, and to maximize positive consequences in other domains and in the long run. The third optimization principle is *diversity;* it requires that goals should be selected so as to avoid excessive selectiveness, which would make the individual too vulnerable. Instead, the individual should remain active in multiple domains, so that narrow dead-end paths are avoided.

The entire model of four control strategies and a set of optimization strategies for adaptive choice of control goals formed the conceptual basis for the development of a measurement instrument, the OPS scales (optimization in primary and secondary control scales; Heckhausen, Schulz, & Wrosch, 1997). These domain-general OPS scales can be modified to form domain-specific OPS scales that are tailored to fit the domain-specific goals (e.g., achieving a promotion in the work domain) and means (e.g., investing more effort) of control. Several such domain-specific scales have been developed, such as those for the domains of work, partnership, child-bearing, getting a new job, coping with disease, and maximizing school achievement. Domain-specific OPS scales are important instruments for research because adaptive control behavior is expected to be specifically tailored to changing opportunities in particular domains of functioning, rather than reflecting spillovers from one domain to all other domains. In fact, one of the hallmarks of adaptive control behavior is to manage inter-domain trade-offs of control investments. Thus, for instance, sharp decreases in opportunities in one particular domain should entice the individual to switch control investments over to a domain in which behavioral investments are more effective.

An Action-Phase Model of Developmental Regulation

The activation of the different primary and secondary control strategies in action cycles of goal engagement and disengagement can be conceptualized in a model of action phases. The *Rubicon Model of Action Phases,* developed by Heinz Heckhausen (1991; Heckhausen & Gollwitzer, 1987; Gollwitzer, Heckhausen, & Steller, 1990) provides the conceptual framework for such a model of developmental regulation. The key assumption of the Rubicon model is that motivational engagement for a given goal does not change in a continuous manner when decisions are made about goals. Instead, Heckhausen and his colleagues showed discrete shifts from a deliberative motivational mind-set in the phase of decision making to an implementational volitional mind-set in the post-decisional phase. Before making a decision, individuals have an open-minded and broad manner of information processing, whereas after the decision, information processing becomes biased and narrowed down to the chosen alternative.

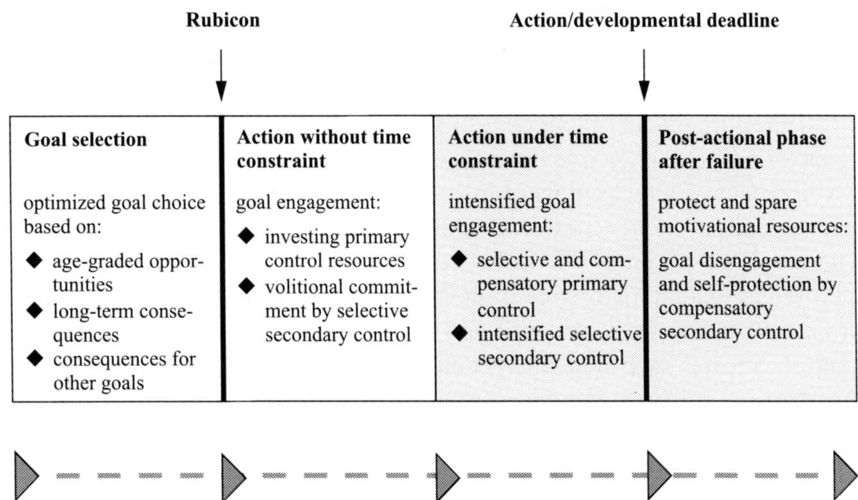

Figure 3. Action-phase model of developmental regulation (adapted from Heckhausen, 1999).

While the Rubicon transition marks the shift from pre-decisional motivation to post-decisional volition, we propose a shift from urgent volitional investment before reaching a deadline for goal attainment to post-deadline motivation (see Figure 3). When approaching the deadline, goal engagement and the involved control processes are expected to be intensified as a response to the perceived urgency of goal pursuit. After passing the deadline, the individual has to shift from intense goal engagement to goal disengagement to avoid futile investments and to protect motivational resources such as self-esteem. The shift to goal disengagement is facilitated by strategies of compensatory secondary control.

Developmental Regulation According to the "Biological Clock" for Child-Bearing

Perhaps the most obvious case of developmental deadline is the deadline for child-bearing associated with the so-called biological clock that involves a rapid decline of fertility and an increase of pre- and perinatal risks in women beyond the age of 40 years. Most people view the age of 40 as the deadline for bearing a child. Women who have not had a child by the age of 40 are expected to remain childless. This renders the developmental goal of child-bearing and the age of 40 highly suitable to study the proposed model of developmental regulation around a deadline. In a series of studies (Heckhausen, Wrosch, & Fleeson, 1999), we therefore recruited subjects in various groups, women without children in their early 30s , their early 40s, and their early 50s, as well as women with children at these ages, and pregnant women. We predicted that women who were in the pre-deadline and urgent condition due to their age would report more child-bearing goals and be more invested in terms of goal engagement control strategies (selective primary, selective secondary, compensatory primary). In contrast, women who were older than the deadline were expected to have disengaged from child-bearing goals, to prefer alternative goals, and to report using more goal disengagement control strategies (compensatory secondary control).

The findings show that women in the urgency group and women with a child nominated more goals related to child-bearing and family than women who had passed the deadline. Women past the deadline were more engaged in goals of self-development, the optimization of personal health, as well as the

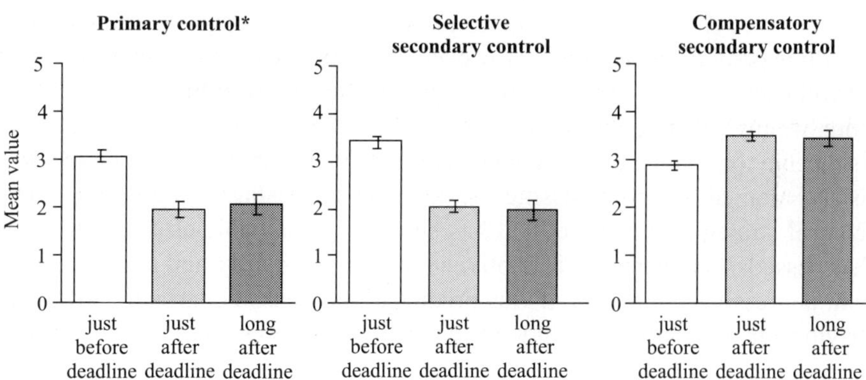

* Aggregate of selective primary control and compensatory primary control.

Figure 4. Developmental deadline "first child": Control strategies for child-bearing rated by pre- and post-deadline women (adapted from Heckhausen et al., 1999).

extension of one's social network. With regard to the control strategies preferred by pre- versus post-deadline groups, the findings strongly supported the action-phase model of developmental regulation.

Figure 4 displays the findings pertaining to the domain-specific control strategies in women in their early 30s (pre-deadline urgency group), 40s (group just past deadline), and 50s (long past deadline). Women in the pre-deadline urgency group reported using control strategies of goal engagement more frequently than women in the two post-deadline groups (early 40s, early 50s). This is shown for the three control strategies of goal engagement: selective primary control, selective secondary control, and compensatory secondary control. Conversely, the compensatory secondary control strategies of goal disengagement were reported more by the post-deadline women compared to the pre-deadline women.

Our research about developmental regulation regarding child-bearing goals also addressed non-intentional, not consciously represented aspects of goal engagement, and goal disengagement. Specifically, we investigated incidental memory indicators of priming information processing for child-bearing goals versus away from child-bearing goals. Women in the urgency group recalled more information about child-bearing related issues (e.g., positive and negative aspects of child-bearing) compared to women who had passed the deadline. The latter showed superior recall for information that was conducive to avoiding self-blame for one's childlessness.

The findings discussed so far support the propositions of the deadline model of action phases in terms of pre-deadline goal engagement and post-deadline goal disengagement. However, we wanted to go one step further and beyond descriptive differences between pre- and post-deadline groups. Therefore, we investigated the adaptiveness of being phase congruent in one's control behavior, that is, using goal engagement control strategies when the goal is still attainable before passing the deadline, and using goal disengagement control strategies when the goal has become unattainable after the deadline has passed. As indicators of adaptiveness we used positive and negative affect and depressive symptoms. It was predicted that phase-congruent control behavior and motivational mind-set (e.g., information-processing bias) would be associated with more positive affect, less negative affect, and less depressive symptomatology.

For the post-deadline women, negative affect was found to be strongly associated with remembering many child-bearing related sentences, particularly those that were concerned with the subjective value of having children, the personal responsibility for not having children, and sentences about grandchildren. Recalling sentences about substitute goals was associated with more positive affect in women who had passed the deadline. Thus, focusing on any child-relevant content was detrimental to a positive affective balance for women who had missed the deadline. Similar findings were obtained for the phase-congruence of control strategies. In the group of pre-deadline women selective primary control was associated with fewer reported depressive symptoms. Conversely, for the older women (early 40s or 50s) greater reported selective primary control striving was associated with elevated levels of depressive symptomatology. This implies that the more women in their early 30s were behaviorally engaged in the goal of bearing a child, the less depressed they were. But in their early 40s and 50s, greater investment in child-bearing goals had negative implications for mental health.

Developmental Regulation Toward or Away From Partnerships in Young and Late-Midlife Adults

The deadline paradigm was then extended to the domain of partnership (Wrosch, 1999; Wrosch & Heckhausen, 1999). The age-related deadline associated with the developmental goal of partnership is not as clearly defined as the deadline for child-bearing. However, population statistics reveal that after a separation, the likelihood of remarrying sharply drops from 80 percent in early adulthood to 20 percent in late midlife (Braun & Proebsting, 1986). Thus, although individuals cannot use a clear and narrow age deadline as a marker for age-based engagement and disengagement with partnership goals, we propose that individuals construct subjective turning points somewhere during midlife, which for them mark the deadline for searching for a new partner on the continuing downward slope of opportunities. Somewhere along the way, when opportunities to meet somebody new and build a new long-term relationship decline, the individual constructs the point in the lifetime after which further efforts are likely to be futile and potentially dangerous for balanced emotionality and self-esteem. Whereas the study reported here used age-groups greatly differing in age, so that they fell clearly either before or after the deadline, further studies should investigate the process by which individuals construct their personal deadline for partnership as well as other important goals. This could be done by comparing groups closer in age, or ideally by conducting longitudinal research.

In the study reported here, young (21- to 35-year-old) and late-midlife (50- to 60-year-old) adults, who were either recently separated or recently committed to a new partner, were compared. Subjects reported their developmental goals for the next five to ten years, completed a domain-specific version of the control strategy scale, performed an incidental memory task of partnership-relevant adjectives, and completed a set of questionnaires on psychological well-being and positive and negative affect.

The rationale of the study was to contrast those adults who, because of their young age, had plenty of opportunities for finding a new partner with those who in late midlife confronted greatly impoverished chances of finding a new partner. It was expected that the younger adults would exhibit a motivational mind-set of goal engagement with the respective control strategies of selective and compensatory primary control and selective secondary control. In contrast, the late-midlife adults were expected to respond to a separation by disengaging from partnership goals and employing control strategies of compensatory secondary control. In addition, we expected that young adults would exhibit information-processing biases favoring positive aspects of partnerships. Older "midlifers," in contrast, would be more inclined to process information bearing negatively on partnerships.

With regard to developmental goals, separated late-midlifers reported the most social goals that were unrelated to partnerships, while recently committed late-midlifers reported the fewest goals of this kind. This pattern of separated late-midlifers being oriented away from partnerships and committed late-midlifers being focused on their recently acquired partnership was repeated in the distribution of gain- versus loss-oriented partnership goals. Gain-oriented partnership goals are those goals that are directed at improving an existing partnership or acquiring a new one. Partnership goals directed at the avoidance of loss are those focusing on preventing deterioration of or loss of an existing partnership. Figure 5 shows the mean number of gain- and loss-oriented partnership goals in the four groups of subjects. Gain-oriented goals predominate among young adults, irrespective of their committed or separated partnership status. By contrast, recently committed late-midlifers focus on avoiding losses more than on achieving improvements. They appear to defensively cherish the recently acquired partnership "against the odds" of an untoward social ecology.

In the service of parsimoniousness, I will focus on the contrast between young and late-midlife separated adults and leave out the findings pertaining to those study participants who were recently committed. As can be seen in Figure 6, young separated adults were more invested in selective primary control, selective secondary control, and compensatory primary control when compared to the late-midlifers. With regard to compensatory secondary con-

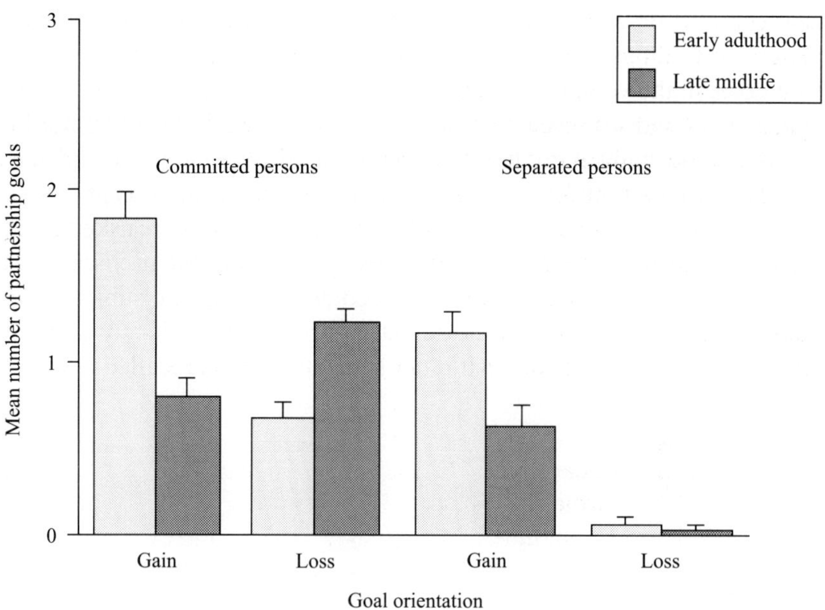

Figure 5. Developmental deadline "partnership": Gain-oriented and loss-avoiding partnership goals in recently committed and separated young and late-midlife adults (adapted from Wrosch & Heckhausen, 1999).

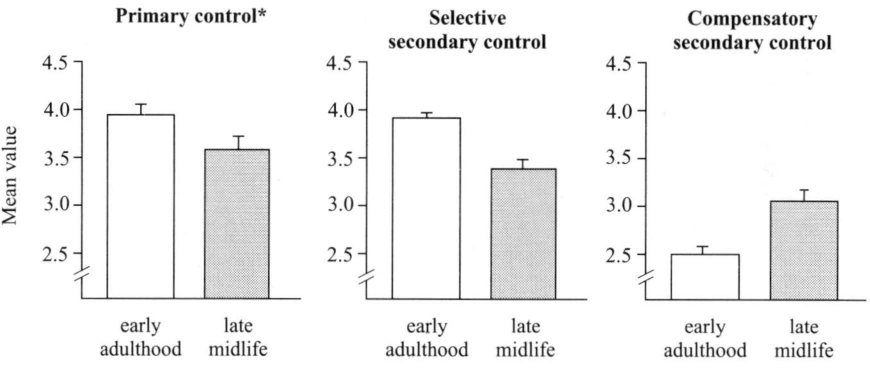

* Aggregate of selective primary control and compensatory primary control.

Figure 6. Developmental deadline "partnership": Control strategies for partnership rated by pre- and post-deadline separated adults (adapted from Wrosch & Heckhausen, 1999) .

trol, late-midlife adults expressed higher preferences than young adults. This pattern of findings represents a more pronounced engagement with partnership goals in the young compared to the late-midlife group, whereas goal disengagement and self-protection was more prominent in the older midlifers.

As in the study about the deadline for child-bearing, we included a measure of non-intentional, preconscious, goal-related information processing, by using an incidental memory test. In this study, subjects were asked to rate adjectives as to the extent they think most people find them characteristic of partnerships. After a ten-minute intermediary activity, the subjects were requested to recall as many of the adjectives they had previously rated as possible. The findings indicate that older separated adults recalled a higher pro-

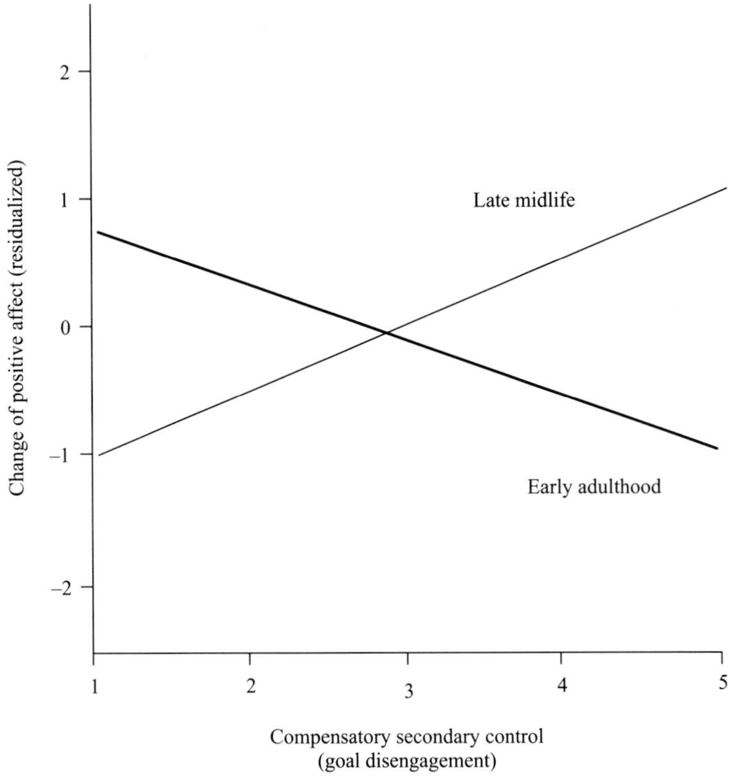

Figure 7. Developmental deadline "partnership": Disengagement from partnership goals in young and older separated adults; predicting change in positive affect (adapted from Wrosch & Heckhausen, 1999).

portion of negative relative to positive adjectives compared to young separated adults. Thus, late-midlife adults after a separation focus more on negative aspects of partnerships than do younger adults.

Again, we asked the question whether interindividual differences in the extent to which goal engagement and disengagement were phase-congruent were associated with psychological well-being. In this study, a longitudinal assessment was employed. Fifteen months after the first assessment subjects were contacted again, among other aspects their positive affect was assessed. Figure 7 displays regression lines pertaining to the relationship between compensatory secondary control and the change in positive affect across the 15-month period, separately for the young separated adults and the late-midlife separated adults. As can be seen in the regression line with the downward slope, young separated adults experienced less favorable change in positive affect the more they used compensatory secondary control. In contrast, late-midlifers profited from compensatory secondary control by enjoying an increase in positive affect over the 15-month period. Thus, phase-congruent goal disengagement and self-protection as captured by compensatory secondary control is beneficial, whereas phase-incongruent goal disengagement was detrimental.

Future Research on Regulation Processes Around Developmental Transitions in Primary Control Potential

The studies discussed in this chapter addressed developmental regulation by comparing different age-groups holding contrasting degrees of control potential with regard to a particular developmental goal (e.g., partnership, childbearing). Such a cross-sequential paradigm involves important problems and limitations with regard to its interpretability and generalizability. Such limitations can be overcome by employing longitudinal designs to study individuals' developmental regulation "in action" as they encounter changes in opportunities to reach certain goals that are important to them. Longitudinal designs avoid the problem of confounded age and target effects, because the same individuals are tracked across age. Moreover, longitudinal methods allow us to track changes in the control- and goal-striving behavior as they unfold across time, and to link sequentially such shifts with changes in the opportunities to attain the goal in question. Finally, longitudinal studies might allow us to identify the processes that lead the individual to construct a certain point in time as the critical deadline.

Specifically, my colleagues and I are pursuing three lines of investigation by employing a longitudinal paradigm to study phenomena related to developmental deadlines: First, a micro-sequential longitudinal study of developmental regulation in German secondary school/junior high school (*Realschule*) students coming up to school graduation and applying for vocational training positions (apprenticeships) (Heckhausen, 1999b). This transition used to be highly normatively regulated. Everybody got an apprenticeship. However, the long-standing economic crisis has rendered this transition a risky passage, with each individual's ability to self-regulate being challenged.

Second, illness and disability can be temporary, reversible, and thus controllable or it can be chronic, irreversible, and uncontrollable. In a prospective health study with elderly caregivers we investigate older adults' control behavior with regard to health problems of the acute controllable kind versus those that are chronic and uncontrollable (Schulz, Wrosch, Yee, & Heckhausen, 1999). Such research can answer several questions: What are adaptive patterns of dealing with illnesses that differ in degree of controllability? How and when do patients decide when the line is crossed to a chronic, uncontrollable illness? How are primary control strivings preserved in disease-ridden elderly? Under which conditions does the system of primary and secondary control fail?

Third, sensory disability may be one of the most severe infringements on primary control potential. One way to study it on-line is to prospectively investigate the control behavior of adults who experience macula degeneration (Horowitz et al., 1998). During early stages of this disease, sensory disability levels are low, and the patient hopes to be spared from more severe disability. However, in most cases this disease leads to complete loss of vision, thus forcing the patient to adapt to a severe loss of primary control potential. How patients make this adaptation, and manage to switch goal engagement to optimizing everyday functioning under the conditions of vision loss, is a fascinating topic of research.

Conclusion

The individual is an active coproducer of his or her own development. Individual efforts to regulate development are organized into action cycles of goal engagement and disengagement. These phases of engagement and disengagement should in the adaptive case follow the age-graded structure of waxing and waning opportunities to achieve developmental goals. Goal engagement and disengagement comprise a set of specific primary and secondary control strategies. Primary control processes are directed at the external world, whereas secondary control processes are directed at the internal world of the individual and serve to focus motivational resources on a chosen goal or to protect motivational resources after a failure or loss.

An action-phase model of developmental regulation was formulated that specifies which control processes should be activated in which phase of action and in response to plentiful versus diminished opportunities. Critical transitions in such action cycles are developmental deadlines, which demarcate the boundary between favorable and unfavorable opportunities for a given developmental goal. Two cross-sectional studies were discussed that provide evidence for the model of adaptive developmental regulation across deadline transitions. Moreover, control behavior conceptualized as phase-congruent by the model was found to be beneficial to psychological well-being and mental health, whereas phase-incongruent control behavior proved to be detrimental.

Future research should employ longitudinal and micro-sequential designs to study action cycles of control behavior in vivo as it is adapted to changes in opportunities to attain important life goals. Such research bears much potential to reveal the adaptive mechanisms of the human control system and thus to uncover its potentials as well as its limits and risks.

References

Baltes, P. B., & Baltes, M. M. (1980). Plasticity and variability in psychological aging: Methodological and theoretical issues. In G. Gurski (Ed.), *Determining the effects of aging on the central nervous system* (pp. 41–60). Berlin, Germany: Schering.

Brandtstädter, J., & Lerner, R. M. (Eds.). (1999). *Action and self-development: Theory and research through the life span.* London: Sage.

Braun, W., & Proebsting, H. (1986). Heiratstafeln verwitweter Deutscher 1979/82 und geschiedener Deutscher 1980/83 [Marriage tables of widowed, 1979/82, and divorced, 1980/83, Germans]. *Wirtschaft und Statistik,* 107–112.

Diener, E. (1999). Introduction to the special section on the structure of emotion. *Journal of Personality and Social Psychology, 76,* 803–804.

Frijda, N. H. (1988). The laws of emotion. *American Psychologist, 43,* 349–358.

Gollwitzer, P. M., Heckhausen, H., & Steller, B. (1990). Deliberative and implemental mindsets: Cognitive tuning toward congruous thoughts and information. *Journal of Personality and Social Psychology, 59,* 1119–1127.

Heckhausen, H. (1991). *Motivation and action.* New York: Springer.

Heckhausen, H., & Gollwitzer, P. M. (1987). Thought contents and cognitive functioning in motivational and volitional states of mind. *Motivation and Emotion, 11,* 101–120.

Heckhausen, J. (1999a). Entwicklungsregulation beim Übergang von der schulischen in die berufliche Ausbildung oder gymnasiale Oberstufe: Anforderungsabhängige Veränderungen im primären und sekundären Kontrollstreben [Developmental regulation during the transition from school to vocational training: Changes in primary and secondary control striving as a function of regulatory challenges]. Grant proposal to the German Research Foundation (No. He3068/3-1). Berlin, Germany: Max Planck Institute for Human Development.

Heckhausen, J. (1999b). *Developmental regulation in adulthood: Age-normative and socio-structural constraints as adaptive challenges.* New York: Cambridge University Press.

Heckhausen, J., & Schulz, R. (1995). A life-span theory of control. *Psychological Review, 102,* 284–304.

Heckhausen, J., & Schulz, R. (1999a). Biological and societal canalizations and individuals' developmental goals. In J. Brandtstädter & R. M. Lerner (Eds.), *Action and self-development: Theory and research through the life span* (pp. 67–103). London: Sage.

Heckhausen, J., & Schulz, R. (1999b). The primacy of primary control is a human universal: A reply to Gould's critique of the life-span theory of control. *Psychological Review, 106,* 605–609.

Heckhausen, J., Schulz, R., & Wrosch, C. (1997). *Optimization in primary and secondary control scales (OPS-scales).* Berlin, Germany: Max Planck Institute for Human Development.

Heckhausen, J., Wrosch, C., & Fleeson, W. (1999). *Developmental regulation before and after a developmental deadline: The sample case of "biological clock" for childbearing.* Manuscript under review.

Horowitz, A., Brennan, M., Reinhardt, J. P., Leonard, R., Benn, D., & Cimarolli, V. (1998). *In their own words: Strategies developed by visually impaired elders to cope with the emotional and functional consequences of vision loss.* New York: The Arlene R. Gordon Research Institute.

Lerner, R. M., & Busch-Rossnagel, N. A. (Eds.). (1981). *Individuals as producers of their development: A life-span perspective.* New York: Academic Press.

Nurmi, J.-E. (1992). Age differences in adult life goals, concerns, and their temporal extension: A life course approach to future-oriented motivation. *International Journal of Behavioral Development, 15,* 487–508.

Nurmi, J.-E., Pulliainen, H., & Salmela-Aro, K. (1992). Age differences in adults' control beliefs related to life goals and concerns. *Psychology and Aging, 7,* 194–196.

Ryff, C. D., & Keyes, C. L. M. (1995). The structure of psychological well-being revisited. *Journal of Personality and Social Psychology, 69,* 719–727.

Schulz, R., & Heckhausen, J. (1996). A life-span model of successful aging. *American Psychologist, 51,* 702–714.

Schulz, R., Wrosch, C., Yee, J. L., & Heckhausen, J. (1999). *Control strategies moderate the relations between physical illness and depression.* Manuscript under review.

Wrosch, C. (1999). *Entwicklungsfristen im Partnerschaftsbereich: Bezugsrahmen für Prozesse der Aktivierung und Deaktivierung von Entwicklungszielen* [Developmental deadlines in the partnership domain: Reference frame for activation and deactivation of developmental goals]. Münster, Germany: Waxmann.

Wrosch, C., & Heckhausen, J. (1999). Control processes before and after passing a developmental deadline: Activation and deactivation of intimate relationship goals. *Journal of Personality and Social Psychology, 77,* 415–427.

Wrosch, C., & Heckhausen, J. (in press). Being on-time or off-time: Developmental deadlines for regulating one's own development. In A. N. Perret-Clermont, J. M. Barrelet, A. Flammer, D. Miéville, J. F. Perret, & W. Perrig (Eds.), *Mind and time.* Göttingen, Germany: Hogrefe & Huber.

11 The Interplay of Work and Family in Young and Middle Adulthood

Bettina S. Wiese and Alexandra M. Freund

The centrality of the domains of work and family for the conduct and meaning of life has long been acknowledged in psychology (cf. Smelser & Erikson, 1980). The major developmental tasks of young and middle adulthood are embedded in the domains of work and family (e.g., Havighurst, 1972; Heckhausen, 1999; Settersten, 1997). Moreover, in the traditional perspective of motivational psychology, the themes of work and family are reflected in research on latent needs and motives (e.g., McAdams, 1985; McClelland,1985), including achievement, power, and affiliation/intimacy. These motivational systems are not bound to a specific domain of functioning, however, the achievement motive is typically associated with personal interest in the professional domain, whereas the need for intimacy is related to being invested in the private sector (cf. Emmons & King, 1989).

Although both domains, work and family, appear to be central for adults' development, there is considerable evidence of potential conflicts between these domains. In the first section of this chapter, we will briefly introduce models of and empirical results on work-family conflict. With reference to the model of selection, optimization, and compensation (SOC; Baltes & Carstensen, 1996; Baltes & Baltes, 1990; Freund & Baltes, in press; Marsiske, Lang, Baltes, & Baltes, 1995), we will then address general strategies of life management that could be useful for the private as well as for the work domain. Finally, we focus on one specific facet of selection: setting priorities in personal life investment. Linking the idea of setting priorities to the work and partnership domains, we propose a concept of goal structures that combines current and prospective engagement in these developmental contexts.

Work and Partnership as Potentially Conflicting Domains of Life Management

The coordination of private and professional life is a challenging task of adulthood that has reached an even higher level of complexity as more and more women have joined the work force. The current discussion of egalitarian gender roles cannot hide that there are pronounced structural conflicts between the domains of work and family (cf. Beck-Gernsheim, 1992). Measures taken by governments or private organizations to enhance the compatibility between work and family (e.g., flexible work schedules, part-time positions), however, need careful evaluation (Starrels, 1992). Workers with part-time jobs, for instance, are able to contribute to the family income (which, of course, often is an economic necessity) and take responsibility for the household at the same time. Yet in the area of establishing themselves professionally, part-time workers might easily fall behind because reaching leading positions is still associated with a career path of continuous full-time employment. Not surprisingly, therefore, Thompson, Beauvais, and Lyness (1999) showed that the perception of a supportive work-family culture in an organization is a central predictor for employees' use of work-family benefits.

With this background of structural incompatibilities as well as possible incompatibilities of motivational strivings (e.g., intimacy vs. power motivation; Zeldow, Daugherty, & McAdams, 1988), it is not surprising that many people perceive difficulties in coordinating their work and family life (e.g., Adams, King, & King, 1996). In psychological models of work-family conflict, domain-specific involvement as well as domain-specific stressors are seen as central conflict predictors (e.g., Frone, Russell, & Cooper, 1992a). Greenhaus and Beutell (1985) distinguish three role-pressure constellations leading to work-family conflict by separating (a) *time-based conflicts,* where the time invested in one role makes it difficult to fulfill the other, (b) *strain-based conflicts* that stem from stress in one domain (e.g., problems with superiors, difficulties in the partnership) interfering with the fulfillment of requirements in the other domain, and (c) *behavior-based conflicts* due to the incompatibility of behavioral modes in the two domains (see Figure 1). Whereas there are only few studies that investigate behavior-based conflicts (e.g., Carlson, 1999), several studies give evidence supporting the predictive role of involvement and stressors in the work and partnership domains for experiencing work-family conflicts (e.g., Frone et al., 1992a; Gutek, Searle, & Klepa, 1991; Loerch, Russell, & Rush, 1989; Voydanoff, 1988).

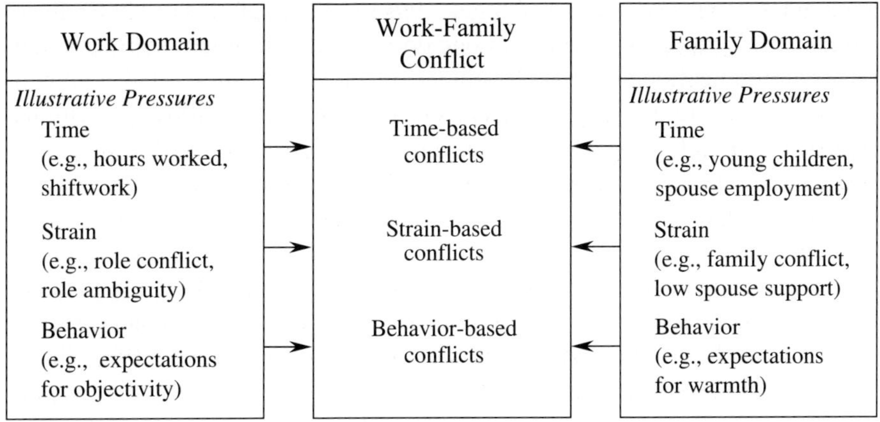

Figure 1. Role-pressure constellations leading to work-family conflict (after Greenhaus & Beutell, 1985).

In addition, a number of studies demonstrate that the reciprocal influences of the domains of work and family have significant effects on various indicators of well-being and psychological functioning (for a review see Kossek & Ozeki, 1998). There is clear evidence that interferences between work and family domains have a negative association with general and domain-specific well-being (e.g., Adams et al., 1996; Netemeyer, Boles, & McMurrian, 1996).

Greenhaus (1988) points to the differentiation between objective and subjective conflicts. A person with long working hours objectively interfering with the family role (e.g., by not being at home for a family dinner), for instance, might subjectively not experience any conflict. This might especially be the case when one evaluates the family domain as less important than the work domain. Hence, the relative importance and salience of specific life domains might moderate the relationship between personal investment and subjective conflicts. This implies that in a situation where high conflicts are expected, setting priorities might help reduce interferences.

Although our focus is on conflictive relations between the work and family domains, note that there is also evidence pointing to *supportive links* (Evans & Bartolome, 1984; Lambert, 1990). A fulfilling family life might have positive effects on the career (cf. Gattiker & Larwood, 1990), and a satisfying and stimulating work situation is known to be positively related to contentment at home (Williams & Alliger, 1994). Positive effects might be due to a transfer of strategies acquired in one domain (e.g., problem-solving strategies, communication style) to the other domain (cf. Crouter, 1984; Lambert, 1990). The differentiation between positive and negative spillover is reminiscent of the sociological positions on multiple roles formulated in the 1960s and 1970s: One hypothesis stated that a high number of roles increases the probability of strain, and therefore decreases well-being (e.g., Goode, 1960). The other position stated that having multiple roles implies being part of different environments each offering resources and stimulation for personal growth (e.g., Sieber, 1974). Empirical research provided evidence for the former as well as for the latter position (e.g., Baruch & Barnett, 1986; Thoits, 1983). Finally, social psychologists, such as Linville (1987), argued that multiple self-defining roles provide a positive effect only in the case of negative events by serving as a buffer for a threatened self (see also Freund, 1995).

Most studies we have cited so far comprise participants with children as well as those without. Carlson (1999) reported that the presence of children in the household is related to time-based, strain-based, and behavior-based work-family conflicts (cf. also Voydanoff, 1988). Especially the presence of young children may create conflicts for working parents (e.g., Greenhaus & Kopelman, 1981). However, Beutell and O'Hare (1987) as well as Bedeian, Burke, and Moffett (1988) did not find a significant relationship between the number of children and the degree of conflicts between work and family domain. The birth of a child might put specific strains on a relationship, and, at least for couples where both partners work outside the home, necessitates satisfying child-care arrangements to minimize work-family conflicts. This does not, however, imply that interferences between the work and private domains occur exclusively in families with children.

Moreover, with regard to life planning in the private and professional domains, not only actual but also anticipated interference might be important. In a study with about 200 employed, so-far-childless adults between the ages of 25 and 36 years, we asked participants to indicate how much the pursuit of their professional goals hinders or promotes goal pursuit in the partnership domain and vice versa (Wiese, in press; Wiese & Freund, in press). Most participants indicated a rather conflicting instead of supporting relationship between their work-related and family-related goals. In addition, the degree of subjectively experienced goal conflict was more pronounced for women. We interpret this finding as indicating that women experience a heavier burden fulfilling both career- and family-related expectations, because they typically have to accomplish more of the household chores and are at the same time under pressure to perform (at least) as well as men in the work domain in order to promote their careers. Our finding of a gender difference in subjective work-family conflicts converges with the results of Frone, Russell, and Cooper (1992b) and Gutek et al. (1991). Other studies, however, could not identify gender differences in the degree of work-family conflicts (e.g., Bedeian et al., 1988). The mixed result pattern might reflect the continuous change in role dynamics in modern society where traditional as well as more egalitarian forms of labor division can be found (cf. Huinink, 1995).

With regard to work-related and partnership-related well-being, we obtained remarkably distinct results (cf. Wiese, in press): Whereas conflicts between work-related and family-related goals were not associated with subjective well-being in the work domain, there were significant negative associations between these conflicts and subjective well-being in the partnership domain. Participants reporting higher degrees of conflict were less satisfied with their partnership, felt emotionally less balanced in this life domain, and rated their development in the partnership domain as less successful than did participants with lower conflict scores. It might be that for a sample of so-far-childless younger adults it is easier to block intrusive thoughts about the partnership while working than to block thoughts about working while with their partners. There is as yet no empirical evidence addressing the question of whether this relationship persists throughout other stages of family and career development.

From a lifespan perspective, one might also wonder whether the intensity of work-family conflicts changes from younger to middle adulthood. At first glance, it seems reasonable to assume that the highest degree of conflict is to be expected in younger adulthood where strong pressures from the work and family domains are evident, particularly if young children are in the household. Young adults have to deal with possibly conflicting demands and responsibilities during a phase of life where a high commitment in both domains is either expected or personally aspired. Greenhaus and Beutell (1985), however, point to the possibility that middle adulthood might represent a period of increasing work-family conflict. In fact, at least for males, some authors do describe mid-life as a period in which adults might question their possible preoccupation with work and try to increase family engagement despite enduringly high demands in the work domain (e.g., Bartolome & Evans, 1979; Levinson, Darrow, Klein, Levinson, & McKee, 1978). In addition, a new source of increasing demands arises when elderly parents need assistance. Not surprisingly, therefore, middle adulthood has been described as being overburdened with roles and responsibilities ("midlife squeeze"; Bengtson, Cutler, Mangen, & Marshall, 1985).

Selection, Optimization, and Compensation as Strategies of Life Management in the Work and Partnership Domains

Given the complexity of coordinating private and professional life, the question arises of how adults deal with the multiple and often conflicting demands associated with work and partnership. The SOC theory (Baltes, 1997; Baltes & Baltes, 1990; Freund & Baltes, in press; Marsiske et al., 1999) guided our search for potentially relevant strategies of life management in the domains of work and partnership. One of the basic assumptions underlying the SOC model is that individual internal and external resources (e.g., time, cognitive capacity, social support) are limited. These limitations and constraints necessitate selective processes that, in turn, provide the basis for processes of goal attainment by means of optimization and compensation.

When applying SOC to an action-theoretical framework, *selection,* the first component of the SOC theory, represents processes that are involved in the structuring and choice of goals. With reference to research in the field of personal goals, Freund and Baltes (in press) summarized a set of possibly adaptive qualitative and quantitative characteristics of goal systems. They postulate, for example, that it is adaptive to concentrate on goals that are perceived to be reachable and that converge with other goals a person wants to achieve. In the domains of work and family, there exist also age-graded opportunity structures and constraints (Freund, 1997; Heckhausen, 1999; Neugarten, Moore, & Lowe, 1965; Settersten, 1997) that might play a role in the process of goal selection (e.g., upper age limits for certain professional positions; restricted time of female fertility). Wrosch and Heckhausen (1999; Heckhausen, 1999) demonstrated that developmental deadlines may operate as anchors for initiating processes of increased or decreased efforts to reach one's goals.

In recent publications (e.g., Freund & Baltes, in press; Freund, Li, & Baltes, 1999), the conceptualization of selection is extended to include a component called "loss-based selection" denoting processes (e.g., lowering of standards) that are supposed to be adaptive whenever compensatory efforts (see below) remain fruitless or outweigh benefits. For reasons of economy, however, the present chapter concentrates on the elective part of selection.

Optimization, the second component of the SOC theory, describes the application of goal-relevant means in order to achieve desired outcomes. On a general level, the investment of time and energy in the acquisition and application of goal-relevant means (e.g., skills) are instances of optimization. The adaptiveness of time investment is convincingly demonstrated in the field of (professional) expertise or other areas where deliberate practice is relevant (e.g., Ericsson, 1996). In the partnership domain, as well, time investment is crucial (e.g., finding enough time for joint activities). Modeling successful others is another instance of optimization. With regard to lifespan development, modeling might be especially important in domains lacking formalized training. In our view, the domain of social relationships might represent such an area with little societal standardization and explicit training. Modeling successful others may also be effective in the work domain. It might, for instance, be helpful to model colleagues who have climbed up in a given professional hierarchy. As a final example for optimization, we want to mention persistence. Persistence is especially important in the case of long-term endeavors and might be strengthened by components like the ability to delay gratification (Mischel, Ebbesen, & Zeiss, 1972).

Compensation, the third component of the SOC model, denotes processes aiming at counteracting anticipated or actual loss in goal-related means. Typical instances of compensation are substituting goal-related means, using external aids (e.g., a hearing aid), or increasing one's efforts. As the probability of losses increases with age, it is not surprising to find numerous examples of compensation in the literature on aging (cf. Dixon & Bäckman, 1995). In young and middle adulthood, losses and subsequent compensatory efforts are often associated with critical life events (e.g., an accident). Losses, however, can also occur gradually. Thinking of marriage, some kind of habituation might take place that leads to decreases in meaningful and pleasurable interactions. In this case, an endeavor to motivate each other to engage in common activities could be a compensatory mean. Other examples of compensation in the partnership domain are the employment of a babysitter in order to regain the possibility of going out together, or resorting to therapeutic help when partnership problems cannot be solved alone. For the work domain, delegating tasks when growing affordances do not leave enough time for them may be viewed as a compensatory strategy. Note, however, that these examples only serve to illustrate what *might* be an adequate behavior. Whether such a behavior would really be adaptive in a specific case, however, needs careful evaluation of the given external and personal situations. To summarize, we believe that (1) selecting from a pool of alternative developmental projects (selection), (2) allocating resources as means of achieving one's goals (optimization), and (3) applying means in order to counteract actual or impending losses (compensation) are key factors for the successful mastery of lifespan demands in different domains of functioning, including the family and professional domains.

There is growing evidence for the predictive utility of SOC as self-reported strategies of life management. Freund and Baltes (1998) examined the usefulness of SOC in a sample of older adults (between 73 and 103 years old). Self-reported SOC behaviors were positively related to several subjective indicators of successful aging (e.g., life satisfaction). In that study age was found to be negatively related to SOC. In another study conducted by Freund and Baltes (1999) comprising participants aged between 14 and 87 years, however, neither optimization nor compensation showed significant relations to age. In contrast to the former study, selection even turned out to be positively related to chronological age. Freund and Baltes (1999) argue that the negative age trajectory of SOC in the sample of old adults might be due to the fact that the implementation of SOC requires resources that themselves decrease in very old age. The positive association between age and selection in younger years, on the other hand, possibly reflects an increasing insight into the limitations of one's developmental potential and resources.

Another example of the usefulness of SOC behaviors is research by Abraham and Hansson (1995) on how adults manage their occupational situations. They obtained a positive link between the use of SOC strategies and subjective ratings of competence maintenance and goal attainment in the work domain. Abraham and Hansson (1995) could not identify a significant link between age and the self-reported use of SOC, but they reported evidence that older employees (49–69 years) profited more from SOC behaviors than did younger employees (40–48 years).

In the study of life management of younger adults mentioned above, we used a work-specific as well as a partnership-specific form of the SOC questionnaire developed by Baltes, Baltes, Freund, and Lang (1999). On a correlational level, our results demonstrated positive relationships between the self-reported use of SOC-related behaviors and the indicators of domain-specific successful life management considered (e.g., work satisfaction, satisfaction with partnership; Wiese, Freund, & Baltes, in press). The positive associations between SOC and subjective indicators of successful life management were quite robust when controlling for other personality (e.g., control beliefs) as well as sociodemographic variables (e.g., education). The associations with domain-specific well-being, however, were not equally strong for all three SOC components. They were mainly due to optimization and compensation, whereas selection turned out to be of lesser importance.

Note that we found pronounced gender differences in SOC behaviors. Women reported using SOC strategies more often than men. As these differences were primarily manifest in the process of compensation, one might speculate whether women are more strongly socialized to deal with losses or to allow and even recruit other people's help. Therefore, it might be easier for women to anticipate and cope constructively with setbacks in different life domains. Our findings converge with results from Wrosch and Heckhausen (1999), who reported that women more often seek social support, advice, and alternative ways to reach their partnership goals than men. One should not, however, conclude that women are more effective in using compensatory means. Comparing women and men, we could not identify differential correlational patterns between the use of compensation and subjective well-being.

In accordance with the assumption that young adults who have just acquired a university degree might be more invested in the occupational domain than nonacademics of the same age, young academics reported a significantly higher number of work-related goals. They did not, however, show more use of self-reported SOC strategies. So far, we do not have enough insight into the role socialization plays for the acquisition of SOC-related knowledge to interpret this finding. Compared to nonacademics, however, young academics more frequently report having a high investment in the work domain but plan to increase their investment in the family domain in the future (see below). This finding indicates that the prolonged duration of career consolidation for academics has to be taken into account when investigating life management in this group.

Setting Priorities in Personal Life Investment as one Facet of Selection in the Face of Competing Demands in the Work and Family Domains

Asking participants to indicate directly their tendency toward specific behavioral modes is only one way to conceptualize and operationalize SOC (Baltes & Carstensen, 1996). On a self-descriptive level, an alternative way to operationalize selection is to take the variability of life investment over a broad range of functional domains as an indicator of selection that has been shown to be positively related to well-being in younger and older age groups (cf. Staudinger, Freund, Linden, & Maas, 1999; Wiese, in press).

With regard to the work and partnership domains, Wiese (in press) recently proposed a concept of goal structure that combines current and prospective commitment in these domains. This concept takes into account that individuals not only differ in the absolute level of commitment in the work and family domains but also in the relative weight they give to these domains in the present and in the future. With this concept in mind, one can differentiate among people with a parallel goal structure who feel equally engaged in the work and family domains, both in the present and in the future, individuals who feel equally engaged in both domains in the present but plan to give priority to one domain in the future, individuals with a sequential goal structure who are currently more invested in one domain but expect to increase engagement in the other domain, and individuals with a monothematic goal structure who are currently more invested in one domain and anticipate that this will also be the case in the future (see Figure 2).

Taking into account normative expectations on developmental sequences that suggest a priority on establishing professionally before founding a family (cf. Huinink, 1995), an equal distribution of the different forms of goal structures is not to be expected. In fact, in our sample the largest proportion of participants could be classified as having a parallel goal structure (i.e., being equally engaged in both domains, both in the present and in the future; 44%), followed by participants having a sequential cluster with current priority in the work domain (25%). Only 9 percent could be classified as monothematic with focus in the professional domain. The small proportion of participants with a monothematic goal structure indicates that cutting off developmental trajectories in a phase of life where such a restriction is not necessary is not considered attractive. One might speculate that the monothematic life view gains importance after a person has passed certain developmental deadlines (e.g., time for having a child for women in mid-life; Heckhausen, 1999). The

		Current Engagement		
		Work > Family	Work = Family	Work < Family
Future Engagement	Work > Family	monothematic (work-oriented)	parallel-sequential (future focus: work)	sequential (current focus: family)
	Work = Family	sequential (current focus: work)	parallel	sequential (current focus: family)
	Work < Family	sequential (current focus: work)	parallel-sequential (future focus: family)	monothematic (family-oriented)

Figure 2. Current and prospective engagement in the work and family domains.

high proportion of young adults having a parallel goal structure, on the other hand, might reflect that an equal engagement in the work and family domains is considered as an ideal in younger cohorts (cf. Spieß, Kaschube, Nerdinger, & von Rosenstiel, 1992).

Comparing the three main groups identified (i.e., parallel, sequential with current focus in the work domain, monothematic with focus in the work domain), personality variables turned out to be of minor importance when used as predictors of goal structuring. Note, however, that in the parallel group work-family conflicts were significantly rarer than in the other groups. The predictive power of the sociodemographic variables (i.e., gender, education) was clearly supported: Compared to men, women were more likely to be classified as having a sequential goal structure with current focus in the work domain but plans for becoming more engaged in the family domain. College graduates belonged more often to the groups with work-focused goal structure than did participants without a college degree. These differences might be explained by sociostructurally based developmental conditions, as for example, the duration of career consolidation and an anticipated traditional labor division between the genders after the birth of a child (e.g., Cowan et al., 1985). A sequential model seems to be part of the normative gender-role life script for women (e.g., Herzog, Bachman, & Johnston, 1983). In fact, surveys on females' work participation in Germany reflect such a model: The professional biography of women is typically divided into a phase of full-time employment before motherhood and a phase without or with part-time employment after the birth of a child (cf. Buba & Schneider, 1996).

With regard to subjective indicators of successful development, participants with a work-oriented goal structure showed higher levels of general as well as work-related well-being than those with a parallel goal structure. These results support the selection assumption of the SOC model that suggests that it is adaptive to set priorities. Concerning the family domain, however, participants in committed relationships who reported prioritizing the work domain felt less successful than individuals with a parallel goal structure. Although participants with an investment focus in the professional domain were not less likely to report having a stable partnership than participants with a parallel structure, they were less satisfied with their development in the present partnership (cf. von Rosenstiel, 1997). Controlling for the absolute level of partnership commitment, however, significantly reduced the association between goal structure and subjective developmental success in the partnership domain, indicating that for ensuring personal growth in the partnership the absolute level of personal investment in this life domain is crucial.

Some Future Research Perspectives

Most studies on work-family conflict and on strategies of life management in the work and partnership domains are restricted to *subjective indicators of functioning*. Future research should pay more attention to *objective indicators* (Baltes & Carstensen, 1996). This seems to be especially important in the work domain where only modest, sometimes even negligible associations between measures of well-being and objective functioning have been found (e.g., Iaffaldano & Muchinsky, 1985). Another limitation of the majority of studies is their cross-sectional design. *Longitudinal studies* would not only allow us to test causal directions, but also to estimate whether variables conceptualized as outcome criteria also play a role as antecedents. Work-related discontent, for instance, could be a starting point for attempts to change one's occupational situation.

From a lifespan perspective, one should differentiate *short-term and long-term effects*. Setting priorities in the work domain, for example, might be highly adaptive for one's career, but an excessive engagement in this domain might have increasingly negative effects for one's private life and health (cf. von Rosenstiel, 1997). But even after reaching one's goals, one might not experience durable feelings of success (cf. McIntosh & Martin, 1992). Some authors even discuss the possibility that the costs of success might outweigh its gains (e.g., Brim, 1992).

Another question is whether individuals are able to give their lives the expected *gestalt*. For instance, do individuals with a sequential goal structure currently focusing on the work domain succeed in being equally engaged in both domains in the future? This is not self-evident. Imagine a sequential person who finally reached the influential managerial position to which he or she aspired. It is well known that leading positions require immense time investments and leave little time for other interests. In addition, changes in the occupational or partnership context might lead to a change in one's goal system and/or in the use of SOC behaviors. In young adulthood the transition into parenthood increases demands in the family domain that necessitate the development of strategies (e.g., time management) that ensure adequate attention to all tasks involved. In mid-life, the departure of the youngest child might require redefining the roles of parents and children.

The last examples also raise another topic, namely, *collective processes of life management*. Daily problem solving and life management are embedded in social contexts (Baltes & Carstensen, 1998; Berg, Meegan, & Deviney, 1998), therefore, it is worthwhile analyzing life management in social units (e.g., couples, families, work groups). Brunstein, Dangelmeyer, and Schultheiß (1996), for instance, report that goal support is related to partnership satisfaction in cases where one accurately knows about the partner's goals. Brandtstädter, Baltes-Götz, and Heil (1990) showed that a high consensus on each other's goals as well as high similarity of goals and values are associated with marital satisfaction. The positive relation, however, did not hold true for all goals. The relation turned out to be even negative when both partners valued professional ambitions rather high. One might speculate that for marital quality, the compatibility rather than the similarity of goals is crucial. From a lifespan perspective, one might ask how the compatibilities of professional and private goals unfold over adulthood as developmental interests and opportunities undergo remarkable changes both for the individual and for social groups.

To conclude, the interplay of work and family is a promising research field for applied scholars as well as for those interested in motivational and behavioral development in adulthood. The simultaneous investigation of current commitments and future projects in the domains of work and family not only takes into account the high salience both domains have in adulthood, it also allows us to discover the interwoven dynamic of developmental pathways associated with these central domains of functioning.

References

Abraham, J. D., & Hansson, R. O. (1995). Successful aging at work: An applied study of selection, optimization, and compensation through impression management. *Journal of Gerontology, 50,* 94–103.

Adams, G. A., King, L. A., & King, D. W. (1996). Relationships of job and family involvement, family social support, and work-family conflict with job and life satisfaction. *Journal of Applied Psychology, 81,* 411–420.

Baltes, M. M., & Carstensen, L. L. (1996). The process of successful ageing. *Ageing and Society, 16,* 397–422.

Baltes, M. M., & Carstensen, L. L. (1998). Social psychological theories and their application to aging: From individual to collective selective optimization with compensation. In V. L. Bengtson & K. W. Schaie (Eds.), *Handbook of theories of aging* (pp. 209–226). New York: Springer.

Baltes, P. B. (1997). On the incomplete architecture of human ontogeny: Selection, optimization, and compensation as foundation of developmental theory. *American Psychologist, 52,* 366–380.

Baltes, P. B., & Baltes, M. M. (1990). Psychological perspectives on successful aging: The model of selective optimization with compensation. In P. B. Baltes & M. M. Baltes (Eds.),

Successful aging: Perspectives from the behavioral sciences (pp. 1–34). Cambridge, UK: Cambridge University Press.

Baltes, P. B., Baltes, M. M., Freund, A. M., & Lang, F. R. (1999). *The measure of selection, optimization, and compensation (SOC) by self-report: Technical Report 1999.* Berlin, Germany: Max Planck Institute for Human Development.

Bartolome, F., & Evans, P. A. L. (1979). Professional lives versus private lives—Shifting patterns of managerial commitment. *Organizational Dynamics, 7,* 3–29.

Baruch, G. K., & Barnett, R. (1986). Role quality, multiple role involvement, and psychological well-being in midlife women. *Journal of Personality and Social Psychology, 51,* 578–585.

Beck-Gernsheim, E. (1992). Anspruch und Wirklichkeit—Zum Wandel der Geschlechterrollen in der Familie [Claim and reality—Changing sex roles in the family]. In K. A. Schneewind & L. von Rosenstiel (Eds.), *Wandel der Familie* [The changing picture of family] (pp. 37–47). Göttingen, Germany: Hogrefe.

Bedeian, A. G., Burke, B. G., & Moffett, R. G. (1988). Outcomes of work-family conflict among married male and female professionals. *Journal of Management, 14,* 475–491.

Bengston, V. L., Cutler, N. E., Mangen, D. J., & Marshall, V. W. (1985). Generations and intergenerational relations. In R. Binstock & E. Shanas (Eds.), *Handbook of aging and the social sciences* (2nd ed., pp. 304–338). New York: Van Nostrand Reinhold.

Berg, C. A., Meegan, S. P., & Deviney, F. P. (1998). A social-contextual model of coping with everyday problems across the life-span. *International Journal of Behavioral Development, 22,* 239–261.

Beutell, N. J., & O'Hare, M. M. (1987). Work-nonwork conflicts among MBAs: Sex differences in role stressors and life satisfaction. *Work and Stress, 1,* 35–41.

Brandtstädter, J., Baltes-Götz, B., & Heil, F. E. (1990). Entwicklung in Partnerschaften: Analysen zur Partnerschaftsqualität bei Ehepaaren im mittleren Erwachsenenalter [Development in partnerships: Analyses of partnership quality of married couples in middle adulthood]. *Zeitschrift für Entwicklungspsychologie und Pädagogische Psychologie, 22,* 183–206.

Brim, O. G. (1992). *Ambition: How we manage success and failure throughout our lives.* New York: Basic Books.

Brunstein, J. C., Dangelmeyer, G., & Schultheiß, O. C. (1996). Personal goals and social support in close relationships: Effects on relationship mood and marital satisfaction. *Journal of Personality and Social Psychology, 71,* 1006–1019.

Buba, H. P., & Schneider, N. F. (Eds.). (1996). *Familie: Zwischen gesellschaftlicher Prägung und individuellem Design* [Family: Between societal shaping and individual design]. Opladen, Germany: Westdeutscher Verlag.

Carlson, D. S. (1999). Personality and role variables as predictors of three forms of work-family conflict. *Journal of Vocational Behavior, 55,* 236–253.

Cowan, C. P., Cowan, P., Heming, G., Garrett, E., Coysh, W. S., Curtis-Boles, H., & Boles, A. J. (1985). Transitions to parenthood. His, hers, and theirs. *Journal of Family Issues, 6,* 451–481.

Crouter, A. C. (1984). Participative work as an influence on human development. *Journal of Applied Developmental Psychology, 5,* 71–90.

Dixon, R. A., & Bäckman, L. (Eds.). (1995). *Psychological compensation: Managing losses and promoting gains.* Hillsdale, NJ: Erlbaum.

Emmons, R. A., & King, L. A. (1989). On the personalization of motivation. In R. S. Wyer & T. S. Srull (Eds.), *Advances in social cognition: Vol. II. Social intelligence and cognitive assessments of personality* (pp. 111–122). Hillsdale, NJ: Erlbaum.

Ericsson, K. A. (1996). *The road to excellence: The acquisition of expert performance in the arts and sciences, sports, and games.* Mahwah, NJ: Erlbaum.

Evans, P., & Bartolome, F. (1984). The changing picture of the relationship between career and the family. *Journal of Occupational Behavior, 5,* 9–21.

Freund, A. M. (1995). *Wer bin ich? Die Selbstdefinition alter Menschen* [Who am I? Self-definition in old age]. Berlin, Germany: Sigma.

Freund, A. M. (1997). Individuating age-salience: A psychological perspective on the salience of age in the life course. *Human Development, 40,* 287–292.

Freund, A. M., & Baltes, P. B. (1998). Selection, optimization, and compensation as strategies of life management: Correlations with subjective indicators of successful aging. *Psychology and Aging, 13,* 531–543.

Freund, A. M., & Baltes, P. B. (1999). *Assessing selection, optimization, and compensation: A questionnaire approach.* Unpublished manuscript, Max Planck Institute for Human Development, Berlin, Germany.

Freund, A. M., & Baltes, P. B. (in press). Selection, optimization, and compensation: An action-theoretical conceptualization of processes of developmental regulation. In W. J. Perrig & A. Grob (Eds.), *Control of human behaviour: Mental processes and consciousness.* Mahwah, NJ: Erlbaum.

Freund, A. M., Li, K. Z. H., & Baltes, P. B. (1999). The role of selection, optimization, and compensation in successful aging. In J. Brandtstädter & R. M. Lerner (Eds.), *Action and development: Origins and functions of intentional self-development* (pp. 401–434). Thousand Oaks, CA: Sage.

Frone, M. R., Russell, M., & Cooper, M. L. (1992a). Antecedents and outcomes of work-family conflict: Testing a model of the work-family interface. *Journal of Applied Psychology, 77,* 65–78.

Frone, M. R., Russell, M., & Cooper, M. L. (1992b). Prevalence of work-family conflict: Are work and family boundaries asymmetrically permeable? *Journal of Organizational Behavior, 13,* 723–729.

Gattiker, U. E., & Larwood, L. (1990). Predictors of career achievement in the corporate hierarchy. *Human Relations, 43,* 703–726.

Goode, W. (1960). A theory of role strain. *American Sociological Review, 25,* 483–496.

Greenhaus, J. H. (1988). The intersection of work and family roles: Individual, interpersonal, and organizational issues. *Journal of Social Behavior and Personality, 3,* 23–44.

Greenhaus, J. H., & Beutell, N. J. (1985). Sources of conflict between work and family roles. *Academy of Management Review, 10,* 76–88.

Greenhaus, J. H., & Kopelman, R. E. (1981). Conflict between work and nonwork roles: Implications for the career planning process. *Human Resource Planning, 4,* 1–10.

Gutek, B. A., Searle, S., & Klepa, L. (1991). Rational versus gender role explanations for work-family conflict. *Journal of Applied Psychology, 76,* 560–568.

Havighurst, R. J. (1972). *Developmental tasks and education* (3rd ed.). New York: Davis McKay.

Heckhausen, J. (1999). *Developmental regulation in adulthood: Age-normative and socio-structural constraints as adaptive challenges.* New York: Cambridge University Press.

Herzog, A. R., Bachman, J. G., & Johnston, L. D. (1983). Paid work, child care, and housework: A national survey of high school seniors' preference for sharing responsibilities between husband and wife. *Sex Roles, 9,* 109–135.

Huinink, J. (1995). *Warum noch Familie? Zur Attraktivität von Partnerschaft und Elternschaft in unserer Gesellschaft* [Why family? On the attractiveness of partnership and family in our society]. Frankfurt a.M., Germany: Campus.

Iaffaldano, M. T., & Muchinsky, P. M. (1985). Job satisfaction and job performance: A meta-analysis. *Psychological Bulletin, 97,* 251–273.

Kossek, E. E., & Ozeki, C. (1998). Work-family conflict, policies, and the job-life satisfaction relationship: A review and directions for organizational behavior-human resources research. *Journal of Applied Psychology, 83,* 139–149.

Lambert, S. J. (1990). Processes linking work and family: A critical review and research agenda. *Human Relations, 43,* 29–47.

Levinson, D. J., Darrow, C. N., Klein, E. B., Levinson, M. H., & McKee, B. (1978). *The seasons of man's life.* New York: Alfred A. Knopf.

Linville, P. W. (1987). Self-complexity as a cognitive buffer against stress-related illness and depression. *Journal of Personality and Social Psychology, 52,* 663–676.

Loerch, K. J., Russell, J. E., & Rush, M. C. (1989). The relationship among family domain variables and work-family conflict for men and women. *Journal of Vocational Behavior, 35,* 288–308.

Marsiske, M., Lang, F. R., Baltes, P. B., & Baltes, M. M. (1995). Selective optimization with compensation: Life-span perspectives on successful human development. In R. A. Dixon & L. Bäckman (Eds.), *Compensating for psychological deficits and declines: Managing losses and promoting gains* (pp. 35–79). Mahwah, NJ: Erlbaum.

McAdams, D. P. (1985). *Power, intimacy, and the life story.* Homewood, IL: The Dorsey Press.

McClelland, D. C. (1985). *Human motivation.* Glenview, IL: Scott, Foresman, & Company.

McIntosh, W. D., & Martin, L. L. (1992). The cybernetics of happiness: The relation of goal-attainment, rumination, and affect. *Review of Personality and Social Psychology, 490,* 222–246.

Mischel, W., Ebbesen, E. B., & Zeiss, A. R. (1972). Cognitive and attentional mechanisms in delay of gratification. *Journal of Personality and Social Psychology, 21,* 204–218.

Netemeyer, R. G., Boles, J. S., & McMurrian, R. (1996). Development and validation of work-family conflict and family-work-conflict scales. *Journal of Applied Psychology, 81,* 400–409.

Neugarten, B. L., Moore, J. W., & Lowe, J. C. (1965). Age norm, age constraints, and adult socialization. *American Journal of Sociology, 70,* 710–717.

Rosenstiel, L. von (1997). Die Karriere—ihr Licht und ihre Schatten [The professional career—its light and shadows]. In L. von Rosenstiel, T. Lang-von Wins, & E. Sigl (Eds.), *Perspektiven der Karriere* [Perspectives on career] (pp. 13–42). Stuttgart, Germany: Schaeffer-Poeschel.

Settersten, R. A., Jr. (1997). The salience of age in the life course. *Human Development, 40,* 257–280.

Sieber, S. (1974). Toward a theory of role accumulation. *American Sociological Review, 39,* 567–578.

Smelser, N. J., & Erikson, E. H. (Eds.). (1980). *Themes of work and love in adulthood.* Cambridge, MA: Harvard University Press.

Spieß, E., Kaschube, S., Nerdinger, F. W., & Rosenstiel, L. von (1992). Das Erleben von Arbeit und Freizeit nach Eintritt in den Beruf—Eine qualitative Studie bei Jungakademikern [The experience of work and leisure time after entering the job—A qualitative study with recent college graduates]. *Zeitschrift für Arbeits- und Organisationspsychologie, 36,* 77–83.

Starrels, M. E. (1992). The evolution of workplace family policy research. *Journal of Family Issues, 13,* 259–278.

Staudinger, U. M., Freund, A. M., Linden, M., & Maas, I. (1999). Self, personality, and life regulation. Facets of psychological resilience in old age. In P. B. Baltes & K. U. Mayer (Eds.), *The Berlin Aging Study: Aging from 70 to 100* (pp. 302–328). New York: Cambridge University Press.

Thoits, P. A. (1983). Multiple identities and psychological well-being: A reformulation and test of the social isolation hypothesis. *American Sociological Review, 48,* 174–187.

Thompson, C. A., Beauvais, L. L., & Lyness, K. S. (1999). When work-family benefits are not enough: The influence of work-family culture on benefit utilization, organizational attachment, and work-family conflict. *Journal of Vocational Behavior, 54,* 392–415.

Voydanoff, P. (1988). Work role characteristics, family structure demands, and work/family conflict. *Journal of Marriage and the Family, 50,* 749–761.

Wiese, B. S. (in press). *Zur Dynamik beruflicher und familiärer Zielstrukturen* [On the dynamics of goal structures in the domains of work and partnership]. Münster, Germany: Waxmann.

Wiese B. S., & Freund, A. M. (in prep.). *All at once or one after the other? Goal structures in the work and family domains.*

Wiese, B. S., Freund, A. M., & Baltes, P. B. (in press). *Selection, optimization, and compensation: An action-related approach to work and partnership.*

Williams, K. J., & Alliger, G. M. (1994). Role stressors, mood spillover, and perceptions of work-family conflict in employed parents. *Academy of Management Journal, 37,* 837–868.

Wrosch, C., & Heckhausen, J. (1999). Control processes before and after passing life-management deadline: Activation and deactivation of intimate relationship goals. *Journal of Personality and Social Psychology, 77,* 415–427.

Zeldow, P. B., Daugherty, S. R., & McAdams, D. P. (1988). Intimacy, power, and psychological health. *Journal of Nervous and Mental Disease, 176,* 172–187.

12 Are Discrepancies Between Developmental Status and Aspired Goals a Sufficient Motivation for Developmental Progression?

Inge Seiffge-Krenke

This chapter analyzes processes of developmental regulation in adolescents with a chronic illness. Given age-normative developmental deadlines (Heckhausen, 1999), this issue is important far beyond this particular age span and valid for diverse groups varying in health status. Based on longitudinal data comparing chronically ill adolescents and healthy peers as well as their families, a unique insight is offered into the capacity of afflicted adolescents to balance adaptation to illness and developmental progression. Several questions were addressed: Do chronically ill adolescents share the same developmental goals as their healthy peers? Is there any indication of a developmental delay in their attainment of age-typical developmental tasks? How does the developmental context contribute to success or failure in the attainment of developmental tasks? Particular consideration is given to the processes of self-regulation by which the adolescents themselves initiate all necessary developmental steps and sequences to reach aspired goals. The adolescents' efforts to prevent or eliminate developmental pressure (as discrepancy between developmental status and aspired goals) depend heavily on the developmental context and result in the emergence of different pathways for solving the dilemma between developmental progression and adaptation to illness.

Developmental Tasks: A "New" Perspective on Adolescent Development

Traditional theories of adolescence have been based on the idea of a crisis. Concepts such as "identity crisis," "generation gap," and "storm and stress" portray the adolescent as a deficient being. This perspective, which pervaded into the 1950s, was strongly influenced by the choice of samples in studies. Although based on highly selective samples of adolescents with clinical disorders and from families with multiple problems or in psychotherapy, the results generalized typical adolescent development. In the 1960s and 1970s, studies of large representative samples were introduced, often with a longitudinal design. These led to a revision of the conceptualization of adolescence as a crisis and confirmed the consistent, stable nature of development. As a consequence of this research, adolescents came to be seen as "producers of their own development" (Lerner, 1987, p. 29) who actively tackle diverse demands and take on new tasks and roles. A concept that had been developed in the 1940s by Havighurst (1953) was revived to give a more precise account of the various tasks of this developmental period. According to Havighurst (1953), a developmental task is

> "(...) a task which arises at or about a certain period in the life of the individual, successful achievement of which leads to happiness and to success with later tasks, while failure leads to unhappiness in the individual, disapproval by society and difficulty with later tasks" (p. 2).

He described eight age-specific developmental tasks for the adolescent period: Adolescents must learn to accept their own body, adopt a masculine or feminine role, develop close relationships with friends, prepare for an occupation and romantic relationships, achieve emotional independence from parents, establish values and an ethical system to live by, and strive for social responsibility. Havighurst's concept of developmental tasks is unique in that it integrates challenges from three different domains: (a) physical development and bodily sensations, (b) adolescent personality and identity, and (c) the expectations of society. In addition, the individual's activity in integrating these demands and linking the developmental tasks of different life phases is stressed. Accordingly, the developmental tasks of adolescence build on developmental tasks of mid-childhood (e.g., learning the skills necessary for everyday life, building a positive attitude toward the self, learning to get along with peers, and achieving personal independence) and are related to tasks in early adulthood (e.g., choosing an occupation, establishing a relationship with a life partner, starting and raising a family, and building a social network).

Coleman's (1978) contribution helped to explain the apparent contradiction between the large number of tasks to be achieved during adolescence and likewise the relatively successful adaptation of the majority of youths facing these demands. Havighurst's ideas also encouraged other investigators to acknowledge the importance of the context in which adolescents develop (Lerner & Foch, 1987), to analyze how biological changes in adolescence interact with and stimulate changes in other domains of development (Brooks-Gunn & Reiter, 1990), and to investigate the adolescents' competence in mastering normative stressors (Petersen, 1988; Seiffge-Krenke, 1995). In 1979, Neugarten's concept of a "social clock" illustrated how societal expectations and subjective "timing" are closely connected. More recently, Galambos and Tilton-Weaver's (1996) concept of subjective age, that is, an individual's perception of being "in time" or "off time" with respect to age-specific development, emphasizes the importance of how society's expectations are interwoven with the subjective understanding of one's own competence and physical maturity. Understanding adolescent development in an age-graded context has become a major issue (Nurmi, 1993).

Developmental Status and Aspired Goals: Age, Gender, and Culture-Specific Influences

Nevertheless, research on adolescent development has not produced conclusive evidence to support the Havighurst theory and more recent conceptualizations. Many questions remain unanswered. Do adolescents see themselves as "producers of their own development," as Lerner (1987, p. 29) suggested? How important are certain developmental tasks for them during specific time periods of adolescence? Do adolescents exercise their own competencies and pursue their own aspirations in accordance with society's expectations?

Despite the key role of developmental tasks, literature on this topic is fairly sparse. More importantly, these questions have not been approached from a longitudinal perspective. A PsychLIT review conducted in 1996 generated 241 entries since 1979 that used the key words "developmental task." In most of these contributions, however, only general reference is made to the theoretical framework of developmental tasks, and only a few provide cross-sectional data about these issues (for a summary see Seiffge-Krenke, 1998a). Earlier studies mainly focused on rating the relative importance of various developmental tasks. They show that work and career are of high subjective importance for both male and female adolescents (Dreher & Dreher, 1985; Engel & Hurrelmann, 1989). Similarly, Grob, Flammer, and Rhyn (1995) were able to demonstrate that society expects adolescents to tackle two developmental tasks in particular, autonomy from parents and developing occupational competence. Female adolescents, compared to males, consistently described their physical development as more accelerated. In addition, the importance of particular tasks varies with age: Establishing romantic relationships and achieving autonomy from parents were much more important to older than younger adolescents.

Although age influences the importance and sequence of developmental tasks, culture also plays an important role (Nurmi, Poole, & Kalakowski, 1994). For example, in comparing Finnish, Australian, and Israeli adolescents, Nurmi, Poole, and Seginer (1995) found a culture-specific timing of certain developmental tasks. Australian youths expected their educational and occupational goals to be realized earlier than Finnish and Israeli adolescents. Discrepancies between desired goals and current developmental status were found in a study comparing German and Polish adolescents (Schoenflug & Jansen, 1995). In addition, family and peer contexts have been found to influence adolescents' performance of developmental tasks. Sessa and Steinberg (1991) have demonstrated how family structure and marital status influence the major task of autonomy development. Conflicts experienced by immigrant or bicultural adolescents in their attempts to master developmental tasks have been identified in several studies (e.g., Gibbs & Moskowitz-Sweet, 1991). In particular, problems related to adolescents' desires to avoid or delay autonomy from parents were reported. Finally, Kirchler, Palmonari, and Pombeni (1993) found that peer group activities can provide the resources that help adolescents to master developmental tasks successfully.

In summary, previous research has emphasized the subjective importance of developmental tasks for the adolescent, thereby calling attention to the diversity of adolescents' perceptions. Age, gender, and culture-specific influences have been noted. Cultural variation in the time span allotted for the mastery of several tasks has been addressed, as well as individual and family factors that contribute to the perceived mastery of developmental tasks.

However, a neglected area of research concerns individual differences in health status. While epidemiological studies have shown that a rather large number of adolescents are afflicted with chronic physical illnesses such as cystic fibrosis, diabetes, arthritis, epilepsy, or cancer (Gortmaker, Walker, Weitzman, & Sobol, 1990), remarkably, little is known about how youths with chronic health conditions complete the transition to adulthood. Are chronically ill adolescents able to cope with various developmental tasks as well as healthy adolescents? Do they aspire to achieve the same developmental goals as their healthy peers? Puberty may be the time when adolescents are most at risk for the effects of chronic illness. In particular, early adolescents are especially vulnerable, due to the cumulative effects of changes in body contour, relationship patterns, and school transition. Are they able to progress developmentally, despite the onset of a severe chronic illness?

The dilemma between adaptation to illness and developmental progression provides the conceptual framework for analyzing the attainment of age-specific tasks in a sample of chronically ill adolescents. In a longitudinal study covering four years from early adolescence (mean age 13.9 years) to late adolescence (17.1 years), we analyzed the developmental goals as well as mastery of developmental tasks in a study of about 100 diabetic adolescents, their parents, siblings, and doctors and about 100 families caring for healthy adolescents of the same age range (Seiffge-Krenke, 2000). Although the afflicted adolescents' capacity to balance medical adaptation and developmental progression was the focus of this study, the developmental context that may have contributed to successful attainment or failure was also explored.

The Dilemma Between Developmental Progression and Adaptation to Illness

Generally, adolescents set personal goals for their own development in view of normative expectations. If their current developmental status deviates from the desired status, they try to prevent or eliminate the developmental pressure of the perceived discrepancy (Lerner & Foch, 1987). This process of self-regulation, by which the adolescents themselves initiate all necessary developmental steps, can have a completely different course in healthy and chronically ill adolescents. The developmental status may also have different connotations for ill and healthy adolescents. Chronically ill adolescents may be severely restricted in their capacities and possibilities, so it is relevant to analyze their aspired norms as well as their mastery of developmental tasks. It is particularly interesting to see how these adolescents deal with discrepancies between their current and desired developmental status. Moreover, developmental tasks are interrelated, so changes in one area can bring about changes in another. Attaining professional competence is often associated with separation from the parental household, and establishing romantic relations occurs at about the same time. Due to these interrelations and the sequential course of developmental tasks, cumulative deficits may occur in chronically ill adolescents.

Various authors have pointed out the strong impact of the outbreak of a chronic illness, speaking of interruption or even "developmental breakdown" (Jamison, Lewis, & Burish, 1986, p. 616). They stress that the adolescents cannot cope appropriately when faced with additional, illness-related stressors (Ben-Sira, 1984). There are a variety of reasons to expect increasing difficulties in successfully tackling the various developmental tasks. For one, having a chronic illness may be associated with increased school absence, due to the illness itself or because of treatment and medical appointments (Weitzman, 1986). Second, academic and vocational performance may be influenced by fatigue, pain, or medication (Cowen et al., 1984). Third, a chronic illness may alter or restrict competencies and future perspectives. Studies have reported that chronically ill adolescents are less likely to acquire a driver's license, and do so later (e.g., Orr, Weller, Satterwhite, & Pless, 1984). Their orientation toward the future may also be altered. Ill adolescents in a study by Fröhlich (1986) reported career plans less frequently, and they favored medical occupations. Fourth, social interactions may be influenced. Medical treatment and physical impairments restrict participation in leisure activities, so the adolescent cannot integrate into the peer group completely (Grey, Genel, & Tamborlane, 1980). Some studies have reported that chronically ill adolescents take up romantic relations later than healthy adolescents (Sinnema, 1986). Finally, there is also evidence that parents of adolescents with a chronic illness exhibit different forms of parenting. It becomes more difficult for the children to separate from the parents, as role expectations and responsibilities within the family change (Becker, 1979) and the ill adolescent becomes the focus of the family's anxiety and attention. Constant parental monitoring and overprotection may hinder separation from the family. Some studies have even demonstrated a "regressive pull" associated with the illness, whereby the adolescents become more dependent and childlike (Hamlett, Pellegrini, & Katz, 1992, p. 41). Although these difficulties are common in a variety of illnesses (Pless & Perrin, 1985), their incidence and extent may depend on the type of chronic illness, particularly on its severity and visibility.

Compared with other chronic illnesses such as arthritis and cancer, diabetes places relatively few restrictions on adolescents, which means they can still participate in nearly all athletic and leisure time activities and are mostly able to pursue the occupation of their choice. Although the diabetic adolescent may not show overt signs of being afflicted with the illness, diabetes management requires that the adolescent constantly exercise extreme self-control. He or she must live by the clock, remembering to eat and administer insulin at predetermined times. Adolescents with diabetes can participate in typical teenager activities, such as eating junk food, experimenting with alcohol consumption, or taking vacations with friends, only by accepting health risks or taking special precautions.

The characteristics just described—that is, the links between illness management and the adolescent's striving for autonomy and family support, the "secret" nature of the illness, and the great importance that the adolescent places on adjustment—make diabetes especially suitable for analyzing developmentally related, opposed to illness-related changes. In fact, one of the most common questions asked by the parents and doctors of adolescents in our study was whether particular behaviors were developmental or illness-specific.

Does Chronic Illness Lead to Developmental Delays?

The results of our study showed (see Seiffge-Krenke, 2000) that most of our adolescents with diabetes coped well with the illness. The majority displayed satisfactory to good metabolic control, a high level of knowledge, good compliance, and a high level of activity in illness management. But what is the impact of the illness on perceived developmental progression in several developmental tasks?

Based on Havighurst's (1953) theory of developmental tasks, we explored the adolescents' current status and future intentions in 11 developmental tasks, among them peer group integration, physical maturity, autonomy from parents, occupational competence, close friendships, and romantic relations (Seiffge-Krenke, 1998a). We asked what the adolescents could already do—that is, their current developmental status—and what they hoped to achieve in the future—that is, their aspired developmental status. The discrepancy between current developmental status and aspired level was termed *developmental pressure.*

It is important to note that the healthy and diabetic adolescents in our study did not differ with respect to their aspired developmental status. They shared the same goals in most of the 11 developmental tasks. Close friendship, autonomy from parents, romantic relationships, and occupational competence were developmental tasks of high importance in both groups. This confirms earlier studies with respect to the importance of these tasks (Dreher & Dreher, 1985; Engel & Hurrelmann, 1989; Grob et al., 1995). However, as early as the first survey in 1991 significant differences between adolescents with diabetes and the healthy control group emerged in achieved developmental status. In developmental tasks involving physical maturity, increasing autonomy from the parents, and developing an individual lifestyle, healthy adolescents had a higher developmental status.

Figure 1 illustrates gender differences in developmental pressure in adolescents with diabetes. The first survey revealed the highest developmental pressure experienced by both male and female adolescents with diabetes in

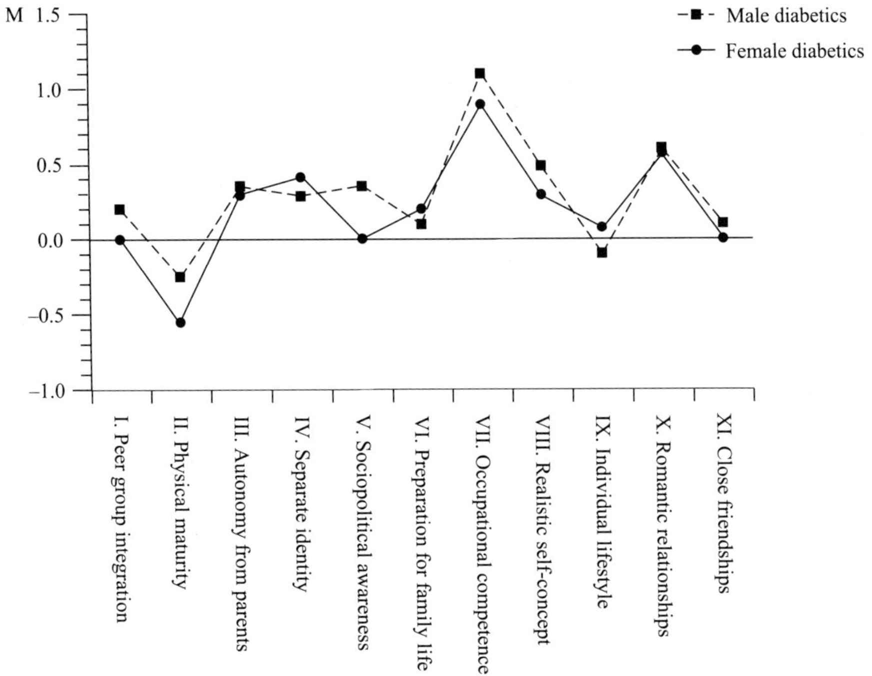

Figure 1. Developmental pressure in male (N = 58) and female (N = 51) adolescents with diabetes.

the field of developing professional competence. This developmental task was also of most concern to healthy adolescents. But in healthy adolescents there was additional developmental pressure with respect to establishing close friendships and romantic relationships. In the group of adolescents with diabetes, males felt significantly more developmental pressure than females regarding sociopolitical awareness. However, as detailed in Figure 1, due to their advanced physical maturity, females experienced less developmental pressure than males in this particular task.

Adolescents with poor metabolic control reported more discrepancies between their current and intended developmental status in several tasks. In addition, their scores in achieved developmental status differed significantly from those of better-adjusted peers in two developmental tasks, namely, autonomy from parents and close friendships. This suggests that adolescents with poor metabolic control of their diabetes are aware of their deficits relative to the typical development of close friendships and do not feel adequately independent in their relationships with their parents. This finding was also substantiated by the pattern of correlations between developmental tasks and metabolic adjustment. Significant correlations emerged between poor metabolic control ($HbA_1 > 9.5$) and the developmental tasks separate identity ($r = -.36$), autonomy from parents ($r = -.47$), and close friendships ($r = -.39$), showing that high HbA_1 values (i.e., poor metabolic control) are associated with low developmental status in these tasks.

These results from the adolescents are only partially confirmed by the reports of their parents and doctors. In the interviews, the parents estimated their children's physical and mental developmental level as average to good. Likewise, the doctors saw a large number of the adolescents they treated as typically developed for their age, both physically and cognitively. Parents seldom mentioned their ill adolescents' social development, while doctors did not discuss it at all. This indicates that adolescents with diabetes perceive delays in their development that are not perceived by their parents and doctors.

The "Unexpected Success Story": Catching Up to the Developmental Level of Healthy Adolescents?

At the beginning of the study, our sample showed developmental delays in the field of relationships. These contrasted sharply with their age-typical development of cognitive capacities and performance and their very strong orientation toward a future career. Their career orientation is remarkable: the developmental task occupational competence exerted by far the greatest developmental pressure, stating that adolescents strive very strongly toward this goal. A strong focus on achievement and career applied to the entire group of adolescents with diabetes but was even more pronounced among adolescents with good metabolic control. In the next step we explored whether the delays in forming relationships found in the first year of the study became even more pronounced with time, or whether the succeeding years were accompanied by adjustment to the developmental level of healthy adolescents. Interestingly, the longitudinal analysis revealed no differences between healthy and diabetic adolescents with respect to desired developmental status. That is, healthy and diabetic adolescents share the same developmental goals. Furthermore, significant time effects in attained developmental status suggest enormous developmental gains in most tasks. Like their healthy peers, diabetic adolescents

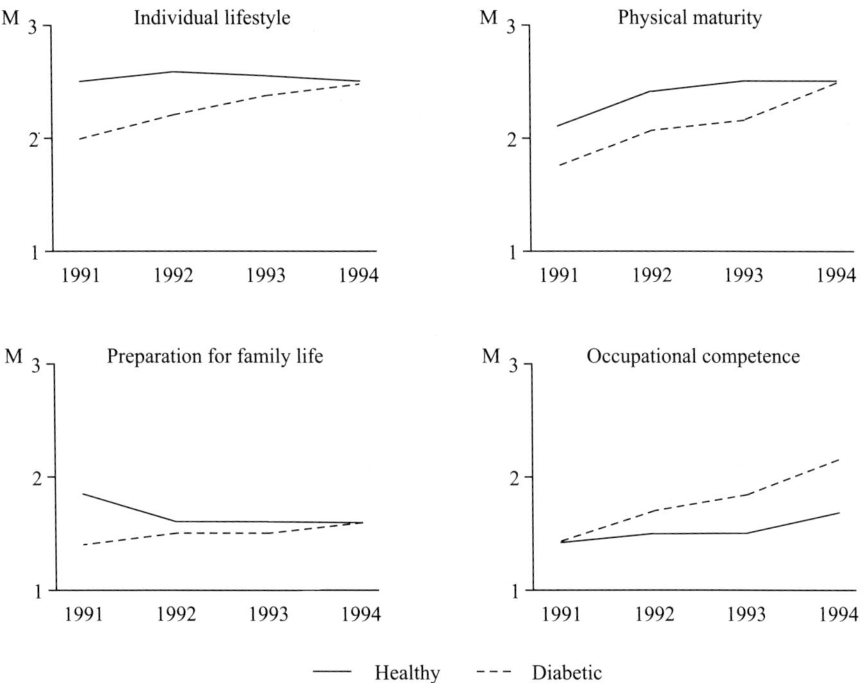

Figure 2. Changes in developmental status in four developmental tasks, perceived by diabetic ($N = 91$) and healthy adolescents ($N = 107$).

perceived significant developmental progression in diverse tasks such as physical maturity, integration into the peer group, establishing a separate identity, and developing occupational competence (Seiffge-Krenke, 1998a). Thus, despite the considerable burdens of the illness, they describe impressive competence in mastering the developmental tasks typical for this age group. Far from being the victims of a major stressor, the diabetic adolescents in our study perceived themselves after four years to be as competent as their healthy peers and judged their development as being "in time" for most of the 11 developmental tasks. Many studies in the past have been conducted to identify adjustment problems in adolescents with a chronic illness. This "unexpected success story," that is, the overall positive adaptation of chronically ill adolescents, is in line with more recent research that emphasizes that positive adaptation is possible (Gortmaker et al., 1993).

However, some differences need to be stressed. At the beginning of our study, adolescents with diabetes scored lower in physical maturity and individual lifestyle. As can be seen in Figure 2, although these differences decreased over the course of four years, they were still evident when the adolescents were about 17 years old. In a third task, occupational competence, the diabetic adolescents started from the same developmental status but perceived enormous gains, surpassing those of their healthy peers.

The Search for Explanation

How can we explain the enormous developmental gains made by chronically ill adolescents in general and the remaining deficits in some tasks in particular? Developmental psychology explains coping with developmental tasks in this stage of life through Coleman's (1978) focal theory. According to this theory, the adolescent focuses on particular relevant developmental tasks and works through them in succession. Thus, the ability to focus on and cope with diverse developmental tasks sequentially is the key to successful developmental progression. Coleman (1984) later described the focussing process more precisely. A promising path emerges if the adolescent is successful in setting priorities and dealing with each goal in turn. On the other hand, developmental stress may result if all the adolescent's knowledge and capacities are not enough to solve a developmental task of high subjective urgency; that is, the more developmental tasks there are simultaneously requiring attention, the more likely the result will be developmental stress.

In our results, it was especially notable that diabetic adolescents handled the accumulation of stressors due to chronic illness and the achievement of developmental tasks by taking illness management to be the single most pressing (and life-preserving) task. This was done at the expense of realizing developmental tasks, tasks that healthy adolescents of their age could deal with. Overall, the developmental progression of the diabetic adolescents was less accelerated compared to the healthy group. But how can one explain the diabetics' developmental setback in some tasks (those related to body concept and individuality) and their strong progression in others tasks (those related to job aspirations and future career)? Apparently, diabetic adolescents cope with diverse tasks sequentially.

Regarding the perceived setback in physical maturity in the group of adolescents with diabetes, it has to be stressed that it had no objective base. The physical development of diabetic males and females was normal for their age.

In this task, there was progression over time in adolescents with diabetes. Individual lifestyle was another developmental task in which diabetic adolescents perceived a lower developmental status than their healthy peers. It is well understood that diabetes forces adolescents to adopt a strict schedule, which leaves them little opportunity to develop individuality. In this task, too, there was developmental progression, probably related to the decrease in compliance found in our sample over time (Hanl & Seiffge-Krenke, 1996). Whereas the strong gains in individual lifestyle can be explained by the need to reduce the gap between current developmental status and aspired goals, the latter being similar for both healthy and diabetic adolescents, the situation is different with respect to occupational competence. There, both healthy and diabetic adolescents started from the same perceived developmental status, but adolescents with diabetes made much stronger gains over time.

Rather unexpectedly, the duration of the illness did not influence developmental progression; that is, adolescents ill for more than five years did not perceive themselves as more developmentally delayed than adolescents ill for less than one year. In addition, metabolic control had no impact on perceived developmental progression. This lends support to the hypothesis that most diabetic adolescents share the same developmental context with similar experiences and limitations. Thus, the impact of the illness seems to be pervasive, irrespective of illness duration and adaptation to the illness.

The Developmental Context: Conditions that Contribute to or Maintain Developmental Delays

Over four years, the developmental progression of diabetic adolescents was impressive. However, the selection of which developmental tasks to tackle requires some explanation. Of all the possible developmental tasks, occupational goals were aimed at more strongly and also attained more often than tasks involving relationships and individuality. This finding was consistent throughout our study. For this reason, we analyzed what conditions contribute to selecting and focusing on certain developmental tasks at the expense of others.

The Adolescents

In our study, a range of evidence suggested that diabetic adolescents approached relationship-based developmental tasks hesitantly because of certain conditions. The most important of these were the poor self-concept and negative body image displayed by our ill adolescents (Seiffge-Krenke, 1996). One consequence of the more negative self-concept could possibly be inhibited use of social support. Adolescents with diabetes see their bodies as more rigid, less flexible, and more childlike. The perception of the body as less mature was not related to delayed maturation processes. No objective group differences were evident in the mean ages of menarche and semenarche. The perceived differences in body concept may have contributed to diabetic adolescents' reserve in establishing close friendships and romantic relationships (Seiffge-Krenke, 1997). Adolescents with diabetes caught up somewhat in their body concept, but even in the third survey in 1993, they still perceived their bodies as less "adult" than those of healthy adolescents. This may explain the continued discrepancies in developmental level regarding romantic relationships and close friendships with peers. Another striking result was the different expectations that adolescents with diabetes had of their close friends and romantic partners. There was a noticeable need for security and a desire for concrete instrumental help (Seiffge-Krenke, 2000). Healthy adolescents were more critical, open to experimentation, and independent in this area and were able to fulfill their sexual needs outside of a fixed partnership. Because of their demanding, atypical expectations, adolescents with diabetes were sometimes disappointed in friendships and romantic relationships, dampening their initiative even further. They put a lot of effort into achievement and were extremely concerned about school and their future profession. Although their developmental status in these tasks was similar to the level of healthy peers at the beginning of our study, they made considerably more progress over time. The results of this study suggest that the family context may help to explain the accelerated progression in this task.

The Families

As described in Seiffge-Krenke (1998b), the family climate in families of adolescents with diabetes differed considerably from that of families of healthy adolescents. Families of ill adolescents were more structured, organized, and controlling, and more strongly oriented toward achievement.

These changes in the family climate indicate functional behavior for coping with the diabetes, although they can lead to a rigid family structure that inhibits the individual family members' further development. This danger was demonstrated in the ill adolescents' low values for personal growth and autonomy, as well as their subjective developmental delay in individual lifestyle. Families of adolescents with diabetes, whether well or poorly adjusted, displayed this highly structured family climate. In addition, family communication was shorter and less elaborate and there was less negotiation about possible solutions of family problems (Fentner & Seiffge-Krenke, 1997). This family functioning persisted over four years, although the metabolic control and generally unproblematic course of the illness in most patients could have allowed the family climate to grow more relaxed and take the adolescents' individual developmental possibilities into account. Once again, there were no differences between families with well- or poorly adjusted adolescents. The very strict family climate we observed over the years supports the adolescents' efforts for achievement but fails to encourage autonomy and individuality. Fathers made a strikingly small contribution to the ill adolescents' acquisition of independence, and the ill adolescents had unusually close relationships with their siblings. Due to the distinctive dynamics of the families, it is reasonable that the adolescents aimed most strongly for and achieved developmental goals that conform to the family's predominant achievement orientation.

The Adolescents' Doctors

Our adolescents generally rated their doctor-patient relationships as extremely important for their coping at the beginning of the study (Seiffge-Krenke & Kollmar, 1996). Evidently, the adolescents not only discuss a variety of illness-related topics with their doctors, but also ask them for advice on many other problems, such as with parents, friends, or school. However, doctor-patient relationships worsened and compliance with the medical regimen decreased over the course of the study, paralleling the increasingly individual lifestyle of adolescents with diabetes. It is important that experts in the medical field—doctors, nurses, dieticians, and so on—be aware of their patients' development and acquire a complex, holistic view of the adolescent. In view of the adolescents' overall development, a more tolerant attitude to deteriorating HbA_1 values and metabolic instability is desirable, at least within a range that rules out the chance of later damage. However, our data show that most doctors failed to notice any deficits in the social field or in important relationships. In this respect, the study may help to guide intervention.

How can parents and doctors help to minimize or prevent developmental delays? It should already be clear that for various reasons, the adolescents can only proceed in their development hesitantly. Focused attention on the most pressing tasks—such as illness management and the diabetes regime—is certainly sensible to avoid overloading. Only when the adolescent can cope reasonably well with this task can he or she turn to other developmental tasks. Coping and illness management are processes that extend over a long period until competence and stability are attained. However, other developmental tasks can rarely be postponed for this long. The adolescent may perceive the conflict between medical requirements and the desire for age-typical development as discrepant and stressful and hanker for a more lenient regime with more freedom to develop. Tolerance and understanding from all parties are necessary. One-sided concentration on the medical aspect of metabolic control—just like excessive parental control and restrictions—could have problematic consequences in the long term.

Different Pathways for Development

The results of our study suggest that the family context (particularly a highly structured and achievement-oriented family climate) and the adolescents' personality (characterized by low self-esteem, a negative body concept, and deficiencies in close relationships) may help to explain the focus on certain tasks as well as the sequence that is chosen. Family conditions, together with the ill adolescent's developmental history, clearly influence the delicate balance between developmental progression and coping with the illness. This basic approach, however, has to be differentiated. As case studies demonstrate (see Seiffge-Krenke, 1997; Seiffge-Krenke, 2000), the dilemma between adhering to the diabetes regime and pursuing developmental tasks is solved in a variety of ways. We found four different pathways.

Adolescents Who Cope by Putting Developmental Tasks on Hold

Some ill adolescents "solve" the dilemma between adhering to the diabetes regime and tackling developmental tasks by relegating development to the back burner. These adolescents fail to resolve important developmental tasks but adjust well to the illness in a medical sense: That is, they maintain satisfactory to good metabolic control and show good compliance. This "solution" seems to be the most common (45% of the adolescents) and is highly endorsed by the parents. But this pathway does affect adaptation to the illness in the long term, too.

Overemphasizing Adolescent Development at the Expense of Metabolic Control

There were also cases among our ill adolescents who ruthlessly pressed on with important developmental tasks, to the detriment of their metabolic control. Twelve percent of adolescents showed this pathway. These adolescents were either poorly adjusted or else deteriorated considerably from an initially good or satisfactory metabolic control. Notably, their development showed a typical adolescent color. These adolescents caused concern to their doctors and parents, not only because of their poor or strongly fluctuating HbA_1 values, but also through their "acting out" and conspicuous social behavior. They demanded the typical possibilities of adolescent development.

Families That Broke Down

In our sample, there were only a few cases (8%) in which the adolescents neither achieved typical developmental tasks nor adjusted to the illness. In each of these cases, it was not so much the individual adolescent as the entire family that experienced negative effects. Some cases involved unsolved neurotic problems within the family, problems that existed before the illness but were intensified by it; in other cases, many additional stressors accumulated after our study began, overtaxing the family's coping capacity. In the latter case, there was often some interaction with pre-existing problems in the family situation.

Families That Adapted Well Overall

About 35% of the cases we studied were characterized by successful adaptation to the illness. The adolescents and their families were able to cope with the illness without causing the adolescents to be delayed developmentally.

When there was developmental delay in certain tasks at the beginning of our study, due to the focus on illness management, the adolescents were still able to make developmental gains over the course of the four years. These cases offer a clear insight into the protective factors that promote adaptation. They suggest that a positive, overall development is not only necessarily dependent on a harmonious, conflict-free family climate, but also depends on the commitment and continuous efforts of all family members to solve this important family task.

Conclusions

There is growing interest in how sociocultural context influences developmental patterns, and in how adolescents influence their own development as agents. Cultural norms and expectations involve standards for age-appropriate developmental tasks, but these tasks cannot be coped with by all adolescents with the same ease. This contribution tries to clarify factors that help to explain developmental progression in adolescence with a focus on adolescents varying in health status. The longitudinal data presented suggests that discrepancies between desired and attained developmental status may well serve as motivation for developmental progression. In healthy adolescents, we found two developmental tasks of high importance, establishing romantic relationships and occupational competence, which places high developmental pressure on them. In both tasks, healthy adolescents made considerable progress over time, demonstrating that developmental pressure can be a motivation for progression. But this is only half of the story, as the results won on a sample of adolescents with diabetes show. Based on similar scores from the beginning of the study and likewise on comparably high developmental pressure as in the healthy group, the diabetics' developmental progress in occupational competence over four years was even higher. In trying to find an explanation for this accelerated progression, we took a closer look at the developmental context. Conditions in the afflicted adolescents, their families, and their attending doctors were discovered that may have contributed to the enormous gains in this particular developmental task. It is, however, a gain at the expense of other developmental tasks pertaining to autonomy and relationship development. In a way, the results reveal an "unexpected success story" in the sample of chronically ill adolescents—but there is still a need for further development in some tasks in order to achieve a more balanced developmental pattern.

References

Becker, R. D. (1979). Adolescents in the hospital. *Israel Annuals of Psychiatry and Related Disciplines,.17,* 328–352.

Ben-Sira, Z. (1984). Chronic illness, stress and coping. *Social Science and Medicine, 18,* 725–736.

Brooks-Gunn, J., & Reiter, E. O. (1990). The role of pubertal processes in the early adolescent transition. In S. Feldman & G. Elliott (Eds.), *At the threshold: The developing adolescent* (pp. 16–53). Cambridge, MA: Harvard University Press.

Coleman, J. C. (1978). Current contradictions in adolescent theory. *Journal of Youth and Adolescence, 7,* 1–11.

Coleman, J. C. (1984). Eine neue Theorie der Adoleszenz [A new theory of adolescence]. In E. Olbrich & E. Todt (Eds.), *Probleme des Jugendalters. Neuere Sichtweisen* [Problems in adolescence. New perspectives] (pp. 49–67). Berlin, Germany: Springer.

Cowen, L., Corey, M., Simmons, R., Keenan, N., Robertson, J., & Levison, H. (1984). Growing older with cystic fibrosis: Psychological adjustment of patients more than 16 years old. *Psychosomatic Medicine, 46,* 363–377.

Dreher, E., & Dreher, M. (1985). Wahrnehmung und Bewältigung von Entwicklungsaufgaben im Jugendalter [The perception and mastery of developmental tasks in adolescence]. In R. Oerter (Ed.), *Lebensbewältigung im Jugendalter* [Coping with life in adolescence] (pp. 30–61). Weinheim, Germany: Edition Psychologie.

Engel, U., & Hurrelmann, K. (1989). *Psychosoziale Belastung im Jugendalter: Empirische Befunde zum Einfluß von Familie, Schule und Gleichaltrigengruppe* [Psychosocial stress in adolescence: Empirical findings regarding the influence of family, school, and contemporaries]. Berlin, Germany: de Gruyter.

Fentner, S., & Seiffge-Krenke, I. (1997). Die Rolle des Vaters in der familiären Kommunikation: Befunde einer Längsschnittstudie an gesunden und chronisch kranken Jugendlichen [The role of the father in family communication: Findings from a longitudinal study involving healthy and chronically ill adolescents]. *Praxis für Kinderpsychologie und Kinderpsychiatrie, 46,* 36–52.

Fröhlich, F. (1986). *Die seelische Verarbeitung lebensbedrohlicher Krankheit im Jugendalter* [The mental processing of a life-threatening illness in adolescence]. Basel, Switzerland: Schwabe.

Galambos, N. L., & Tilton-Weaver, L. (1996). *The adultoid adolescent: Too much, too soon.* Paper presented at the Biennial Meeting of the Society for Research on Adolescence, Boston, MA.

Gibbs, J. T., & Moskowitz-Sweet, G. (1991). Clinical and cultural issues in the treatment of bisocial and bicultural adolescents. *Families in Society, 72,* 579–592.

Gortmaker, S. L., Perrin, J. M., Weitzman, M., Halmer, C. J., & Sobol, A. M. (1993). An unexpected success story: Transition to adulthood in youth with chronic physical health conditions. *Journal of Research on Adolescence, 3,* 317–336.

Gortmaker, S. L., Walker, D. B., Weitzman, M., & Sobol, A. M. (1990). Chronic conditions, socio-economic risks, and behavioral problems in children and adolescents. *Pediatrics, 85,* 267–276.

Grey, M. J., Genel, M., & Tamborlane, W. V. (1980). Psychological adjustment of latency-aged diabetics. Determinants and relationship to control. *Pediatrics, 65,* 69–73.

Grob, A., Flammer, A., & Rhyn, H. (1995). Entwicklungsaufgaben als soziale Normsetzung. Reaktionen Erwachsener auf Lösungsmodi von Entwicklungsaufgaben [Developmental tasks for the setting of social norms. The reactions of adults regarding the mode of problem solving in developmental tasks]. *Zeitschrift für Sozialisationsforschung und Erziehungssoziologie, 15,* 45–62.

Hamlett, K. W., Pellegrini, D. S., & Katz, K. S. (1992). Childhood chronic illness as a family stressor. *Journal of Pediatric Psychology, 17,* 33–47.

Hanl, J., & Seiffge-Krenke, I. (1996). Krankheitsbezogene Einstellungen und ihr Bezug zur medizinischen Anpassung [Illness-related attitudes and their relationship to medical adaptability]. *Diabetes und Stoffwechsel, 5,* 259–265.

Havighurst, R. J. (1953). *Developmental tasks and education.* New York: Longmans, Green & Co.

Heckhausen, J. (1999). *Developmental regulation in adulthood.* Cambridge, UK: Cambridge University Press.

Jamison, R. N., Lewis, S., & Burish, T. G. (1986). Psychological impact of cancer on adolescents: Self-image, locus of control, perception of illness and knowledge of cancer. *Journal of Chronic Disease, 39,* 609–617.

Kirchler, E., Palmonari, A., & Pombeni, M. L. (1993). Developmental tasks and adolescents' relationships with their peers and their family. In S. Jackson & H. Rodriguez-Tomé (Eds.), *Adolescence and its social world* (pp. 145–168). Hillsdale, NJ: Erlbaum.

Lerner, R. M. (1987). A life-span perspective for early adolescence. In R. M. Lerner & T. T. Foch (Eds.), *Biological-psychosocial interactions in early adolescence: A life-span perspective* (pp. 9–34). Hillsdale, NJ: Erlbaum.

Lerner, R. M., & Foch, T. T. (Eds.). (1987). *Biological-psychosocial interactions in early adolescence: A life-span perspective.* Hillsdale, NJ: Erlbaum.

Nurmi, J. E. (1993). Adolescent development in age-graded context: The role of personal beliefs, goals, and strategies in the tackling of developmental tasks and standards. *International Journal of Behavioral Development, 16,* 169–189.

Nurmi, J. E., Poole, M. E., & Kalakowksi, V. (1994). Age differences in adolescent future-oriented goals, concerns, and related temporal extension in different sociocultural contexts. *Journal of Youth and Adolescence, 23,* 471–487.

Nurmi, J. E., Poole, M. E., & Seginer, R. (1995). Tracks and transition: A comparison of adolescent future-oriented goals, explorations, and commitment in Australia, Israel, and Finland. *International Journal of Psychology, 30,* 355–375.

Orr, D. P., Weller, S. C., Satterwhite, B., & Pless, I. B. (1984). Psychosocial implications of chronic illness in adolescence. *The Journal of Pediatrics, 104,* 152–157.

Petersen, A. C. (1988). Adolescent development. *Annual Review of Psychology, 39,* 583–607.

Pless, I. B., & Perrin, J. M. (1985). Issues common to a variety of illnesses. In N. Hobbes & J. M. Perrin (Eds.), *Issues in the care of children with chronic illness* (pp. 41–60). San Francisco: Jossey-Bass.

Schoenflug, K., & Jansen, X. (1995). Self-concept and coping with developmental demands in German and Polish adolescents. *International Journal of Behavioral Development, 18,* 385–405.

Seiffge-Krenke, I. (1995). *Stress, coping, and relationships in adolescence.* Mahwah, NJ: Erlbaum.

Seiffge-Krenke, I. (1996). Selbstkonzept und Körperkonzept bei chronisch kranken und gesunden Jugendlichen [The issue of self-concept and body concept regarded by chronically ill and healthy adolescents]. *Zeitschrift für Gesundheitspsychologie, 4,* 247–269.

Seiffge-Krenke, I. (1997). The capacity to balance intimacy and conflict: Differences in romantic relationships between healthy and diabetic adolescents. In S. Shulman & W. A. Collins (Eds.), *Romantic relationships in adolescence: Developmental perspectives* (pp. 53–68). San Francisco: Jossey-Bass.

Seiffge-Krenke, I. (1998a). Chronic disease and perceived developmental progression in adolescence. *Developmental Psychology, 34,* 1073–1084.

Seiffge-Krenke, I. (1998b). The highly structured climate in families of adolescents with diabetes: Functional or dysfunctional for metabolic control? *Journal of Pediatric Psychology, 23,* 313–322.

Seiffge-Krenke, I. (2000). *Diabetic adolescents and their families. Stress, coping, relationships and adaptation.* New York: Cambridge University Press.

Seiffge-Krenke, I., & Kollmar, F. (1996). Der jugendliche Diabetiker und sein Arzt: Diskrepanzen in der Einschätzung der Arzt-Patienten-Beziehung und der Compliance [The adolescent diabetic and his doctor: Discrepancies in estimating the doctor-patient relationship and accompanying compliance]. *Kindheit und Entwicklung, 4,* 240–249.

Sessa, F. M., & Steinberg, L. (1991). Family structure and the development of autonomy during adolescence. *Journal of Early Adolescence, 11,* 38–55.

Sinnema, G. (1986). The development of independence in chronically ill adolescents. *International Journal of Adolescent Medicine and Health, 2,* 1–14.

Weitzman, M. (1986). The use of school absence rates as outcome measures in studies of children with chronic illness. *Journal of Chronic Disease, 39,* 799–808.

13 Cohort Change in Adolescent Developmental Timetables After German Unification: Trends and Possible Reasons

Rainer K. Silbereisen and Margit Wiesner

After German unification in 1990 Western societal institutions were transferred to the Eastern part of the country and implemented rather quickly. People, however, change their minds and attitudes much more slowly. For instance, even a decade after unification the population from the East still expects more support and guidance from state authorities than their counterparts in the West (Zapf & Habich, 1999).

In this chapter we deal with a particular effect of the social and political transformations after unification on adolescent development. Adolescence can be characterized by a series of biographical transitions, or developmental tasks (Havighurst, 1972). Both the entire life course and single transitions (e.g., from school to work) reflect the intersection of social and historical factors with psychological development (particularly personal goals and aspirations) and biological growth. The relative importance of these components depends on the particular transition—the more personal and private a transition (e.g., first romantic involvement), the less influential the role of normative, societal expectations implemented by social institutions.

Consequently, the exchange of social institutions after German unification primarily should affect transitions that are subject to institutional influences. The Western three-track school system implemented in the East, for example, presumably will not change the basic biological, psychological, and social processes related to romantic involvement. In contrast, quite a substantial influence can be expected on the development of vocational preferences because social constraints crucial for the accomplishment of this task changed after unification. However, new constraints (and opportunities) certainly will not translate directly into a revision of individual goals for adolescent development. Rather, this linkage between social change and individual development represents a "loose coupling" (Elder & O'Rand, 1995) because many factors within the family and individuals' personalities contribute to the linkage, thereby producing individual differences in adaptation.

The accomplishment of a developmental task can be described by its specific substantive outcome (e.g., the particular vocational preference that was developed), but also by several more formal aspects of such transitions (e.g., the timing, i.e., the age at which a certain task was resolved, or the sequence, i.e., the temporal order of accomplishments across tasks). In a series of previous studies, we (Juang, Silbereisen, & Wiesner, 1999; Silbereisen, 2000; Silbereisen, Schwarz, & Rinker, 1996; Silbereisen, Vondracek, & Berg, 1997) have concentrated on the timing aspect across several domains of adolescent transitions.

The basic methodological approach was to compare data gathered on large quota samples from East and West in 1991 (the Shell Youth Study, which encompassed about 4,000 young people aged between 13 and 29; see Fischer, 1992), with data collected on equivalent replication samples in 1996, which encompassed about 3,000 young people of the same age range (see Wiesner & Pickel, 1996). Such a cohort design has its limitations but we had no alternative (for further details see Masche & Reitzle, 1999).

Thereby, the particular emphasis was on the potential impact of the social and political transformations in Germany on changes of the timing of transitions compared to preunification times. In line with traditions in life-course research, we pursued two types of analyses (George, 1993). First, mean trends (i.e., "median transition ages") were compared between cohorts and regions. The second approach aims at a better understanding of the mechanisms that connect the timing of transitions with antecedents that also may differ in their role between East and West.

In this chapter, we deal with selected transitions for 13- to 19-year-old participants: first romantic involvement (more specifically, falling in love, steady friendship, and sexual experiences) and first vocational preferences. Participants were asked whether they had already experienced the issues mentioned, and if so, at what age—in full years—this had occurred. Taking results from research on acculturation among immigrants, which has shown that adaptation to the developmental timetables in the host country happens faster the more proximate the influence of new institutions and, generally speaking, the pragmatics of life (Feldman & Rosenthal, 1990; Schmitt-Rodermund & Silbereisen, in press), as a model, we had the following expectations.

Concerning first vocational preferences, a clear timing difference in 1991 in favor of earlier commitments in the East was expected. Before unification, relevant decisions were deemed an issue of high public interest in the East, as evidenced by extensive guidance and control by the schools and other state authorities (Kornadt, 1996). Consequently, such preferences became crystallized rather early. In the West, such decisions were less scrutinized and restricted by social institutions, early decisions were not demanded, and "floundering" (Hamilton, 1990) was more acceptable. Furthermore, as the change in the school system after unification, which took place in 1992, affected large parts of the replication sample relatively late in life, and also mindful of the concept of loose coupling mentioned earlier, we did not expect the differences observed in 1991 to have disappeared entirely in 1996.

In contrast to such "socioinstitutional" categories of developmental tasks (Dekovic, Noom, & Meeus, 1997), in more personal transitions that are not influenced in any proximal way by the social institutions affected by German unification we did not expect to find differences between the samples from East and West, neither in 1991 nor in 1996. More specifically, the timing of first romantic involvement should not reveal marked differences because of the shared cultural heritage (Silbereisen & Wiesner, 1999). Note that this does not apply to transitions such as marriage or birth of the first child, which were more heavily influenced by societal regulations.

These expectations basically were supported in previous analyses (some exemplary results are reported in the next section). Thus, in extension of the hypotheses mentioned so far, we thought it would be plausible to assume that those affected by such changes the most would reveal a more pronounced delay. Naturally this would only apply if a trend toward a more delayed timing of first vocational preferences in 1996 compared to 1991 in the East is indeed rooted in people's reaction to the political and social transformations after unification. Note that by assuming such a relationship we implicitly claim that the actual mechanism is individuals' active processing of their experiences with unification consequences. In contrast, people could simply do what is perhaps almost automatically induced by the opportunities available in the changed circumstances.

To record interindividual differences in the degree to which (Eastern) participants were confronted with new challenges after unification, we had to rely on indirect measures. After a careful search in the database, we came up with several characteristics (see Table 1, last seven entries). In our judgment they would make a family more vulnerable to negative side effects of unification, or indicate an already experienced negative outcome. The *number of children,* for instance, was included because support for families, from kindergarten to after-school care, became more expensive after unification. Also due to its roots in structural changes in the industries, *unemployment of parents* and *adolescents* should convey the need to adapt to the new challenges most closely.

Table 1
Distribution of Stratification Variables and Vulnerability Indices in the 1991 and 1996 Samples

	1991 (N = 1,561)		*1996 (N = 909)*	
	West (65%)	*East (35%)*	*West (50.4%)*	*East (49.6%)*
Age	χ^2 ns		χ^2 ns	
13	139 (13.7%)	90 (16.5%)	52 (11.4%)	59 (13.1%)
14	171 (16.8%)	95 (17.4%)	62 (13.5%)	51 (11.3%)
15	129 (12.7%)	61 (11.2%)	60 (13.1%)	72 (16.0%)
16	141 (13.9%)	72 (13.2%)	92 (20.1%)	66 (14.6%)
17	129 (12.7%)	64 (11.7%)	60 (13.1%)	70 (15.5%)
18	138 (13.6%)	65 (11.9%)	67 (14.6%)	59 (13.1%)
19	168 (16.6%)	99 (18.1%)	65 (14.2%)	74 (16.4%)
Gender	χ^2 ns		χ^2 ns	
Male (1)	483 (47.6%)	263 (48.2%)	226 (49.3%)	214 (47.5%)
Female (2)	532 (52.4%)	283 (51.8%)	232 (50.7%)	237 (52.5%)
Education	$\chi^2 = 146.56$; $df = 2$; $p < .001$		$\chi^2 = 8.51$; $df = 2$; $p = .014$	
Lower track (1)	255 (25.1%)	27 (4.9%)	109 (23.8%)	85 (18.8%)
Middle track (2)	356 (35.1%)	325 (59.5%)	195 (42.6%)	235 (52.1%)
College track (3)	404 (39.8%)	194 (35.5%)	154 (33.6%)	131 (29.0%)
Community size	$\chi^2 = 10.65$; $df = 1$; $p = .001$		$\chi^2 = 10.11$; $df = 1$; $p = .001$	
< 20,000 (1)	455 (44.8%)	292 (53.5%)	156 (34.1%)	200 (44.3%)
> 20,000 (2)	560 (55.2%)	254 (46.5%)	302 (65.9%)	251 (55.7%)
Adversities before the age of 9	χ^2 ns		χ^2 ns	
No (0)	923 (90.9%)	500 (91.6%)	424 (92.6%)	413 (91.6%)
Yes (> 1 times) (1)	92 (9.1%)	46 (8.4%)	34 (7.4%)	38 (8.4%)
Sexual experience	χ^2 ns		χ^2 ns	
No, never (0)	552 (54.4%)	273 (50.0%)	236 (51.5%)	217 (48.1%)
Yes (1)	463 (45.6%)	273 (50.0%)	222 (48.5%)	234 (51.9%)
First falling in love	$\chi^2 = 9.73$; $df = 1$; $p = .002$		χ^2 ns	
No, never (0)	270 (26.6%)	107 (19.6%)	118 (25.8%)	98 (21.7%)
Yes (1)	745 (73.4%)	439 (80.4%)	340 (74.2%)	353 (78.3%)
Steady friendship	$\chi^2 = 7.80$; $df = 1$; $p = .005$		χ^2 ns	
No, never (0)	438 (43.2%)	196 (35.9%)	213 (46.5%)	205 (45.5%)
Yes (1)	577 (56.8%)	350 (64.1%)	245 (53.5%)	246 (54.5%)
First vocational preferences	$\chi^2 = 54.72$; $df = 1$; $p <.001$		$\chi^2 = 16.17$; $df = 1$; $p < .001$	
No, never (0)	368 (36.3%)	102 (18.7%)	178 (38.9%)	119 (26.4%)
Yes (1)	647 (63.7%)	444 (81.3%)	280 (61.1%)	332 (73.6%)
Attitude towards unification	χ^2 ns		χ^2 ns	
Rest (0)	984 (96.9%)	536 (98.2%)	440 (96.1%)	441 (97.8%)
Against (1)	31 (3.1%)	10 (1.8%)	18 (3.9%)	10 (2.2%)
Housing	$\chi^2 = 99.18$; $df = 2$; $p < .001$		$\chi^2 = 22.88$; $df = 2$; $p < .001$	
Tenant (1)	412 (40.6%)	321 (58.8%)	213 (46.5%)	254 (56.3%)
Owner (2)	568 (56.0%)	170 (31.1%)	221 (48.3%)	152 (33.7%)
Rest (3)	35 (3.4%)	55 (10.1%)	24 (5.2%)	45 (10.0%)
Number of children	χ^2 ns		χ^2 ns	
0–3 (0)	935 (92.1%)	503 (92.1%)	446 (97.4%)	438 (97.1%)
≥ 4 (1)	80 (7.9%)	43 (7.9%)	12 (2.6%)	13 (2.9%)
Loss of parent	χ^2 ns		χ^2 ns	
No (0)	970 (95.6%)	510 (93.4%)	410 (89.5%)	394 (87.4%)
Yes (1)	45 (4.4%)	36 (6.6%)	48 (10.5%)	57 (12.6%)
Parental unemployment	$\chi^2 = 190.48$; $df = 1$; $p < .001$		$\chi^2 = 120.31$; $df = 1$; $p < .001$	
No (0)	999 (98.4%)	423 (77.5%)	416 (90.8%)	273 (60.5%)
Yes (1)	16 (1.6%)	123 (22.5%)	42 (9.2%)	178 (39.5%)
Adolescent unemployment	$\chi^2 = 27.40$; $df = 1$; $p < .001$		χ^2 ns	
No (0)	997 (98.2%)	507 (92.9%)	447 (97.6%)	438 (97.1%)
Yes (1)	18 (1.8%)	39 (7.1%)	11 (2.4%)	13 (2.9%)
Gave up apprenticeship	$\chi^2 = 10.00$; $df = 1$; $p = .002$		χ^2 ns	
No (0)	996 (98.1%)	520 (95.2%)	451 (98.5%)	439 (97.3%)
Yes (1)	19 (1.9%)	26 (4.8%)	7 (1.5%)	12 (2.7%)

Note. χ^2 statistics given for comparisons across regions within periods.

We have to admit that the variables are rather crude indicators of whether families were affected by the unification strains. Nevertheless, further analyses of the covariation between them and/or with sociodemographics (not reported in detail) supported the view that they probably reflect real differences. For instance, the rate of unemployed adolescents and parents was higher in the East German sample. The variables (hereafter called "vulnerability indices") chosen plus additional information on the sociodemographics are shown in Table 1, together with percentages for regions and periods.

Constancy and Change in Median Transition Ages

For the analyses, we used various models of event history analysis (see Willett & Singer, 1991). This allowed for the inclusion of so-called censored cases, that is, participants for which the event of interest had not occurred yet. The results of the analyses are shown in Table 2.

Concerning the estimated median transition ages (survival analyses), neither in 1991 nor in 1996 was there a significant difference in the timing of romantic involvement between East and West. This confirms our hypothesis that these transitions are not related to the societal changes of German unification. In addition, the ascending order of transition ages from first falling in love to first sexual experience is exactly what one would have expected from the literature (Silbereisen & Wiesner, 1999). The Cox regressions reflect this lack of a difference in the nonsignificant risk ratios (numbers larger [smaller] than 1 would indicate that students from the East reported earlier [later] transition ages). Also, as expected, adding the vulnerability indices did not change the results.

The results in regard to first vocational preferences, however, show a different picture. As can be seen in Table 2, there was quite a remarkable difference in median transition age in 1991, in favor of an earlier timing in the East. This, and the fact that there was still a difference in the same direction in 1996, although much smaller, supports our line of arguments. Apart from that, the results of the Cox regressions were disappointing. First vocational preferences were formed earlier in the East, but the vulnerability indicators were irrelevant. Whether or not people had had such experiences did not affect the timing of the transition. Thus, we were not able to demonstrate that the diminished differences in the timing of first vocational preferences (1996 compared to 1991) differed as a function of the personal situation vis-a-vis unification.

Table 2
Survival Analyses and Cox Regressions of the Transition Ages

	Falling in love	*Steady friendship*	*Sexual experiences*	*Vocational preferences*
1991				
Median transition age				
West (1)	14.86	16.17	16.73	16.04
East (2)	14.60	15.96	16.62	14.51
Wilcoxon Test	ns	**	ns	***
Cox Regression by region (risk ratio)	1.08	1.12+[a]	1.09	1.86***
Cox Regression by region, controlled for the vulnerability indices[b] (risk ratio)	1.12 (adolescent unemployment =.78+)	1.07 (loss of parent =1.31*)	1.08 (tenant = 1.17+, rest = 1.26+)	1.85*** (number of children = 1.24*)[c]
1996				
Median transition age				
West (1)	14.77	16.43	16.73	15.95
East (2)	14.57	16.46	16.62	15.52
Wilcoxon Test	ns	ns	ns	*
Cox Regression by region (risk ratio)	1.06	1.02	1.10	1.31***[a]
Cox Regression by region, controlled for the vulnerability indices[b] (risk ratio)	1.04 (number of children = 1.77*)	1.02 (number of children = 1.62+)	1.10 (loss of parent = 1.31+)	1.29**[c]

[a] The statistical assumption of proportional hazard rates was not met.
[b] That is, controlled for gender, education, community size, adolescent unemployment, apprenticeship given up, negative attitudes toward unification, housing, number of children, parental unemployment, and loss of parent.
[c] Not controlled for adolescent unemployment and apprenticeship given up.
$+ p < .10$; $* p < .05$; $** p < .01$; $*** p < .001$.

Constancy and Change in Predictors of Individual Differences in Transition Ages

As mentioned before, past research on the timing of psychosocial transitions also pursued a second approach that was aimed at a better understanding of the mechanisms that connect the timing of biographical transitions with antecedents in people's biographies. Thus, rather than perhaps prematurely finishing our attempt to control for differential experiences with unification consequences, we now turn to this second topic. Note that the inclusion of the vulnerability indices in the Cox regressions reported above already corresponded to this approach. The conditions investigated, however, were concurrent. In the following we focus instead on individual experiences during childhood and early adolescence, which unfortunately had to be gathered retrospectively (but see Brewin, Andrews, & Gotlib, 1993; Scott & Alwin, 1998).

As reported in various papers (Silbereisen & Schwarz, 1998; Silbereisen & Wiesner, 1999; Vondracek, Reitzle, & Silbereisen, 1999), basically the expectation was that predictors indicating active, self-directed, and peer-oriented activities would have a differential effect on the developmental timetables. More specifically, the timing of first romantic involvement would be accelerated, whereas the timing of first vocational preferences would be delayed. In regard to differences between East and West, the idea was that there should be no differences between the regions, neither in 1991 nor 1996, as far as first romantic involvement is concerned. With regard to first vocational preferences, however, we expected in 1991 (and perhaps maintained in 1996) a stronger role of individual factors in the West. The reason behind this expectation was that the former Eastern system gave less leeway to individual decisions (Heinz, 1996).

As was done in the analyses of the median transition ages, we added the sociodemographics and the vulnerability indices to the variables indicating experiences during childhood and adolescence. In summarizing the results across all three indicators of first romantic involvement, the data revealed, beyond many particularities (and even more nil effects), two or three fairly consistent effects across regions and periods that were in line with our basic expectation (for details see Silbereisen & Wiesner, 1999). Furthermore, there were almost no differences between East and West at both times. Finally, also as expected, the level of presumed affectedness by negative events related to German unification did not change the patterns of predictions (nor have a consistent effect on its own).

The variables we used in the prediction of first vocational preferences were not the same as in the previous analyses. This is to be consistent with earlier publications. The global adversity index was replaced with relocation. We also added a measure of identity beliefs. Otherwise the basic outline was the same.

As can be seen from Table 3, wherever there was a significant effect, it tended to be different between the two political regions (see the effects of school track, early negative experiences with relocation, and identity beliefs). Unfortunately, the vulnerability characteristics again did not function as we had hoped. However, two interesting differences compared to 1991 turned up in 1996. Now identity beliefs played a comparable role in East and West (due to their stronger effect in the East in 1996 compared to 1991), thus indicating a similar association between first vocational preferences and broader identity

Table 3
Hierarchical Cox Regressions Predicting Timing of First Vocational Preferences in 1991 and 1996: Risk Ratios

	West		*East*	
Variables	*1991*	*1996*	*1991*	*1996*
Female	1.04	.80	1.04	1.22
Lower school track[a]	1.59***	1.42+	.67	1.30
Middle school track[a]	1.35**	1.14	.89	1.24
≥ 20,000 residents	.74***	.87	1.14	.91
Relocation[b]				
< 9 years old, severe	1.29+	1.90*	1.82**	.56+
< 9 years old, not severe	1.09	1.32	1.38*	1.02
≥ 9 years old, severe	1.22	.95	1.13	1.07
≥ 9 years old, not severe	1.24	1.38	1.22	.86
Negative attitude toward unification	.92	.90	.90	1.10
Tenant[c]	.97	.86	.97	1.05
Rest[c]	1.25	.76	.93	1.15
≥ 4 children	1.29+	1.23	1.29	.68
Loss of parent	.89	1.02	1.03	1.13
Parental unemployment	.68	1.32	1.01	1.03
Cultural encourgement	.97	.92	1.16	1.15
School involvement	1.12	1.15	1.10	1.07
Leisure activities				
Peers	1.03	1.15	1.04	.84
Culture	.88	1.31*	1.06	1.07
Family	1.11+	1.17+	1.08	1.13
Self-improvement	.93	1.01	.92	.96
Identity beliefs[d]				
Moratorium	1.33*	1.24	.92	1.60**
Foreclosure	1.63***	2.24***	1.22	1.96***
Achievement	2.12***	2.35***	1.54*	2.11***
Planfulness	1.08	.75*	.83+	.87
χ^2	93.05	61.82	51.95	37.41
(df)	(24)	(24)	(24)	(24)
p	***	***	***	*
Percent censored	36.3	38.9	18.7	26.4

[a] Dummy coding; adolescents with college track aspirations as reference group.
[b] Dummy coding; adolescents who did not relocate as reference group.
[c] Dummy coding; adolescents residing in house/apartment owned by parents as reference group.
[d] Dummy coding; adolescents in identity diffusion as reference group.
+ $p < .10$; * $p < .05$; ** $p < .01$; *** $p < .001$.

beliefs. Further, the role of early relocation seemed reversed in the East—in 1996 adolescents with such experiences took more time to come up with vocational preferences (for a discussion of this effect see Vondracek et al., 1999; Silbereisen et al., 1997).

Conclusions

We found consistent, although not particularly strong support for our view that the "reshuffling" of social institutions (particularly those related to family and school as the primary developmental contexts of the young) should be reflected in the resolution of developmental tasks that are relatively closely influenced by such forces. The tentative convergence of East and West in the timing of first vocational preferences and the higher similarity of the association between identity beliefs and vocational preferences in both regions in 1996 was our case in point. Consistent with our line of argumentation, none of the above applied to the timing of first romantic involvement.

Yet, a crucial result remains that was not to our delight. We had hoped to trace the missing link between the changed social institutions and the developmental timetables to individual differences in the degree to which people were actually challenged by the unification strains. Although some of the available vulnerability indices were heavily skewed, this cannot explain our failure to meet our goals. In the remainder of this chapter, we discuss some of the possible reasons.

First of all, it could be that the differences and commonalities we found between the (Eastern) cohorts in 1991 and 1996 were actually much less solid than we thought. In other words, the differences with regard to first vocational preferences (the only instance of an institution-influenced psychosocial transition dealt with in this chapter) could have been unsystematic. Moreover, one could argue that the nexus between institutional changes and the developmental timetables studied is less proximal than we claimed, and that thus the entire framework for the interpretation needs to be revised anyway.

Fortunately, we have good reasons not to believe this because when we analyzed biographical transitions in early adulthood that represent clearer demarcations than those reported thus far, the period effects were even stronger. For instance, Juang and Silbereisen (in press) studied the timing and sequence of leaving home, giving birth to the first child, and marriage for our 20- to 29-year-old participants. In 1991, soon after unification, especially Eastern women who had followed the vocational track in school gave birth and married (often in this order) much earlier than their counterparts from the West. This result was as expected and mainly seems to be rooted in the system of social benefits provided by the former East German state (parenthood increased the likelihood of getting an apartment in an otherwise totally state-regulated housing market). Because by 1996 many of the former East German infrastructures and services had disappeared, a delay particularly in giving birth to the first child among women of this educational track was expected in 1996 compared to 1991. This is exactly what we found.

On top of that, in another investigation we were able to pinpoint the causes for a change in the transition ages in more detail. Reitzle and Silbereisen (1999) examined the timing of financial self-support and, again, found analogous changes in the East between 1991 and 1996. Moreover, about half of the individual differences in the timing could be explained by unification-related life experiences, namely, spells of unemployment and whether one had attended professional retraining courses offered by the state.

Therefore, we deem it fair to conclude that the cohort differences in the East between 1991 and 1996 indeed reflect a precipitation of the social and institutional changes inherent to German unification. Why, then, did we not find any indication that our vulnerability variables made a difference despite the fact that the changes in social institutions, as mentioned above, had an impact?

One answer is that the conditions we introduced were too distal and/or too unspecific. For instance, negative attitudes toward the new Germany can cover many different things and may not even be conducive for actions at all (as is well known in survey research on public opinion, people very often claim a state of emergency for the state but nevertheless report their personal circumstances as being quite favorable).

The plausibility of this argument seems obvious when one compares what we did with attempts by Elder and colleagues to bridge the gap between social change and individual adaptation. In their case, the economic hardships were first translated into immediate perceptions and reactions with regard to saving potentials, such as reduced expenditures for the household or for services, and only this in turn had an effect on psychological well-being (Conger, Ge, Elder, Lorenz, & Simons, 1994; Elder, Conger, Foster, & Ardelt, 1992). Seen in this way, our vulnerability indices were certainly remote and unspecific.

And yet we do not believe this remoteness to be the actual (at least not the only) reason. Interestingly enough, our own analyses of the present samples' coping with economic changes and hardships, utilizing a model designed in the style of Elder and Conger, give a hint. Whereas parts of the model worked in East and West as expected, a remarkable difference turned up concerning the role of experienced economic hardships for well-being. In the West those stricken by hardships showed correspondingly higher levels of depressive mood; in the East, however, almost no such effects were observed (Forkel & Silbereisen, in press). The most plausible explanation left had to do with the particular characterization of hardships in the East as "collective fate." We speculated this exerted a protective shield (even if not justified in a particular case) that would help to maintain one's psychological health (see Winefield, Tiggeman, & Winefield, 1992).

This is not to say that people would not adapt to new challenges, but, due to attributions of failures to the social system rather than the person, negative effects are minimized, and consequently attempts to avoid them cannot be the key to adaptation. Rather, particularly with regard to the developmental timetables, we believe people adjust easily when "collective molds" are provided. Seen in this vein, the delay of parenthood as observed in Eastern females of the lower educational track would not require the experience of any personal drawbacks, such as a recent spell of unemployment. Instead, it would be enough to live in an area where such events are frequently reported, to listen to family sagas where such reactions are described as adequate, or to observe models in the media.

In the extensive debate on the mechanisms of value change, similar arguments play a role with regard to current influences rather than effects of early socialization experiences (Flanagan, 1982). More specifically, the question is whether features of the macrocontext (like unemployment rates) or individual experiences are decisive. Interestingly enough, a recent study on value change in former East Germany found a rather weak role of individual experiences (which were more topic-specific than our vulnerability indices) such as disappointments with social justice (Zelle, 1998).

Although we have to admit that our analyses at best scratched the surface of the processes linking the macro level of the changed institutions and the micro level of individuals' personality developments, we were able to add a bit more substance to what loose coupling as introduced by Elder and O'Rand (1995) could mean. Given the fact that the analyses utilized retrospective data of a psychometrically rather weak nature, and bearing in mind the cross-sectional cohort design, more caveats apply. The advantage we had was a rather fresh look at an unprecedented social change, which surprised almost everybody, including social scientists.

References

Brewin, C. R., Andrews, B., & Gotlib, I. H. (1993). Psycho-pathology and early experience: A reappraisal of retrospective reports. *Psychological Bulletin, 113,* 82–98.

Conger, R. D., Ge, X., Elder, G. H., Lorenz, F. O., & Simons, R. L. (1994). Economic stress, coercive family process, and developmental problems of adolescents. *Child Development, 65,* 541–561.

Dekovic, M., Noom, M. J., & Meeus, W. (1997). Expectations regarding development during adolescence: Parental and adolescent perceptions. *Journal of Youth and Adolescence, 26,* 253–272.

Elder, G. H., Conger, R. D., Foster, E. M., & Ardelt, M. (1992). Families under economic pressure. *Journal of Family Issues, 13,* 5–37.

Elder, G. H., & O'Rand, A. M. (1995). Adult lives in a changing society. In K. S. Cook, G. A. Fine, & J. S. House (Eds.), *Sociological perspectives on social psychology* (pp. 452–475). Needham Heights, MA: Allyn & Bacon.

Feldman, S. S., & Rosenthal, D. A. (1990). The acculturation of autonomy expectations in Chinese high schoolers residing in two Western nations. *International Journal of Psychology, 25,* 259–281.

Fischer, A. (1992). Zur Stichprobe [On the sample]. In Jugendwerk der Deutschen Shell (Ed.), *Jugend '92* (Vol. 4, pp. 59–63). Opladen, Germany: Leske + Budrich.

Forkel, I., & Silbereisen, R. K. (in press). Family economic hardship and depressed mood of young adolescents from former East and West Germany. *American Behavioral Scientist.*

George, L. K. (1993). Sociological perspectives on life transitions. *Annual Review of Sociology, 19,* 353–373.

Hamilton, S. F. (1990). *Apprenticeship for adulthood: Preparing youth for the future.* New York: The Free Press.

Havighurst, R. J. (1972). *Developmental tasks and education* (3rd ed.). New York: Longmans, Green.

Heinz, W. R. (1996). Berufsverläufe im Transformationsprozeß [Career trajectories during the social and political transformation]. In S. E. Hormuth, W. R. Heinz, H.-J. Kornadt, H. Sydow, & G. Trommsdorff (Eds.), *Individuelle Entwicklung, Bildung und Berufsverläufe* (pp. 273–329). Opladen, Germany: Leske + Budrich.

Juang, L., & Silbereisen, R. K. (in press). Family transitions for young adult females in the context of a changed Germany: Timing, sequence, and duration. *American Behavioral Scientist.*

Juang, L. P., Silbereisen, R. K., & Wiesner, M. (1999). Predictors of leaving home in young adults raised in Germany: A replication of a 1991 study. *Journal of Marriage and the Family, 61,* 505–515.

Kornadt, H.-J. (1996). Erziehung und Bildung im Transformationsprozeß [Socialization and education during the social and political transformation]. In S. E. Hormuth, W. R. Heinz, H.-J. Kornadt, H. Sydow, & G. Trommsdorff (Eds.), *Individuelle Entwicklung, Bildung und Berufsverläufe* (pp. 201–272). Opladen, Germany: Leske + Budrich.

Masche, J. G., & Reitzle, M. (1999). Stichprobe und Design [Sample and design]. In R. K. Silbereisen & J. Zinnecker (Eds.), *Entwicklung im sozialen Wandel* (pp. 39–62). Weinheim, Germany: PVU.

Reitzle, M., & Silbereisen, R. K. (1999). *The impact of structural factors on the timing of transitions into work: The example of social change in Eastern Germany.* Manuscript submitted for publication.

Schmitt-Rodermund, E., & Silbereisen, R. K. (in press). Determinants of differential acculturation of developmental timetables among adolescent immigrants to Germany. *International Journal of Psychology.*

Scott, J., & Alwin, D. (1998). Retrospective versus prospective measurement of life histories in longitudinal research. In J. Z. Giele & G. H. Elder (Eds.), *Methods of life-course re-*

search. Qualitative and quantitative approaches (pp. 98–127). Thousand Oaks, CA: Sage.

Silbereisen, R. K. (2000). German unification and adolescents' developmental timetables: Continuities and discontinuities. In L. Crockett & R. K. Silbereisen (Eds.), *Negotiating adolescence in times of social change* (pp. 104–122). Cambridge, UK: Cambridge University Press.

Silbereisen, R. K., & Schwarz, B. (1998). Predicting the timing of first romantic involvement: Commonalities and differences in the former Germanys. In J. E. Nurmi (Ed.), *Adolescents, cultures, and conflicts: Growing up in Europe* (pp. 129–148). New York: Garland.

Silbereisen, R. K., Schwarz, B., & Rinker, B. (1996). The timing of psychosocial transitions in adolescence: Commonalities and differences in unified Germany. In J. Youniss (Ed.), *New directions in child development: Vol. 70. After the wall: Family adaptation in East and West Germany* (pp. 23–38). San Francisco: Jossey-Bass.

Silbereisen, R. K., Vondracek, F. W., & Berg, L. A. (1997). Differential timing of initial vocational choice: The influence of early childhood family relocation and parental support behaviors in two cultures. *Journal of Vocational Behavior, 50,* 41–59.

Silbereisen, R. K., & Wiesner, M. (1999). Erste romantische Beziehungen bei Jugendlichen aus Ost- und Westdeutschland: Ein Vergleich der Prädiktoren von 1991 und 1996 [First romantic relationships among adolescents from East and West Germany: A comparison of predictors for 1991 and 1996]. In R. K. Silbereisen & J. Zinnecker (Eds.), *Entwicklung im sozialen Wandel* (pp. 101–118). Weinheim, Germany: PVU.

Vondracek, F. W., Reitzle, M., & Silbereisen, R. K. (1999). The influence of changing contexts and historical time on the timing of initial vocational choices. In R. K. Silbereisen & A. von Eye (Eds.), *Growing up in times of social change* (pp. 151–169). New York: de Gruyter.

Wiesner, M., & Pickel, G. (1996). Stichprobe und Methoden [Sample and methods]. In R. K. Silbereisen, L. A. Vaskovics, & J. Zinnecker (Eds.), *Jungsein in Deutschland* (pp. 369–380). Opladen, Germany: Leske + Budrich.

Willet, J. B., & Singer, J. D. (1991). How long did it take? Using survival analysis in educational and psychological research. In L. M. Collins & J. L. Horn (Eds.), *Best methods for the analysis of change: Recent advances, unanswered questions, future directions* (pp. 310–327). Washington, DC: American Psychological Association.

Winefield, A. H., Tiggemann, M., & Winefield, H. R. (1992). Unemployment distress, reasons for job loss and causal attributions for unemployment in young people. *Journal of Occupational and Organizational Psychology, 65,* 213–218.

Zapf, W., & Habich, R. (1999). *Die Wohlfahrtsentwicklung in der Bundesrepublik Deutschland 1949 bis 1999* [Welfare trends in the Federal Republic of Germany 1949 to 1999]. Wissenschaftszentrum Berlin: Jahrbuch. Berlin, Germany: Wissenschaftszentrum.

Zelle, C. (1998). Soziale und liberale Wertorientierungen: Versuch einer situativen Erklärung der Unterschiede zwischen Ost- und Westdeutschen [Social and liberal value orientations: An approach toward situative explanations of differences between East and West Germans]. *Aus Politik und Zeitgeschichte, 41/42,* 24–36.

Acknowledgment

The research reported in this chapter was conducted with the support of the German Research Council (Si 296/14-3; Principal Investigator R. K. Silbereisen). We want to thank the other principal investigators of our interdisciplinary research consortium (J. Zinnecker, L. Vaskovics) and all the participants of the studies.

PART FOUR

Work, Love, and Children: Individual Motivation and Societal Conditions for Mastering Developmental Tasks in Adulthood

2000 Elsevier Science B.V.

14 Motivation and Volition in Pursuing Personal Work Goals

Lutz von Rosenstiel, Hugo M. Kehr, and Günter W. Maier

Developmental psychology, some time ago, claimed not only to comprise the study of childhood and adolescence, but the life span as a whole (Baltes, Reese, & Lipsitt, 1980; Oerter & Montada, 1998). In this chapter we will concentrate on the age group of young adults, primarily on those who graduated from university. For young adults, intimacy versus isolation is the characteristic crisis of this period in life, as Erikson (1950) has described in his brave and somewhat speculative eight developmental phases. During this stage two important issues, among others, are building solidarity with a group and simultaneously rejecting influences that could jeopardize one's own identity.

The transition from leaving university to entering an occupation marks a critical developmental step (von Rosenstiel, Nerdinger, & Spieß, 1991, 1998; von Rosenstiel, Nerdinger, Spieß, & Stengel, 1989). The socialization climate at universities is clearly different from the socialization climate at business organizations and public administrations where most university graduates start their career. As a consequence, a mismatch of values can be expected that university graduates may experience as a "reality shock" when confronted with their new organizational environment. Furthermore, this passage is prone to anxiousness due to heightened unemployment rates among university graduates (cf. von Rosenstiel, 1998). Hence, the beginning of a career can from several perspectives be seen as a critical life event (Filipp, 1981), decisively influencing the individual development of university graduates.

After having started a business career, further vocational activities provide additional impulses in the occupational development of the young adult. Particularly training programs are a systematic instrument used to prepare and qualify employees for new tasks in an organization. Because university graduates are most frequently employed in leadership positions they are more likely to be offered management training to improve their leadership skills than technical training (cf. Kehr, Bles, & von Rosenstiel, 1999a).

To meet the demands of these two core steps in career development—entering the workplace and acquiring leadership skills through training—the individual's motivation and volition are of utmost importance. The search for a suitable position requires self-initiative that goes beyond internalized norms. Nowadays, university graduates are often employed as highly specialized professionals, usually being better qualified than their supervisors. This has shifted the supervisors' functional relevance: Formerly, supervisors stood out because of their exceptional expert knowledge, whereas contemporarily their leadership function mainly consists of coordinating specialists as members of their teams. On the other hand, the specialists themselves are responsible for setting their own goals and monitoring themselves. Etzioni's (1967) reasoning is still valid here, because performance is determined less by external forces or by basic exchange principles (e.g., performance for money), and more through the individual's identification with her or his task, team, and organization. In effect, internal pressure continuously replaces external pressure. The psychological mechanisms that translate internal pressure into successful action must be understood in terms of motivation (Herzberg, Mausner, & Snyderman, 1959; Maslow, 1943; von Rosenstiel, 1975; Vroom, 1964) and volition (Kehr, 1999; Kuhl & Beckmann, 1994; Sokolowski, 1996).

In this chapter the enigmatic constructs of motivation and volition will be closely examined, specifically with regard to their relevance for occupational development. We begin with a brief description of some outstanding motivational concepts related to industrial and organizational psychology. We then present some recent work of our research team concerning the relevance of motivation and volition in entering the workplace and in acquiring leadership skills in management training. Finally, we conclude with some remarks concerning the value of including concepts of motivation and volition in research about organizational socialization and vocational development.

Motivational Theories in Industrial and Organizational Psychology

By looking at subject and author indexes in textbooks of industrial and organizational psychology (I/O psychology) and human resource management, the reader finds references to motivational theories and authors that are only occasionally or not at all mentioned in handbooks or readers of motivational psychology. One can speculate about the reasons for this omission. Perhaps it takes several decades until current research in general motivational (e.g., Heckhausen, 1991; Weiner, 1996) and volitional psychology (e.g., Kuhl &

Beckmann, 1994; Sokolowski, 1996; cf. Kehr, 1999) becomes acknowledged in I/O psychology. Another explanation could be that even though some models may be questioned for theoretical or empirical reasons from the perspective of general psychology, they may nevertheless be preferred in I/O psychology, because of their pragmatic stance and closeness to applied settings. This is true, for example, of Maslow's (1943) hierarchical theory of needs and of Vroom's (1964) value-instrumentality-expectation (VIE) model. Both models underwent considerable critique because of their theoretical conceptualization and empirical validation. Nevertheless, in I/O psychology they are considered prototypes of content and process models of motivation, respectively (Campbell & Pritchard, 1976; Nerdinger, 1994; von Rosenstiel, 2000).

Content Theories: Maslow and the Consequences

Several categories can be used to classify motives. However, the most convincing category, at least in lay psychology, is the content of a motive. One speaks more about need content such as drinking, eating, sleeping, social contact, sexual activity, social esteem, and so forth than about categories like innate versus environmentally determined or central versus peripheral motives. The desire for simplicity and plausibility is satisfied with Maslow's (1943, 1954) hierarchical theory of needs. Five motives (physiological needs, safety needs, social needs, esteem needs, self-actualization needs) are—at least in one of several versions of Maslow's model—arranged in the form of a pyramid where lower needs have to be satisfied before needs of the next step can be activated.

Although neither Maslow's taxonomy nor the hierarchical order were supported by empirical research (Huizinga, 1970; Miner & Dachler, 1973), for practitioners the model did not lose its popularity. Too well does Maslow's hierarchical theory of needs seem to fit naive psychological assumptions, to mirror everyday life experiences ("food first, moral second ..."), and to meet expectations of social desirability (i.e., the striving for self-actualization is socially highly valued). In the organizational realm, the model provides implicit recommendations for managerial action. The hierarchically arranged need categories are suggestive in terms of which organizational incentives (e.g., cafeteria, organizational security systems, teamwork, status symbols, delegation as a leadership principle) match the needs at the various levels. However, the empirical questions still remain unanswered whether these incentives actually do satisfy the needs on the targeted levels and whether the desired achievement behaviors are thereby aroused. Alternative content theories of motivation, such as Alderfer's (1972), albeit being empirically better sustained than Maslow's approach, generally are much less widespread among practitioners.

Process Theories—Vroom and the Consequences

Rarely has an assumption been so widely accepted in organizational and social sciences as the Bernoulli principle. It postulates that a preference should be given to the alternative that maximizes the product of utility and probability of success. While economic and behavioral theories tend to use objective measures for utility and probability indicators most psychological theories such as decision models (Edwards, 1962) or motivational theories (e.g., Lewin, 1939; Tolman, 1932) rather tend to use subjectively based measures. Vroom's (1964) VIE model has extended these conceptions with instrumentality considerations: An action is performed when it is subjectively perceived as being a means (I = instrumentality) to reach a highly valued goal (V = valence) and when the probability of successful execution is high (E = expectancy). Although the VIE approach seems to be overly cognitive (Heckhausen, 1991), it is considerably well accepted in I/O psychology, as it is in the behavioral sciences, presumably because its rational conceptualization corresponds to the common way of thinking in these areas. Its usefulness for application purposes lies in the concept of instrumentality. The organizationally desired achievement behavior should be seen as instrumental to reach one's personal highly valued goals. Nevertheless, the VIE theory—although being formally highly structured—does not predict which goal an individual will value in a given situation. From case to case, this needs to be empirically established. Various authors have criticized other aspects of the VIE theory (e.g., Blickle, 1997; van Eerde & Thierry, 1996) and it has been differentiated and modified in several ways (e.g., Graen, 1969; Lawler, 1973). But still it is by far the most frequently cited and the most recognized process theory in I/O psychology.

Some other motivational theories that were either influential in I/O psychology or that even were developed within this domain cannot be unambiguously classified as content or process theories, mainly because they contain propositions regarding content and process alike. This is the case for theories of achievement motivation (Atkinson, 1964; Heckhausen, 1965; McClelland, Atkinson, Clark, & Lowell, 1953), several equilibrium assumptions (Adams,

1963; Patchen, 1961), and for the concept of flow experience (Csikszentmihalyi, 1975).

Further Motivational Concepts in I/O Psychology

In the attempt to carry out applied research that is both theoretically and empirically valid, researchers afforded neither Maslow's hierarchical theory of needs nor Vroom's VIE theory a dominant role. Instead, two additional models have to be mentioned here that stimulated considerable and occasionally controversial discussion: the two-factor theory by Herzberg et al. (1959) and the goal-setting theory by Locke and Latham (1990).

"The Motivation to Work"—Herzberg's Controversial Concept

The study of Herzberg and his colleagues (Herzberg et al., 1959), which was to become one of the most cited studies in I/O psychology, started with rather vague theoretical considerations that lead to unexpected empirical findings. Using Flanagan's (1954) critical incident technique, Herzberg et al. interviewed employees about in which situations they were particularly satisfied and how this influenced their achievement orientation. Then they reversed the question and asked in which specific situations the employees were particularly dissatisfied and how this again influenced their achievement orientation.

To summarize the results, Herzberg et al. (1959) found that so-called "motivators" such as previous achievements, assigned responsibility, and the opportunity for mental growth are most basic for experiencing satisfaction. It is a core feature of these motivators that they are directly linked to the content of the work process ("content variable") and thus relate to intrinsic motivation and the willingness to achieve alike. In contrast, so-called "hygiene factors" such as interpersonal relations, company policies, working conditions, and payment, are predominant causes for dissatisfaction at work. Hygiene factors relate to the framework conditions of work ("context variable"), which at best may contribute to the removal of the existing dissatisfaction but directly cause neither satisfaction nor the willingness to achieve.

The findings reported by Herzberg et al. (1959) were replicated whenever the same method was used. However, if different methods were used, the expected results could almost never be obtained. Equally problematic seems to be the theoretical argument that the participants' responses may be biased according to a tendency to maintain self-esteem: The causes for satisfaction are attributed to oneself, for example, one's own achievements, whereas the causes for dissatisfaction are attributed to external causes, for example, the supervisor. But neither these nor further critical arguments regarding Herzberg's method, categorization system, and theory (cf. Gebert & von Rosenstiel, 1996; Locke & Henne, 1986; Neuberger, 1974; Vroom, 1964) hampered the widespread use of Herzberg's theory in applied settings. This may be due to the specific recommendations derived from the theory on how to shape work content and work environment to stimulate work motivation. Other models, such as the job characteristics theory by Hackman and Oldham (1974), while being more carefully defined, have not received the same attention as Herzberg's approach.

Goal Setting Theory—Locke's Empirically Well-Established Approach

A vast body of evidence has demonstrated the validity of Locke and his colleagues' basic proposition that difficult goals that are specifically defined lead to increased achievement in contrast to do-your-best goals that are ill-defined (cf., for an overview, Locke & Latham, 1990). Additional factors that are important for the impact of goal setting on job performance are the employee's acceptance of the goal and the feedback given on the progress made towards reaching the goal. Meta-analyses such as Guzzo, Jette, and Katzell's (1985) show that adequate goal-setting programs increase achievement considerably and are comparably effective as financial incentives or work-structuring methods. Nevertheless, goal-setting theory leaves open several questions of motivational and volitional relevance, for example, how goals relate to motives (cf., Brunstein, Schultheiss, & Maier, 1999), which psychological mechanisms mediate the goal-setting process (e.g., conflicts between goals, volitional conflict resolution strategies, etc.; cf. Kehr, 1999; Kuhl, 1996; Sokolowski, 1996), and how goals actually translate into action (cf. Carver & Scheier, 1981).

All approaches discussed so far were almost exclusively used to provide supervisors with scientifically based help in motivating subordinates (Comelli & von Rosenstiel, 1995). Thus, the models serve chiefly to motivate *others* (von Rosenstiel, 1988), rather than to motivate *oneself.* Taking into consideration that highly qualified specialists, either in organizational leadership positions or as self-employed professionals, primarily have to motivate *themselves,* it seems more appropriate to consider those models that emphasize self-motivation. This applies for the concept of personal goals (Brunstein & Maier, 1996) and for models of volitional action control (Kehr, 1999; Kuhl & Beckmann, 1994; Sokolowski, 1996) alike. Our research team has primarily investigated the relevance of such concepts for organizational socialization processes.

Motivation and Volition During Organizational Socialization

Organizational socialization is defined as the learning process in the course of which abilities, values, and attitudes are acquired that are necessary to execute successfully a role in an organization (e.g., Ashford & Taylor, 1990; Fisher, 1986; Van Maanen, 1976; Van Maanen & Schein, 1979). As an attempt to systematize the main demands employees are confronted with during each of the several stages of organizational socialization, phase models were developed (e.g., Buchanan, 1974; Feldman, 1976; Porter, Lawler, & Hackman, 1975; Van Maanen, 1976; Wanous, 1992). Accordingly, typical phases of organizational socialization include the time period prior to membership in an organization, the initial integration into an organization, as well as subsequent horizontal or vertical progression (Maier & Rappensperger, 1999). The traditional research approach of organizational socialization examines primarily effects of socialization procedures on employees, where employees are viewed largely as passive recipients of such procedures. Examples of such socialization procedures are the realistic job preview (e.g., Wanous, 1989; Waung, 1995), mentoring (e.g., Chao, Walz, & Gardner, 1992; Scandura, 1992), or training (e.g., Tannenbaum & Yukl, 1992). These traditional approaches are now supplemented by a more modern view, namely the approach of "proactive socialization." Based on the assumption that newcomers need to gather information to make sense of their new environment (Louis, 1980), their *active* efforts in seeking information were theoretically discussed (Ashford & Taylor, 1990; Miller & Jablin, 1991; Taylor & Giannantonio, 1993) and empirically studied (Ashford & Cummings, 1985; Brett, Feldman, & Weingart, 1990; Morrison, 1993a, 1993b). The concept of "sense making" and the associated feedback seeking can best be understood in terms of striving for personal work goals, because individuals seek feedback particularly for behavior that relates to their goals (cf., Ashford, 1986).

Personal Work Goals and Organizational Socialization

In our first series of studies we focused on the proactive assumptions, that (new) employees not only are passive recipients of organizational socialization practices but also take an active part in the socialization process. Central to the newcomers' active involvement are the goals they strive for. The concept of personal goals (Brunstein & Maier, 1996; Emmons, 1996) is particularly useful in investigating this assumption. Personal goals are plans and ventures of individuals for which they currently strive and that they seek to attain in the future. In a series of studies it was shown that several characteristics of personal goals, such as commitment to personal goals, goal attainability, or perceived strain in goal striving, are linked to subjective well-being (for an overview, cf. Brunstein et al., 1999).

In our first study we examined whether progress in personal work goal achievement mediates the effect of newcomer socialization practices on organizational integration (Rappensperger, Maier, & Wittmann, 1998). We recruited 910 university graduates to participate in this longitudinal study. The initial testing period took place about half a year after entering the organization (Time 1); the second one was one year later (Time 2). At Time 1, the following independent variables were assessed: newcomer's experience of social support (quantity and quality) and estimates of how realisticly participants perceived their job preview (realistic job preview). Previous studies have demonstrated that social support during organizational entry (Feldman & Brett, 1983; Fisher, 1985; Nelson & Quick, 1991) and realistic job preview (e.g., Phillips, 1998) are beneficial for organizational integration. At Time 2, successful integration in the new organization was measured using the following dependent variables: job satisfaction, organizational commitment, and intentions to leave the job (cf. Major, Kozlowski, Chao, & Gardner, 1995). To gather information on the mediating variables, responses to a list of 29 potential personal work goals were assessed at Times 1 and 2. At Time 1, the university graduates were asked to check which of the goals they actually pursued, and at Time 2, they estimated their progress in reaching these goals.

In line with earlier research, our study replicated findings concerning the favorable effects of social support and realistic job preview during organizational entry: Social support and realistic job preview in tandem accounted for a significant portion of variance of successful integration 12 months later ($.04 < R^2 < .09$). However, of particular interest is that these relationships were mediated by progress in goal attainment at Time 2. Goal attainment correlated significantly with social support and realistic job preview as well as with successful integration. The direct test of mediation demonstrated, for example, that—goal progress being partialed out—the portion of variance in job satisfaction accounted for by social support and realistic job preview declined from 9% to 6%. Thus, our findings supported the notion that successful striving for personal work goals has to be seen as an important mediating factor in the process of organizational entry. Helpful socialization practices facilitate the newcomer's progress in personal work goal achievement, which in turn leads to successful adaptation to the new organization.

Our next study was to extend the findings on the mediating function of goal progress by looking for goal-specific factors that enable newcomers to reach goal progress (Maier, 1996; Maier & Brunstein, 2000). This study was based on the goal commitment × goal attainability model of subjective well-being (Brunstein et al., 1999): According to this model, newcomers should be successfully integrated into an organization if they perceive favorable conditions for reaching their goals. This effect should be particularly high if newcomers are strongly committed to their goals. The postulated interaction effect of goal commitment and goal attainability for successful integration should be mediated by progress in reaching personal work goals.

These hypotheses were examined in a longitudinal study with three testing periods covering eight months. At Time 1, the respondents had been working in their organization for about 20 weeks. At that time we assessed their personal work goals, estimates of goal commitment and goal attainability, as well as indicators of successful integration (job satisfaction and organizational commitment). Data collection for Times 2 and 3 took place four and eight months after Time 1, respectively. At Times 2 and 3 job satisfaction and organizational commitment were measured again, and in addition, progress on goal attainment was assessed.

Hierarchical regression analyses revealed that the interaction of goal commitment and goal attainability was significantly related to changes in job satisfaction and organizational commitment. This interaction effect was of the expected direction: First, for individuals with *high goal commitment,* who reported having *favorable* conditions to attain their goals, job satisfaction and organizational commitment increased from Time 1 to Times 2 and 3, respectively. Second, for individuals with high goal commitment, but who reported *unfavorable* conditions, job satisfaction and organizational commitment decreased from Time 1 to Times 2 and 3, respectively. Third, for individuals with *low goal commitment* job satisfaction and organizational commitment were independent from goal attainability. The interaction effect remained significant even if goal-unspecific resources at the workplace (e.g., control at work, social support at work) were statistically controlled. Further, we could show that the influence of the interaction on job satisfaction and organizational commitment was mediated by progress in goal attainment.

These results clearly support the proposition that newcomers should be seen as active participants in the process of organizational socialization. This active role can be studied within the framework of personal work goals. Provided employees are committed to pursuing their personal work goals, the success of their integration into the new organization depends to a high degree on their goal-specific resources: If appropriate goal-specific resources are available, integration will succeed; if they are lacking, it may fail.

Volitional Factors in Management Training Transfer

After the entry into an organization, further vocational activities guide the course of the individual's organizational socialization. Particularly, organizational training efforts intend appropriate attitudinal and behavioral changes of the employee, and thus, to contribute to her or his development. However, generally speaking, management training transfer is quite low. Research on factors influencing training transfer has led to an increased interest in motivational variables, for example, self-efficacy (Mathieu, Martineau, & Tannenbaum, 1993), commitment and motivation (Kehr, Bles, & von Rosenstiel, 1999c; Tannenbaum, Mathieu, Salas, & Cannon-Bowers, 1991), or motive dispositions (Sokolowski & Kehr, 1999).

Taking for granted Tannenbaum and Yukl's (1992, p. 414), remark that "it is widely accepted that learning and transfer will occur only when trainees have both the ability ("can do") and volition ("will do") to acquire and apply new skills," it seems surprising that in research on training transfer, volitional factors have been widely neglected. The study reported here (cf. Kehr, Bles, & von Rosenstiel, 1999b) serves as an example of the efforts to bridge this gap. It focuses on the impact of volitional factors on training transfer, particularly on management training transfer, as our concern is mainly in the development of university graduates, who often tend to occupy management positions.

The theoretical background of the Kehr et al. (1999b) study is the theory of volitional action control (Kuhl, 1996; Kuhl & Fuhrmann, 1998; Kuhl & Goschke, 1994a; Sokolowski, 1996). This theory conceptualizes volition as an array of conflict-resolution mechanisms and strategies to overcome difficulties in the action process caused by competing action tendencies (Kehr, 1999; Kuhl & Goschke, 1994a; Sokolowski, 1996). With respect to training transfer, old habits, tempting alternatives, or simply a lack of motivation are typical difficulties that may arise when individuals attempt to reach their goals and to realize what they have learned.

Kuhl (1996; Kuhl & Fuhrmann, 1998) distinguishes two modes of volition: self-regulation and self-control. Self-regulation is a self-integrating ("democratic") style of action control whereas self-control is a self-disciplined ("authoritarian") style. How self-regulation and self-control presumably influence management training transfer will be illustrated in detail by introducing the dependent variables used in this study: goal memory, emotions when enacting goals, and success of training transfer.

To empirically address the relevance of the theory of volitional action control in management training transfer we conducted a longitudinal field study with a sample of managers of a German insurance company (Kehr et al., 1999b). The managers attended a two-day management training course, the objectives of which were behavioral techniques for the recruitment and leadership of employees. Self-regulation and self-control were assessed at the outset of the training course (Time 1) using two scales of the Volitional Components Inventory (VCI), a self-report questionnaire that was developed and experimentally validated by Kuhl and Fuhrmann (1998). At the end of the training course (Time 2) the managers were asked to formulate three idiosyncratic goals for how to implement what they have learned. The dependent variables—goal memory, emotions, success of training transfer—were assessed three months after the course (Time 3).

Goal Memory. During management training courses, managers set themselves goals specifying how to implement what they have learned. The faculty to keep these goals in memory is an important prerequisite for training transfer (cf. Bjork, 1994). Adapting the theory of action control (Kuhl, 1996; Kuhl & Fuhrmann, 1998) to the process of setting training transfer goals, it is to be expected that a trainee scoring high on self-regulation will form these goals in a self-integrating manner. He or she might carefully weigh the trainers' proposals against his or her own needs, predilections, and habits. A manager scoring high on self-control, on the other hand, will tend to adopt willingly the goals proposed by trainers and supervisors while ignoring his or her own preferences. It seems plausible that self-congruent goals can be assumed to be more realistic than self-incongruent goals (cf. Brunstein et al., 1999). In combination with the finding that realistic goals are better remembered than unrealistic goals (Kuhl & Goschke, 1994b), we expected that self-regulators should be better able to remember their goals than self-controllers.

Goal memory (free recall at Time 3 of the three idiosyncratic goals assessed at Time 2) was compared for the two extreme groups: self-regulation high and self-control low (Group 1: *self-regulators*) versus self-regulation low and self-control high (Group 2: *self-controllers*). The results show that self-regulators recall significantly more intentions ($M = 2.2$) than self-controllers ($M = 1.5$; $p < .05$).

Emotions Elicited by Enacting Goals. Emotions play an important role in the action process. Action can be conceptualized as an interaction of emotional and cognitive processes operating as parallel systems (Kuhl & Goschke, 1994a; Leventhal & Scherer, 1987). One major proposition of the Kuhl model is that the self-regulation mode activates a reward system that is accompanied by positive emotions whereas the self-control mode activates a punishment system that is accompanied by negative emotions (Kuhl, 1996; Kuhl & Fuhrmann, 1998). Therefore, we hypothesized that self-regulation is associated with positive emotions, whereas self-control is associated with negative emotions.

Emotions experienced by managers while trying to enact their training transfer goals were measured using a bipolar emotion scale (low scores indicate negative emotions; high scores indicate positive emotions). A regression analysis revealed that high self-regulation at Time 1 led to experiencing positive emotions while enacting the goals, whereas high self-control led to experiencing negative emotions. Taken together, both predictors accounted for 32% of the variance of the managers' emotional experience.

Success of Training Transfer. As can be seen in the aforementioned comparison of self-regulation and self-control, the theory of action control, generally speaking, clearly favors the self-regulation mode (Kuhl, 1996; Kuhl & Fuhrmann, 1998). Therefore, we expected that self-regulation increases the success of training courses, whereas self-control impedes the success of training courses.

Two indicators for success of training courses were used: goal realization (perceived progress in attaining the personal training transfer goals) and criteria fulfillment (degree to which a set of nomothetic criteria were met). The results of the study reveal that self-regulation significantly increases the success of management training transfer, both in terms of goal realization and criteria fulfillment. However, the expected negative effect of self-control on success of training transfer could only be sustained with respect to goal realization. The postulated negative effect of self-control on criteria fulfillment, however, fails to be statistically significant (p = .057).

The results obtained by the Kehr et al. (1999b) study encourage the discussion of possible implications for teaching and training. Compared to self-control, self-regulation seems to offer several advantages for training transfer, particularly with respect to goal memory, emotions, and success. This indicates that training methods that allow self-regulation should be favored over those that reinforce self-control. Thus, training courses should stimulate the trainees' self-determination (cf. Deci & Ryan, 1985): Instead of insisting on preformulated training goals, trainers should allow trainees to elaborate their personal need structure when developing individual training goals.

Furthermore, training courses could be specifically designed to improve self-regulatory skills. Our research team is currently developing an intervention program to improve managers' meta-motivational and meta-volitional skills (for an elaboration of this distinction, see Kehr, 1999). It aims at enhancing self-regulation and at the same time reducing excessive self-control (over-control). Specifically, managers should develop their ability to form self-congruent goals (meta-motivation) and to flexibly employ volitional strategies whenever barriers to action arise (meta-volition).

Conclusion

Traditionally, both applied concepts on work motivation and organizational socialization models have conceptualized employees as being passively exposed to organizational influences. Classical work motivation theories generally give advice on how the staff is led to be motivated. In a related vein, traditional models of organizational socialization primarily focus on the practices and mechanisms that adjust employees to organizational settings. Practitioners have widely shared the view of the organization being dominant in the socialization process and have recognized the employees' active part only insofar as abilities and skills were concerned.

Recent developments in motivational and volitional theories, however, portray employees as being active agents in the socialization process. In mastering important developmental steps employees set themselves personal work goals, mobilize resources of their organizational environment, and strive to accomplish their goals. The studies reported here have adopted this view. We were mainly interested in analyzing the role of motivational and volitional factors in personal development, specifically during entering an organization and during further vocational training. With respect to organizational entry we found that goal commitment, availability of goal-relevant resources, and goal attainment improves successful integration. With respect, to further vocational training we demonstrated that a flexible mode of volitional action control (i.e., self-regulation), in contrast to a more rigid mode of action control (i.e., self-control), enhances management training transfer.

Taken together, these results illustrate the relevance of personal work goals with respect to their motivational and volitional significance in organizational socialization. Nevertheless, when studying motivational and volitional processes in organizational settings several question remain to be answered. Which factors influence the choosing and setting of personal work goals? How are personal work goals linked to related psychological constructs such as implicit motives? Which internal conflicts and external obstacles may hinder their realization and how are these overcome? Research in this challenging field may help to find solutions to the old question of how to integrate the demands of the organization and the development of the individual.

References

Adams, J. S. (1963). Toward an understanding of inequity. *Journal of Abnormal and Social Psychology, 67,* 422–436.

Alderfer, C. P. (1972). *Existence, relatedness, and growth. Human needs in organizational settings.* New York: The Free Press.

Ashford, S. J. (1986). Feedback-seeking in individual adaption: A resource perspective. *Academy of Management Review, 29,* 465–487.

Ashford, S. J., & Cummings, L. L. (1985). Proactive feedback seeking: The instrumental use of the information environment. *Journal of Occupational Psychology, 58,* 67–79.

Ashford, S. J., & Taylor, M. S. (1990). Adaption to work transitions: An integrative approach. *Research in Personnel and Human Resources Management, 8,* 1–39.

Atkinson, J. W. (1964). *An introduction of motivation.* Princeton, NJ: Van Nostrand.

Baltes, P. B., Reese, H. W., & Lipsitt, L. P. (1980). Life-span developmental psychology. *Annual Review of Psychology, 31,* 65–110.

Bjork, R. A. (1994). Memory and metamemory considerations in the training of human beings. In J. Metcalfe & A. P. Shimamura (Eds.), *Metacognition: Knowing about knowing* (pp. 185–205). Cambridge, MA: MIT Press.

Blickle, G. (Ed.). (1997). *Ethik in Organisationen* [Ethics in organizations]. Göttingen, Germany: Verlag für Angewandte Psychologie.

Brett, J., Feldman, D. C., & Weingart, L. R. (1990). Feedback-seeking behavior of new hires and job changers. *Journal of Management, 16,* 737–749.

Brunstein, J. C., & Maier, G. W. (1996). Persönliche Ziele: Ein Überblick zum Stand der Forschung [Personal goals: A state-of-the-art review]. *Psychologische Rundschau, 47,* 146–160.

Brunstein, J. C., Schultheiss, O. C., & Maier, G. W. (1999). The pursuit of personal goals: A motivational approach to well-being and life-adjustment. In J. Brandstädter & R. M. Lerner (Eds.), *Action and development: Theory and research through the life span* (pp. 169–196). Thousand Oaks, CA: Sage.

Buchanan, B. (1974). Building organizational commitment: The socialisation of managers in work organizations. *Administrative Science Quarterly, 19,* 533–546.

Campbell, J. P., & Pritchard, R. D. (1976). Motivation theory in industrial and organizational psychology. In M. D. Dunnette (Ed.), *Handbook of industrial and organizational psychology* (pp. 63–130). Chicago, IL: Rand McNally.

Carver, C. S., & Scheier, M. F. (1981). *Attention and self-regulation: A control-theory approach to human behavior.* New York: Springer.

Chao, G. T., Walz, P. M., & Gardner, P. D. (1992). Formal and informal mentorships: A comparison on mentoring functions and contrast with nonmentored counterparts. *Personnel Psychology, 45,* 619–636.

Comelli, G., & Rosenstiel, L. von (1995). *Führung durch Motivation. Mitarbeiter für Organisationsziele gewinnen* [Leadership by motivation. How to win employees for organizational goals]. München, Germany: Beck.

Csikszentmihalyi, M. (1975). *Beyond boredom and anxiety.* San Francisco: Jossey-Bass.

Deci, E. L., & Ryan, R. M. (1985). *Intrinsic motivation and self-determination in human behavior.* New York: Plenum Press.

Edwards, W. (1962). Subjective probabilities inferred from decisions. *Psychological Review, 69,* 109–135.

Emmons, R. A. (1996). Striving and feeling: Personal goals and subjective well-being. In P. M. Gollwitzer & J. A. Bargh (Eds.), *The psychology of action: Linking motivation and cognition to behavior* (pp. 313–337). New York: Guilford Press.

Erikson, E. H. (1950). *Childhood and society.* New York: Norton.

Etzioni, A. (1967). *Soziologie der Organisation* [Sociology of the organization]. München, Germany: Juventa.

Feldman, D. C. (1976). A contingency theory of socialization. *Administrative Science Quarterly, 21,* 433–452.

Feldman, D. C., & Brett, J. M. (1983). Coping with new jobs: A comparative study of new hires and job changers. *Academy of Management Journal, 26,* 258–272.

Filipp, S. H. (1981). *Kritische Lebensereignisse* [Critical live events]. München, Germany: Urban & Schwarzenberg.

Fisher, C. D. (1985). Social support and adjustment to work: A longitudinal study. *Journal of Management, 11,* 39–53.

Fisher, C. D. (1986). Organizational socialisation: An integrative review. *Research in Personnel and Human Resource Management, 4,* 101–145.

Flanagan, J. G. (1954). The critical incident technique. *Psychological Bulletin, 51,* 327–358.

Gebert, D., & Rosenstiel, L. von (1996). *Organisationspsychologie.* Stuttgart, Germany: Kohlhammer.

Graen, G. B. (1969). Instrumentality theory of work motivation: Some experimental results and suggested modifications. *Journal of Applied Psychology, 53,* 1–21.

Guzzo, R. A., Jette, R. D., & Katzell, R. A. (1985). The effects of psychologically based intervention programs on worker productivity: A meta-analysis. *Personnel Psychology, 38,* 275–291.

Hackman, J. R., & Oldham, G. R. (1974). *The job diagnostic survey.* New Haven, CT: Yale University Press.

Heckhausen, H. (1965). Leistungsmotivation [Achievement motivation]. In H. Thomae (Ed.), *Handbuch der Psychologie: Vol. 2. Allgemeine Psychologie. 2 Motivation* (pp. 602–702). Göttingen, Germany: Hogrefe.

Heckhausen, H. (1991). *Motivation and action.* New York: Springer.

Herzberg, F., Mausner, B., & Snyderman, B. (1959). *The motivation to work.* New York: Wiley & Sons.

Huizinga, G. (1970). *Maslow's need hierarchy in the work situation.* Groningen, The Netherlands: Wolters-Noordhoff.

Kehr, H. M. (1999). Entwurf eines konfliktorientierten Prozeßmodells von Motivation und Volition [Outline of a process-oriented conflict model of motivation and volition]. *Psychologische Beiträge, 41,* 20–43.

Kehr, H. M., Bles, P., & Rosenstiel, L. von (1999a). Motivation von Führungskräften: Wirkungen, Defizite, Methoden [Motivation of managers: Effects, deficits, and methods]. *Zeitschrift Führung und Organisation, 68,* 4–9.

Kehr, H. M., Bles, P., & Rosenstiel, L. von (1999b). Self-regulation, self-control, and management training transfer. *International Journal of Educational Research, 31,* 487–498.

Kehr, H. M., Bles, P., & Rosenstiel, L. von (1999c). Zur Motivation von Führungskräften: Zielbindung und Flußerleben als transferfördernde Faktoren bei Führungstrainings [Motivation and management training: Goal commitment and flow as transfer-enhancing factors]. *Zeitschrift für Arbeits- und Organisationspsychologie, 43* (N.F. 17), 83–94.

Kuhl, J. (1996). Wille und Freiheitserleben: Formen der Selbststeuerung [Volition and the experience of feedom: Styles of self-regulation]. In J. Kuhl & H. Heckhausen (Eds.), *Enzyklopädie der Psychologie, Serie Motivation und Emotion: Vol. 4. Motivation, Volition und Handlung* (pp. 665–765). Göttingen, Germany: Hogrefe.

Kuhl, J., & Beckmann, J. (1994). *Volition and personality: Action versus state orientation.* Seattle, WA: Hogrefe & Huber.

Kuhl, J., & Fuhrmann, A. (1998). Decomposing self-regulation and self-control: The volitional components inventory. In J. Heckhausen & C. Dweck (Eds.), *Lifespan perspectives on motivation and control* (pp. 15–49). Hillsdale, NJ: Erlbaum.

Kuhl, J., & Goschke, T. (1994a). A theory of action control: Mental subsystems, modes of control, and volitional conflict resolution strategies. In J. Kuhl & J. Beckmann (Eds.), *Volition and personality: Action versus state orientation* (pp. 93–124). Seattle, WA: Hogrefe & Huber.

Kuhl, J., & Goschke, T. (1994b). State orientation and the activation and retrieval of intentions in memory. In J. Kuhl & J. Beckmann (Eds.), *Volition and personality: Action versus state orientation* (pp. 127–153). Seattle, WA: Hogrefe & Huber.

Lawler, E. E. (1973). *Motivation in work organizations.* Monterey, CA: Brooks/Cole.

Leventhal, H., & Scherer, K. R. (1987). The relationship of emotion to cognition: A functional approach to semantic controversy. *Cognition and Emotion, 1,* 3–28.

Lewin, K. (1939). *The conceptual representation and the measurement of psychological forces.* Durham, NC: Duke University Press.

Locke, E. A., & Henne, D. (1986). Work motivation theories. In C. L. Cooper & I. T. Robertson (Eds.), *International review of industrial and organizational psychology 1986* (pp. 1–35). Chichester, UK: Wiley.

Locke, E. A., & Latham, G. P. (1990). *A theory of goal setting and task performance.* Englewood Cliffs, NJ: Prentice Hall.

Louis, M. R. (1980). Surprise and sense making: What newcomers experience in entering unfamiliar organizational settings. *Administrative Science Quarterly, 25,* 226–251.

Maier, G. W. (1996). *Persönliche Ziele im Unternehmen: Ergebnisse einer Längsschnittstudie bei Berufseinsteigern* [Personal goals at the work place: A longitudinal study with a sample of newcomers]. Unpublished doctoral dissertation, Ludwig Maximilians University, München, Germany.

Maier, G. W., & Brunstein, J. C. (2000). *Personal work goals and newcomer socialization: Longitudinal effects on job satisfaction and organizational commitment.* Manuscript submitted for publication.

Maier, G. W., & Rappensperger, G. (1999). Eintritt, Verbleib und Aufstieg in Organisationen [Entrance, staying, and promotion within organizations]. In C. Graf Hoyos & D. Frey (Eds.), *Arbeits- und Organisationspsychologie* (pp. 50–63). Weinheim, Germany: Beltz.

Major, D. A., Kozlowski, S. W. J., Chao, G. T., & Gardner, P. D. (1995). A longitudinal investigation of newcomer expectations, early socialization, and the moderating effects of role development factors. *Journal of Applied Psychology, 80,* 418–431.

Maslow, A. H. (1943). A theory of human motivation. *Psychological Review, 50,* 370–396.

Maslow, A. H. (1954). *Motivation and personality.* New York: Harper.

Mathieu, J. E., Martineau, J. W., & Tannenbaum, S. I. (1993). Individual and situational influences on the development of self-efficacy: Implications for training effectiveness. *Personnel Psychology, 64,* 125–147.

McClelland, D. C., Atkinson, J. W., Clark, R. A., & Lowell, E. L. (1953). *The achievement motive.* New York: Appleton-Century-Crofts.

Miller, V. D., & Jablin, F. M. (1991). Information seeking during organizational entry: Influences, tactics, and a model of the process. *Academy of Management Journal, 16,* 92–120.

Miner, J. B., & Dachler, H. P. (1973). Personnel attitudes and motivation. *Annual Review of Psychology, 24,* 379–402.

Morrison, E. W. (1993a). Longitudinal study of the effects of information seeking on newcomer socialization. *Journal of Applied Psychology, 78,* 173–183.

Morrison, E. W. (1993b). Newcomer information seeking: Exploring types, modes, sources, and outcomes. *Academy of Management Journal, 36,* 557–589.

Nelson, D. L., & Quick, J. C. (1991). Social support and newcomer adjustment in organizations: Attachment theory at work? *Journal of Organizational Behavior, 12,* 543–554.

Nerdinger, F. W. (1994). *Zur Psychologie der Dienstleitung* [Psychology of services]. Stuttgart, Germany: Schäffer-Poeschel.

Neuberger, O. (1974). *Theorien der Arbeitszufriedenheit* [Theories of job satisfaction]. Stuttgart, Germany: Kohlhammer.

Oerter, R., & Montada, L. (1998). *Entwicklungspsychologie* [Developmental psychology] (4th ed.). Weinheim, Germany: Psychologie Verlags Union.

Patchen, M. (1961). *The choice of wage comparisons.* Englewood Cliffs, NJ: Prentice Hall.

Phillips, J. M. (1998). Effects of realistic job previews on multiple organizational outcomes: A meta-analysis. *Academy of Management Journal, 41,* 673–690.

Porter, L. W., Lawler, E. E. III, & Hackman, J. R. (1975). *Behavior in organizations.* New York: McGraw-Hill.

Rappensperger, G., Maier, G. W., & Wittmann, A. (1998). Die Bedeutung von Mitarbeiterzielen bei der Einarbeitung [The role of personal work goals during early organizational socialization]. In L. von Rosenstiel, F. W. Nerdinger, & E. Spieß (Eds.), *Von der Hochschule in den Beruf: Wechsel der Welten in Ost und West* (pp. 115–126). Göttingen, Germany: Verlag für Angewandte Psychologie.

Rosenstiel, L. von (1975). *Die motivationalen Grundlagen des Verhaltens in Organisationen—Leistung und Zufriedenheit* [The motivational foundations of behavior in organizations—Performance and satisfaction]. Berlin, Germany: Duncker & Humblot.

Rosenstiel, L. von. (1988). Motivationsmanagement [Motivation management]. In M. Hofmann & L. von Rosenstiel (Eds.), *Funktionale Managementlehre* (pp. 214–264). Berlin, Germany: Springer.

Rosenstiel, L. von (1998). Einstieg und Aufstieg—Selektion und Sozialisation von Hochschulabsolventen in den 80er und 90er Jahren beim Übergang vom Bildungs- ins Beschäftigungssystem [Entry and promotion—Selection and socialization of university graduates in the 80s and 90s at the transition from educational systems to work organizations]. In L. von Rosenstiel & H. Schuler (Eds.), *Person—Arbeit—Gesellschaft* (pp. 65–96). Augsburg, Germany: Wißner.

Rosenstiel, L. von (2000). *Grundlagen der Organisationspsychologie: Basiswissen und Anwendungshinweise* [Foundations of organizational psychology: Basic knowledge and applied suggestions] (4th ed.). Stuttgart, Germany: Schaeffer-Poeschel.

Rosenstiel, L. von, Nerdinger, F., & Spieß, E. (1991). *Was morgen alles anders läuft* [Changes of tomorrow]. Düsseldorf, Germany: Econ.

Rosenstiel, L. von, Nerdinger, F., & Spieß, E. (Eds.). (1998). *Von der Hochschule in den Beruf* [From university to vocation]. Göttingen, Germany: Verlag für Angewandte Psychologie.

Rosenstiel, L. von, Nerdinger, F., Spieß, E., & Stengel, M. (1989). *Führungsnachwuchs im Unternehmen* [Leadership candidates in companies]. München, Germany: Beck.

Scandura, T. A. (1992). Mentorship and career mobility: An empirical investigation. *Journal of Organizational Behavior, 13,* 169–174.

Sokolowski, K. (1996). Wille und Bewußtheit [Volition and consciousness]. In J. Kuhl & H. Heckhausen (Eds.), *Enzyklopädie der Psychologie, Serie Motivation und Emotion: Vol. 4. Motivation, Volition und Handlung* (pp. 485–530). Göttingen, Germany: Hogrefe.

Sokolowski, K., & Kehr, H. M. (1999). Zum differentiellen Einfluß von Motiven auf die Wirkungen von Führungstrainings (MbO) [Differential impact of motive dispositions on the effects of management trainings (MbO)]. *Zeitschrift für Differentielle und Diagnostische Psychologie, 20,* 192–202.

Tannenbaum, S. I., Mathieu, J. E., Salas, E., & Cannon-Bowers, J. A. (1991). Meeting trainees' expectations: The influence of training fulfillment on the development of commitment, self-efficacy, and motivation. *Journal of Applied Psychology, 76,* 759–769.

Tannenbaum, S. I., & Yukl, G. (1992). Training and development in work organizations. *Annual Review of Psychology, 43,* 399–441.

Taylor, M. S., & Giannantonio, C. M. (1993). Forming, adapting, and terminating the employment relationship: A review of the literature from individual, organizational, & interactionist perspective. *Journal of Management, 19,* 461–515.

Tolman, E. (1932). *Purposive behaviors in animals or men.* New York: Century.

van Eerde, W., & Thierry, H. (1996). Vroom's expectancy models and work-related criteria: A meta analysis. *Journal of Applied Psychology, 81,* 575–586.

Van Maanen, J. (1976). Breaking in: Socialisation to work. In R. Dubin (Ed.), *Handbook of work, organization and society* (pp. 67–130). Chicago, IL: Rand McNally.

Van Maanen, J., & Schein, E. H. (1979). Toward a theory of organizational socialization. *Research in Organizational Behavior, 1,* 209–264.

Vroom, V. H. (1964). *Work and motivation.* New York: Wiley.

Wanous, J. P. (1989). Installing a realistic job preview: Ten tough choices. *Personnel Psychology, 42,* 117–134.

Wanous, J. P. (1992). *Recruitment, selection, orientation and socialization of newcomers* (2nd ed.). Reading, MA: Addison-Wesley.

Waung, M. (1995). The effects of self-regulatory coping orientation on newcomer adjustment and job survival. *Personnel Psychology, 48,* 633–650.

Weiner, B. (1996). *Human motivation* (3rd ed.). Newbury Park, CA: Sage.

Motivational Psychology of Human Development – J. Heckhausen (Editor)

15 Self-Starting Behavior at Work: Toward a Theory of Personal Initiative

Doris Fay and Michael Frese

In this article we would like to look at the importance of self-starting behavior, particularly in future work settings. After we have established its importance we will try to understand it. Self-starting behavior has traditionally been framed within concepts of intrinsic motivation. We think that there are several conceptual problems when using intrinsic motivation in applied settings. We present the personal initiative theory with which we seek to overcome some of these problems. The personal initiative theory attempts to resolve the theoretical contradiction that exists in the occurrence of self-starting behavior in the context of externally given tasks; it allows for the simultaneous occurrence of extrinsic *and* intrinsic motivation for a behavior, and it enlarges our understanding of the role of positive and negative affect in the enactment of a self-starting behavior.

The Future of Work and the Relevance of Self-Starting Behavior

Both scientific and popular writing indicate that the domain of work is undergoing large-scale changes (Bridges, 1995; Howard, 1995; Rifkin, 1995). Advancing globalization and technological developments strongly influence and alter the demands placed on those at work. We will briefly present a general idea of the changes to come.

In the Western world, the number of available jobs in large companies is declining due to technological development and global competition. In some cases, complete business sectors and industries are becoming superfluous. This requires more activity to find a job—or even to create one's own job. It also makes the "cradle-to-grave" concept of employment—to be trained and to stay in one profession for one's whole working life, probably in the same organization—untenable. This changing job market might force people to hold different occupations over their lifetime. Life-long learning is then critical to keep up with the changing demands (Hall & Mirvis, 1995). Individuals now need to be responsible for their own careers; they have to observe and respond to changing job demands and job markets to maintain or increase their employability.

Increasing worldwide competition promotes a faster rate of innovation. This continuous change of job content requires the "users" of an innovation (e.g., job incumbents who work with new computer software) constantly to learn new skills. There is also an increasing use of management systems that delegate responsibility to lower levels of the organization (Womack, Jones, & Roos, 1990). These empowering strategies require individuals to act more independently. Innovations and improvements to technology, organizational processes, and procedures are no longer brought about solely by higher management and change experts, but by regular employees who have good ideas about what and how things can be improved. This requires one to be able to realize one's ideas independently.

What is needed to participate successfully in this world of changing demands? We argue here that individuals need to show more *self-starting behavior.* Self-starting means to develop one's own goals deliberately and to execute them without external order or demand—to initiate actions without external pressure. To better understand what enables people to deal with this changing world and how they can be enabled, we need to study theories explaining self-starting behaviors. Self-starting behavior in terms of voluntary action has been described in the field of intrinsic motivation.

Intrinsic Motivation

Behavior is intrinsically motivated if it is done freely because of the inherent interest, satisfaction, and enjoyment in doing the activity. Behavior is extrinsically motivated if its purpose is to gain material or social reward, that is, when the goal of the activity is the pursuit of a valued outcome and not the activity itself. Several theoretical approaches have been developed over time that seek to account for the bases of intrinsically motivated behavior. There are theoretical perspectives that stress stimulation, optimum level of arousal, incongruity, and discrepancy motives (Berlyne, 1966; Hunt, 1965). They are distinctly different from theories emphasizing the experience of effectance and mastery (White, 1959). A third group of theories focuses on self-determination, personal causation, and personal control (deCharms, 1968; Deci,

1975; cf. Heckhausen, 1991; Malone & Lepper, 1987). The different approaches have in common—despite their diversity—"that intrinsic behavior occurs for its own sake or for the sake of closely connected goal states, that it is not merely a means to a different purpose" (Heckhausen, 1991, p. 456).

One approach fruitfully integrated the themes of competence and personal causation to account for the origin of intrinsic motivation: the cognitive evaluation theory (Deci & Ryan, 1985). According to this theory, intrinsic motivation is rooted in humans' innate needs for competence and self-determination. Similar concepts are the need for self-actualization (Maslow, 1954), growth need (Alderfer, 1969), effectance motivation (White, 1959), and need for autonomy (Murray, 1938). These intrinsic needs energize a broad range of behaviors, with which the individual seeks and tries to master optimal challenges. A challenge is optimal for a given individual if it requires the stretching of that person's abilities. The rewards of intrinsically motivated activities are the experience of effectance and autonomy (hence, the satisfaction of the two needs), and the experience of positive emotions such as enjoyment and excitement. Sometimes, people experience flow when intrinsically motivated (Csikszentmihayli, 1975).

The cognitive evaluation theory assumes that external events that initiate or regulate behavior differ in their capacity to enhance or decrease intrinsic motivation. Two types of situational aspects are seen as important precursors for intrinsic motivation: First, the degree of self-determination for the activity allowed by the context affects the individual's perceived locus of causality (deCharms, 1968). When an individual perceives oneself as the cause of an activity, for example, one's own interest, one is said to have an internal locus of causality for the action; this promotes intrinsic motivation. In contrast, if an individual perceives the activity to be executed for a reason external to oneself, for example, to obtain a reward or to escape negative experience, one has an external perceived locus of causality; this decreases intrinsic motivation. Situational aspects that affect locus of causality relate to the degree of self-determination. If they reduce self-determination, they are called *controlling aspects* of a situation. Rewards, constraints, one's self-esteem being at risk, or surveillance and punishment are considered controlling aspects because they pressure people to behave in a certain way. This reduces self-determination. In contrast, choice allows self-determination, promotes an internal locus of causality, and enhances intrinsic motivation.

Second, aspects of external events can influence intrinsic motivation by means of affecting one's perception of one's own capacities and how they are related to the task. If an individual faces a challenging situation, intrinsically motivated behavior is more likely if one perceives one's capacities to be high. Environmental aspects that are *informational,* which provide feedback about effectance and performance, promote intrinsic motivation. In contrast, environmental aspects that convey that goals cannot be achieved are *amotivational.* This is the case, for example, for persistent negative feedback or continuous failure; they negatively affect the perception of capacity.

To summarize, according to the cognitive evaluation theory, humans have an innate need for competence and self-determination. As a consequence, individuals develop an intrinsic motivation for an activity if the activity allows an internal perceived locus of causality, if they feel a high competence for the task, and if the task allows a stretching of the competencies. Additionally, the activity must be interesting. Central to the cognitive evaluation theory, however, are environmental variables that influence intrinsic motivation. Environmental aspects are cognitively evaluated, thereby influencing how much a person experiences itself in a given situation to be self-determined and competent. It is this evaluative process that makes intrinsic motivation contingent on the environment. Situational aspects that have the capacity to regulate behavior are informational, controlling, and amotivating aspects (cf. Deci & Ryan, 1985).

The overjustification effect—central for research on intrinsic motivation—is used to describe situations in which there are detrimental effects of rewards and when extrinsic rewards corrupt intrinsic ones. Results of recent meta-analyses predominantly confirm the negative effect of rewards (Deci, Koestner, & Ryan, 1999; Eisenberger & Cameron, 1996; Rummel & Feinberg, 1988; Tang & Hall, 1995). It appeared that rewards do not always decrease intrinsic motivation; the overjustification effect depends on the interplay of many factors, such as type of reward (praise vs. tangible reward), predictability of the reward (expected vs. unexpected), and condition for the reward (reward obtained for participation in the study, performance level, or for executing the task), to name a few. The overjustification effect appears robustly (i.e., independently of type of sample, research design, and operationalization of intrinsic motivation) if study participants obtain a material, expected reward that is given contingent on doing a task (Tang & Hall, 1995; see similar results in Eisenberger & Cameron, 1996). Most of the results conform to the predictions of the cognitive evaluation theory.

Intrinsic motivation has received a high degree of attention since it is seen as an important motivator of learning and growth in competencies, and it is associated with flexibility, persistence, and performance (cf. Deci & Ryan, 1985). This has made intrinsic motivation relevant for a diversity of research areas, such as education, developmental psychology, sports psychology, and work psychology.

Intrinsic Motivation and Cognitive Evaluation Theory in Work and Organizational Psychology

The cognitive evaluation theory has found wide application in sports psychology and educational psychology (cf. Ambrose & Kulik, 1999). Unfortunately, to our knowledge there has not been a direct test of the theory in an organizational setting (Ambrose & Kulik, 1999; Deci & Ryan, 1985).

Some of the predictions in the cognitive evaluation theory regarding the occurrence of intrinsic motivation can be found in one of the most influential theories of work motivation: the job characteristics theory (Hackman & Oldham, 1976). The job characteristics theory states that several core job characteristics lead to three specific psychological states, which in turn promote organizationally highly desirable outcomes such as internal work motivation, satisfaction with work, quality of work performance, low absenteeism, and low turnover. Internal work motivation was defined as "the degree to which the employee is *self*-motivated to perform effectively on the job—that is, the employee experiences positive internal feelings when working effectively on the job …" (Hackman & Oldham, 1975, p. 162, emphasis in original). Intrinsic work motivation according to Hackman and Oldham implies enjoyment of performance of a task (in the context of organizational behavior) under the condition that performance is high; this is similar to the general concept of intrinsic motivation.

The five core job characteristics were hypothesized to lead to the following psychological states: skill variety, task identity, and task significance promote the experienced meaningfulness of one's work; work autonomy leads to experienced responsibility for work outcomes; and task feedback leads to knowledge of actual results of work outcomes. The relationships between the core job characteristics, the psychological states, and the outcomes are conditioned on the degree of a personality variable: the individual's growth need strength. The job characteristics theory posits that the relationships only hold for individuals with high growth need strength. Many studies have supported the assumption of the job characteristics theory that the core job characteristics affect internal motivation; the relevance of growth need strength has also been substantiated (cf. meta-analysis: Fried & Ferris, 1987).

The job characteristics theory and the cognitive evaluation theory make similar assumptions about the factors promoting intrinsic motivation. The job characteristics theory posits that work autonomy promotes intrinsic motivation; according to the cognitive evaluation theory, having autonomy at work allows a high degree of self-determination, leading to a high internal locus of causality, which in turn promotes intrinsic motivation. Task feedback is another determinant of intrinsic motivation in the job characteristics theory; this is similar to the assumption in the cognitive evaluation theory that informational feedback (i.e., learning how well one is performing in comparison to others) promotes intrinsic motivation. Furthermore, the role of an individual's growth need strength in the job characteristics theory is similar to the postulate of humans' need for growth in the cognitive evaluation theory. The job characteristics theory has received considerable empirical support (Fried & Ferris, 1987); we suggest that this can also be seen as indirect support for the assumptions of the cognitive evaluation theory.

Intrinsic Motivation: A Theory of Self-Starting Behavior at Work?

While there is empirical evidence as discussed above for intrinsic motivation, there are conceptual problems and paradoxes that make it difficult to apply intrinsic motivation concepts at work. We think that there are three major problems.

First, at work, one usually gets to do tasks. These tasks are most of the time externally given and not self-developed. Therefore, one cannot speak of work being "done freely" as required in definitions of intrinsic motivation.

Second, as in most applied settings, on the job behavior is affected by a multitude of factors. Some of these are external rewards (e.g., money) and some of them are internal (e.g., interest in a certain type of task). However, one very important motivator at work is probably money. People expect (and usually obtain) a monetary reward. Withholding the salary would reduce the behavior to zero (people usually do not come to work if they are not paid). This would occur even if someone enjoyed her job very much. Many other extrinsic rewards are involved in work, for example, receiving approval from a supervisor or colleagues, getting a promotion, or exerting power over people.

According to the intrinsic motivation literature, the overjustification effect implies that there is a reciprocal relationship between internal and external rewards. The more one gets extrinsic rewards, the smaller is the intrinsic motivation. Therefore, the ubiquitous presence of extrinsic motivators in the domain of work excludes the possibility of work behavior being truly intrinsically motivated.

Third, the hallmark of intrinsic motivation is the experience of positive feelings such as enjoyment, satisfaction, and pleasure. Using intrinsic motivation as a framework to understand self-starting behavior at work requires self-starting behaviors to be accompanied by positive emotions and positive affect. This is untenable. There are some, albeit small, positive relationships between positive emotions at work (i.e., job satisfaction) and work behavior (i.e., performance) (Iaffaldano & Muchinsky, 1985); but it is sometimes a negative emotion, for example dissatisfaction, that leads to self-starting behavior. Sometimes dissatisfaction causes behavior because someone wants to change something for the better.

The concept of intrinsic motivation has certain difficulties in being applied to the domain of work. We think that our theory of personal initiative may be more useful to understand self-starting behaviors at work.

Personal Initiative Theory

The concept of personal initiative was developed in the context of research in East Germany initiated after the fall of the wall. East Germany's economy was in a poor state. Technological reasons such as outdated technology and mismanagement were held responsible for this; additionally, employees' behavior contributed to the poor economic performance: they were lacking initiative. We developed measures of personal initiative and have shown their validity and usefulness (Frese, Kring, Soose, & Zempel, 1996; Frese, Fay, Hilburger, Leng, & Tag, 1997).

Three Aspects of Personal Initiative: Self-Starting Behavior, Proactivity, and Persistence

Showing personal initiative means being self-starting, proactive, and persistent. *Self-starting* implies that an individual pursues a goal without having been explicitly told to do so. Furthermore, the goal pursued goes beyond the formal requirements of the job (e.g., as implied in the job description) and beyond the explicit work role. Responding to the job description is not considered to be self-starting. *Proactivity* often implies that one develops self-starting goals. Proactivity means not waiting until one *must* respond to a demand.

Instead, there is a long-term focus on work that enables the individual to consider things to come (new demands, new or reoccurring problems, emerging opportunities) *and* to proactively do something about them.

Imagine, for example, a secretary of a university department who books tickets for the travels of her boss. The secretary's formal task is to phone the travel agency with which the university has negotiated discounts in order to book the tickets. On one occasion, she is not satisfied with the service and finds the discount unattractive. Therefore, she decides to find out whether she can get a better deal somewhere else. She phones different agencies, checks options on the internet, negotiates, and finally comes up with a better agency. This secretary has taken initiative: She self-started an activity, because she went beyond her role and the formal requirements. The secretary acted in a proactive manner, since she anticipated that she will have to take care of the travel arrangements in the future and that service and prices will not improve by themselves. This example also illustrates that personal initiative affects changes in the environment.

Taking initiative requires self-setting a goal. This goal can be based on an idea developed by the person but it is also indicated when someone takes charge of an idea or a project that is based on a well-known idea in a given context but that had not previously been put into action. In other words, personal initiative often requires that somebody really takes charge of an idea that has been around for a while.

When taking initiative, *persistence* is often necessary to reach one's goal. Generally, personal initiative implies that something is being changed: A process, a procedure, or a task is added. These might be minor changes (as in the case of the secretary), but personal initiative can also bring about major changes. Changes never work out perfectly from the very beginning; they often involve setbacks and failure. People affected by the changes may not like that they have to adapt to something new and that they are forced to abandon their routines. This requires persistence from the person taking initiative in order to master technical barriers and to overcome others' resistance and inertia. Sometimes, persistence also has to be shown in dealing with supervisors, who may not like it if their subordinates go beyond the boundary of their authority.

Thus, self-starting implies that one has long-term goals that are usually proactive and that one takes future problems and opportunities into consideration. Since personal initiative changes the environment and since changes make it difficult to use old routines, personal initiative leads to difficulties and barriers. These barriers may be caused by the person itself who has shown personal initiative (own routines do not work and one has to relearn how to do things), by other people, or by organizations.

These three aspects of personal initiative reinforce each other to a large extent. A proactive stance leads to developing self-starting goals because an active orientation toward the future makes it more likely to develop goals that go beyond what one is expected to do. Self-starting goals lead to the need to overcome barriers because of the changes inherent in the implementation of these goals. Overcoming barriers also leads to self-starting goals, because unusual solutions often require self-starting behavior. Finally, self-starting implies that one looks at potential future issues and, therefore, there is a higher degree of proactivity.

On the other hand, there is no automatic relationship between these three aspects. One may be self-starting and still not overcome barriers and not be proactive. For example, one might start to change something at work but back down from the initiative when problems arise. Sometimes personal initiative is also simply reactive, for example, when one takes over work because another person has been sick. In this case, there is little proactivity. Still, there is a tendency for these three issues to co-occur (Frese et al., 1997). Therefore, we propose that there is a relationship between these three aspects of personal initiative: self-starting, proactive, and overcoming barriers.

Self-Starting Behavior in the Context of Organizational Goals and Tasks

At work, people are usually confronted with tasks embedded in an organizational structure. How do people at work generate self-starting goals? We propose that personal initiative is the result of a deeper analysis of these tasks. Imagine a white-collar worker who learns that the company he works for will be taken over by an American organization. He anticipates that it will be useful to have a solid knowledge of the English language in the future. He convinces his colleagues that learning English will be a worthwhile investment and organizes professional English lessons for all of them. Additionally he persuades the supervisor that part of the English course can be done on company time. This is an example of initiative taking: The person is not responding to an immediate but to a future demand. At the moment when personal initiative is shown, it is based on a self-set goal, however. Thus, a deeper task analysis implies that one sees the implications for one's tasks when changes occur and that one proactively develops knowledge and skills to deal with future task demands.

One could argue that this is not self-starting in the true sense of the word. After all, the example implies a response to future task demands. Just responding to a task is not self-starting. A similar problem for the concept of self-starting appears when certain jobs demand personal initiative as part of the job requirements. For example, higher managers and entrepreneurs have as an explicit task to anticipate future challenges, opportunities, and threats and to act accordingly (proactively). In their case, they are required to show personal initiative, and since personal initiative is then an in-role behavior it does not seem to be self-starting. On the other hand, high-ranking managers and entrepreneurs need to be described on the dimension of personal initiative as well, and many show it to a high degree.

These problems have led us to conceptualize self-starting to mean that there is a great psychological distance from some path taken as part of personal initiative and the "normal" path. If something is obviously going to happen in the future, the psychological distance to take appropriate steps now is not high. However, if it is something not obvious or is difficult to do, the psychological distance is high. If a high-ranking manager takes up an innovation that is "in the air," that other managers also talk about, and that has been discussed in manager magazines, it is not personal initiative. The psychological distance is small in this case. However, if the same suggestion comes from an assembly line worker, the psychological distance is much higher and this would, therefore, constitute personal initiative. It is also personal initiative if the high-ranking manager takes an approach that is unusual (at least for the industry of the company concerned), because there is also a high psychological distance in this case between the course taken by the manager and the normal one.

It is sometimes easier to describe the other pole—non-self-starting behavior. If a task is prescribed in detail and the person follows the prescription, there is no self-starting behavior. The more the person deviates from the prescription, the more the person shows personal initiative.

The Functional Value of Personal Initiative

A self-starting action has to have functional value for the individual (or the group) showing this self-starting action; otherwise it is not considered personal initiative. As pointed out, the more a person deviates from the prescription, the more the person shows personal initiative. However, we require that personal initiative has to show functional value, which means that the task needs to get done well or even better than when just following the prescriptions; otherwise the deviation from the prescribed path is due to inefficiency or mistakes.

People can also take initiative that has functional value for them but that is at the same time harmful for the organization. If a hairdresser who is employed in a shop offered to give his or her clients the same haircut as usual in his or her off-work time at home, charging them a discount price, the hairdresser would be pursuing a self-starting goal. It would be proactive if the hairdresser intended to open his or her own business. As the hairdresser harms his or her employer's business there is no functional value for the organization, therefore it is not personal initiative. For the time being, we take the perspective of the organization—a self-starting goal must have functional value and must not be harmful to the organization. Personal initiative is task related and we only measure personal initiative that is conceptualized to help do the tasks and/or to help advance the group or the organization.

We propose that initiative taking is energized by the expectation of several outcomes or results; each occurrence of personal initiative may have its own pattern of motivators. Consider the person organizing the English language course for his colleagues and himself. He can anticipate several positive outcomes of his doing so: He might have a feeling of increased job security because he is well prepared for the new organizational culture to come, or he might anticipate social rewards in the form of appreciation by his colleagues. Hence, in terms of psychological needs (Maslow, 1954) he satisfies his needs for security or "belongingness" and love. The secretary searching for a new travel agency expects to gain better service when booking tickets, which makes her work easier, and positive feedback from her supervisor, since she managed to reduce travel costs. There are many other outcomes motivating individuals to take personal initiative; presumably making one's work easier and being prepared for the future are outcomes frequently involved.

In a few cases of personal initiative there are monetary rewards involved. For blue-collar workers who work on assembly lines (or similarly constrained workplaces; cf. section on antecedents of personal initiative) it is very difficult to take initiative. Many companies have introduced suggestion schemes to which workers can submit their improvement suggestions. This is one case of initiative (cf. Frese, Teng, & Wijnen, 1999). When an improvement suggestion is implemented, it is usually rewarded. Even if there is no official suggestion scheme, bringing about an improvement is often rewarded (e.g., a bonus or better career opportunities). Thus, an external reinforcement can sometimes play a role in personal initiative.

We propose that personal initiative is motivated by multiple goals: the outcome itself (i.e., facilitation of work, an improvement, the functional value of personal initiative, as described in the previous section), effects directly related to the outcome (an increase in competencies as in the case of the English language course), and "side-effects" of the outcome (the satisfying feeling of achievement, pride, recognition of valued others, such as co-workers, supervisor).

We assume that the biological functionality of personal initiative developed alongside work. Humankind has always lived in a continuously changing environment (with periods of slower and faster changes). This requires a steady adaptation to the altering environmental situation. We assume that personal initiative increased the long-term survival chances of genes. The most immediate mechanism responsible for such a development may have been the following: Personal initiative increases the survival value of genes through providing a higher and a more steady degree of food for the offspring due to proactivity and future orientation. A self-starting and proactive stance allows an individual to find and catch food at places that other people do not know or find.

Antecedents of Personal Initiative

Aspects of the workplace and individual difference variables are antecedents of personal initiative. At the workplace, the most important factors promoting personal initiative are control at work and complexity of work (Frese et al., 1996). Having control means that the individual can make relevant decisions, for example, over the timing of work and over how to do the work. Task complexity is high if one is, for example, required to make difficult decisions and to increase one's qualifications. Lack of control and complexity imply that people are told in detail of how they have to do their job. This tight regulation of work makes it difficult to show self-starting behavior since there is no stimulation to engage in deeper task analysis. Furthermore, with narrow task prescriptions it is not functional to show personal initiative (e.g., personal initiative is not functional on an assembly line because one cannot try out another way to do one's work—the only possibility is to propose a formal suggestion). Job-related qualifications are antecedents because people need to know their work well before they can develop better strategies to do their work.

In the area of personality, we think a proactive personality is an important antecedent of personal initiative (Fay, Böckel, Kamps, Wotschke, & Frese,

1999). Proactive personality is defined as a "relatively stable tendency to effect environmental change" (Bateman & Crant, 1993, p. 103). Proactive persons are believed to be change agents; they grasp opportunities to influence and change their environment instead of adapting to or enduring the environment. Beyond specific job qualifications, people need general mental abilities (intelligence) to handle successfully a departure from routine paths of work and to show personal initiative (Fay, 1998; Frese, Krauss, & Friedrich, 2000). Finally, personal initiative needs to be feasible. This implies that one should expect positive outcomes (outcome expectancy) and that one is able to show the necessary actions (self-efficacy) (Bandura, 1997).

We propose that there are resources in the workplace (control, complexity) and in the person (qualifications, ability, expectancies, proactive personality) that increase the chances to show personal initiative. Personal initiative does not exist in a situation of low control and complexity, in which detailed instructions of what to do are given, as long as the person conforms to the instructions.

Consequences of Personal Initiative

Our studies have supported the notion that personal initiative has positive outcomes for the person exhibiting it, and that personal initiative contributes to the overall effectiveness of an organization. Unemployed persons who have a high degree of personal initiative get a job faster than those with a low degree of personal initiative (Frese et al., 1997). Personal initiative is related to developing clear career plans and to executing them (Frese et al., 1997). Personal initiative is positively related to individual performance: For example, in a sample of university students, those with higher personal initiative had the better high school grades (Fay et al., 1999). Students with high personal initiative are more self-reliant and independent when they have to acquire new knowledge. In an experiment, the students had to learn a computer program from exploration. Students with a higher degree of personal initiative sought less help and reassurance from the trainer and tried to overcome problems by themselves (Fay & Frese, 1998). Furthermore, personal initiative benefits organizations when it is widespread within a company. Small-scale business owners' personal initiative is related to their firms' success in East Germany (Zempel, 1999), in Uganda (Koop, De Reu, & Frese, in press) and in Zimbabwe (Krauss, Frese, & Friedrich, 1999). In a sample of medium-sized German companies, a pro-initiative climate was substantially related to the profitability of the company. This means that a widespread use of personal initiative in the organization makes the organization better able to deal with challenges. One particular challenge is the introduction of process innovations (e.g., process re-engineering or just-in-time production). Those process innovation efforts resulted in higher profitability only when the company also showed a high degree of a pro-initiative climate (Baer & Frese, 1999).

Thus, we propose that exhibiting initiative brings about positive outcomes both for the individual and for the organization because personal initiative means dealing actively with the world, which furthers individual self-development and contributes to organizational success. At least in those environments in which it is necessary to deal with a changing world, personal initiative is important.

Conclusion

The goal of this chapter was to find a theoretical framework for self-starting behaviors at work. The discussion of intrinsic motivation showed that intrinsic motivation has conceptual problems when applied to work and organizational settings. We think that the personal initiative theory allows us to overcome some of the conceptual problems that beset intrinsic motivation and the cognitive evaluation theory.

First, the personal initiative theory is not worried about the fact that there are tasks at work. Whereas the execution of an externally given task causes us to question attributing this performance to intrinsic motivation (in the sense of the behavior being shown freely because of its inherent interest), externally given tasks do not exclude the occurrence of self-starting behavior. Self-starting behavior is possible if the tasks are not spelled out in detail. The specification of the task given must allow for a psychological distance between the task and the completion by the job incumbent. The more tasks are spelled out, the less there is the possibility of self-starting behavior.

Second, both intrinsic as well as extrinsic rewards can be related to self-starting behavior. This seems to stand in contrast to intrinsic motivation theory. However, we suggest a departure from the dichotomy of behavior being extrinsically *or* intrinsically motivated. Furthermore, we suggest studying the overjustification effect from a different perspective.The overjustification effect is probably contingent on the *prescription of specific behavior* and not so much on the external reward. If a reward is given for a certain outcome and the individual is allowed to choose with what kind of behavior to achieve the outcome (i.e., giving room for self-determination), the overjustification effect might diminish. This agrees with the meta-analytic result that rewards for performance *level* (in contrast to task execution) appear not to reduce intrinsic motivation (Tang & Hall, 1995). However, this is still a speculative account, but it might explain how an extrinsic reward would not counteract intrinsic motivation. Thus, the personal initiative theory allows us to understand that self-starting behavior can be motivated by both intrinsic aspects of the task and extrinsic rewards, such as money.

Third, the personal initiative theory does not demand that people's feelings have to be positive. As a matter of fact, one of the antecedents of personal initiative is stress at work (a negative feeling) (Fay, Sonnentag, & Frese, 1998). It makes sense that we often self-start an action when we find the situation negative but changeable. Consider the person organizing the English language course. Even if he is one of those people who like to organize things and make things happen, it is quite unlikely that he will enjoy all of his actions. Organizing such a course can become quite a nuisance; for example, he must convince everybody of its worth, consider conflicting schedules, and so forth. He will be confronted with social resistance and organizational problems. Showing personal initiative often involves nuisance and one needs stamina and persistence to realize one's ideas against inertia or resistance and sometimes an initiative does not work out at all.

Clearly, there is a large overlap between personal initiative and intrinsic motivation. Many antecedents are similar, for example, control and complexity of the task at hand. We suggest that most cases of intrinsic motivation at work occur when people take initiative. As personal initiative is based on a self-set goal, personal initiative is a self-determined action. Taking initiative means leaving routine paths of action; therefore, one can test and enhance one's abilities and competencies (both work related and non-work related, for example, having the competence to persuade other people to support one's action).

We suggest that the personal initiative theory overcomes some of the problems involved with intrinsic motivation when accounting for self-starting behavior at work. We furthermore propose that concepts of intrinsic motivation need to be revised to make them usable in applied settings: The facts of externally given tasks, mixed motives, and the presence of rewards need to be integrated into the concept.

Obviously we did not mean to be critical of the concept of intrinsic motivation. In contrast, we think it is a very important concept for work psychology as well as for other applied settings. It is, of course, also possible to start the other way around and to integrate some ideas of the personal initiative theory into intrinsic motivation theory. However, we hope to have shown that it is both possible and necessary to talk about self-starting behavior within the context of task-driven and rewarded behavior and that the most important issue that reduces self-starting behavior is not the reward itself but the tight prescription of behaviors (which often goes along with rewards). We have limited ourselves to work psychology because this is the area of our expertise. However, we think that much of what we have said can also be integrated into other applied settings, for example, the school or even psychotherapy. In all of these settings, professionals are presenting tasks to allow people to be eventually self-starting.

References

Alderfer, C. P. (1969). An empirical test of a new theory of human needs. *Organizational Behavior and Human Performance, 4,* 142–175.

Ambrose, M. L., & Kulik, C. T. (1999). Old friends, new faces: Motivation research in the 1990s. *Journal of Management, 25,* 231–292.

Baer, M., & Frese, M. (1999). *Pro-initiative climate, psychological safety climate, process innovation and firm performance: Innovation is not enough.* (Manuscript in prep.)

Bandura, A. (1997). *Self-efficacy: The exercise of control.* New York: Freeman.

Bateman, T. S., & Crant, J. M. (1993). The proactive component of organizational behavior: A measure and correlates. *Journal of Organizational Behavior, 14,* 103–118.

Berlyne, D. E. (1966). Curiosity and exploration. *Science, 153,* 25–33.

Bridges, W. (1995). *Jobshift.* London: Allan & Unwin.

Csikszentmihayli, M. (1975). *Beyond boredom and anxiety.* San Francisco: Jossey-Bass.

deCharms, R. (1968). *Personal causation.* New York: Academic Press.

Deci, E. L. (1975). *Intrinsic motivation.* New York: Plenum Press.

Deci, E. L., Koestner, R., & Ryan, R. M. (1999). A meta-analytic review of experiments examining the effects of extrinsic rewards on intrinsic motivation. *Psychological Bulletin, 125,* 627–668.

Deci, E. L., & Ryan, R. M. (1985). *Intrinsic motivation and self-determination in human behavior.* New York: Plenum Press.

Eisenberger, R., & Cameron, J. (1996). Detrimental effects of reward: Reality or myth? *American Pychologist, 51*(11), 1153–1166.

Fay, D. (1998). *Personal initiative: Construct validation of a new concept of performance at work.* Unpublished doctoral dissertation, University of Amsterdam, The Netherlands.

Fay, D., Böckel, A., Kamps, A., Wotschke, G., & Frese, M. (1999). *Personal initiative and organizational citizenship behavior: Overlaps and distinctions.* (Manuscript submitted for publication)

Fay, D., & Frese, M. (1998, April). The nature of personal initiative: Self-starting orientation and proactivity. In S. Parker, S. Kozlowski, & M. Frese (Chair), Proactivity and learning.

Symposium conducted at the Annual Conference of the Society for Industrial and Organizational Psychology, Dallas, TX.

Fay, D., Sonnentag, S., & Frese, M. (1998). Stressors, innovation, and personal initiative: Are stressors always detrimental? In C. L. Cooper (Ed.), *Theories of organizational stress* (pp. 170–189). New York: Oxford University Press.

Frese, M., Fay, D., Hilburger, T., Leng, K., & Tag, A. (1997). The concept of personal initiative: Operationalization, reliability and validity in two German samples. *Journal of Occupational and Organizational Psychology, 70,* 139–161.

Frese, M., Krauss, S., & Friedrich, C. (2000). *Micro-enterprises in Zimbabwe: On the function of socio-demographic factors, psychological strategies, personal initiative, and goal setting for entrepreneurial success.* Westport, CT: Greenwood.

Frese, M., Kring, W., Soose, A., & Zempel, J. (1996). Personal initiative at work: Differences between East and West Germany. *Academy of Management Journal, 39,* 37–63.

Frese, M., Teng, E., & Wijnen, C. J. D. (1999). Helping to improve suggestion systems: Predictors of giving suggestions in companies. *Journal of Organizational Behavior, 20,* 1139–1155.

Fried, Y., & Ferris, G. R. (1987). The validity of the job characteristics model: A review and meta-analysis. *Personnel Psychology, 40,* 287–322.

Hackman, J. R., & Oldham, G. R. (1975). Development of the job diagnostic survey. *Journal of Applied Psychology, 60*(2), 159–170.

Hackman, J. R., & Oldham, G. R. (1976). Motivation through the design of work: Test of a theory. *Organizational Behavior and Human Performance, 16,* 250–279.

Hall, D. T., & Mirvis, P. H. (1995). Careers as lifelong learning. In A. Howard (Ed.), *The changing nature of work* (pp. 323–361). San Francisco, CA: Jossey-Bass.

Heckhausen, H. (1991). *Motivation and action.* New York: Springer.

Howard, A. (1995). A framework for work change. In A. Howard (Ed.), *The changing nature of work* (pp. 3–44). San Francisco, CA: Jossey-Bass.

Hunt, J. M. (1965). Intrinsic motivation and its role in psychological development. In D. Levine (Ed.), *Nebraska Symposium on Motivation* (Vol. 13, pp. 189–282). Lincoln, NE: University of Nebraska Press.

Iaffaldano, M. T., & Muchinsky, P. M. (1985). Job satisfaction and job performance: A meta-analysis. *Psychological Bulletin, 97*(2), 251–273.

Koop, S., De Reu, D., & Frese, M. (2000). Socio-demographic factors, entrepreneurial orientations, personal initiative and environmental problems in Uganda. In M. Frese (Ed.), *Success and failure of microbusiness owners in Africa: A new psychological approach.* Westport, CT: Greenwood.

Krauss, S. I., Frese, M., & Friedrich, C. (1999). *Entrepreneurial orientation and personal initiative: A psychological model of success in Zimbabwean micro and small business owners.* (Manuscript in prep.)

Malone, T. W., & Lepper, M. R. (1987). Making learning fun: A taxonomy of intrinsic motivation for learning. In R. E. Snow & M. J. Farr (Eds.), *Aptitude, learning, and instruction: Conative and affective process analyses* (Vol. III, pp. 223–253). Hillsdale, NJ: Erlbaum.

Maslow, A. H. (1954). *Motivation and personality.* New York: Harper & Row.

Murray, H. A. (1938). *Explorations in personality.* New York: Oxford University Press.

Rifkin, J. (1995). *The end of work.* New York: Putnam.

Rummel, A., & Feinberg, R. (1988). Cognitive evaluation theory: A meta-analytic review of the literature. *Social Behavior and Personality, 16,* 147–164.

Tang, S. H., & Hall, V. C. (1995). The overjustification effect: A meta-analysis. *Applied Cognitive Psychology, 9,* 356–404.

White, R. (1959). Motivation reconsidered: The concept of competence. *Psychological Review, 66,* 297–333.

Womack, J. P., Jones, D. T., & Roos, D. (1990). *The machine that changed the world.* Chichester, UK: Wiley.

Zempel, J. (1999). Selbständigkeit in den Neuen Bundesländern. In K. Moser, B. Batinic, & J. Zempel (Eds.), *Unternehmerisch erfolgreiches Handeln* (pp. 69–92). Göttingen, Germany: Verlag für Angewandte Psychologie.

Motivational Psychology of Human Development – J. Heckhausen (Editor)

16 Stability and Change in Romantic Relationships

Hans-Werner Bierhoff and Elke Rohmann

The study of love has flourished during the last 25 years. This is documented by two journals (*Personal Relationships, Journal of Social and Personal Relationships*) that regularly publish studies on love. Since most of these studies are carried out with undergraduates, relatively little is known about stability and change of love over the life span. In this contribution we offer data that may help to bridge the gap. First, we will discuss the meaning of love using the hierarchical model of love proposed by Barnes and Sternberg (1997). In addition, we turn to the measurement of love emphasizing the approach of Lee (1973) and Hendrick and Hendrick (1986; Hendrick, Hendrick, & Dicke, 1998). Second, we will delineate hypotheses on the link between age and love using the approach of age-adjusted control processes (Heckhausen & Schulz, 1995; Wrosch & Heckhausen, 1999). Finally, we will describe the results of two studies that address our hypotheses. In discussing the relation between age and love we will take the modifying influence of relationship duration into account.

Barnes and Sternberg (1997) have developed a hierarchical model of love. They assume that different structural theories and processes of love may be combined into a comprehensive model that takes the level of generality of the theories into account. Analogous to theories of intelligence, the broad concept of love can be broken down into two facets: passionate love and companionate love (cf., Berscheid & Walster, 1974). The love styles as described by Lee (1973) are located on the next lower level of the hierarchical model.

Lee (1973) developed the theory of love styles that emphasizes the complexity of the experience of love. After collecting love descriptions in literature and philosophy and on the basis of structural interviews, he developed a multidimensional typology of love styles. The analogy of colors of love was chosen by Lee to emphasize that different love styles may be combined into new love styles. In addition, the preference for a specific color depends on taste. In the same vein, the attitude toward different love styles depends on individual preferences.

Lee distinguished primary and secondary love styles. Primary love styles include romantic love (Eros), game-playing love (Ludus) and best-friends love (Storge).

(1) Romantic love refers to immediate attraction to the loved person as expressed in love at first sight. Attractiveness and sexual passion play an important role in the development of this love style.

(2) Game-playing love represents a form of passionate affection in which seduction, sexual freedom, and sexual adventure stand in the foreground. Orientation toward longer-term investments is less emphasized.

(3) Best-friends love develops from a previous friendship. The interpersonal orientation is characterized by common interests and mutual trust and tolerance.

Secondary love styles include possessive love (Mania), pragmatic love (Pragma), and altruistic love (Agape).

(4) Possessive love is an extreme version of romantic love since it accentuates passionate and seemingly irrational dependent behavior. Idealization of the partner and possessiveness elicit strong feelings that may be either positive (achieving fusion with the partner) or negative (jealousy, because the partner does not seem to give himself or herself fully).

(5) Pragmatic love represents a certain contrast to the emotional ebullience of possessive love, because rational considerations help determine the choice of partner. The relationship is intended to create pleasant living conditions or serve particular goals (e.g., end loneliness, have children).

(6) Altruistic love exists where partners are prepared to make sacrifices for one another. Lovers who emphasize this type of love are willing to put their interests last if this contributes to the well-being of their partner.

The hierarchical model of love assumes that love may be subdivided into passionate and companionate love. Eros, Ludus, and Mania are summarized under passionate love; they all refer to emotional experiences that are the focus of this type of love. In contrast, Pragma, Storge, and Agape are examples of companionate love. They focus on practical goals that are related to the partnership.

Following Lee's approach, several questionnaires were developed for the measurement of these six love styles (LAS: Hendrick & Hendrick, 1986; MEIL: Bierhoff, Grau, & Ludwig, 1993). Whereas the LAS includes seven items per love style, the MEIL is based on ten. Recently, Hendrick, Hendrick, and Dicke (1998) have developed a short version of the LAS that includes only four items in each subscale.

Love and partnership are complex phenomena. Is it possible to measure love like other psychological variables? Or is the combination of feelings, thoughts, and behavioral tendencies that occurs in close relationships so highly idiosyncratic that it is impossible to measure it by a questionnaire? The answer to such critical questions depends on the issue of internal and external validity of the love-style questionnaire (Amelang, 1991). Bierhoff and Grau (1999) and Hendrick and Hendrick (1997) have collected some evidence that indicates that the love-style typology is valid.

In the following we delineate hypotheses on the level of passionate love and companionate love. By implication, these hypotheses apply to Eros, Ludus, and Mania (examples of passionate love) and to Pragma, Storge, and Agape (examples of companionate love).

Age-Graded Love Styles

The topic of love across the life span has not received much attention in the past. One exception is the analysis of attachment behavior in infancy, adolescence, adulthood, and old age by Koski and Shaver (1997), who note that attachments are a main factor for life satisfaction in all age groups. Although their analysis is only indirectly relevant for our discussion, since it refers to attachment styles and not to love styles, we will mention some of their conclusions because they apply to the analysis of love styles as well. Unfortunately, no quantitative evidence on the life-span perspective for love styles is available to us. Koski and Shaver (1997) emphasize the continuities in the development of attachment; but they also acknowledge certain differences comparing different phases over the life span. For example, cognitive abilities contribute to the improvement of the communication pattern. In addition, the roles that the individuals assume change within the life span. The concept of developmental tasks as developed by Havighurst (1953) focuses on those tasks that the individual has to solve during a certain life period. In general, these developmental tasks are derived from biological and cultural factors that influence individual expectations and aspirations. Examples are child-bearing and mate selection. Both examples are related to the development and maintenance of romantic relationships. If it is true that people set priorities in their goals depending on developmental tasks, the experience of romantic relationships at different ages might be affected by the presence or absence of these developmental tasks. In addition, people might—depending on the importance of certain developmental tasks at their current age—use different problem-solving techniques, which include effort expenditure, aggression, assimilation of the individual to fulfill situational or social demands, defense, and "leaving the situation" (Lehr, 1977).

This idea has been developed further by Wrosch and Heckhausen (1999), who argue that the realization of life goals depends on opportunity structures that increase or decline depending on age. For example, the goal of partnership formation is characterized by age-graded opportunity structures because the chances of finding an appropriate partner are higher in early adulthood than in late midlife. As a consequence age-normative factors exert an influence on the chances to fulfill certain expectations with respect to the initiation and maintenance of partnerships. Partners may adapt to this opportunity structure and adopt the strategy to set age-related goals in their partnership.

If there is an age timing of opportunity structures it is likely that partners' love orientation changes over their life span. For example, younger partners are likely to be involved in highly romantic relationships, whereas older partners emphasize friendship and solidarity. Therefore, a possible age-related sequence is that the emphasis on passionate love in early adulthood is replaced by an emphasis on friendship and cooperation in late midlife. This hypothesis agrees with sociobiology (cf., Buss & Shacklewood, 1997), which assumes that younger partners and especially younger women are more intensely orientated toward passionate feelings than older partners.

Heckhausen and Schulz (1995) have distinguished between control strategies that serve the realization of goal attainment and compensatory strategies that are used as a technique of goal disengagement. The possibility exists that people in late midlife turn to goals like the fulfillment of common interests as a compensatory strategy when the availability of romantic experiences diminishes. Consequently, love styles are assumed to be related to age. Whereas it is assumed that passionate love will be highest in early adulthood and decreases afterwards, the importance of companionate love is assumed to increase in a compensatory way. This might be considered an example of compensatory strategies. From a theoretical point of view we cannot predict which love styles from the passionate cluster will decrease in importance over the life span and which love styles from the companionate cluster will increase. For example, it might turn out that one passionate love style (e.g., Eros) decreases, whereas one companionate love style (e.g., Pragma) increases. We would consider such evidence as empirical support for the assumed compensation of passionate love by companionate love. It is unlikely that all passionate love styles lose importance over the middle life span, and all companionate love styles gain importance. Instead, it is likely that the expected compensation is manifested on the basis of specific love styles. For example, the possibility exists that specific companionate love styles are more easily employed as compensation devices than others.

Wrosch and Heckhausen (1999) note that some opportunity structures change quite rapidly (e.g., childbearing), whereas others change more slowly (e.g., mate selection). We assume that the opportunity structures that are important for love orientations change only gradually. Although we must admit that opportunity structures with respect to mate selection and starting a romantic affair change very slowly, we hardly doubt that such a deterioration of chances takes place over the life span.

Love styles that are related to passionate love are assumed to decrease in importance during middle age. This hypothesis refers to romantic love, game-playing love, which is highly passion-driven, and possessive love, which is dominated by affection and anxieties about the potential loss of the loved partner. Possessive love is an expression of an anxious-ambivalent attachment style as described by Bowlby (1969) and Koski and Shaver (1997).

Furthermore, love styles that are related to companionate love are assumed to be emphasized more strongly in later adulthood than in early adulthood. This hypothesis refers to best-friends love, altruistic love, and pragmatic love. Whereas selfless love is an example of denial of personal needs and urges, pragmatic love is characterized by avoidance of romantic feelings and emphasis on practical considerations.

In this chapter we will present data on the link between age and love styles. We start with the assumption that love includes two "superordinate clusters" (Barnes & Sternberg, 1997, p. 91) that can be described as passionate love and companionate love. The hypotheses imply that the passionate-love cluster (including Eros, Ludus, and Mania) decreases from early to late adulthood, whereas the companionate-love cluster (including Storge, Pragma, and Agape) increases.

Note that our approach is in agreement with the hierarchical model of love as outlined by Barnes and Sternberg (1997), which assumes that higher-order love may be separated into different love styles at a lower level of analysis. Whereas our hypothesis refers to companionate love and passionate love at a high level of abstraction, the love styles represent these general orientations at a lower level of abstraction.

The general research strategy is the following: The relationship between age and love styles is investigated using samples composed of partners in romantic relationships ranging in age from early adulthood to late adulthood. Since relationship duration is correlated with age and may exert specific influences on love styles, we take the influence of relationship length into account. For example, romantic love may decrease as a function of the amount of experience in the relationship as measured by the length of the relationship. In contrast, best-friends love may increase as a function of the number of common experiences in the partnership. Therefore, for analytical reasons the distinction between age of partners and relationship duration is important.

Finally, research on developmental tasks indicates that gender plays an important role (cf., Lehr, 1977). For example, men emphasize the importance of problems at work, whereas women place more emphasis on partnership and children. Therefore, we report results on gender differences with respect to love styles and take gender as a covariate into consideration when we look at the link between age and love styles.

Method

The results are based on two samples. In Sample 1 the respondents ranged in age from 19 to 54 years, with a mean age of 29 years ($SD = 7$). Eleven percent had a low educational level, 15% a middle level, and 77% a high education level. The sample is not representative of the population, since persons with a high educational level are over-represented. Length of partnership is quite high. It ranged from 1 month to 35 years, with a mean relationship length of 72 months. Twenty-eight percent were married and 34% had children. The participants in Sample 2 ranged in age from 18 to 65 years. The mean relationship length was 91 months. Moreover, 53% were married and 28% had children. Whereas in Sample 1 all six love styles were measured once, in Sample 2 only measures on romantic, best-friends, and possessive love were obtained at three time points within a 14-month period. Love styles were measured by the MEIL (Bierhoff, Grau, & Ludwig, 1993).

Results

We first report results on the general response level and the intercorrelations of love styles. Figure 1 presents the means obtained in Sample 1. The means indicate that romantic love is preferred most, followed by best-friends love and altruistic love. The means of game-playing love are lower. The mean dif-

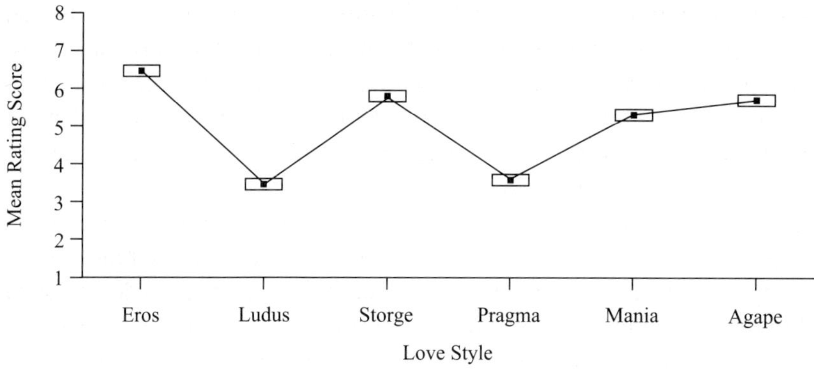

Figure 1. Mean assessment of love styles (N = 1,308; data from Bierhoff, Grau, & Ludwig, 1993). Confidence intervals are indicated by boxes.

ferences between love styles are highly significant ($F = \frac{5}{1302}$) = 760.6; $p <$ .001.

In general, the correlations among the six scales are quite low (see Table 1). An exception is the relatively high correlation between romantic and altruistic love: Higher values for romantic love are associated with more willingness to sacrifice. In addition, the correlations between altruistic love and possessive love are substantial: Higher jealousy is associated with stronger altruistic orientation.

Table 2 presents an overview of the correlations between love scales and age, length of relationship, and gender, in Sample 1. The highest correlation

Table 1
Correlations of Love Styles According to Gender

	Eros	*Ludus*	*Storge*	*Pragma*	*Mania*	*Agape*
Eros	–	–.31**	.09*	–.04	.24**	.41**
Ludus	–.32**	–	.08*	.09*	–.08*	–.17**
Storge	.08*	–.11	–	.34**	.13**	.27**
Pragma	–.01	.06	.29**	–	.13**	.23**
Mania	.18**	–.00	.08	.12**	–	.45**
Agape	.38**	–.28**	.27**	.25**	.37**	–

Note. Above diagonal: men (N = 678); below: women (N = 629); * $p < .05$, ** $p < .01$.

is obtained for pragmatic love, which is higher in long-lasting relationships. In addition, pragmatic love increases with age. The correlation of duration of relationship and altruistic love is also substantial, indicating that partners in long-lasting relationships report more altruistic love. Finally, several other correlations are significant. For example, men express less possessive love and more altruistic love than women.

The interpretation of these correlations depends in part on the correlations among age, relationship duration, and gender. As expected, a strong overlap between age and duration of relationship occurs: Respondents who are older tend to be in long-lasting relationships. In addition, a small but significant negative correlation emerges between age and gender. Male respondents tend to be older than female respondents. Whereas this last result reflects peculiarities of the sample, the high correlation between age and relationship duration leads us to the conclusion that statistical methods should be applied that control for relationship duration in order to obtain pure age effects.

As a consequence, partial correlations were computed. For example, duration, gender, and marital status were partialled out in all correlations including age. As expected, partial correlations are attenuated compared with simple correlations. The basic picture of results is the same as in Table 2: Women score higher on possessive love than men, whereas men score higher on altruistic love than women. Relationship duration is positively correlated with pragmatic and altruistic love as well as with best-friends love. Romantic love decreases with age.

Whereas correlations reflect the strength of linear relationships, it is possible that the relationships between age and love styles are nonlinear. For example, U-shaped relationships cannot be detected by correlations. Therefore,

Table 2
Correlations of Love Styles With Age, Relationship Length, and Gender in Sample 1

	Age	*Duration*	*Gender*
Eros	–.08**	–.07*	.01
Ludus	–.02	–.03	–.06*
Storge	.03	.15**	.06*
Pragma	.23**	.33**	.03
Mania	–.00	.03	.17**
Agape	.10**	.24**	–.15**

Note. Gender is coded 1 = male, 2 = female. * $p < .05$, ** $p < .01$.

age was coded into 14 levels. In a multivariate analysis of variance with the six love styles as dependent variables, the recoded age variable as independent variable, and relationship duration as covariate, a significant age effect emerged (Wilks Lambda = .87; F (58,5338) = 1.75; p < .001; Sample 1). In univariate tests the age effect is significant for romantic, altruistic, game-playing, and best-friends love on the 1% level. In addition, the age effect is significant for pragmatic love on the 5% level.

The hypotheses assume, in agreement with the hierarchical model of love, that love may be subdivided into passionate and companionate love. Therefore, the results are illustrated graphically for passionate love (i.e., Eros, Ludus, and Mania) and companionate love (i.e., Pragma, Storge, and Agape) separately.

The results for romantic love are displayed in Figure 2. Observed and adjusted means do not differ. Therefore, length of relationship does not influence these results. In general, there seems to be a tendency that romantic love decreases with age, although in the oldest subgroup a reversal of this trend is visible. This pattern of results agrees quite well with the hypothesis. Note that the change in romantic love is not dramatic, since it is not larger than one scale point.

Additional evidence is offered by the results of the second sample, which confirm the trend in Sample 1. Data obtained at all three measurement points indicate that romantic love decreases with age, whereas in the highest age groups there is a reversal of this trend.

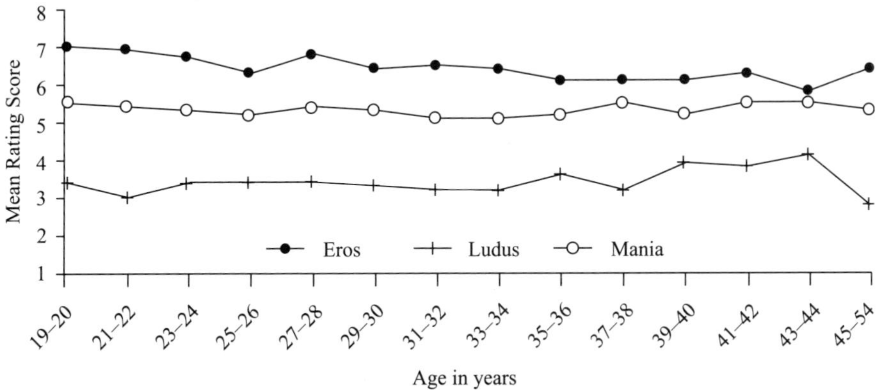

Figure 2. Mean assessments of passionate love depending on age (N = 987).

Next, we turn to game-playing love, which is also dependent on age (see Figure 2). Observed and adjusted means are close together, indicating that relationship duration does not modify the relationship between age and game-playing love. Whereas game-playing love is at a constant level for younger respondents, it increases in the age range of 35–45 and then decreases. This reversed U-shaped relationship that was not detected by correlations confirms the hypothesis only for late midlife.

Possessive love seems to be independent of age influences (see Figure 2). This result is confirmed in the second sample. In addition, the influence of relationship duration is very small. In summary, neither age nor relationship duration seem to exert a systematic influence on possessive love, which is present at a constant level in all phases of the life span that were included in our analyses.

Next the results for companionate love are presented. For pragmatic love the pattern of correlations is confirmed. It increases with age (see Figure 3) and with relationship duration. Therefore, the curve of adjusted means is flatter than the curve of observed means. Older respondents and persons who have a longer relationship tend to respond in a more pragmatic way. The increase in pragmatic love which agrees with the hypothesis is strongest in late midlife.

The importance of best-friends love varies over the age range studied (see Figure 3). In late midlife a small increase is visible. In Sample 2 no significant

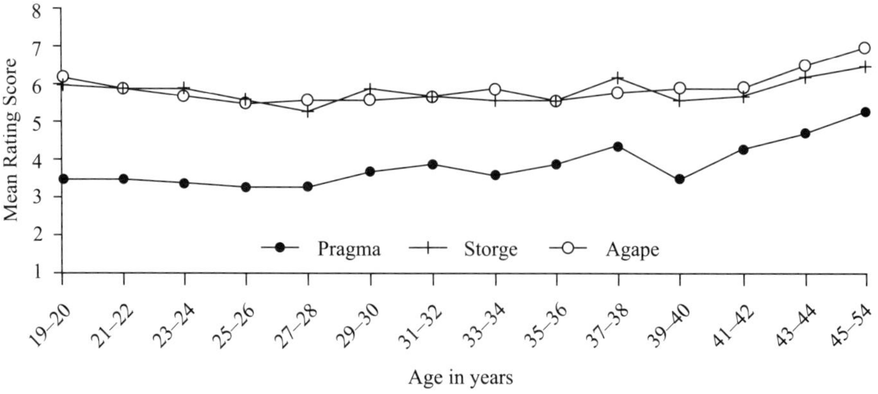

Figure 3. Mean assessments of companionate love depending on age ($N = 987$).

age influences on best-friends love are observed. All in all, the age effect on best-friends love is quite small. In Sample 2 it follows no systematic pattern.

Altruistic love is dependent on age (see Figure 3). A U-shaped relationship is visible. Altruistic love is lower in the middle age range and higher for younger and older respondents. Controlling for length of relationship reduces these differences. These results confirm the hypothesis for late midlife.

Discussion

In summary, linear age effects are observed only for romantic love, which decreases with age, and for pragmatic love, which increases with age. Both age effects were predicted in the hypotheses. In contrast, the relationship between game-playing love and altruistic love, on the one hand, and age, on the other hand, is U-shaped. In the middle age range, game-playing love is more important and altruistic love is less important than in the younger and older age groups. The results for best-friends love and possessive love seem to indicate that only minimal age effects are present, especially if relationship duration is controlled for.

The hypotheses on passionate and companionate love are only supported in part by the data. The results for romantic love confirm the hypothesis quite strongly, since data supporting it are found in both samples. In addition, a detailed analysis of Sample 2 data indicates that the means of the third measurement point for romantic love are lower than the means of the first measurement point. This is further evidence based on longitudinal data for a decrease of romantic love depending on age.

We had expected a general increase in pragmatic love over the age range studied. The results confirm this hypothesis. But the increase in pragmatic love occurs only in late midlife. Whereas the change in romantic love is more gradual, it is sharper for pragmatic love. The tentative interpretation that the increase in pragmatic love has a compensatory function is in agreement with the pattern of results if we assume that the compensation is delayed.

Altruistic love was expected to increase with age. The results do not agree with this expectation. Instead a U-shaped relationship emerges with higher altruistic love in the younger and older age groups. Why do these changes occur? It may be that altruistic love is emphasized early in the relationship as an indication of selfless affection, whereas it is emphasized in late midlife as a result of compensatory processes that are related to the reduction in romantic love as assumed in the hypotheses. The results for best-friends love are similar but less pronounced. Possibly, best-friends love is an indication of intimacy that is relevant for the experience in romantic relationships in all age groups.

With respect to game-playing love, the hypothesis on passionate love implies that it decreases with age. The results show that the influence of age on game-playing love is more complex than assumed because game-playing love increases in the middle age groups and is lower in the younger and older groups. This pattern of results is difficult to explain on the basis of our assumptions. A speculative interpretation is that the increase in the middle age groups reflects the influence of factors that may be summarized under the heading of midlife crisis.

Finally, the results for possessive love are not in agreement with our hypotheses. It is not clear why the hypotheses on passionate love were not confirmed for possessive love. The tendency to experience jealousy seems to be quite strong in all age groups. It is possible that jealousy reflects basic anxieties of the individuals in romantic relationships and is therefore more under the control of personality than under the control of opportunity structures (cf., Bierhoff & Grau, 1999).

In sum, the hypotheses received the strongest support for romantic and pragmatic love. This is encouraging since romantic love is part of the passionate love cluster, whereas pragmatic love is part of the companionate love cluster. Therefore, the interpretation is feasible that the increase in pragmatic love is compensatory with respect to the decrease in romantic love.

Relationship duration is a competing factor influencing the experience in romantic relationships, which is highly correlated with age. Results indicate that age and relationship duration exert independent influences on love styles. In general, the relationships of love styles with age are reduced if relationship duration is taken into account. The most obvious influence of relationship duration is observed for pragmatic love, which increases with length of relationship. A more comprehensive understanding of the development of love styles is possible by including relationship duration besides age as explanatory concepts. Whereas this chapter focuses primarily on age-graded influences, relationship duration is another important independent explanatory variable that considerably overlaps with age.

The results that were reported are preliminary in several respects. For example, we do not know whether similar results would have been found in the 1950s, 1960s, or 1970s. In addition, we must admit that we have no data on love among adolescents and the elderly. Another open question is how love styles develop in a longitudinal perspective. We have only limited data on this point since we could only consider a time span of 14 months in Sample 2. In the future we plan to collect longitudinal data over a larger time span. Although the limitations of our longitudinal sample are obvious, it is interesting to note that for romantic love, the results point in the same direction as in the cross-sectional sample. This convergence of results is encouraging for future research.

References

Amelang, M. (1991). Einstellungen zu Liebe und Partnerschaft: Konzepte, Skalen und Korrelate [Love attitudes and partnership: concepts, scales, and correlates]. In M. Amelang, H. J. Ahrens, & H.-W. Bierhoff (Eds.), *Attraktion und Liebe* [Attraction and love] (pp. 153–196). Göttingen, Germany: Hogrefe.

Barnes, M. L., & Sternberg, R. J. (1997). A hierarchical model of love and its prediction of satisfaction in close relationships. In H. J. Sternberg & M. Hojjat (Eds.), *Satisfaction in close relationships* (pp. 79–101). New York: Guildford Press.

Berscheid, E., & Walster, E. (1974). A little bit about love. In T. L. Huston (Ed.), *Foundations of interpersonal attraction* (pp. 355–381). New York: Academic Press.

Bierhoff, H.-W., & Grau, I. (1999). *Romantische Beziehungen* [Romantic relationships]. Bern, Switzerland: Huber.

Bierhoff, H.-W., Grau, I., & Ludwig, A. (1993). *Marburger Einstellungsinventar für Liebesstile* [Marburg Love Style Inventory]. Göttingen, Germany: Hogrefe.

Bowlby, J. (1969). *Attachment and loss: Vol. 1. Attachment* (1st ed.). New York: Basic Books.

Buss, D. M., & Shacklewood, T. K. (1997). In H. J. Sternberg & M. Hojjat (Eds.), *Satisfaction in close relationships* (pp. 79–101). New York: Guildford Press.

Havighurst, R. J. (1953). *Human development and education.* London, UK: Longmans.

Heckhausen, J., & Schulz, R. (1995). A life-span theory of control. *Psychological Review, 102,* 284–304.

Hendrick, C., & Hendrick, S. (1986). A theory and method of love. *Journal of Personality and Social Psychology, 50,* 392–402.

Hendrick, C., Hendrick, S. S., & Dicke, A. (1998). The love attitudes scale: short form. *Journal of Social and Personal Relationships, 15,* 147–159.

Hendrick, S., & Hendrick, C. (1997). Love and satisfaction. In H. J. Sternberg & M. Hojjat (Eds.), *Satisfaction in close relationships* (pp. 56–78). New York: Guildford Press.

Koski, L. R., & Shaver, B. R. (1997). Attachment and relationship satisfaction across the life span. In H. J. Sternberg & M. Hojjat (Eds.), *Satisfaction in close relationships* (pp. 26–55). New York: Guildford Press.

Lee, J. H. (1973). *The colours of love.* Englewood Cliff, NJ: Prentice Hall.

Lehr, U. (1977). *Psychologie des Alterns* [Psychology of old age]. Heidelberg, Germany: Quelle und Meier.

Wrosch, C., & Heckhausen, J. (1999). Control processes before and after passing a developmental deadline: Activation and deactivation of intimate relationship goals. *Journal of Personality and Social Psychology, 77,* 415–427.

17 Motivation for Parenthood and Early Family Development: Findings of a Five-Year Longitudinal Study

Klaus A. Schneewind

Over the last decades Germany has experienced a sharp decline in birthrates. While in 1965, 100 women in their reproductive phase gave birth to 250 children, in 1996 the corresponding number of children was 139 in the Western part of Germany. In East Germany, due to the imponderabilities of the German reunification, the birthrate even dropped to a remarkable low of 96 births per 100 women (Engstler, 1998). Some demographers and social politicians view this as an alarming sign of a changing German society. In 1988, the predecessor of the present Federal Department of the Family, Seniors, Women, and Youth initiated a joint sociological and psychological prospective longitudinal study on the development of young couples and families to explore these demographic changes in greater detail.

Developmental Paths of Young Couples and Families: A Quasi-Experimental Longitudinal Study

Two research teams, one with a sociological focus directed by Laszlo Vaskovics at the University of Bamberg and my own team at the University of Munich stressing a psychological point of view, tried to tackle the complex problem of analyzing the dynamics of early couple and family development. The joint project started in 1989 and was finished in 1994 (Schneewind et al., 1992, 1994, 1997). In the following I shall exclusively refer to the psychological part of this joint study. Moreover, some selected findings will be presented that, in the present context, might be of special interest.

Before turning to five questions that will be addressed in this contribution I shall briefly report on the background of our study. First, from a family developmental point of view, as has been proposed by several authors (e.g., Aldous, 1996; Carter & McGoldrick, 1988; Rodgers & White, 1993), we focused in particular on two stages of the family life cycle, namely, (a) the joining of families through marriage and (b) the raising of young children, each of them entailing specific key issues and developmental tasks.

We were not the first, of course, to be interested in the process of family formation. Although I will not elaborate on the history of research that has been carried out in this field summarized elsewhere (see, e.g., Reichle & Werneck, 1999; Schneewind et al., 1997), I would nevertheless like to mention two major projects that, in my view, constitute milestones in studying the transition to parenthood. One is the "Pennsylvania Infant and Family Development Project" (Belsky, Gilstrap, & Rovine, 1984) that was conducted at Pennsylvania State University during the 1980s and early 1990s by Jay Belsky and his collaborators, based on his process model of the determinants of parenting (Belsky, 1984). The other is Philip and Carolyn Cowan's "Becoming a Family Project" at the University of California at Berkeley (Cowan & Cowan, 1992). The Cowans based their research on a structural model comprising of five domains (Cowan & Cowan, 1990): (a) the characteristics of each individual in the family, (b) the husband-wife relationship, (c) the relationship between each parent and child, (d) the patterns connecting the new family and the two families of origin, and (e) the parents' external sources of stress and support, with special emphasis on social networks and jobs or careers.

After intensive consultation with both research groups we finally came up with our own contextualistic process model. Figure 1 gives an idea of the major components of this model, which, as can be seen, are related to a time line discerning past, present, and future. In addition, Figure 1 provides an overview of the major topics that we tried to assess empirically using a variety of assessment instruments (described in detail elsewhere, see Schneewind et al., 1989).

To implement the study, a sample of 180 couples was recruited from a screening sample of more than 1,100 couples in the Munich area according to specified criteria such as age, duration of marriage, nationality, and so forth. In particular, we divided our sample into five subgroups according to their strength of motivation for parenthood at the first measurement point in spring 1989. We finally came up with five groups: (a) couples in transition to parenthood ($n = 48$), (b) couples intending to become parents within the next five years ($n = 46$), (c) couples intending to become parents in more than five years ($n = 20$), (d) couples being undecided as to whether to become parents at all ($n = 48$), and (e) voluntarily childless couples ($n = 18$).

We used a quasi-experimental design; that is, all five groups were assessed synchronically at eight measurement points over a period of five years,

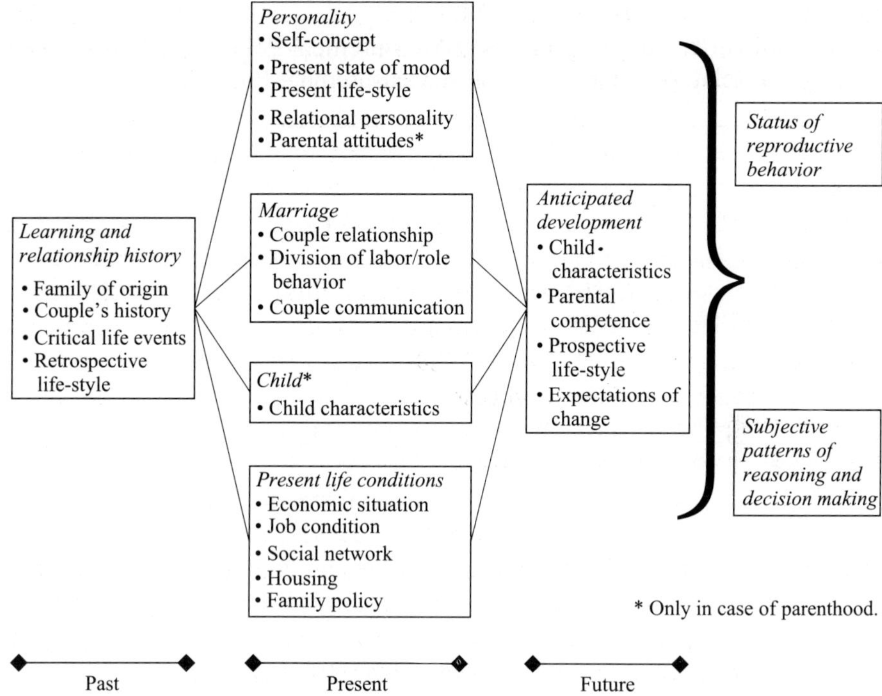

Figure 1. Contextualistic process model of motivation for parenthood and early family development.

thus allowing for a longitudinal comparison across groups. As might be expected, we had some attrition of the sample across the five years. At the final measurement point in 1994 we ended up with 130 of the initial 180 couples. Considering that in 1994 20 couples were separated or divorced, we actually lost 30 couples or 17 percent of the initial sample.

As a first objective indication of the couples' development, Table 1 gives an overview of the number of births and pregnancies in 1994 in relation to the initial status of the five groups of couples in 1989.

As can be inferred from Table 1, the majority of the couples in the parents' group (group 1) moved on to having two or even three children. Also, the other groups are pretty much in accordance with their original plans to have or not to have children. A somewhat different but also more differentiated view of the same situation is provided in Table 2, which, however, refers only to groups 2 through 5, taking into account individual rather than couple data.

Table 1
Number of Births and Pregnancies at Measurement Point (MP) VIII (1994) in Relation to Group Status at Measurement Point I (1989)

	No child	*1 child*	*2 children*	*3 children*
Group 1: Parents ($n = 37$)		6	25	6 (1)
Group 2: Child within 5 years ($n = 36$)	12	10 (2)	14 (5)	
Group 3: Child after 5 years ($n = 14$)	8	5 (2)	1	
Group 4: Undecided ($n = 31$)	17	11 (2)	3	
Group 5: Voluntarily childless ($n = 12$)	12			

Note. Numbers in parentheses refer to pregnancies.

Table 2
Correspondence of Initial Group at Measurement Point (MP) I (1989) and Motivation for Parenthood at Measurement Point VIII (1994)

	Groups at MP I				
Motivation for parenthood at MP VIII	*Group 2: Child within 5 years*	*Group 3: Child after 5 years*	*Group 4: Undecided*	*Group 5: Voluntarily childless*	*Sum*
Pregnant/ with child	48++	12	28	0–	88 48.4%
Pro child	16	13++	8–	0–	37 20.3%
Undecided	4–	2	20++	4	30 16.5%
Voluntarily childless	3–	0–	5–	19++	27 14.8%
Sum	71 39.0%	27 14.8%	61 33.5%	23 12.6%	182 100%

++ Significantly overrepresented in corresponding group; – significantly underrepresented in corresponding group.

Again, it becomes evident that our subjects stick to their prior plans. The double pluses in the main diagonal of Table 2 indicate that the initial motivation for parenthood is still significantly overrepresented in the corresponding groups. Thus, for instance, a major segment of those belonging to the undecided group in 1989 were still undecided five years later.

What Are the Pros and Cons of Parenthood?

I now turn to the first of the five questions to be addressed, that is, the subjective reasons for and against parenthood held by the different groups of couples at the beginning of the study. To answer this question we used different approaches including an open-ended interview, a card sort method, and a novel technique that I am going to focus on in the following. We provided our subjects with a set of index cards and spread them out in front of them. Each index card represented a particular aspect such as "my personality," "my relationship," or "my job" that might be considered either conducive to having children or as interfering with parenthood. In addition, we gave our subjects two sets of plastic chips, 40 white and 40 black, the white ones symbolizing a pro-child attitude and the black ones the opposite. We then asked our subjects to assign as many white and/or black chips to the various index cards as they thought was true for them. One advantage of this procedure is that our subjects could decide not only on the pro or con direction of each argument but also on the relevance of the respective argument in relation to all the other arguments, thus yielding something like a gestalt of the subjective reasoning pattern.

Figure 2 presents some of the results using this procedure. For the sake of simplicity, only the findings of group 1 (parents-to-be), group 4 (undecided couples) and group 5 (voluntarily childless couples) are being shown using the data of both spouses. The length of the bars indicates how important a particular aspect is as a pro or con parenthood argument.

There are several points that deserve mentioning. First, it is quite evident that it is mainly the personality and relationship aspects that turned out to be most important, whereas, for instance, the relationship with the family of origin or the job situation were less salient. Second, some arguments differ quite considerably between the three groups. Again, it is the personality and relationship area where the differences are most pronounced. The voluntarily childless couples, for example, are rather ambivalent about their own personality and parenting competence as well as their partner's personality and their relationship, whereas all these aspects are by far on the positive side for the parents-to-be. Third, there are some arguments, in particular those concerning jobs and the general political and economic situation, that are tipping the balance toward the negative side, although even more so for the groups with a more-or-less distant motivation for parenthood.

On the whole, these findings point to the fact that a great deal of the perceived motivational potential pro or con parenthood resides in the personality

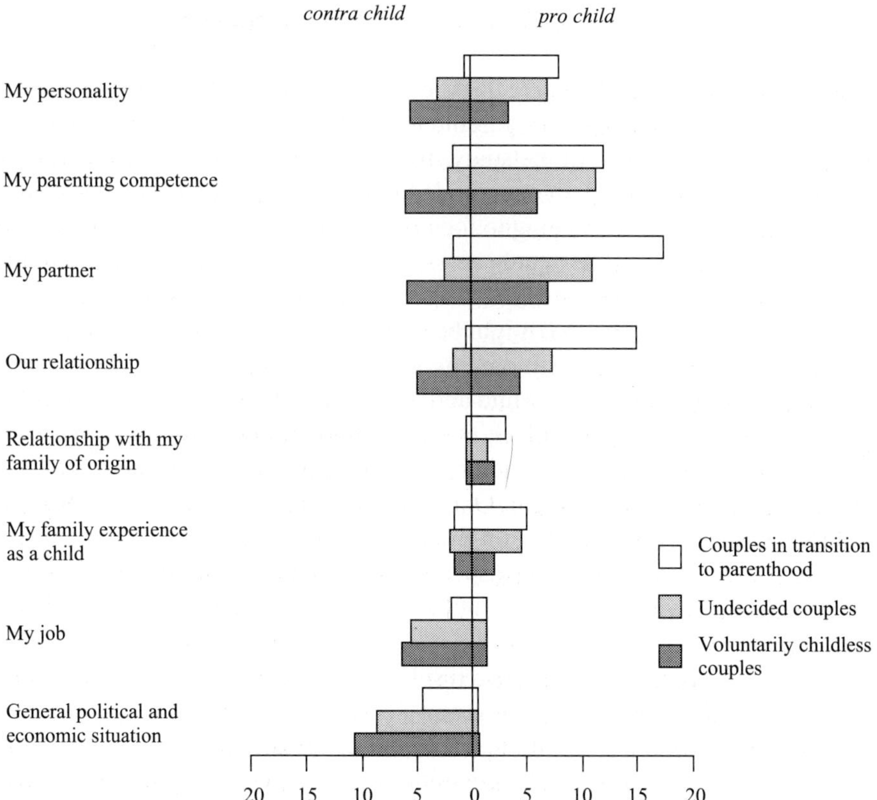

Figure 2. Subjective reasons pro and con parenthood for three groups of couples.

and relationship realm, suggesting that more attention should be directed to these particular aspects. Yet this does not mean, for example, that the financial or housing situation or the occupational status play a minor role in parenthood decision making. Rather, our data suggest that these aspects are obvious and necessary prerequisites. This may be the reason why these aspects are less salient at the subjective level. On the other hand, even if material and status resources are abundant, they do not qualify as sufficient reasons for parenthood. Rather, it seems that in addition to them personal and relationship resources are of utmost importance.

What Conditions Are Conducive to Second-Time Parenthood?

When turning to the next question, that is, the conditions for second-time parenthood, we took a special look at the personality and relationship development of young mothers and fathers. Based on the perceived pros and cons of parenthood just mentioned, we expected that, first, the quality of the couple relationship and, second, a positive relational personality pattern comprising such aspects as general social competence, empathy, and emotional stability (Vierzigmann, 1995) might be important prerequisites to venture having a second child. Overall there was no such effect. However, when we analyzed our data separately for young mothers and fathers we made a rather interesting finding. While we were not able to find any significant correlations for the young mothers this was not the case for the young fathers. Figure 3 provides the results for fathers endowed with a positive, intermediate, or negative relational personality and corresponding changes to their perceived marital relationship with respect to the number and timing of second births.

Based on the relational personality dimensions mentioned above and a set of indicators of the marital relationship such as couple climate, couple competence, or sexual satisfaction we used latent class analysis (Rost, 1990) to divide the whole group of first fathers into three subgroups characterized by positive, intermediate, and negative relationship development. Remember that all first-time fathers made their transition to parenthood in early 1989. Two years later almost 80% of the first-time fathers belonging to the positive relational development group had become second-time fathers whereas none of the fathers in the negative group had a second child, with the intermediate group scoring somewhere in between. The following year, that is, in 1992, all of the fathers in the positive group had become second-time fathers in contrast to about 50% in the negative and 70% in the intermediate group. Still another two years later the negative group hovers around 60% and the intermediate group turns out about 80% second-time fathers.

Although, as already stated, we found similar subgroups of positive, intermediate, and negative patterns of personality and marital relationship development in young mothers they were not associated with the number and timing of second births. This may lead to the conclusion that it is particularly the young fathers' relational personality and perceived relationship development that, all things being equal, predisposes young families to continue with their family-building process. In fact, these findings suggest that young fathers play a more prominent role in family formation than formerly believed.

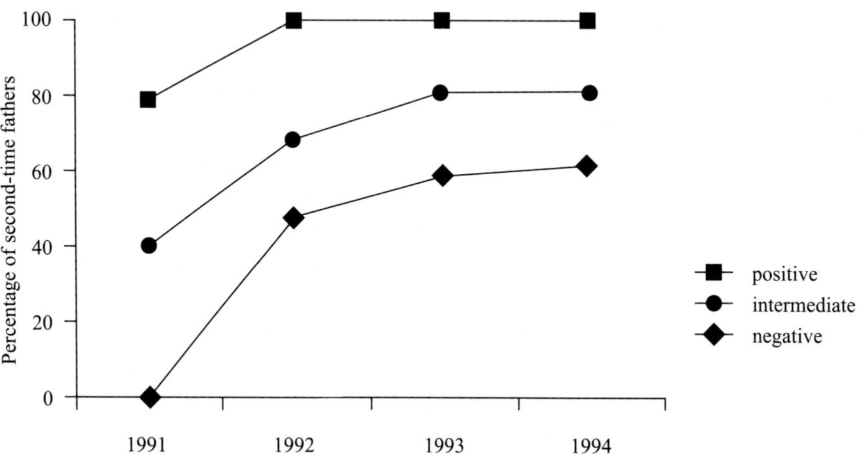

Figure 3. Number and timing of second births for three groups of fathers with differing of relational personality and quality of marital relationship development.

When Does a Child Become a "Stressor" in Marital Relationships?

We now proceed to the question of whether and under what circumstances the birth of a child and, in particular, the subsequent challenges of child care become a "stressor" for the couple relationship. This is not a new question. In fact, quite a few studies have addressed this issue, especially those in the early tradition of a "parenthood-as-crisis" paradigm (e.g., Dyer, 1963; Hobbs, 1965; LeMasters, 1957). Quite a few studies have demonstrated a more-or-less marked decline in marital relationship quality upon the arrival of a child. However, with the notable exception of the study by Belsky and Rovine (1990), what has received less attention in respective empirical studies is a differential perspective, that is, singling out different developmental paths of marital relationship quality emerging in couples with and without children.

In the following, some findings will be presented that refer exactly to such a differential perspective. To begin with, we looked at different clusters of the couples' relationship climate consisting of three main dimensions: cohesion, activity, and control (for a more detailed description of the couple climate scales see Schneewind, 1993). Using again latent class analysis we arrived at two distinct clusters. The first cluster combines a relatively high degree of cohesion and activity with low mutual control. The second cluster is made up of the opposite configuration, that is, low cohesion and activity combined with a high degree of control. For the sake of simplicity, we call the first cluster "positive couple climate" and the second one "negative couple climate."

Next, we looked at each couple's correspondence between the husband's and wife's perceived couple climate across a period of two years yielding three types of stable couple constellations. Thus, we got one type ($n = 41$ couples, 6 with and 35 without a child) where both husband and wife belonged to the positive climate cluster. The next type ($n = 51$ couples; 20 with and 31 without a child) represents a mixed couple constellation, that is, either the husband belongs to the positive and the wife to the negative cluster or vice versa. Finally, the third type ($n = 37$ couples; 10 with and 27 without a child) consists of spouses who both belong to the negative cluster.

Let us now look at the development of marital quality as a function of the initial couple climate constellation and family status. To illustrate this point, I focus on marital satisfaction as one of the prominent defining variables of the concept of relationship quality which, in our case, was measured using a German translation of Hendrick's (1988) "Relationship Assessment Scale." The findings of this analysis are shown in Figure 4.

First, when referring to the data for the couples with a divergent view of their couple climate it turns out that, not quite unexpectedly, marital satisfaction in this group declines rather considerably over time. However, there is virtually no difference between the couples with and without a child. Next, when we turn to the couples with a consistently positive couple climate we find that there is almost no change across a two-year period. Both groups of couples, that is, those with and without a child, remain at a high level of marital satisfaction—the young parents even somewhat more so than the nonparents, although the difference is statistically not significant. As we now take a look at the last group, that is, the one where both spouses tend to perceive their couple climate in a rather negative way, it does not come as a surprise that, compared to the other groups, these couples score on a considerably lower level of marital satisfaction. More importantly, however, it is in this group where we find a seemingly different development of marital satisfaction depending on whether the couples are parents or nonparents. While the decline of marital satisfaction is rather moderate in the nonparents' subgroup there is a much sharper drop in the parents' subgroup that, despite the small number of parents in this group, turns out to be statistically highly significant.

What can be concluded from these findings? First of all, our data suggest that the advent of a child is not a stressor per se for all couples. Rather, it de-

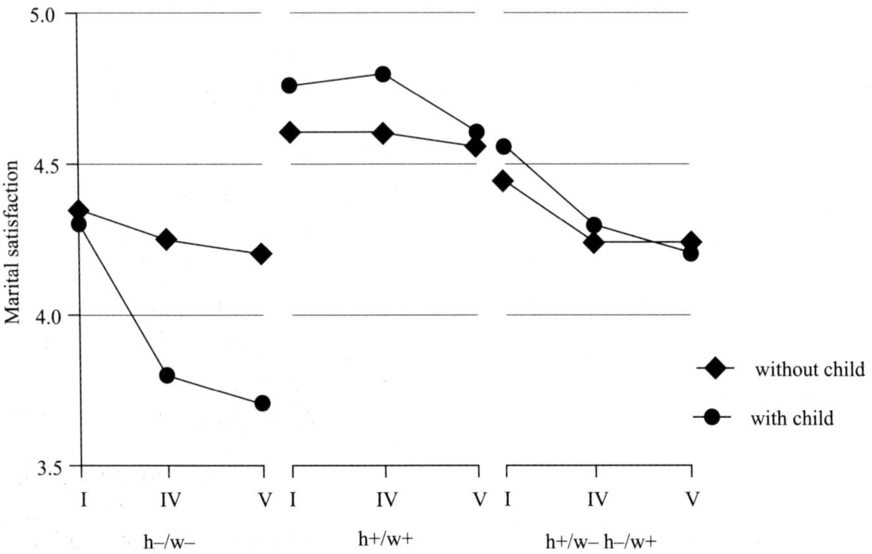

h = husband; w = wife; + = positive couple climate; – = negative couple climate. I = 1st measurement point (MP); IV = 4th measurement point (1 year after 1st MP); V = 5th measurement point (2 years after 1st MP).

Figure 4. Mean marital satisfaction for parents and non-parents belonging to three types of couple climate patterns.

pends on the initial level of a couple's relationship climate whether the birth and subsequent care of a child have a detrimental impact on various aspects of marital quality. Second, if that is a valid conclusion, it would make sense to take steps to improve the quality of the marital relationship *before* couples proceed to the stage of family formation. Moreover, this is a nice example of the interrelatedness of non interventive predictive or prospective longitudinal studies on the one hand, and interventive, or rather preventive studies on the other hand. At this point, it should be mentioned that we have developed a preventive decision-making program focusing on the question "Children: yes or no?" that contains, among others segments, a module on the prospective changes of the marital relationship following the birth of a child and that attempts to teach specific communication skills to deal with these changes (a detailed description and evaluation of this program can be found in Schneewind, 1991).

How Compatible Is Work and Family Life?

The fourth question deals with the compatibility of "work" and "family" as perceived by young mothers and fathers, again in comparison with nonparents. In the following some of the major findings are briefly summarized:

(1) It is only the young mothers who substantially reduce their number of work hours or temporarily give up their jobs. In contrast, young fathers remain at about the same level of time that they devote to their jobs before and after their transition to parenthood.

(2) Wives who, in general, have a positive motivation for parenthood but nevertheless tend to delay childbearing demonstrate a particularly strong commitment to their jobs just before they enter pregnancy. Moreover, they dwell on intrinsic job motivation such as joy and interest in the job while husbands, especially young fathers, put more emphasis on extrinsic job motivations, such as the necessity to earn money.

(3) Job commitment and job strain has increased considerably during the last years, especially for men, regardless of their parental status, and for childless women.

(4) A particularly interesting finding refers to the job and career situation of the male part of our sample. The more important the job was for the young husbands in 1989, the higher the likelihood that they belonged to the group putting in 50 or more work hours per week in 1994. In addition, among those with a high load of work hours we found only 45% fathers. In contrast, the group working somewhat around 40 hours per week, which, incidentally, reflects the "normal" situation in Germany, consists of more than 80% fathers. Moreover, the longer-working husbands attribute to themselves more intrinsic job motivations, whereas those with fewer work hours felt more extrinsically motivated.

All in all, we may conclude that an increasing importance of work and commitment to the job accompanied by intrinsically motivating job conditions make it less probable that husbands, particularly young husbands, will develop into fathers. It should be noted that this finding contrasts with the one reported earlier in which young husbands' relational personality and perceived marital relationship development contributed to the likelihood of (a) having more children and (b) having them earlier in time. Future research should try to disentangle these two motivational tendencies.

What Are the Intra- and Extrafamilial Arrangements for Child Care?

The fifth question focuses on the intra- and extrafamilial arrangements of child care. Again, a few points will be summarized in the following:

(1) First, we found that, at least for our sample, almost all parents took care of their children exclusively by themselves. This holds particularly true for families with young children up to age 3. From age 3 on, kindergarten and grandparents, or a combination of both, became the most frequent modes of child care.

(2) The attitude concerning extrafamilial child care depends much on the age of the child. At measurement point VIII (1994) we asked our parents whether they would entrust their child to a day-nursery or kindergarten, a day-care mother, or family relatives on a "non-regular basis," to a "limited extent" or "without hesitation." The results are presented in Table 3.

The findings speak quite convincingly to the fact that the parents are rather reluctant to consign the care of their child to extrafamilial institutions, especially if the child is very young. It should be realized, however, that the situation in East Germany, where day-nurseries used to be a very common institution in the former German Democratic Republic, might be quite different. On the other hand, kindergarten becomes a very much accepted mode of complementary child care as soon as the child has reached the age of 3. It should also be noted that most parents are very sensitive concerning the quality of extrafamilial child care as assessed by a set of dimensions such as "quality of socio-emotional relationships," "stimulation of the child's development," and "flexible time arrangements" (Schneewind et al., 1997).

(3) What about intrafamilial child care? Here we find a very clear trend toward a traditionalization of family roles, that is, the mothers take over most if not all of the various child care responsibilities—at least during the week, while, in general, the fathers remain astonishingly uninvolved. To put it more

Table 3
Attitudes Towards Extrafamilial Child-Care in % ($n = 125$)

	Age of child: ≤ 3			*Age of child: 3–6*		
	Day nursery	*Day-care mother*	*Family relatives*	*Kinder-garten*	*Day-care mother*	*Family relatives*
Non-regular base	37	35	18	2	21	13
Limited extent	54	49	59	31	41	46
Without hesitation	9	16	23	67	38	41

concretely, on average, the mothers carry out 85% of the child-care activities, and for one third of the mothers it is even a full 100%. The traditionalization effect is even stronger for families with two children: while in one-child families 80% of the child-care tasks are attended to by the mothers the corresponding figure is 87% for mothers with two children. The situation becomes somewhat more balanced when the mothers work 20 hours or more per week. Then their share of child care drops to 70%.

These numbers reflect the "real situation" as perceived by both parents. We also asked them what, in their view, an "ideal situation" of child care and parenting would look like. In this case, the numbers approached almost a 50/50 balance with some variance due to the extent of both parents' job involvement. When we computed difference scores by subtracting the values of the "real situation" from those of the "ideal situation" we thought that large differences should be a good indicator of the couples' overall lack of satisfaction with their child-care arrangements. Contrary to what we expected and also to empirical findings of some other studies (e.g., Belsky, Lang, & Huston, 1986; Reichle, 1994; Ruble, Fleming, Hackel, & Stagnor, 1988), this was not the case. Nor was there a substantial correlation between the difference scores and marital satisfaction. Thus, it seems that the traditionalization effect, although it turned out to be rather strong, is seen as something quite "natural"—perhaps because of the young fathers' more prominent role as the family bread-winner. In any case, differences between actual and preferred modes of shared child care apparently do not have detrimental effects on the couple relationship. In this respect some aspects of interparental behavior such as differences in parenting, lack of interparental solidarity, or specific parent-child coalitions excluding the other parent, although they can not be reported here in detail, turned out to be much more powerful correlates of marital satisfaction.

As can be inferred from Table 3, kindergarten becomes the most preferred institution of complementary extrafamilial child care when the child has reached the age of 3. This is the point at which a great number of young mothers who, up to that time, have taken care of their child themselves would like to return to work, preferably to an interesting and well-paid part-time job that would give them enough time to spend with their child after kindergarten. However, although in the view of many young mothers this would be an ideal arrangement to solve the work-family compatibility problem, it does not work for many of them, first, because particularly in West Germany there are not enough kindergarten openings, and second, because in both the West and even more so the East there are not enough attractive part-time jobs available.

Concluding Remarks: What Should Be Done?

Looking back on the results reported in this contribution, I should like to draw some conclusions with a particular eye on family policy.

First, although I dealt primarily with psychological and, in particular, relational aspects, I want to make quite explicit that financial, occupational, and infrastructural issues are of vital importance for most couples considering starting a family. If we keep in mind that in Germany, only about 20% of the actual costs of children are covered by corresponding governmental transfer payments, it becomes quite evident that young families, as compared to childless couples, are relatively deprived economically. This does not even include the so-called opportunity costs of the mothers' nonparticipation in the labor force, which in Germany, as some economists have found out, amount to about DM 800,000.00 over a period of 18 years (Bundesministerium für Familie und Senioren, 1994; Lampert, 1989). This is quite a respectable sum that could easily be used to buy a nice family home. In addition, the occupational and infrastructural conditions are, as we have already seen above, not very conducive to having children. In fact, it has been argued that in Germany a "structural recklessness" against families makes it difficult to rear children properly (e.g., Bundesministerium für Familie und Senioren, 1994; Kaufmann, 1995). In any case, a solid financial and also occupational base, supported by adequate infrastructural conditions, are indispensable prerequisites for the nest-building phase in the family life cycle. Nevertheless, this is only half the story.

The other half is the quality of the relational personality at the individual level and the quality of marital relationships at the couple level. The good news is that both basic research and applied prevention studies demonstrate quite convincingly that particularly the quality of relationships can be influenced for the better—especially via the main vehicle of appropriate communication and psychologically informed relationship skills (for reviews see Hahlweg, Baucom, Bastine, & Markman, 1998; Schneewind & Graf, 2000; van Widenfeldt, Markman, Guerney, Behrens, & Hosman, 1997). By the latter I mean that strengthening relationship skills should take into account a differential perspective at the individual, couple, or family level with respect to the corresponding experiential and relationship histories (e.g., Schneewind & Gerhard, 2000). For many reasons, the best strategic point to start strengthening relationship competence is the couple relationship. Later on, specific aspects concerning the parent-child relationship could be added as the children move through their individual and family life cycle.

In sum, psychology has not only the know-how but also well-researched technologies to enhance relationship competence, which, in turn, empowers young couples and families to cope better with difficult events and transitions in their lives. What at least in Germany is still missing, however, is to sensitize people to and bring them in touch with this knowledge base on a large scale (for a discussion of this point see Baucom, 1998; Hahlweg, Schröder, & Lübke, 2000). In my view, this is an important and worthwhile challenge for family policy.

References

Aldous, J. (1996). *Family careers. Rethinking the developmental perspective.* Thousand Oaks, CA: Sage.

Baucom, D. H. (1998). Maßnahmen zur Prävention von Beziehungsstörungen und Scheidung [Treatments for preventing partnership problems and divorce]. In K. Hahlweg, D. H. Baucom, R. Bastine, & H. J. Markman (Eds.), *Prävention von Trennung und Scheidung—Internationale Ansätze zur Prädiktion und Prävention von Beziehungsstörungen* (pp. 13–26). Stuttgart, Germany: Kohlhammer.

Belsky, J. (1984). The determinants of parenting: A process model. *Child Development, 55,* 83–96.

Belsky, J., Gilstrap, B., & Rovine, M. (1984). The Pennsylvania Infant and Family Development Project: I. Stability and change in mother-infant and father-infant interaction in a family setting at one, three and nine months. *Child Development, 55,* 692–705.

Belsky, J., Lang, M., & Huston, T. L. (1986). Sex typing and division of labor as determinants of marital change across the transition to parenthood. *Journal of Personality and Social Psychology, 50,* 517–522.

Belsky, J., & Rovine, M. (1990). Patterns of marital change across the transition to parenthood: Pregnancy to three years postpartum. *Journal of Marriage and the Family, 52,* 5–19.

Bundesministerium für Familie und Senioren (Ed.). (1994). *Familien und Familienpolitik im geeinten Deutschland—Zukunft des Humanvermögens. Fünfter Familienbericht.* Bonn, Germany: Universitäts-Druckerei.

Carter, B., & McGoldrick, M. (Eds.). (1988). *The changing family life cycle: A framework for family therapy* (2nd ed.). New York: Gardner Press.

Cowan, C. P., & Cowan, P. A. (1992). *When partners become parents. The big life change for couples.* New York: Basic Books.

Cowan, P. A., & Cowan, C. P. (1990). Becoming a family: Research and intervention. In I. Sigel & G. Brody (Eds.), *Family research* (Vol. 1, pp. 1–51). Hillsdale, NJ: Erlbaum.

Dyer, E. D. (1963). Parenthood as crisis. A restudy. *Marriage and Family Living, 25,* 196–201.

Engstler, H. (1998). *Die Familie im Spiegel der amtlichen Statistik* [???]. Brühl, Germany: Chudeck Druck Service.

Hahlweg, K., Baucom, D. H., Bastine, R., & Markman, H. J. (Eds.). (1998). *Prävention von Trennung und Scheidung—Internationale Ansätze zur Prädiktion und Prävention von*

Beziehungsstörungen [Prevention of separation and divorce—International approaches for predicting and preventing partnership problems]. Stuttgart, Germany: Kohlhammer.

Hahlweg, K., Schröder, B., & Lübke, A. (2000). Prävention von Paar- und Familienproblemen: Eine nationale Aufgabe [Prevention of problems in couples and families—A national task.]. In K. A. Schneewind (Ed.), *Familienpsychologie im Aufwind: Brückenschläge zwischen Forschung und Praxis* (pp. 249–274). Göttingen, Germany: Hogrefe.

Hendrick, S. S. (1988). A generic measure of relationship satisfaction. *Journal of Marriage and the Family, 50,* 93–98.

Hobbs, D. F. Jr. (1965). Parenthood as crisis: A third study. *Journal of Marriage and the Family, 27,* 367–372.

Kaufmann, F.-X. (1995). *Zukunft der Familie im vereinten Deutschland* [Future of the family in unified Germany]. München, Germany: Beck.

Lampert, H. (1989). Familie heute—sozialökonomische Analyse ihrer Lebenslage [Family today—Socio-economic analysis of families' welfare]. In M. Wingen (Ed.), *Familie im Wandel—Situation, Bewertung, Schlußfolgerungen* (pp. 92–120). Bad Honnef, Germany: Eigenverlag des Katholisch-Sozialen Instituts.

LeMasters, E. E. (1957). Parenthood as crisis. *Marriage and Family Living, 19,* 352–355.

Reichle, B. (1994). *Die Geburt des ersten Kindes—eine Herausforderung für die Partnerschaft.* Bielefeld, Germany: Kleine.

Reichle, B., & Werneck, H. (Eds.). (1999). *Übergang zur Elternschaft* [Transition to parenthood]. Stuttgart, Germany: Enke.

Rodgers, R. H., & White, J. M. (1993). Family development theory. In P. G. Boss, W. J. Doherty, R. LaRossa, W. R. Schumm, & S. K. Steinmetz (Eds.), *Sourcebook of family theories and methods: A contextual approach* (pp. 225–254). New York: Plenum Press.

Rost, H. (1990). *LACORD. Latent class analysis for ordinal variables. A FORTRAN Program.* Kiel, Germany: Institut für die Pädagogik der Naturwissenschaften.

Ruble, D.N., Fleming, A.S., Hackel, L.S., & Stagner, C. (1988). Changes in the marital relationship during the transition to first time motherhood: Effects of violated expectations concerning division of household labor. *Journal of Personality and Social Psychology, 55,* 78–87.

Schneewind, K. A. (1991). *Familienpsychologie* [Family psychology]. Stuttgart, Germany: Kohlhammer.

Schneewind, K. A. (1993). Paarklima—die "Persönlichkeit" von Partnerschaften [Couple climate—the "personality" of partnerships]. In H. Mandl, M. Dreher, & H.-J. Kornadt (Eds.), *Entwicklung und Denken im kulturellen Kontext* (pp. 145–161). Göttingen, Germany: Hogrefe.

Schneewind, K. A., & Gerhard, A.-K. (2000). *Relationship personality, conflict resolution styles and marital satisfaction: Mediational analyses across the first five years of marriage.* Unpublished manuscript, Department of Psychology, University of München, Germany.

Schneewind, K. A., & Graf, J. (2000). Beziehungstraining—Wissen und Handeln im Kontext von Partnerschaft und Familie [Relationship training—Knowledge and action in the context of partnership]. In H. Mandl & J. Gerstenmaier (Eds.), *Die Kluft zwischen Wissen und Handeln: Empirische und theoretische Lösungsansätze* (pp. 157–196). Göttingen, Germany: Hogrefe.

Schneewind, K. A., Knopp, V., Schmidt-Rinke, M., Sierwald, W., & Vierzigmann, G. (1989). *Optionen der Lebensgestaltung junger Ehen und Kinderwunsch. Materialband. Teil II: Psychologische Teilstudie* [Life planning options of young families and childwish. Volume II: Psychological investigation]. Unpublished research report, Department of Psychology, University of München, Germany.

Schneewind, K. A., Vaskovics, L. A., Backmund, V., Buba, H.-P., Schneider, N., Sierwald, W., & Vierzigmann, G. (1992). *Optionen der Lebensgestaltung junger Ehen und Kinderwunsch* [Life planning options of young families and childwish]. Stuttgart, Germany: Kohlhammer.

Schneewind, K. A., Vaskovics, L. A., Backmund, V., Gotzler, P., Rost, H., Salih, A., Sierwald, W., & Vierzigmann, G. (1994). *Optionen der Lebensgestaltung junger Ehen und Kinderwunsch. Zweiter Projektbericht* [Life planning options of young families and childwish. Second project report]. Stuttgart, Germany: Kohlhammer.

Schneewind, K. A., Vaskovics, L. A., Gotzler, P., Hofmann, B., Rost, H., Schlehlein, B., Sierwald, W., & Weiß, J. (1997). *Optionen der Lebensgestaltung junger Ehen und Kinderwunsch. Endbericht* [Life planning options of young families and childwish. Final report]. Stuttgart, Germany: Kohlhammer.

van Widenfeldt, B., Markman, H. J., Guerney, B., Behrens, B. C., & Hosman, C. (1997). Prevention of relationship problems. In W. K. Halford & H. J. Markman (Eds.), *Clinical handbook of marriage and couples intervention* (pp. 651–675). New York: Wiley.

Vierzigmann, G. (1995). Entwicklung von Skalen zur Erfassung individueller Beziehungskompetenzen (SEBE) [Development of scales for assessing individuals' competenecies in social relationships]. *Zeitschrift für Differentielle und Diagnostische Psychologie, 16,* 103–112.

Name Index

Subject Index